Urbanization in
Southeast Asia

The **Centre for Liveable Cities (CLC)** was set up in 2008 by the Ministry of National Development and the Ministry of the Environment and Water Resources, based on a strategic blueprint developed by Singapore's Inter-Ministerial Committee on Sustainable Development. The Centre's mission is to distil, create and share knowledge on liveable and sustainable cities. CLC distils key learning points from Singapore's experiences over the last half-century, while creating knowledge to address emerging challenges. It also shares knowledge with, and learns from, other cities and experts. Guided by the CLC Framework for Liveable and Sustainable Cities, the Centre works across three main areas — Research, Training, and Promotions. *http://www.clc.org.sg*

The **ASEAN Studies Centre** of the Institute of Southeast Asian Studies in Singapore is devoted to working on issues that pertain to the Association of Southeast Asian Nations as an institution and a process, as distinct from the broader concerns of the Institute with respect to Southeast Asia.

Through research, conferences, consultations, and publications, the Centre seeks to illuminate ways of promoting ASEAN's purposes — political solidarity, economic integration and regional cooperation — and the obstacles on the path to achieving them. Through its studies, the Centre offers a measure of intellectual support to the ASEAN member-countries and the ASEAN Secretariat in building the ASEAN Community, with its political/security, economic and socio-cultural pillars. The Centre aims to conduct studies and make policy recommendations on issues and events that call for collective ASEAN actions and responses.

The Centre seeks to work together with other intellectual centres, institutes, think-tanks, foundations, universities, international and regional organizations, government agencies, and non-governmental organizations that have similar interests and objectives, as well as with individual scholars and the ASEAN Secretariat.

The **Institute of Southeast Asian Studies (ISEAS)** was established as an autonomous organization in 1968. It is a regional centre dedicated to the study of socio-political, security and economic trends and developments in Southeast Asia and its wider geostrategic and economic environment.

The Institute's research programmes are the Regional Economic Studies (RES, including ASEAN and APEC), Regional Strategic and Political Studies (RSPS), and Regional Social and Cultural Studies (RSCS).

ISEAS Publishing, an established academic press, has issued more than 2,000 books and journals. It is the largest scholarly publisher of research about Southeast Asia from within the region. ISEAS Publications works with many other academic and trade publishers and distributors to disseminate important research and analyses from and about Southeast Asia to the rest of the world.

Urbanization in Southeast Asia
ISSUES & IMPACTS

EDITED BY Yap Kioe Sheng AND Moe Thuzar

CENTRE for
LiveableCities
SINGAPORE

ASEAN
Studies Centre
Institute of Southeast Asian Studies

ISEAS

INSTITUTE OF SOUTHEAST ASIAN STUDIES
SINGAPORE

First published in Singapore in 2012 by
ISEAS Publishing
Institute of Southeast Asian Studies
30 Heng Mui Keng Terrace
Pasir Panjang
Singapore 119614

E-mail: publish@iseas.edu.sg
Website: <http://bookshop.iseas.edu.sg>

Co-published with
Centre for Liveable Cities
45 Maxwell Road
#07-01 The URA Centre
Singapore 069118
http://www.clc.org.sg

The responsibility for facts and opinions in this publication rests exclusively with the authors and their interpretations do not necessarily reflect the views or the policy of the publishers or their supporters.

ISEAS Library Cataloguing-in-Publication Data

Urbanization in Southeast Asia : issues and impacts / edited by Yap Kioe Sheng and Moe Thuzar.
1. Urbanization—Southeast Asia.
2. Sustainable urban development—Southeast Asia.
3. Municipal government—Southeast Asia.
I. Yap, K. S.
II. Moe Thuzar.
HT147 A9U73   2012

ISBN 978-981-4380-02-7 (soft cover)
ISBN 978-981-4380-04-1 (e-book, PDF)

Typeset by Superskill Graphics Pte Ltd
Printed in Singapore by Fabulous Printers Pte Ltd

CONTENTS

MESSAGE from
Head, ASEAN Studies Centre

The Centre for Liveable Cities and the ASEAN Studies Centre initiated a series of three regional workshops in December 2009 that brought together experts, academics, and practitioners from Southeast Asian countries to discuss urbanization issues in the region, particularly the challenges and prospects for regional collaboration on this matter. The regional workshops would not have been possible without the keen interest and enthusiasm of Andrew Tan, who headed the Centre for Liveable Cities at the time, and who first mooted the idea of convening the workshop series to find a pathway towards closer collaboration in the region's actions and responses on this issue.

Through the workshops, we attempted to identify priority issues that Southeast Asia — and ASEAN member states — need to tackle to ensure that urbanization occurs as an integral part of regional efforts to realize the open, dynamic and resilient ASEAN Community envisioned by leaders of ASEAN. When the workshops concluded in July 2010, ASEAN's efforts for greater connectivity among and within its member states provided an additional impetus for our suggestions to facilitate closer partnerships among ASEAN member states to address urbanization concerns that would inevitably arise from greater regional connectivity.

The workshop recommendations, which were brought to the attention of high- and working-level ASEAN meetings, support the larger strategic objectives of ASEAN community building. Papers presented at the workshop have been developed into thoughtful contributions to help policymakers understand what we as a region face in addressing challenges associated with rapid urbanization, and also identify, for ASEAN as a collective, opportunities to overcome these challenges and enhance the region's prospects.

The ASEAN Studies Centre hopes that this publication will be the catalyst for similar exercises that assist responses to urbanization concerns at the regional and national levels in ASEAN. At the very least, the workshops have created a space for discussion and debate on what countries face in addressing urbanization in their local context. Information sharing will help further identify and clarify concerns that merit closer attention.

RODOLFO C. SEVERINO
Head
ASEAN Studies Centre
Institute of Southeast Asian Studies
Singapore

MESSAGE from Executive Director, Centre for Liveable Cities

The story of urbanization gaining pace is a familiar one in many parts of the world. The Southeast Asian region is no different. In 1950, the rate of urbanization was only 15.4 per cent. The rate today stands at slightly over 40 per cent and is projected to increase to 49.7 per cent by 2025.

While the circumstances surrounding each city within Southeast Asia are unique, the challenges that cities can identify with and collectively address as a region are common. Overburdened cities struggle to supply essential urban infrastructure, services, and shelter to residents, but they have also lifted hundreds of millions out of poverty. Cities are now also more interconnected and share more anxieties — from financial crises and rising inequality to climate change.

Governments need to find creative mechanisms to mobilize the private sector and civil society to generate economic growth and reduce poverty, improve productivity and living conditions, protect the environment, and adapt to climate change.

Against this backdrop, liveability and sustainability have become central concerns for many urban leaders. At the Centre for Liveable Cities (CLC), we believe that good urban governance and integrated planning, demonstrated through sound policies and effective legal and institutional frameworks that mobilize human and financial resources, can result in a city being adaptable to changes in environmental, social, and economic systems over the long term.

Over a series of three workshops, the CLC was most fortunate to have partnered the ASEAN Studies Centre (ASC) in bringing together experts in the region to gain a better understanding of urbanization trends in Southeast

Asia. This included an Expert Panel Session at the World Cities Summit 2010 (WCS) in Singapore on 30 June 2010, which provided a platform for regional leaders to share and discuss experiences on the subject. In all, the workshops had allowed for regional urban researchers and policymakers to exchange views on challenges, identify opportunities, and exchange experiences and practices associated with rapid urbanization.

I am happy that the research arising from the proceedings and discussions of the workshops has been captured in the rich and diverse discourse in this book on Southeast Asian cities. This will extend the influence of the ideas and best practices far beyond the workshops and summit.

KHOO TENG CHYE
Executive Director
Centre for Liveable Cities
Singapore

ABOUT THE CONTRIBUTORS

Fitria Pramudina Anggriani ARIFIN is a knowledge-worker in community and urban development. She is also A LEAD (Leaders in Environmental and Development) Fellow for Sustainable City. She is currently involved in developing sustainable city indicators.

Alex B. BRILLANTES, Jr. is Professor at the National College of Public Administration and Governance (NCPAG), University of the Philippines (UP), President of the Philippine Society for Public Administration (PSPA), and Board Member of the Asian Association for Public Administration (AAPA). He earlier served as Secretary General of the Association of Schools of Public Administration of the Philippines (ASPAP), Deputy Secretary General of the Eastern Regional Organisation for Public Administration (EROPA), and Chairman of the Philippine Social Science Council (PSSC).

Anthony T.H. CHIN is Associate Professor of Transportation Economics at the Department of Economics, National University of Singapore. He is a Fellow of the Society of Logisticians of Malaysia, Chief Editor, *Journal of Logistics and Sustainable Transport*, Associate Editor, *Singapore Economic Review*, Member of the Networking Committee, Air Transport Research Society and Track Leader, Centre for Maritime Studies, National University of Singapore (NUS).

Herisadel P. FLORES is a researcher at the Centre for Local and Regional Governance (CLRG), National College of Public Administration and Governance, University of the Philippines (UP).

GOH Ban Lee is Senior Research Fellow of the Penang Institute, Penang. He is also a columnist for the *Sun* newspapers in Malaysia, focusing on issues related to urban governance, housing, and urban planning.

Anna Maria M. GONZALES is Sustainability Manager of Ayala Land Inc. She is an architect and environmental planner by training, and a social development worker by avocation. During the time this book was being written, she was working with the Partnership of Philippine Support Service Agencies (PHILSSA) as part of the National Project Monitoring Office of Urban Partnerships for Sustainable Upliftment, Renewal Governance and Empowerment (UPSURGE).

Chuthatip MANEEPONG is Affiliate Faculty at the School of Politics and Global Studies, Arizona State University (ASU).

Nutavoot PONGSIRI is Assistant Governor (Human Resources and Organisation Development Group) at the Bank of Thailand. He is also Visiting Researcher at the Centre on Regulation and Competition (CRC), United Kingdom.

Wicaksono SAROSA is Executive Director of the Partnership for Governance Reform (or Kemitraan), a multi-stakeholder organization and trust fund aimed at promoting good governance in Indonesia.

Victor R. SAVAGE is Associate Professor in the Department of Geography and Environmental Studies Programme (BES) in the National University of Singapore (NUS). He also teaches in the Southeast Asian Studies Department. He is the Deputy Director of the Masters in Environmental Management Programme (MEM) in NUS. His research interests are on historical-cultural landscapes, cross-cultural and eco-development issues in Singapore and Southeast Asia.

Felix SEEBACHER is Managing Director and Partner of Donauconsult and a resource person for the Environment and Development Division of UNESCAP.

Rony SOERAKOESOEMAH is Assistant Director and Head of the Initiative for ASEAN Integration & Narrowing the Development Gap Division of the ASEAN Economic Community Department at the ASEAN Secretariat.

TAN Ern Ser is Associate Professor of Sociology, Academic Convener of the Singapore Studies Programme, and former Vice-Dean of Students at the

National University of Singapore (NUS). Dr Tan was Principal Consultant of the National Orientations of Singaporeans (NOS) survey series I–IV. He is also Principal Investigator of the Asian Barometer-Singapore and World Values Survey-Singapore. He is a member of Singapore's Economic and Social Research Network, the Family Research Network, and the HDB Research Advisory Panel. He also chaired REACH's policy study workgroup on integration.

TAN Peng Ting has been Senior Associate at the Centre for Liveable Cities, Singapore, since 2009. She is currently pursuing a Masters of Social Sciences in Geography at the National University of Singapore (NUS). A nature lover and volunteer nature guide, she organizes capacity-building workshops for other volunteers in her free time.

TI Le-Huu is the Chief of Sustainable Development and Water Resources Section of the United Nations Economic and Social Commission for Asia and the Pacific (UNESCAP).

TOH Mun Heng is Associate Professor of the Department of Strategy and Policy, NUS Business School, National University of Singapore. He serves as Economic Consultant to the Ministry of Trade and Industry and is the Associate Editor of the *Asian Economic Journal* and the *Singapore Economic Review*.

Myo THANT is Principal Economist at the Asian Development Bank (ADB) in Manila, the Philippines. He is at present the focal person for regional public goods in the ADB.

Moe THUZAR is Lead Researcher (ASEAN Socio-Cultural Community) at the ASEAN Studies Centre of the Institute of Southeast Asian Studies in Singapore.

YAP Kioe Sheng retired from UNESCAP in Bangkok in June 2009. Before his retirement, he was Chief, Social Protection and Social Justice Section at UNESCAP, and in charge of the Centre for the Alleviation of Poverty through Secondary Crops (CAPSA) in Bogor, Indonesia. He is currently Honorary Professor at the Cardiff School of City and Regional Planning, Cardiff University.

INTRODUCTION

Yap Kioe Sheng and Moe Thuzar

It is not easy to identify challenges common to the cities and towns of Southeast Asia as the region is diverse in demographic, economic and sociocultural terms. All Southeast Asian countries strive for better standards of living and sustainable livelihoods, but the urban scenarios across the region require different prescriptions for their development goals. However, ASEAN member states are also moving towards regional and economic integration by improving connectivity between existing and potential centres of economic activity. This will have immense repercussions for urbanization and urban development in the member states.

To assist policymakers address these challenges, the ASEAN Studies Centre at the Institute of Southeast Asian Studies (ISEAS) and the Centre for Liveable Cities (CLC) of Singapore organized a series of regional workshops on urbanization in Southeast Asian countries from December 2009 to July 2010 to:

- Provide opportunities for ASEAN countries to learn from one another by sharing information and exchanging good practices;
- Assess the preparedness of countries in the region for an increasingly urban future; and
- Discuss and recommend options on how regional cooperation could assist national and subregional efforts in addressing urbanization issues.

The workshop discussions helped to identify urbanization issues that ASEAN member states could address at national and regional levels. The recommendations that resulted from the discussions were submitted in the form of a preliminary report to relevant ASEAN ministerial and senior officials meetings and the ASEAN Summit. These recommendations now appear in this book together with papers presented and discussed at the regional workshops.

The authors contributing to this book have tried to go beyond an analysis of a particular set of urban challenges within one city or one country, and instead have drawn conclusions and lessons for all the countries of the region. In the opening chapter, Yap Kioe Sheng provides an overview of the urban challenges that Southeast Asian countries face. He summarizes the key challenge as "to promote urban economic growth, while reducing urban (and rural) poverty and protecting the local, national, regional and global environment". Another challenge he identifies is enabling a more effective and efficient delivery of urban services through decentralization and privatization, when many local governments lack the capacity (and willingness) to use measures for the benefit of the city as a whole. Capacity development and good governance are critical to making urban areas productive, inclusive, and sustainable.

Cities drive economic growth in Southeast Asia, but they need to remain competitive in the global economy to sustain the growth. In his chapter, Toh Mun Heng argues that cities allow agglomeration to happen. This facilitates economic growth, but enabling factors are needed concurrently to make growth possible. The government must play an active role as facilitator by developing infrastructure, promoting R&D to improve products and processes, and encouraging trade. Cities should apply principles of globalization, localization, diversity, sustainability, and responsibility to generate a diverse local economy that is protected from market volatility. The development of industry clusters is the key to the development of a competitive urban economy which guards against diseconomies. Developing a competitive economy is more than maximizing business efficiency. There must be a dynamic equilibrium between wealth creation and social cohesion.

Cities in Southeast Asia need to develop urban infrastructure to support economic development, but costs are a serious obstacle. Public-private partnerships are seen as a possible solution. Nutavoot Pongsiri identifies issues and challenges in the area of public-private partnership for infrastructure provision and finance in Southeast Asia. He notes both successes and failures in the region and stresses the importance of an effective legal and regulatory framework to enable the smooth and efficient delivery of infrastructure services. Underlying this is the implementation of good governance and accountability frameworks. Failures are often the result of a lack of adequate guarantees for long-term investment return and of political interventions by local government. He warns that private investors will stay away and seek more hospitable places to invest unless there is a limited, transparent, fair, and consistent regulatory regime, and the government keeps its promises.

Urban development is not just a sub-national issue; it is also shaped and affected by regional cooperation. Myo Thant observes that international trade facilitation has a profound impact on the urban landscape, particularly on the growth of secondary cities and small towns. Regional cooperation and trade facilitation encourage two types of cross-border development: growth triangles (such as the Singapore-Johor-Riau cooperation) and economic corridors. Cross-border economic corridors link production, trade, and infrastructure in a geographic region with a clear economic rationale for such links. Myo Thant sees positive impacts of an economic corridor on urbanization: it reduces uncertainty about urban areas likely to grow; it affects intermediate-sized cities in the interior rather than primate cities and coastal areas; and it changes the relationship between urban areas within and across borders. There are also challenges, including the lack of institutional capacity to deal with cross-border economic activities and their social impacts.

Chuthatip Maneepong analyses rural-urban linkages in Southeast Asia in her chapter. Cities do not function in isolation from the surrounding rural areas in the same or a different country. Their relationship and the impact they have on one another intensify and grow more complex due to peri-urban developments, increased connectivity, growth of rural industries, regional migration, and cross-border trade. Mitigating the unintended impact of economic growth on the environment and longer-term sustainability of development through cooperation and coordination of development efforts is essential. Other priorities are support for human resource development, capacity development of local government and other stakeholders, private sector involvement in the development of peri-urban areas, the development of accessible and affordable communications systems, and the facilitation of labour mobility. Regional cooperation is thus imperative to facilitate these processes.

As cities in Southeast Asia grow through internal and international migration, their populations become more diverse. Nowhere in Southeast Asia is this more apparent than in Singapore where almost one in four residents comes from another country. What happens in Singapore is a likely precursor to what will happen in other cities of Southeast Asia. Tan Ern Ser reviews the multi-ethnic character of public housing in Singapore, where the government consciously prevents the formation of ethnic, class, and generational enclaves. He asks if the diversity spells social tensions and conflict involving opposing values and interests, but concludes that although social divides are present, they do not lead to social conflict. Social distance has narrowed through the development of social capital and communities. Conditions in Singapore differ from those in other cities in Southeast Asia, but important lessons can be drawn from its experience. Community building policies and programmes and infrastructural designs and town planning that facilitate social interactions can transform public housing into more than just a physical shelter in a high-density urban environment.

Victor Savage sees dealing with the impacts of climate change as one of the greatest challenges facing Southeast Asia and its cities. He does not expect governments to adopt adaptive measures proactively, given the lack of specific information on the impacts of climate change. In Savage's view, tackling the impact of climate change is not a problem of knowledge, but of management and decision making. Governments must review their long-term developmental programmes and bridge the economic and environmental divide. They must find environmentally sustainable ways to deal with consumerism, capitalism, the growth fetish, and the industrial production process. Climate change thus delves into philosophical issues about human morality and about manageable, politically desirable, and generally expedient ways of dealing with these challenges.

Felix Seebacher and Ti Le-Huu present the outlines of a "Waste water Revolution in Asia" to reduce untreated urban waste water that pollutes water bodies. Treating waste water is important because the available per capita water is dropping in Southeast Asia due to climate change, increased demand for water as a result of urbanization, and other trends. The authors estimate that the urban population in Southeast Asia of almost 250 million produces more than 30 million cubic metres of waste water daily. Much of it is discharged untreated into open water courses or seeps underground. They see compact, small waste water treatment plants as a solution. The technology has improved and space requirements are much reduced; even in crowded spaces they can operate. Advantages include the feasibility of rapid, local decision-making and implementation, and unit costs within an affordable range.

Green space is an important contributor to urban liveability; the quality of urban life depends largely on the amount and quality of green space within it or close to it. In her chapter, Tan Peng Ting notes the multiple benefits of urban green spaces for the social, environmental, and economic well-being of urban communities and for environmental sustainability. To achieve this well-being, cities need good urban governance, including integrated master planning and a competitive economy. Unfortunately, cities in Southeast Asia do not give green spaces a high priority due to a lack of capability, funding, or perhaps political will. In fact, urbanization and economic growth are often associated with deforestation. Regional exchanges amongst cities in the region on issues ranging from creative infrastructure financing and practices to implementation woes may help provide a plethora of solutions for cities to consider.

Goh Ban Lee reviews the reality of good governance in Southeast Asian cities with a focus on accountability: those who hold power or influence decision-making that affects the lives of others must be held responsible for their actions. Key players are politicians and bureaucrats, civil society, and corporate capital. The mechanism of accountability is the periodic election, but an election alone does not guarantee accountability; the entire electoral process is important. Corruption and bribery of politicians and bureaucrats often influence decision-making in Southeast Asia. The accountability of NGO leaders also requires scrutiny: they may be true to the causes of their members, but their voices do not always reflect the wishes of the majority of the people. The ubiquitous act of non-compliance in most Southeast Asian cities is a clear sign of the lack of accountability and a reason Southeast Asian cities are not among the top internationally recognized liveable cities. Goh calls for studies on the lack of accountability in Southeast Asian cities.

Wicaksono Sarosa and Anggriani Arifin seek to identify the challenges of engaging local government in sustainable urban development. They distinguish five ways to do so: national policies and programmes, donor-funded or donor-initiated programmes, civil society led initiatives, peer-to-peer learning, and visionary and innovative local leadership. These modalities are well known, but implementation is not easy. There is a lack of human and financial resources; the legal framework often does not allow for the introduction of good urban practices; local governments do not understand the goals of decentralization. There is also the problem of sustainability. A good practice introduced by an external actor may not continue after the end of the programme and local initiatives depend on local leaders. National government must provide guidance, opportunity, and facility for local governments to enhance skills and change mindsets. Civil society should put pressure on local government and advocate the adherence to sustainable urban development principles.

Alex Brillantes and Herisadel Flores note that decentralization seems unable to improve public service delivery despite its perceived advantages. Some problems are the result of the hesitant, half-hearted way decentralization is implemented; other problems are temporary, but inevitable consequences of the transition. There is also the self-serving behaviour of those who try to take advantage of the new situation. Local governments become self-centred and efforts by national and local governments to pursue development are often uncoordinated, leading to duplication and misallocation of funds. Decentralization has also spawned good practices in urban management based on values such as equity, transparency, accountability, participation, and environmental protection. Some local governments built alliances with the private sector and civil society to address common problems. Because it is relatively new; decentralization requires capacity building that equips local governments with appropriate knowledge and skills on effective urban management.

Rony Soerakoesoemah and Moe Thuzar explore how ASEAN can address urbanization under the regional cooperation framework. They highlight the importance for ASEAN to consider urbanization as part of the regional agenda. Recognizing the diversity of the ASEAN landscape and the need to bridge developmental and other gaps between the member states, they see the Initiative for ASEAN Integration as a vehicle for ASEAN to put urbanization on the regional agenda, in support of the implementation of the Master Plan on ASEAN Connectivity adopted by the 17th ASEAN Summit in 2010. To ensure coherence in the activities, they propose an ASEAN Regional Forum on Urbanization as a platform for discussions on urbanization issues, and also as a platform for an ASEAN Cluster on Urbanization to present its recommendations and to institutionalize the informal network of urban experts, policymakers, and practitioners created by the regional workshop series of the ASEAN Studies Centre and the Centre for Liveable Cities.

Urbanization is a process that comes in tandem with development and, therefore, has economic, social, environmental, and political implications. Faced with continuing urbanization and growing populations, countries in the region need to build — individually and collectively — the capacity of cities and towns to promote economic growth and development, to make urban development more sustainable, to mitigate and adapt to climate change, and to ensure that all groups in society share in the development. This book highlights urbanization issues that have implications for ASEAN cooperation and provides practical recommendations for policymakers. It is a first step in assisting ASEAN members to navigate the cross-sectoral importance of urbanization, and take advantage of existing collaborative partnerships to address the urban transformation challenges facing countries in the region.

URBANIZATION IN SOUTHEAST ASIAN COUNTRIES
Recommendations

Yap Kioe Sheng and Moe Thuzar

Southeast Asia is urbanizing and the challenges emanating from the urbanization are numerous and complex. The ASEAN Studies Centre (ASC) and the Centre for Liveable Cities (CLC) jointly organized three workshops in December 2009 and March and July 2010 in Singapore to discuss these challenges on the basis of a regional overview paper and a number of other topical papers. Based on the overview paper, the thematic papers, and discussions by participants in the workshops, the following recommendations were formulated for ASEAN's consideration.

NETWORKING

1. ASEAN currently does not have a formal network of researchers on urbanization in Southeast Asia. With the CLC-ASC regional workshops as the starting point, ASEAN can develop a network of urban researchers and practitioners in the ASEAN member states, leading towards the establishment of a network of experts on urbanization in Southeast Asia.
2. Most countries of ASEAN have an association or league of municipalities in one form or another. These associations/leagues can be formed into a regional federation of associations/leagues of municipalities to

facilitate cooperation, the exchange of information and experiences, and their capacity development.

3. Networking can be further enhanced through regular annual round tables which bring together urban researchers, policymakers and the private sector, with the aim of developing recommendations for more responsive policies to address the challenges of urbanization in Southeast Asia, for consideration by ASEAN decision-makers.

DEVELOPING MORE RESPONSIVE POLICIES

4. Urban-specific data are required to formulate effective policies on critical urban issues, especially data on the impact on urbanization and urban settlements of increased connectivity and economic integration in the region. Building on the CLC-ASC regional workshop series. ASEAN can further develop a series of workshops for policymakers, statistical offices, and researchers from member states to discuss the collection and use of urban-specific data.

5. Economic globalization, decentralization, privatization, and climate change mitigation and adaptation are largely uncharted territory for cities and towns in Southeast Asia. It is timely for ASEAN to commission a series of studies on good practices in urban development under these conditions.

INCREASING CAPACITY

6. Many local governments lack the capacity to make use of the opportunities offered by decentralization, privatization and economic globalization, and to deal with climate change. This hampers the development of cities and towns. In conjunction with the commissioned studies on good practices in urban development, ASEAN can organize seminars at national and regional levels for local governments to review good practices in urban development.

7. In order to develop the capacity of local governments on a sustainable basis, ASEAN should identify research and training institutes in member states that can provide training on urban issues for local governments through existing or new training programmes, and encourage member states to facilitate participation by local government staff.

1

THE CHALLENGES OF PROMOTING PRODUCTIVE, INCLUSIVE, AND SUSTAINABLE URBANIZATION

Yap Kioe Sheng

URBANIZATION

Urbanization Trends

Demographically, 2008 was a global milestone, as the world became predominantly urban (UNPD 2010). The United Nations Population Fund wrote in its State of the World Population 2007 report (UNFPA 2007, p. 1) that:

> For the first time in history, more than half its human population, 3.3 billion people, will be living in urban areas. By 2030, this is expected to swell to almost 5 billion. Many of these new urbanites will be poor. Their future, the future of cities in developing countries, the future of humanity itself, all depend very much on decisions made now in preparation for this growth.

Southeast Asia is also steadily urbanizing. Today (2010), 41.8 per cent of the population or 246.7 million people in the region live in urban areas. This was only 15.5 per cent in 1950. The region's urban population is expected to increase to 49.7 per cent in 2025 (see Table 1.1).

Table 1.1
Urbanization in Southeast Asia (1950–2050)

Country	1950	1975	2000	2025	2050
Brunei	26.8	62.0	71.1	80.9	87.2
Cambodia	10.2	4.4	16.9	26.3	43.8
Indonesia	12.4	19.3	42.0	50.7	65.9
Lao PDR	7.2	11.1	22.0	49.0	68.0
Malaysia	20.4	37.7	62.0	80.5	87.9
Myanmar	16.2	23.9	27.8	44.4	62.9
Philippines	27.1	35.6	48.0	55.4	69.4
Singapore	99.4	100.0	100.0	100.0	100.0
Thailand	16.5	23.8	31.1	42.2	60.0
Vietnam	9.9	14.6	24.3	36.4	54.9
Timor Leste	11.6	18.8	24.5	40.5	59.0
Southeast Asia	15.5	23.3	38.2	49.7	65.4

Source: UNPD 2010.

Levels of urbanization vary widely between countries of the region, with a clear link between urbanization and economic development. The countries can be divided into three categories. The first category consists of countries with a high level of urbanization (over 65 per cent) and a high level of economic development in terms of GDP per capita: Singapore, Brunei, and Malaysia. The second category consists of economically less advanced countries with a low level of urbanization (less than 34 per cent): Cambodia, Timor Leste, Vietnam, Lao PDR, and Myanmar. Thailand, Indonesia, and the Philippines form a category in between. The region has an average annual urban growth rate of 2.22 per cent, but that of the least urbanized countries is much higher: 5.0 per cent for Timor Leste, 4.9 per cent for Lao PDR, and 3.2 per cent for Cambodia (see Table 1.2).

Official urbanization statistics do not fully reflect the urban reality. The numbers used above are provided by the United Nations on the basis of statistics supplied and endorsed by the governments of the countries concerned. They present the population living within the boundaries of an area defined as "urban". The data are useful for some purposes,

Table 1.2
Urbanization, Urban Growth Rate, and GDP per capita

Country	Population in 2010			Urban annual growth rate (2010–2015)	GDP per capita ($, 2009)*
	Urban ('000)	Total ('000)	% urban		
Singapore	4,837	4,837	100.0	0.9	52,840
Brunei	308	407	75.7	2.2	48,714
Malaysia	20,146	27,914	72.2	2.4	14,275
Thailand	23,142	68,139	34.0	1.8	8,479
Indonesia	102,960	232,517	44.3	1.7	4,380
Philippines	45,781	93,617	48.9	2.3	3,604
Vietnam	27,046	89,029	30.4	3.0	3,104
Timor Leste	329	1,171	28.1	5.0	2,677
Lao PDR	2,136	6,436	33.2	4.9	2,401
Cambodia	3,027	15,053	20.1	3.2	2,084
Myanmar	16,990	50,496	33.6	3.0	1,244
Southeast Asia	246,701	589,615	41.8	2.2	

Note: * Based on purchasing power parity (PPP); current international $
Source: UNPD 2010; IMF 2010.

but have serious limitations for the formulation of policies dealing with urbanization because the fastest population growth often occurs just outside urban boundaries (Cohen 2004) and is counted as rural population growth or as urban population growth in a different municipality (Jones and Douglass 2008, p. 5).

Understanding Urbanization

Urbanization can be defined as a shift in the ratio of people living in urban and in rural areas, but what are urban and what are rural areas? Surprisingly, there is no definition of rural; it is simply all that is not urban. Equally surprising is that there is no agreed definition of urban. Each country has its own definition (see Box 1.1). The definitions used in Thailand and the Philippines explain the anomaly in their levels of urbanization relative to economic development: Thailand's urbanization level appears too low in relation to its level of economic development, while that of the Philippines appears too high.

Box 1.1
Definitions of "Urban" in the Latest Census

Country	Components of definition
Brunei	Municipalities and areas having urban socio-economic characteristics
Cambodia	Municipalities and other urban centres
Indonesia	Municipalities, regency capitals, and other places with urban characteristics
Lao PDR	The five largest towns
Malaysia	Gazetted areas with their adjoining built-up areas and with a combined population of 10,000 persons or more
Myanmar	n/a
Philippines	All cities and municipalities with a density of at least 1,000 persons per sq. km; administrative centres, barrios of at least 2,000 inhabitants, and those barrios with at least 1,000 inhabitants which are contiguous to the administrative centre, in all cities and municipalities with a density of at least 500 persons per sq. km; and all other administrative centres with at least 2,500 inhabitants.
Singapore	City of Singapore
Thailand	Municipalities
Timor Leste	—
Vietnam	Places with 4,000 inhabitants or more

Source: UNPD 2004, pp. 111–28.

Much of the migration in Thailand in the 1980s was to areas surrounding Bangkok; these were often still classified as rural in the 1990 census. Based on municipal areas alone, the annual rate of urban growth between 1980 and 1990 was 2.53 per cent, against 5.55 per cent in the previous decade. If rural areas surrounding the municipality were included, the annual urban growth rate was 2.82 per cent for 1980–85, and 3.23 per cent for 1985–88 (Pejaranonda et al. 1995, p. 183). The classification of an area as "urban" can have political motives (Jones 2002, p. 5). Municipalities in Thailand have special administrative status, and not all towns are so defined, although they can be quite large. Non-municipal towns remain under the control of the provincial governor, while municipalities have popularly elected local governments. In the Philippines, on the other hand, some small villages with populations of only 1,000 are considered urban.

If fringe areas are included, some cities have a much larger population than the official data show. Jones (2008, p. 42) calculated the population size of Bangkok, Ho Chi Minh City, Jakarta, and Manila using the 1990 and 2000 census. He distinguished three zones: (a) an urban core with a population density exceeding 5,000 persons per km^2; (b) an inner zone with a density exceeding 1,000 persons per km^2 and employment in agriculture of less than 10 per cent; (c) an outer core: the remainder of the administratively defined region surrounding the core and the inner zone, excluding areas with more than 40 per cent employment in agriculture. The actual population of Bangkok, Jakarta, and Manila proved to be more or less double the official one (see Table 1.3).

Census data are also just a snapshot of the population at a particular moment. There can be a chronic undercount of the urban population because some people are overlooked, and for some it is difficult to determine where the person should be recorded (Jones 2008, p. 44). Many Southeast Asian cities and towns have large numbers of migrants who leave their rural or urban home to earn a living in a different locality. Their stated intention is usually to stay only temporarily, but some stretch their actual stay indefinitely; others come and go on a regular basis. Many remain registered in their place of origin, although they have been away most of

Table 1.3
Population of Mega-urban Regions (1990, 2000)

Mega-Urban Region	Population ('000)			Mega-Urban Region	Population ('000)		
	MUR		City		MUR		City
	1990	2000	2000		1990	2000	2000
Jakarta			8,390	Manila			9,958
Core	8,223	8,347		Core	7,907	9,880	
Inner Zone	5,434	9,435		Inner Zone	4,183	6,365	
Outer Zone	3,442	3,407		Outer Zone	3,819	5,368	
Total	17,098	21,190		Total	15,909	21,613	
Bangkok			6,332	HCM City			4,336
Core	5,445	5,876		Core	2,320	3,203	
Inner Zone	1,596	2,380		Inner Zone	904	1,078	
Outer Zone	1,593	2,163		Outer Zone	700	756	
Total	8,634	10,419		Total	3,924	5,037	

Note: MUR: Mega-urban region; City: population within administrative boundary.
Source: Jones 2008, p. 52; UNPD 2010.

the time. Jones (2000, p. 3) suspects a census undercount of two million people in Jakarta (but provides no evidence).

Urbanization is more than just numbers. Urban areas differ from rural areas in demography, economy, administrative status, physical landscape, and social features, although rural areas are increasingly adopting urban characteristics. An urban settlement displays a set of interrelated characteristics:

- Demographic: it has a relatively large, dense, and diverse population.
- Economic: its population is predominantly engaged in non-agricultural activities, i.e., industry and services.
- Administrative: it often has the status of a municipality or a capital of a district or province.
- Physical: it has a high density of buildings and network infrastructure, such as paved roads, electricity, water supply, and drainage.

Urban areas benefit from economies of scale and agglomeration. The size, density, and diversity of an urban population lead to innovation, division of labour, economic growth, and prosperity. Economic growth, prosperity, and employment attract people to urban areas, thereby further increasing its size, density, and diversity. The high concentration of people and economic activities requires infrastructure and rules and regulations to minimize negative impacts and enhance efficiency. Urban settlements are granted municipal authority to set such rules and regulations, mobilize funds, and develop infrastructure.

Urban densities make the provision of services such as education, health care, clean water, and safe sanitation more efficient. In 2006, 86 per cent of the population of Southeast Asia had access to improved water supply; the coverage was 92 per cent in urban areas and 81 per cent in rural areas. Better access to services improves the health and education of the population and its productivity. A well-skilled labour force attracts investments which generate more employment and more prosperity.

Urban Culture

The size, density, and diversity of the city lead people to live a life that differs from that in a small town, village, or rural area. According to Wirth (1938), the clock and the traffic signal are symbolic of the basis of our social order in the urban world, although the importance many Southeast Asians attach to the clock and the traffic signal shows that the urban culture is actually a mixture of urban and rural elements.

Urbanization leads to changes in population dynamics. Urban areas provide better access to health and education services, in particular for women and girls; education offers a pathway for upward economic mobility. Faced with the monetary nature of the urban economy and the high cost of urban living, and enabled by better education, a large percentage of women in urban areas of Southeast Asia participate in the labour force outside their home. This makes women independent income earners and contributes to their emancipation and empowerment.

In urban areas, many women focus on their careers and postpone marriage or do not marry at all (see Table 1.4). Family planning tends to become the norm and fertility rates decline. Because of low infant mortality rates in urban areas and career opportunities that tend to delay marriage, many women choose to have fewer children. The total fertility rate in many cities of Southeast Asia is now at or below the replacement level of 2.1 and this trend is spreading to other urban areas as well as rural areas (see Table 1.5).

Lower fertility rates and higher life expectancy lead to the ageing of the population in many parts of Southeast Asia. The ageing of a population has economic and social consequences: a shrinking of the labour force and increased dependency on fewer workers, increased costs of health care, and the need for changes in the way houses are built, and cities and towns designed. Eventually it may lead to a need to promote international immigration. Low fertility forced the Government of Singapore to change its slogan from "Stop at two!" to "Have three, if you can afford it!"

Table 1.4
Percentage of Women Never Married at Ages 35–39 (1970–2000)

	1970	1980	1990	2000
Indonesia	1.4	1.9	2.7	3.5
Myanmar	7.0	8.9	13.8	18.6
Philippines	8.0	8.0	8.7	9.5
Singapore	5.1	8.5	14.8	15.1
Thailand	5.2	7.3	9.6	11.6

Source: Jones 2010, p. 20.

Table 1.5
Total Fertility Rates in Urban and Rural Areas of Southeast Asia

Country			
Cambodia	Total fertility rate	2000	2005
	Urban	3.1	2.8
	Rural	4.2	3.5
	Phnom Penh	2.1	2.5
Indonesia	Total fertility rate	1970–76	2007
	Urban	4.72	2.3
	Rural	5.34	2.8
	Jakarta		2.1
Philippines	Total fertility rate	1993	2003
	Urban	3.50	3.0
	Rural	4.80	4.3
	National Capital Region		2.8
Thailand	Total Fertility Rate	1987	
	Urban	1.68	
	Rural	2.57	
	Bangkok	1.64	
Vietnam	Total fertility rate	1989	2002
	Urban	2.2	1.40
	Rural	4.3	1.99
	Ho Chi Minh City	—	1.51

Notes: Total fertility rate: average number of children born to a woman over her lifetime.
Sources: Cambodia: NIS et al. 2001, pp. 60–61 and NIPH et al. 2006, pp. 61, 63; Indonesia: Tjiptoherijanto and Hasmi 2005, and Statistics Indonesia and Macro International 2008, pp. 48, 50, 170; Philippines: Orbeta 2002, p. 2, and NSO and Macro 2004, pp. 41, 42; Thailand: Chayovan et al. 1988, p. 38; Vietnam: Trinh et al. 2005, p. 307, and Committee for Population, Family and Children and Macro 2003, p. 28.

Urbanization can affect care of the elderly (Mason 1992, p. 4). There may be a loss of parental power over, and loyalty and obedience by, younger generations due to the separation of economic production from the household. Increased labour force participation by women reduces their availability to provide care to the elderly, while lower fertility reduces the number of potential caregivers. With an increase in migration, the number of multi-generational households decline, but rising income makes traditional financial safety nets less critical and gives the elderly greater independence.

An urban way of life can change the relationship between the family and the state. Smaller housing units and the need to work long hours outside the home constrain the time spent in care for vulnerable members. If the family and the community are less available to look after them, there is more pressure on the state to perform social functions. Schools play a larger role in the education of children, but as parents are busy working, the media and the "street" also play a role that is not always positive.

Urbanization leads to changes in living arrangements. The cost of urban housing is high and most housing units can only accommodate a nuclear family, not an extended one. It is not unusual in urban areas of Southeast Asia to see a household split up to take advantage of differences in the cost of living and to reduce transport costs. The wife and school going children live in a suburban area; the husband and income-earning children live near centres of employment; the grandparents live in the rural areas with the very young children.

A significant development in Southeast Asia is the rise of the urban middle class. Although defined in many ways, there is an agreement that the middle class is well educated, has stable employment as a professional, often in the formal sector, and an adequate income to spend beyond the basic necessities of food and shelter on items such as a car and a home. Stability of income and employment and home-ownership give the middle class a stake in society and the economy (Shiraishi 2004).

The urban middle class in Southeast Asia is often seen as a supporter of order, harmony, and consensus to give the government a free hand to meet their material needs (Peerenboom 2005, p. 131). The environmental movement places its hope on the education and awareness of the urban middle class to move society and the economy into a more sustainable direction. Yet economic growth driven by domestic demand relies on the consumerism of the urban middle class. The sport utility vehicle (SUV) and organic food are probably both symbols of the urban middle class in Southeast Asia.

The use of public space is another challenge of urban living as it requires an "urban" type of behaviour to deal with its intensive use by diverse people. An example is the way drivers of cars, motorcycles, and bicycles use public roads. In Southeast Asian cities, many appear unaware of traffic rules (and traffic signals) and precedence is determined by the status of the car. Another example is the use of semi-public space in residential multi-storyed buildings. The interior of housing units tends to be impeccably clean, but semi-public space seems no one's concern. The

Government of Singapore has taught its residents how to behave in a way that fits urban conditions and enforces rules with steep fines.

Cultural changes pose a dilemma for policymakers. Official ideologies describe the cities of Southeast Asia as a symbiosis of both tradition and modernity, but the combination is not an easy one (Evers and Korff 2000, p. 5). Southeast Asian cities feel the need to modernize in order to compete with world cities, and to appear a part of the global economy. They replace traditional shophouses with shopping malls and glass-and-steel office towers, and allow McDonalds and Burger King to set up shop on every street corner. Cities such as Singapore, Bangkok, and Hanoi risk losing their traditions, and start to look like any other city in the world.

At the same time, people are not expected to "Americanize" with cola, pizza, and burgers, and to lose their unique national or local identity. But constantly rising land prices make preserving cultural heritage difficult. Many cities regret too late the losses incurred. An international conference on urban culture stated: "a city can only be reborn successfully, if it does not lose its unique cultural identity" (Beijing Declaration 2007, pp. 4–7).

Cultural changes do not remain confined to urban areas, but spread to rural areas, facilitated by the increased mobility of the population and the penetration of the education and the media into rural areas (Thompson 2007). In Thailand, migrant women take "social remittances" (ideas, patterns of behaviour, identities, attitudes, skills, and practices) back to their rural families. Learning the importance of education, they send money for the education of other children (Clawen 2002, p. 61). As rural populations adopt urban norms and values and an urban way of life, urbanization as a social process spreads to cover ever wider areas.

CONCERNS ABOUT URBANIZATION

Social critics and policymakers in Southeast Asia have raised concerns about the urbanization of the region. Some of the concerns relate to urbanization per se and to the arrival of poor rural migrants in urban areas; other concerns relate to the pace, form, and impact of urbanization.

Anti-urbanization

Some social critics argue that Southeast Asia is and should remain a predominantly agrarian society. They deplore its urbanization, and seem to say that urbanization is a new trend in a traditionally rural region.

However, Southeast Asia was already highly urbanized in the sixteenth and seventeenth centuries. Evers and Korff (2000, pp. 30, 40) distinguish three types of traditional Southeast Asian cities: commercial coastal cities such as Melaka, Brunei, Cebu, Hanoi, Surabaya, and Patani; sacred cities such as Angkor, Mandalay, Yogyakarta, Ayutthaya, and Hue; and smaller, intermediate cities.

Southeast Asia's commercial peak period (1570–1630) led to rapid urbanization with some established cities growing and new ones emerging. In this period, an estimated 5 per cent of the total population of the region (one million people) lived in cities with 30,000 inhabitants or more. Colonialism brought the demise of many cities and towns. It was one reason so few Southeast Asians lived in cities in the century before 1940. Colonial powers did not encourage (or even disallowed) the local population to migrate to the city (Reid 1993, pp. 67–90, 303).

There is some nostalgia for the time when cities in Southeast Asia were small, orderly, pleasant, and quiet. In the first half of the twentieth century, cities such as Bangkok, Batavia, Phnom Penh, and Saigon were small (see Table 1.6), as the majority of the population lived in the rural areas. However, life in the rural areas was far from idyllic in those days. The national life expectancy reflects the harsh conditions in the villages. In 1950–55, life expectancy at birth was just 37.5 years for Indonesia, 39.4 years for Cambodia and 48.5 years for Malaysia. Today, all countries in Southeast Asia have a life expectancy at birth of sixty years or more (UNPD 2009).

Table 1.6
Estimated Population of Selected Cities in Southeast Asia (1900–50)

	c.1900	c.1910	c.1920	c.1930	c.1940	c.1950
Jakarta	115,000	160,000	290,000	533,000	545,000	1,661,000
Saigon-Cholon	192,000	260,000	300,000	300,000	460,000	1,500,000
Manila City	257,000	n/a	293,000	451,000	661,000	984,000
Singapore	228,000	303,000	418,000	557,000	680,000	938,000
Bangkok	600,000	629,000	n/a	890,000	800,000	782,000
Rangoon	245,000	293,000	342,000	400,000	501,000	737,000
Hanoi	80,000	n/a	n/a	n/a	n/a	568,000
Kuala Lumpur	32,000	47,000	80,000	111,000	n/a	176,000
Phnom Penh	42,000	n/a	n/a	103,000	108,000	111,000

Source: Rimmer and Dick 2009, p. 9.

Some hold the view that cities are the places for the political and religious leadership, and that the common Southeast Asian men and women should live on and off the land. These views go back to the days of the sacred cities, when only the elite and their immediate servants populated the centres of political and religious authority, while the major marketplace was at the river mouth on the coast, at the societal periphery (Hall 2007, p. 1). Referring to the political situation in Thailand, Satrusayang (2010) noted that "[m]any among my peers have even gone so far as to say the ideal Thai state revolves around the classic Siamese peasant who was both simple and happy."

Some governments have actively tried to keep the rural population out of the urban areas. In Cambodia, the Khmer Rouge took the most extreme position. After taking power in Phnom Penh in 1975, it vacated the urban areas and drove the entire urban population to the countryside where hundreds of thousands died of starvation and maltreatment. After its victory in 1975, the Government of Vietnam sent many rural families from Ho Chi Minh City to new economic zones in the rural areas to reduce the size of the city population (Thrift and Forbes 1986, pp. 153–55).

Restricting rural-urban migration has proven to be not only difficult, but often also counterproductive. Ali Sadikin, governor of Jakarta (1966–77), tried to stop migration into Jakarta by introducing a residency permit system that allowed only those who could prove they were employed to enter the city. He had to abolish the system when the city faced a shortage of low-cost labour. Vietnam has a household registration system (*ho khau*) similar to China's *hu kou* system. Although gradually being relaxed, the regulations still result in a two-tier system of urban residents with full registration, and those with temporary registration (Locke et al. 2008).

Others realized that urbanization can have a positive impact. In 1970, Mahathir bin Mohamad wrote in *The Malay Dilemma* that: "we must seek to urbanize the Malays" (2008, p. 136). He argued that:

> The importance of urbanization in the progress of a community lies in the more complex organization which the towns and the cities provide. This makes urban dwellers sharper and more knowledgeable. The rural dwellers on the other hand are cut off from these experiences and are subjected only to the age-old pattern of life that characterizes the countryside. Their sum total of knowledge is therefore minimal and their capacity for change limited. The rural community is thus more static when compared with the urban community. In short, there is inequality of development between the urban and the rural areas. (2008, p. 105)

As a result of affirmative policies, Malays, who formed 27.6 per cent of the urban population in 1970, increased their proportion of the urban population to 43.9 per cent by 2000 (Tey 2005, p. 215).

Today's concerns about urbanization focus on its environmental impact (Newman 2006). Households, industry, and services in urban settlements generate immense amounts of pollution and waste. The domestic and industrial sectors discharge untreated waste water in the rivers, lakes, and seas, and industries and fossil-fuelled vehicles emit greenhouse gases in the atmosphere, resulting in global warming. According to the Global Footprint Network (2009), the ecological footprint of Singapore in 2005 was 4.5 global hectares per capita, while its biocapacity was 0.0 global hectares per capita.

It is, however, unfair to blame urbanization for all environmental evils. Urban areas pollute more than rural areas because of the high concentration of economic activities and urban prosperity. Many industries are urban-based, but they do not produce only for the urban population, but also for the rural one. Moreover, it is not just the size or the growth of the urban population that drives the increase in greenhouse gas emissions, but its consumption level due to increases in prosperity (Satterthwaite 2009). Once the rural population reaches the same level of prosperity as the urban population, rural pollution levels will also rise.

Besides, urban areas can spearhead efforts to mitigate climate change. Urban density and spatial organization influence energy consumption. By concentrating people and economic activities in a limited area, cities can make more efficient use of natural resources and services. Emissions can be reduced if the population relies more on public transport. Cities that align their consumption with realistic needs, produce more of their own food, and put more of their waste to use, can improve efficiency in water, materials, food, and energy use (O'Meara 1999, pp. 7–9). Local governments have the authority to influence urban activities through market incentives and regulations, and law enforcement is easier in urban than in rural areas. Finally, cities are centres of technological innovation, places where solutions can be developed (WWF 2009).

Components of Urban Growth

Poor rural migrants are often blamed for urbanization, but urban growth has three components: (a) natural population growth, (b) migration and

(c) reclassification. The share of each component differs from country to country and also over time. Natural population growth may contribute 40–50 per cent of the urban population growth, but as urban fertility rates in Southeast Asia decline and economic opportunities in urban areas increase, the impact of natural population growth declines in favour of rural-urban migration (see Table 1.7).

Rural-urban migration is the second component, but people migrate not only from rural to urban areas. Between 1995 and 2000, 29.5 per

Table 1.7
Components of Urban Growth (%)

Indonesia		1961–70	1971–80
	Natural growth	68	48
	Net migration	32	52
	Total	100	100

Source: World Bank quoted in Tjiptoherijanto and Hasmi 2005, p. 161.

Malaysia		1957–70	1991–2000
	Natural growth	60	46
	Net migration	20	33
	Reclassification	20	21
	Total	100	100

Source: Tey 2005, p. 189.

Philippines		1980–90
	Growth and migration	43.5
	Reclassification	56.5
	Total	100.0

Source: Gultiano and Flieger 1993, p. 270

Vietnam		1989–99
	Natural growth	41
	Migration	32
	Reclassification	27
	Total	100

Source: Trinh et al. 2005, pp. 290–91.

cent of the migrants in Thailand were rural-rural migrants, 28.6 per cent
were rural-urban migrants, 21.4 per cent were urban-urban migrants,
and 12.4 per cent were urban-rural migrants; the origin of the remainder
was unknown. In Vietnam, 37.0 per cent of the migrants were rural-rural
migrants and 27.2 per cent rural-urban migrants between 1994 and 1999
(Guest 2009, pp. 360–61).

Migration motives are mainly economic, but migrants are rarely
poor and destitute. They are usually younger, better educated, and more
entrepreneurial than non-migrants. Most rural migrants find a better
income in the urban areas. So, rather than by push factors alone, rural-
urban migration is explained by the consistently higher productivity per
worker in urban than in rural areas (see Table 1.8).

Table 1.8
Output per Worker by Economic Sector (2000)

	Output per worker, most recent year (constant 2000 US$)		
	Agriculture	Industry	Services
Cambodia	320	1,445	789
Indonesia	738	5,394	2,351
Lao PDR*	479	2,290	2,331
Malaysia	6,095	17,670	8,487
Philippines	1,163	5,789	3,268
Thailand	751	9,710	5,470
Vietnam	359	2,294	1,491

Note: * 2001
Source: ILO 2007, p. 36.

A type of migration that has not received much attention in urbanization
studies is international migration, although such migration to, from, and
within Southeast Asia is quite substantial. Benton-Short et al. (2004) argue
that skilled international labour migration has become a vital ingredient of
world cities. Disaggregated data are hard to find, but available data show
that in 2000 18.3 per cent of the population of Singapore was foreign born
(mainly from Malaysia and China) and the figure was 6.7 per cent for Kuala
Lumpur. For Jakarta and Bangkok, it was only 0.9 per cent.

The third component is the reclassification of rural areas into urban
areas. This occurs for two reasons: (a) rural areas surrounding a city or town

are incorporated into the urban administration; (b) rural settlements are reclassified and provided with an urban status because they underwent a structural transformation; as they grew and densified, their non-agriculture employment increased and urban infrastructure and services developed.

The proportion of each of these components of urbanization is difficult to determine. However, available data show that natural urban population growth was initially the main component of urban growth because fertility rates, even in urban areas, were high. As family planning became more common in urban areas, the share of the natural growth component in urban growth started to decline. At the same time, urban economic growth accelerated, resulting in an increase in rural-urban migration. Reclassification, which occurs in leaps and bounds, played an important role in the urbanization in some countries (for example, in the period 1980–90 in the Philippines).

Over-urbanization

Some policymakers have raised concerns about the pace of urbanization. In the 1950s and 1960s, many believed that developing countries were over-urbanized because migrants were pushed from rural areas due to population pressure (perhaps due to rural overpopulation?), rather than pulled into urban areas because of better opportunities. Urban population growth that exceeded the growth of the urban economy resulted in unemployment, poverty, homelessness, etc.

Today, rural households earn an increasing share of their income outside agriculture because it offers a pathway out of poverty and a way to manage risk. The rural non-farm economy contributes 40–45 per cent of the income in Southeast Asia, while urban income may contribute another 25–30 per cent (DFID 2002, p. 1). Off-farm sources of income accounted for 64.5 per cent of total rural income in Indonesia and 37.8 per cent in Vietnam, where 99.0 per cent of the rural households continued to do some on-farm work. However, only 64.3 per cent did so in Indonesia (Davis et al. 2010, pp. 48–52).

In ASEAN, employment in agriculture is expected to decline by 6.6 million between 2005 and 2015, while employment in industry and services will expand by 24 million and 35 million respectively. The service sector will be the main source of job creation by 2015, and the largest sector in terms of employment, with 40 per cent of ASEAN's total employment.

The share of agriculture will drop from 47.8 per cent to 37.6 per cent, and the share of industrial employment will grow from 17.4 per cent to 22.2 per cent (ILO 2007, p. 72).

Urbanization is essential for economic growth, says the *World Development Report* 2009, "Reshaping Economic Geography". Countries cannot grow economically without industrialization and urbanization. Economic growth requires higher densities, shorter distances, and fewer divisions; cities, migration, and trade have been the main catalysts of progress in the developed world over the past two centuries, and that is what they should be for developing countries (World Bank 2009).

Megacities

Many have expressed their concerns over the rise of megacities. The United Nations defines a megacity as a city with ten million inhabitants or more. Thus, there is only one real megacity in Southeast Asia: Manila with 11.1 million inhabitants in 2007. However, Southeast Asia has several mega-urban regions with total populations of more than ten million: Bangkok, Jakarta, and Manila.

Megacities are undoubtedly more difficult to manage than small towns. They may require new approaches and new institutions, but problems of size can be overcome. Tokyo with thirty-six million inhabitants is not only the most populous city in the world, but also its richest with an estimated GDP of $1.5 billion (Hawksworth et al. 2009, p. 31). Despite its traffic congestion, Bangkok continues to attract foreign direct investment.

Urban primacy, defined as a high concentration of the urban population in a single city, has also raised concerns (see Table 1.9). The United Nations

Table 1.9
Urban Primacy in the 1990s

Country	Ratio*	Country	Ratio*
Thailand	21.4	Malaysia	4.1
Cambodia	17.8	Indonesia	3.9
Philippines	9.2	Vietnam	1.9
Myanmar	4.2	Lao PDR	1.8

Note: * Ratio between the largest city and the second-largest city in terms of population
Source: Dutt and Song 1994, p. 172.

calls a city "primate" if its population represents at least 40 per cent of a country's total urban population (UNPD 2004, p. 97). Phnom Penh is a primate city, as its population is almost half of the total urban population of Cambodia. Others measure primacy by the ratio of the population of the largest city to that of the second-largest city, or of the total population of the second to the fourth largest cities.

Urban primacy is explained by the need to use scarce resources efficiently. In the early stages of development, when financial resources are scarce, investments are made where the return is highest, usually the capital or the largest city. In addition, governments want to keep their decision-making centralized in the capital, where the best minds of the country are concentrated. Given the value attached to face-to-face contacts and social networks in decision-making in Southeast Asia, a presence in the capital is often considered essential. The capital also has a nation-building function: it needs to be beautiful and a place the nation can be proud of.

National urban concentration tends to change with economic growth. Studying 80–100 countries between 1960 and 1995, Henderson (2000, pp. 25–26) found that urban concentration increases sharply as income rises, up to a per capita income of about $5,000 (PPP), when it declines modestly. He notes that economic growth losses from significant, non-optimal urban concentrations can be large, and mentions Thailand, which has an excessive concentration, and Malaysia, with too little primacy.

With all the attention on megacities, it is often forgotten that a large majority of the urban population lives in small cities and towns (see Table 1.10): 67.0 per cent of the urban population of Southeast Asia (165 million people) live in urban settlements with fewer than 500,000 inhabitants. Only 13.8 per cent live in cities with more than five million inhabitants (UNPD 2010). The functions of small cities and towns differ from those of megacities; they have an important role in the development of agriculture and the rural areas.

A majority of the population and a majority of the poor in Southeast Asia live in the rural areas. The region's total population is estimated at 594 million and more than 300 million of them live in the rural areas. UN ESCAP (2008, p. 121) estimates that around 18.9 per cent of the population of Southeast Asia or some 100 million people lived on less US$1.25 a day in 2005. Their exact number is unknown; it is often assumed that two-thirds to three-quarters (around 65–75 million) of these poor live in the rural areas.

Table 1.10
Urban Population by Size of Settlement (2010)

	<0.5 million		0.5–1 million		1–5 million		>5 million		Total	
	abs (m)	%	abs (m)	%	abs (m)	%	abs (m)	%	abs (m)	%
BRU	308	100.0		0.0		0.0		0.0	308	100.0
CAM	1,464	48.4		0.0	1,562	51.6		0.0	3,026	100.0
IND	76,696	74.5	5,123	5.0	11,931	11.6	9,210	8.9	102,960	100.0
LAO	1,304	61.1	831	38.9		0.0		0.0	2,135	100.0
MAL	14,171	70.3	3,328	16.5	2,647	13.1		0.0	20,146	100.0
MYA	10,582	62.3		0.0	6,408	37.7		0.0	16,990	100.0
PHI	29,703	64.9	2,931	6.4	1,519	3.3	11,628	25.4	45,781	100.0
SIN		0.0		0.0	4,837	100.0		0.0	4,837	100.0
THA	16,165	69.9		0.0		0.0	6,976	30.1	23,141	100.0
VIE	329	100.0		0.0		0.0		0.0	329	100.0
TLS	14,523	53.7	1,571	5.8	4,784	17.7	6,167	22.8	27,045	100.0
SEA	165,245	67.0	13,784	5.6	33,688	13.7	33,981	13.8	246,698	100.0

Source: UNPD 2010.

Addressing the challenges of urbanization must not be done at the expense of the rural population or of agriculture. Reducing rural poverty and increasing agricultural productivity remain critical for development, but it is difficult to improve agricultural productivity and reduce rural poverty without well-managed cities and towns. The most unproductive agriculture is found in the most thoroughly rural countries. To be productive, agriculture needs many goods and services produced in or transplanted from cities (Jacobs 1970, pp. 7–11).

Towns can perform several functions for surrounding rural areas: (a) as markets and transport hubs for agricultural produce from rural areas; (b) as centres for the production and distribution of goods and services to the rural areas; (c) as centres for the growth and consolidation of rural non-farm activities and employment; and (d) as centres to reduce migration pressure on larger urban centres (Tacoli 2004, pp. 4–5). Thus, the development of small towns not only benefits the urban population, but also the rural population.

Small towns often lack the urban management capacity to perform these functions efficiently. The development of urban management capacity in local governments of small towns is essential for economic growth and poverty reduction in these towns and the surrounding rural areas. Urban development and rural development are not two separate agendas, but are a single challenge.

Urbanization Policies

There have been many policies and programmes in Southeast Asia to guide urbanization and to achieve a better population distribution, but planning or guiding urbanization is extremely difficult. Population (re)distribution policies have more often failed than succeeded (UNCHS 1985, p. 63), as they tend to have unrealistic goals and do not take into account economic and financial forces at work. These forces are not only market forces that attract labour and investments to other locations, but are also economic policies with spatial implications that undermine urbanization policies. Programmes are often also focused on too many cities and towns at the same time, and tend to select cities and towns that have political importance rather than economic potential. Finally, guiding the urbanization process is a slow and long-term process for which many politicians simply lack the patience.

Failing to redistribute the population at a national level, some governments try to decongest at least the capital city by building a new capital. In 1999, Malaysia inaugurated Putrajaya, the new administrative capital, consisting of government buildings, a mosque, monuments, and housing for civil servants. Like in the traditional city, the common people, represented by parliament, and the commercial leadership remained in the major marketplace, Kuala Lumpur. Myanmar moved its capital from Yangon to Naypyidaw in 2005. Thailand and Indonesia are still considering the idea. UNCHS (1985, p. 40) has called the relocation of the capital an undesirable strategy, as the costs are massive and the communication diseconomies resulting from geographical separation of the administrative capital from the primary city can be substantial. However, the primary objective in master planning capital cities is to construct, communicate, and normalize national identity to the citizenry. Putrajaya is a showpiece for the country. It demonstrates to Malaysians and the world that Malaysia is a stable, prosperous, progressive, and technologically sophisticated Muslim country, but it also showcases Malaysia's roots in traditional culture and religion (Moser 2010, p. 1).

Rather than trying to direct people and investments to places that the government considers important, policies should aim at stimulating the economic development of secondary cities and provincial towns (and the surrounding rural areas) that have economic potential in a particular region by linking them strategically through urban infrastructure and services. This is what city-cluster development attempts to do. An interesting example of city-cluster development is the trans-border Singapore-Johor-Riau growth triangle that makes use of the comparative advantages of human, financial, and natural resources in three different countries (ADB 2008a).

The Singapore-Johor-Riau growth triangle is a planned development based on cooperation agreements between three countries. Trans-border urban development also occurs in a more ad hoc manner. Examples are the Thai-owned garment and fish- and seafood-processing factories at the Myanmar-Thailand border that employ cheap (often illegal) labour from Myanmar, and the casinos along the border of Cambodia that cater mainly to Thai customers. Such investments often give rise to further urban development without proper planning and management (e.g., in Poipet in Cambodia).

URBAN CHALLENGES

Urbanization is never a smooth process as there are always tensions between its different components: the urban population grows faster than the urban economy; the urban economy grows, but does not reduce urban poverty significantly; the urban environment deteriorates as the economy grows; and urban management capacity is lacking. Some would argue that a synchronization of these processes cannot be achieved because of the need to prioritize the use of scarce resources. The *World Development Report* 2009 (World Bank 2009, p. 27) argues that "policymakers must show patience in dealing with these imbalances".

The "Kuznets curve" is often used to justify the imbalances. It indicates that income inequality increases in early stages of development, but declines when a certain income level is reached (World Bank 2009 p. 293). Similarly, the "Environmental Kuznets curve" is said to show that environmental conditions worsen in early development, but improve afterwards. The idea that conditions will improve after they deteriorated is, however, hardly consolation for policymakers and the poor (and sounds more like a modern version of Marx's "opium of the people").

The links between economic growth, poverty, and the environment are more complex than the Kuznets curves show. Urban economic growth can leave many urban residents in poverty, with a lack of access to essential services such as water supply, sanitation, housing, education and health care, and credit. With the formal and the informal economy highly integrated in Southeast Asia, there may be a trickling down of benefits, but there would need to be a pouring down of benefits to make an impact. The exclusion of the urban poor from the benefits of urban development, because they live in informal settlements or because they are migrants, will create social divisions in the city or town.

There are different types of urban environmental problems (Bai and Imura 2000): those related to poverty (e.g., lack of adequate water supply, sanitation, drainage, solid waste collection), those related to industrialization (e.g., air, soil, and water pollution), and those related to prosperity (e.g., greenhouse gas emissions). Over time, these problems develop in different ways: poverty related problems decline if economic growth leads to poverty reduction; industry related problems initially increase and then decline; prosperity related problems increase with growth (McGranahan 2007). In some cities the three types occur sequentially, with some overlap.

The transitions do not occur through natural economic behaviour, but depend on policy interventions, and require political pressure for them to happen. The poverty related problems make only a local impact (that is, mainly on the poor), but the poor usually lack the power to influence decision-making on poverty related problems. Industry related problems have a wider impact and are felt by the urban middle class who can and will put pressure on politicians to intervene. Prosperity related problems are global and long-term. They are initially not felt by anyone in particular and therefore there is hardly any pressure to take action.

Thus, the different types of problems often occur simultaneously in the same city or town. Many urban residents live in extreme poverty under poor environmental conditions and excluded from the benefits of urban development despite the city's or town's rapid economic growth. Elsewhere, old and new rich live a life of conspicuous consumption inside gated communities. As the economy develops, industry moves out of the city; environmental problems are exported to small towns and rural areas where regulations do not exist or are not enforced.

Eventually social and political tension will rise because disparities are too visible. The rich may not see the poverty in their city, but the poor will see the prosperity. Politicians in Southeast Asia are learning through experience that today's urban (and rural) poor are becoming better educated, better informed, and better organized. Leaving wide disparities unresolved will undermine political stability, while there is growing awareness that some environmental trends are irreversible and that action needs to be taken as early as possible.

The urban challenge faced by the countries of Southeast Asia is, therefore, to achieve, within available resources, better synchronization between different, but related processes:

- Urbanization in a demographic sense of growth of the urban population relative to the rural population.
- Urban economic development, including the generation of sufficient urban employment to reduce poverty.
- The reduction of urban poverty and disparities through inclusive policies on urban land, housing, basic infrastructure, and services.
- Protection of the urban environment, including mitigation of and adaptation to climate change.

Urban Economy

Competitive Cities

Many cities in Southeast Asia function as engines of economic growth. A ranking of the richest cities in the world by GDP (see Table 1.11) shows Tokyo first with a GDP of $1,479 billion in 2008 (Hawksworth et al. 2009). Eight cities in Southeast Asia were included: Singapore ($215 billion), Metro Manila ($149 billion), Bangkok ($119 billion), Jakarta ($92 billion), Ho Chi Minh City ($58 billion), Hanoi ($42 billion), Yangon ($24 billion), and Bandung ($21 billion).

Not all cities and towns in Southeast Asia have had their share of rapid economic growth. Some cities and towns are better situated, better equipped, and/or better managed than others. Much of the region's

Table 1.11
Richest Cities in Southeast Asia (2008)

City	GDP (US$bn) (2008)	City	GDP (US$bn) (2008)
Singapore	215	Ho Chi Minh City	58
Manila	149	Hanoi	42
Bangkok	119	Yangon	24
Jakarta	92	Bandung	21

Source: Hawksworth et al. 2009.

economic development has been based on export-oriented industrialization, and cities with ports and along trade routes have had a clear advantage. However, no city or town can be complacent.

Cities and towns need further economic growth to create jobs, upgrade infrastructure, improve the quality of life, and reduce poverty. In a globalized economy, they must compete for investments that bring economic growth. In early stages of development, the low costs of labour and other factors of production made Southeast Asia attractive to foreign investors. Today China and South Asia can offer labour at a lower cost than Southeast Asia. Cities and towns must attract higher value added manufacturing and services, and issues such as the quality and productivity of labour start to play a role in the investment decision (Begg 1999).

The World Economic Forum defines competitiveness as the set of institutions, policies, and factors that determine productivity. It lists twelve pillars for competitiveness, each with a set of indicators: (a) institutions; (b) infrastructure; (c) macroeconomic stability; (d) health and primary education; (e) higher education and training; (f) goods market efficiency; (g) labour market efficiency; (h) financial market sophistication; (i) technological readiness; (j) market size; (k) business sophistication; (l) innovation (Schwab 2009, pp. 4–7, 45–47).

The Global Urban Competitiveness Project (2008) defines urban competitiveness as a city's ability to create more wealth in a faster and better way than other cities. It measured the competitiveness of 500 cities in terms of nine indexes: GDP, GDP per capita, per unit area GDP, labour productivity, the number of multinational enterprises, the number of patent applications, price advantage, employment rate, and economic growth rate. Except for Singapore, cities in Southeast Asia do not score well in competitiveness surveys.

The 2007–8 report of the Global Urban Competitiveness Project (GUCP 2008) ranked New York first and included fifteen cities in Southeast Asia, but their ranking was quite low (see Table 1.12). MasterCard (2008, pp. 12–14) ranked seventy-five cities around the world (see Table 1.13). London scored the best; Singapore ranked fourth. Other Southeast Asian cities scored low in the areas of financial flow (with indicators such as financial services networks, transactions, and traded contracts), business centre (e.g., volumes of goods and services at ports and airports, numbers of hotels, and commercial real estate development), but in particular in knowledge creation and information flow.

Table 1.12
Global Urban Competitiveness Index Ranking (2007–8)

Rank	City	Score	Rank	City	Score
1	New York	1.000000	336	Rayong	0.183110
8	Singapore	0.645897	368	Medan	0.155998
155	Bangkok	0.330798	371	Bandung	0.155608
209	Kuala Lumpur	0.276306	384	Phnom Penh	0.144471
248	Jakarta	0.245050	392	Penang	0.137771
317	Hanoi	0.192682	427	Yangon	0.116008
318	HCM City	0.192522	436	Malacca	0.111536
323	Manila	0.190379	460	Cebu	0.103958

Source: GUCP 2008.

Southeast Asia is still attracting its fair share of foreign direct investment (FDI). Singapore is in the top five destination cities in the Asia-Pacific in terms of capital investment, despite a decline of 8 per cent in actual projects in 2008. Bangkok doubled its market share to almost 2 per cent due to a growth in capital investment of 130 per cent (FDI Intelligence 2009, pp. 3–4, 14). However, they need to work hard to avoid the "middle-income trap".

In the global knowledge economy, competitiveness depends increasingly on the ability to create knowledge. Quality of education and an environment that encourages innovation, creativity, and information flows are critical. They are usually associated with cities that have a multiplicity of large and thriving universities and research institutions with a global reputation due to their researchers, scientific publications, and citations (MasterCard 2008, p. 14). In the ranking of the top 200 of world universities, Southeast Asia is represented by only four universities: two from Singapore, one from Thailand, and one from Malaysia (see Table 1.14).

"Quality of place" also becomes important, as highly skilled workers (human capital) determine the comparative advantage of a firm in a knowledge economy. Such workers are increasingly footloose, can work anywhere in the world, and are attracted by the "quality of place" (OECD 2005, p. 5). Singapore has an active policy of attracting young and highly educated and skilled labour in view of its need to compete in the global economy and the ageing of its population, although "buying in" of research and knowledge is, according to MasterCard (2008, p. 14), no substitute for long-term investment in education, research, and knowledge creation.

Table 1.13
Competitiveness of Southeast Asian Cities (2008)

	1. London	4. Singapore	42. Bangkok	50. Kuala Lumpur	68. Jakarta	71. Manila
Legal & Political Framework	85.17	90.32	71.29	69.26	53.48	54.62
Economic Stability	89.66	89.74	82.78	78.90	58.04	76.99
Ease of Business	79.42	82.82	61.56	65.95	45.46	47.95
Financial Flow	84.70	42.15	27.07	24.54	20.49	7.76
Business Centre	67.44	62.58	44.21	25.66	24.98	22.63
Knowledge Creation, Information Flow	62.35	39.45	15.48	8.61	11.17	6.38
Liveability	91.00	84.94	67.75	74.19	58.63	69.56
Index Value	79.17	66.16	48.23	45.28	35.40	35.15

Source: MasterCard 2008, pp. 20–21.

Table 1.14
Top 200 World Universities 2009

	Top 200		Top 50									
	Overall		1		2		3		4		5	
	rk.	sc.	rk.	sc.	rk.	sc.	rk.	sc.	rk.	sc.	rk.	sc.
NUS	30	84.3	14	57.5	20	57.4	27	50.7	20	57.3	23	55.0
NTU	73	72.0	33	45.3	—	—	—	—	—	—	—	—
Chula	138	62.3	—	—	—	—	—	—	—	—	40	40.7
UM	180	56.5	—	—	—	—	—	—	—	—	—	—

Notes: 1: engineering and IT; 2: life sciences and bio-medics; 3: natural sciences; 4: social sciences; 5: arts and humanities; rk. rank; sc. score.
NUS: National University of Singapore; NTU: Nanyang Technological University; Chula: Chulalongkorn University; UM: University Malaya
Source: Times Higher Education 2009.

Another factor in investment decisions is governance. Malesky (2004) lists four critical dimensions of local governance for investors in Vietnam: (a) implementation of central laws and directives, (b) transparency and accountability, (c) reduction of bottlenecks and transaction costs, and (d) local governments that are dynamic and proactive in solving problems. These issues have an impact on the scale of FDI, but foreign investors can also contribute to an improvement of local governance by pointing out the shortcomings to local governments.

Competition is not only about foreign direct investments and highly skilled labour. There is fierce competition in Southeast Asia for tourists. It involves many secondary cities and towns such as Bali, Pattaya, Phuket, Luang Prabang, Siem Reap, and Yogyakarta. Besides conventional tourism, Southeast Asian cities and towns compete for meetings, incentives, conferences/conventions, and events/exhibitions (MICE). Medical tourism is a growing subsector in some countries because medical services tend to be much cheaper in Southeast Asia than in developed countries. One study estimated that 1,280,000 medical tourists visited Thailand in 2006, 448,000 visited Singapore, and 350,000 visited Malaysia (Gupta 2008).

The growth in travel and tourism, the deregulation of the airline industry, and the emergence of low-cost carriers have led to competition between airports for destination traffic, connecting traffic, and cargo traffic (Tretheway and Kincaid 2005, pp. 4–6). Today, Singapore's Changi Airport, Bangkok's Suvarnabhumi Airport, and the Kuala Lumpur International

Airport compete to be the major hub in Southeast Asia for passengers from Europe and North America (see Table 1.15). The competition is again not limited to capital cities, but includes secondary cities (e.g., Chiang Mai, Cebu City, Surabaya, and Penang) that use lower landing fees and less congestion as attractions (Rimmer and Dick 2009, pp. 102–12).

Table 1.15
Southeast Asian Airports in Global Top 30 Ranking (2008)

	Passenger traffic		Cargo traffic	
Airport	Rank	Passengers	Rank	Cargo*
Bangkok	18	38.6 million	20	1.2 million
Kuala Lumpur	—	—	27	0.7 million
Singapore	19	37.7 million	10	1.9 million

Note: * metric tonnes
ACI 2009 <www.airports.org>.

Urban Employment

Despite rapid economic growth, some urban areas experience a slow growth of employment (see Tables 1.16 and 1.17). A study that included Cambodia, Indonesia, Malaysia, the Philippines, and Thailand found that, except for Malaysia, economic growth was not as employment-intensive as in the East Asian miracle. The causes are not clear, but it may be a loss of competitiveness in labour-intensive exports, or the emergence of new opportunities for low labour-intensive activities (Khan 2007, p. 43).

Table 1.16
GDP and Employment Growth in the Formal Sector (2000–2008)

Country	Average annual growth rate		Country	Average annual growth rate	
	GDP	Employment		GDP	Employment
Cambodia	9.0	5.7	Singapore	5.5	4.1
Indonesia	5.2	1.6	Thailand	4.8	1.6
Malaysia	5.1	2.1	Vietnam	7.5	2.3
Philippines	5.0	2.3			

Notes: Cambodia: GDP growth: 2000–2005, Employment growth: 2000–2006; Indonesia: GDP growth: 2001–8; Malaysia: GDP growth: 2001–8; Vietnam: Employment growth: 2000–2006.
Source: Prasad 2009, p. 40.

Table 1.17
Productivity and Employment Growth in Southeast Asia (1991–2006)

	Average Annual Growth rate					
	Labour Productivity			Employment		
	91–95	95–00	00–05	91–95	95–00	00–05
Brunei	—	—	—	2.9	2.8	2.2
Cambodia	2.4	5.1	7.3	2.4	3.5	3.2
Indonesia	5.7	0.5	3.5	2.2	2.5	1.0
Lao PDR	—	—	—	2.9	2.7	3.0
Malaysia	7.0	3.5	2.7	3.1	3.6	2.6
Myanmar	6.2	7.2	11.7	2.2	2.1	1.7
Philippines	0.7	1.8	2.5	3.7	2.0	4.4
Singapore	6.2	3.6	2.1	2.0	3.0	1.5
Thailand	7.3	–0.5	4.3	0.8	1.0	1.4
Timor Leste	—	—	—	1.7	–3.2	8.5
Vietnam	6.8	5.5	6.3	2.6	2.4	2.4
Southeast Asia	5.7	1.3	3.9	2.2	2.2	1.9

Source: UN ESCAP 2008, p. 110.

Almost 75 per cent of the added employment in Southeast Asia involves own-account workers or contributing family workers (UN ESCAP 2008, pp. 105–6). This could indicate that employment is growing mainly in the urban informal sector, which is very dominant in the urban areas of Southeast Asia. It covers a wide range of economic activities: from food hawkers in the streets to sweatshops producing items for global brands. It includes own-account workers who have found a small market niche and large companies that try to avoid regulations and taxes.

The economic importance of the informal sector is by definition hard to measure, but is thought to be very large. UNDP (2007, pp. 299–300) estimated employment in the urban informal sector as a percentage of non-agricultural employment at 78 per cent in Indonesia (1998), 70 per cent in the Philippines (1995), and 72 per cent in Thailand (2002). The informal sector outside agriculture generated 31 per cent of the non-agricultural GDP of Indonesia (1998), and 32 per cent of that in the Philippines (1995) (ILO 2002b, pp. 23–24).

Own-account workers in the informal sector often show great entrepreneurship and alertness to income-generating opportunities. They meet a demand for goods or services that the formal sector is unable or unwilling to meet due to labour costs, regulations, and the small size and low purchasing power of the market. The capacity to innovate perhaps lies not in the area of engineering or design, but in that special taste of the noodle soup that attracts patrons from across the entire city.

The informal economy is expected to remain massive in Southeast Asia. Between 2006 and 2015, the number of contributing family workers in ASEAN will decline by ten million, but the number of own-account workers will increase by more than forty-three million. On the whole, the informal economy will account for at least 60 per cent of ASEAN's total employment by 2015 (ILO 2007, p. 72).

The role of the informal sector is evident in the supply of food, transport, and housing. Informal-sector food vendors, housing in informal settlements, and motorcycle taxis keep the costs of urban living low, and this improves the competitiveness of the city or town. The informal sector not only caters to the urban poor, but also to the urban middle class and the formal sector. Often close links exist between the formal and the informal sectors (Daniels 2004, p. 505) and a major link is subcontracting (Bunjongjit and Oudin 1992, pp. 36–37).

Low productivity and low incomes are said to characterize the urban informal sector, but that is not always the case. Incomes in the informal sector sometimes exceed those in the formal sector, and poor working conditions and low wages are not limited to the informal sector. The formal sector often also pays low wages, forces workers to put in long hours, and operates under poor working conditions. That is not to say that all is well in the informal sector: working conditions tend to be extremely poor and wages extremely low.

Cities in Southeast Asia face a dilemma in dealing with the informal sector. The sector is a convenient and low-cost way to create employment and generate income, but it exposes some of the worst forms of exploitation and inhuman working conditions. The best option is a gradual accommodation of the informal sector in the formal economy through selective and staged interventions (such as microfinance, access to market information, and training) that lead to improved conditions while preserving the sector's viability (ILO 2002*a*, p. 1).

Urban Poverty

There is a concern that rapid urbanization is moving poverty from rural to urban areas. Ravallion, Chen, and Sangraula (2007) analysed 208 household surveys in eighty-seven countries and found that the urbanization of poverty differs from region to region. East Asia (that is, Cambodia, Indonesia, Lao PDR, the Philippines, Thailand, Vietnam, and Mongolia) is the region with the least urbanized income poverty problems. From 1993 to 2002, more than 33 million people in the region escaped poverty: almost 28 million in the rural areas and about 5.5 million in the urban areas. Rural poverty declined by 36.4 per cent, while urban poverty declined by 30.8 per cent. There was a small increase in the urban share of poverty from 18.96 per cent to 20.28 per cent between 1993 and 2002 (see Table 1.18).

Table 1.18
Urban and Rural Poverty in East Asia (1993–2002)

| | Urban and rural poor | | | | | |
| | millions | | | % | | |
	urban	rural	total	urban	rural	total
1993	17.73	75.79	93.52	18.96	81.04	100.00
1996	12.39	59.94	72.68	17.05	82.47	100.00
1999	12.60	47.46	60.05	20.98	79.03	100.00
2002	12.27	48.22	60.49	20.28	79.72	100.00
Change 1993–2002	5.46	27.57	33.03	−16.53	−83.47	−100.00

Notes: East Asia here includes Cambodia, Indonesia, Lao PDR, Mongolia, Philippines, Thailand, and Vietnam, but excludes China. Poverty line of $1.08/day (in 1993 PPP)
Source: Ravallion, Chen and Sangraula 2007, p. 38.

What is most visible in urban areas is the contrast between the rich and poor. Intra-urban income inequality is, however, difficult to calculate with available data and estimates must be viewed with caution. UN-HABITAT (2008, pp. 74–75) estimated the Gini coefficient for urban Asia at 0.39, and for selected cities as follows: Jakarta: 0.32 (2002); Phnom Penh: 0.36 (2004); Hanoi: 0.39 (2002); Manila: 0.41 (2003); Bangkok: 0.48 (2006); and Ho Chi Minh City: 0.53 (2002). Suryadarma et al. (2006, p. 16) calculated the Gini coefficient for the urban areas of Indonesia in 2004: 0.44 against 0.35 for rural areas. Healy and Jitsuchon (2007, p. 739) found a Gini coefficient of 0.463 for urban areas in Thailand, and 0.400 for Bangkok.

Poverty is not just a lack of income; it is a multidimensional condition. Very important in urban areas are the lack of access to basic services (water, sanitation, education, health care, etc.) and the lack of power to influence decision-making. Most urban residents in Southeast Asia have access to improved water sources (see Table 1.19), ranging from a household connection to a public standpipe, but "improved water source" does not imply an adequate quantity or quality of water. Water may be supplied intermittently and this could lead to contamination of the water when pressure declines and waste is sucked into the pipes. If households rely on public water standposts and water is supplied intermittently, household members may have to queue for hours to fetch water and water may have to be stored under unsanitary conditions.

The urban poor are generally better off than the rural poor, but there is often a wide gap between the urban poor and the urban non-poor. A comparison of access to water supply and sanitation for the rural population, the urban poor, and the urban non-poor in Indonesia, the Philippines, and Thailand (NRC 2003, p. 175) found that 29 per cent of the rural households, 17.5 per cent of the urban poor households, and a negligible percentage of the urban non-poor lacked adequate water supply, sanitation, and electricity (see Table 1.20).

Table 1.19
Access to Improved Water Sources and Sanitation (1990–2006)

| | Urban Population with Access (%) | | | | | | | |
| | Improved Water Sources | | | | Improved Sanitation | | | |
	1990	1995	2000	2008	1990	1995	2000	2008
Brunei	—	—	—	—	—	—	—	—
Cambodia	52	54	64	81	38	40	50	67
Indonesia	92	91	90	89	58	60	63	67
Lao PDR	—	78	77	72	—	56	62	86
Malaysia	94	96	99	100	88	91	94	96
Myanmar	87	85	80	75	—	77	81	86
Philippines	93	93	93	93	70	73	76	80
Singapore	100	100	100	100	99	99	100	100
Thailand	97	98	98	99	93	94	94	95
Timor Leste	—	—	69	86	—	—	55	76
Vietnam	88	91	94	99	61	70	79	94
Southeast Asia	92	92	92	92	69	71	71	79

Source: JMP 2010, pp. 38–52.

Table 1.20
Access to Services in Selected Countries of Southeast Asia

	Access to Services (1980s–90s)					
	Piped water on Premises	Water in Neighbour-hood	Flush Toilet	Pit Latrine	Electricity	Lacks 3 Services
Rural	18.6	53.7	55.5	24.3	50.8	29.4
Urban Poor	34.0	53.7	61.8	22.9	68.9	17.5
Urban Non-Poor	55.8	40.1	89.0	9.4	97.4	0.6

Source: NRC 2003, p. 175.

A key problem for the urban poor is a lack of affordable housing in a suitable location. This forces them to rent accommodation in dilapidated buildings in a central part of the city or town, or to squat, without the owner's consent, on public or private land. There, they rent, build, or buy a house that lacks proper permits and authorization. Because the settlements are unauthorized, the residents face the constant threat of eviction. This discourages them from investing in the improvement of the house (see Table 1.21), while it is a reason for the authorities not to provide basic infrastructure. UN-HABITAT (2008, p. 92) uses the term "slum" for all forms of inadequate housing, meaning lacking security of tenure, access to improved water and sanitation, sufficient living area, and structural quality and durability.

Most governments are unwilling to invest in water supply, drainage, or roads in unauthorized neighbourhoods. Thus, the urban poor's lack of access to infrastructure is not so much a matter of lack of infrastructure or lack of government funding, but a deliberate decision to exclude informal settlements and, thereby, many urban poor from access to basic services. Without a formal status, houses do not have a proper address and residents are stigmatized for living in such settlements.

Overall, economic growth has nevertheless resulted in improved housing conditions across the region. The combination of higher incomes, the emergence of private-sector housing developers, and developments in the housing finance sector have increased the effective demand for and the supply of middle and lower-middle-income housing, usually in the form of row-houses and condominiums. Still, many cities and towns in Southeast Asia face a massive housing shortage for low- and lower-middle-income groups.

Table 1.21
Slum Populations in Southeast Asia (2005)

Country	Slum population ('000) (2005)	Urban population ('000) (2005)	Slum population as % of urban population
Brunei	—	275	—
Cambodia	2,309	2,926	78.9
Indonesia	28,159	107,068	26.3
Lao PDR	969	1,222	79.3
Malaysia	—	17,345	—
Myanmar	7,062	15,487	45.6
Philippines	22,768	52,101	43.7
Singapore	—	4,327	—
Thailand	2,061	7,927	26.0
Timor Leste	—	357	—
Vietnam	9,192	22,257	41.3
Southeast Asia	72,520	208,988*	34.7*

Note: * excluding Brunei, Malaysia, Singapore and Timor Leste
Source: UN-HABITAT 2010.

Governments have tried to address urban housing problems with various degrees of success. Singapore has been the most successful. It provided public-sector housing with transport links to employment centres as part of planned urban development from its early stages of economic development. The approach is difficult to replicate in other countries because of the unique character of Singapore: a strong and stable government, a relatively small population and no rural hinterland, a rapidly growing economy, and a population that works predominantly in the formal sector.

Resettlement of squatters and slum dwellers has produced mixed results. Most resettlement sites are situated outside the city where land is less costly. Some resettled households from Phnom Penh found themselves in a location without infrastructure, far from centres of employment, and with a high risk of flooding. The resettlement of canal-bank squatters in Ho Chi Minh City benefited some, but excluded those with a temporary residence permit; it raised housing-related costs and led to a drop in income for some (Castiglioni et al. 2010, pp. 114–15).

Some governments have launched programmes to improve living conditions in slums and squatter settlements. The programmes aim at regularization of land tenure, the provision of infrastructure, and the improvement of housing conditions with strong community involvement.

Good practices include the Community Mortgage Programme (CMP) in the Philippines, the Kampung Improvement Programme (KIP) in Indonesia, and the Baan Mankong Programme in Thailand.

In places where land or land occupancy rights are freely traded in the market, legalizing land tenure of squatter settlements is difficult. Because of the complexities of granting land tenure to squatters, some settlements are upgraded without security of tenure. Their residents continue to face the threat of eviction when the urban economy booms and market pressure on urban land increases. If they obtain legal titles, the urban poor are often tempted or forced to sell to high-income groups.

In many cities and towns of Southeast Asia, the housing problems of the urban poor have not been solved.

> The importance of allocating attention and resources to addressing the housing problems in the cities of Southeast Asia cannot be overstated. Persistence of the problem reflects not only on the lack of political will among governments at addressing the issues involved, but also the disparities in the distribution of wealth as well as the share in the benefits from the rapid economic growth seen in the region (Ooi 2005, p. 88).

Urban Environment

Urban areas, or rather, activities in urban areas such as industry, transport, and mass consumption cause serious damage to the environment. Urban areas in Southeast Asia are no exception, and their residents experience daily the impact of various types of pollution on their health. The most direct links between urban environmental degradation and health are air pollution and respiratory diseases, water pollution and diarrhoea and cholera, solid waste and the plague, and toxic waste and toxicity-related cancers and neurological problems (Brandon 1998, p. 38).

Air pollutants are emitted by factories, motor vehicles, power plants, etc. Many cities and towns in Southeast Asia are vast construction sites, and dust from construction also pollutes the air. Over the past twenty years, air quality in Southeast Asia seems to have improved nevertheless (see Table 1.22), possibly because popular pressure forced governments to take mitigating measures. Unlike poverty-related environmental problems, particulate matter in the air is a type of problem that all urban dwellers (including the influential middle class) notice.

Increasing prosperity leads to rapid growth in the generation of solid waste (see Table 1.23). Local governments face huge problems disposing

Table 1.22
Concentration of PM$_{10}$ in Urban Areas (1990–2005)

	Micrograms per m^3			
	1990	1995	2000	2006
Brunei	28.0	42.0	54.0	46.0
Cambodia	116.0	66.0	70.0	62.0
Indonesia	138.0	115.0	120.0	96.0
Lao PDR	73.0	48.0	51.0	47.0
Malaysia	37.0	32.0	27.0	25.0
Myanmar	116.0	91.0	76.0	63.0
Philippines	55.0	58.0	48.0	26.0
Singapore	106.0	53.0	44.0	40.0
Thailand	88.0	85.0	79.0	77.0
Timor Leste	—	—	—	—
Vietnam	124.0	78.0	70.0	61.0
Southeast Asia	103.7	86.6	84.4	67.4

Notes: Particulate matter (PM) is the term for fine solid or liquid particles from various sources found in the air. PM$_{10}$ is particulate matter smaller than 10 micrometres in the air. The standard for PM$_{10}$ is 50 microgram per m^3.
Source: UN ESCAP 2008, p. 191.

Table 1.23
Municipal Solid Waste Generated (2001) (kg/capita/day)

Country	Solid waste generated per capita per day	Country	Solid waste generated per capita per day
Brunei	1.4 kg	Myanmar	n.a.
Cambodia	n.a.	Philippines	0.50 kg
Indonesia	n.a.	Singapore	1.86 kg
Lao PDR	0.75 kg	Thailand	1.0 kg
Malaysia	0.68 kg	Vietnam	0.61 kg

Source: ASEAN 2006, p. 70.

the waste generated in urban areas. In poorer countries, informal-sector street collectors separate solid waste for recycling and reuse. When the urban population prospers and the supply of waste increases, households pay collectors to remove the recyclables rather than sell the waste to them. Some cities and towns have a well-developed recycling industry in the formal or informal sector, but the industry tends to focus on the most profitable materials in the waste only.

Common disposal methods for solid waste in Southeast Asia are open dumping and landfill (see Table 1.24), but it becomes more and more difficult for an urban local government to find a suitable site within municipal boundaries. Situating a dump or landfill site in a neighbouring district is usually completely out of the question. Incineration is regularly mentioned as a disposal method. Because much of the waste in Southeast Asia (64 per cent) consists of organic matter (fruits and vegetables), and has a high moisture content, high temperatures are required, which makes incineration costly. Incineration also has a negative environmental impact.

The lack of infrastructure and of law enforcement has led to extensive water pollution in Southeast Asia:

- Only seven cities in the Philippines have piped sewer systems, which cover a small percentage of the population. Most domestic waste water enters directly or via septic tanks into the groundwater, public canals, or drainage systems and eventually rivers and other water bodies. In Metro Manila, only 15 per cent of the population is connected to a sewer system; 192,000 tons of domestic waste enters the drainage system and groundwater yearly after only minor

Table 1.24
Disposal Methods for Municipal Solid Waste

| Country | Disposal Method | | | | |
	Composting	Open Dumping	Landfill	Incineration	Others
Brunei	2	0	70	0	28
Indonesia	15	60	10	2	13
Malaysia	10	50	30	5	5
Myanmar	5	80	10	–	5
Philippines	10	75	10	–	5
Singapore	–	–	10	90	–
Thailand	10	65	5	5	15
Vietnam	10	70	–	–	20

Source: ASEAN 2006, p. 74.

treatment in largely unmaintained septic tanks (World Bank 2007, p. 19).

- Rivers in Vietnam's urban areas, especially its major cities, are seriously polluted by untreated industrial waste water. Lakes, streams, and canals within cities increasingly serve as sinks for domestic sewage and municipal and industrial wastes (World Bank 2003*a*, pp. 22–23).
- In urban areas of the Lao PDR, pollutants from roads, commercial and industrial areas, and private properties wash into the drains and watercourses. Litter, dust and dirt, oil and grease, particles of rubber compounds from tyres, metal, glass, and plastic from vehicles, and lead are common pollutants. Drains act as secondary sewers carrying industrial discharges, septic tank seepage and overflows in wet weather. Sewage is disposed into surface drains and drainage channels (World Bank 2005*b*, pp. 33–34).
- Indonesia has one of the lowest rates of sewage and sanitation coverage in Asia. Industries have expanded without much regard for the environment and led to serious environmental degradation. Domestic sewage, industrial effluents, agricultural run-off, and mismanaged solid waste are polluting surface and groundwater in Indonesia (World Bank 2003*b*, pp. 20–21).

Southeast Asia contributed 12 per cent (5,187 $MtCO_2$-eq) of the global greenhouse gas emissions in 2000. The sources were mainly the decline in biomass stocks of forestland through deforestation (see Table 1.25). Of the emissions, 59 per cent came from Indonesia, 6 per cent from Thailand, 4 per cent from the Philippines, 2 per cent from Vietnam, and 1 per cent from Singapore; the remaining came from the rest of Southeast Asia (ADB 2009*a*, pp. 125–26). Per capita emissions are higher than the global average, but still low compared with developed countries (ADB 2009*a*, p. 5).

Climate change is a very serious challenge facing Southeast Asia in the twenty-first century as the region is extremely vulnerable to climate change. It has a long coastline of 173,251 kilometres and high concentrations of population and economic activities in coastal areas which will be exposed to sea level rises of 1.3 ±0.7 mm per year over the next decades (see Table 1.26). The most conservative scenario estimates a sea level rise in Southeast Asia of about 40 cm above today's level by the end of the twenty-first century (ADB 2009*a*, p. 32).

Table 1.25
GHG Emissions in Southeast Asia (1990–2000) (MtCO$_2$-eq.)

Sector	1990	1995	2000
Energy	432.6	635.5	971.8
Industrial Process	25.4	46.4	50.8
Agriculture	336.7	369.3	407.0
Land Use Change and Forestry	3,232.4	3,832.2	3,861.0
Waste	64.1	70.5	76.6
Total	4,091.2	4,944.9	5,187.2

Source: ADB 2009a, p. 125.

Table 1.26
Share of Population within 100 Kilometres from the Coast (2005)

Country	%	Country	%
Indonesia	98.4	Thailand	39.5
Philippines	88.6	Vietnam	77.9
Singapore	84.4	Southeast Asia	80.2

Source: ADB 2009a, p. 9.

An urban low-elevation coastal zone (LECZ) is a contiguous land area up to 100 kilometres from the coast that is 10 metres or below in elevation. In Southeast Asia, it represents 29.4 per cent of the total urban land area (see Table 1.27). The urban population living in these zones is 12.3 per cent of the total population, and 36.0 per cent of the total urban population (CIESIN 2006). The urban poor are likely to be affected disproportionally as they tend to live in very-low-elevation areas.

A sea level rise of 59 cm could result in loss of mangroves, coastal erosion, and land loss for Singapore. Rising sea levels, combined with land subsidence due to overexploitation of groundwater, will move the coastline in Indonesia inland with a higher risk of flooding. If the sea level rises 0.25, 0.57, or 1.00 cm per year, floods will affect about 40, 45 or 90 sq. km respectively of North Jakarta in 2050. If the mean sea level rises by 0.5 metres and land subsidence continues, parts of six subdistricts of North Jakarta and Bekasi will be permanently inundated (ADB 2009a, pp. 49–50).

A 30 cm sea level rise in the Philippines by 2045 could affect 2,000 ha of land and about 500,000 people. A rise of 100 cm by 2080 will inundate

Table 1.27
Urban Population at Risk from Sea Level Rise (1995, 2000)

Country	2000 Population ('000)			1995 Land Area (km²)		
	Total	Urban	Urban in LECZ	Total	Urban	Urban in LECZ
Brunei	328	222	25	5,901	1,117	256
Cambodia	13,082	1,886	288	179,505	672	136
Indonesia	212,068	81,367	22,705	3,213,908	32,398	8,174
Lao PDR	5,278	892	0	230,230	1,134	0
Myanmar	47,749	12,452	4,509	669,310	4,698	1,084
Malaysia	22,172	13,902	3,684	329,945	14,090	3,774
Philippines	75,290	24,866	6,807	295,408	8,596	1,872
Singapore	4,018	3,926	550	597	543	62
Thailand	62,610	20,787	12,472	516,922	27,525	9,191
Timor Leste	737	33	1	14,789	134	7
Vietnam	78,136	17,406	12,863	328,535	5,959	3,872
SEA	521,468	177,739	63,904	5,785,050	96,866	28,428

Note: LECZ: Low-elevation coastal zone, i.e., contiguous land area up to 100 kilometres from the coast that is 10 metres or below in elevation.
Note that the data used in this table may differ from the official data.
Source: CIESIN 2006; McGranahan, Balk and Anderson 2006, p. 23.

over 5,000 ha of the Manila Bay coastal area and affect more than 2.5 million people. The risks intensify if sea surges associated with intense storms increase. In Thailand settlements along rivers and coastal areas will be at risk from the threat of sea level rise and coastal storm surges; increasing coastal erosion is expected, with a serious impact on the tourism industry. In Vietnam, a sea level rise of 100 cm could lead to flooding of 5,000 km² of the Red River Delta and 15,000–20,000 km² of the Mekong Delta (ADB 2009a, pp. 50–51).

Port cities in Southeast Asia are vulnerable to climate change due to their location in low-lying delta areas (see Table 1.28). Nicholls et al. (2008) studied the impact of climate change on port cities with more than one million inhabitants in 2005. In twelve port cities in Southeast Asia, more than five million people and assets worth US$114 billion are already exposed to coastal flooding due to storm surges and damage due to high winds. In 2070, twenty-eight million people and assets worth US$2,900 billion could be exposed to climate change.

A possible indirect impact of global warming in Southeast Asia is refugees. People may flee their rural homes due to persistent droughts,

Table 1.28
Exposure of Port Cities to Climate Change (2005, 2070)

	Pop. 2005 ('000)	Delta	Current City (2005)		Future City (2070)	
			Exposed ('000)	Exposed Assets (US$ b)	Exposed Pop. ('000)	Exposed Assets (US$ b)
Indonesia						
Jakarta	13,215	D	513	10.11	2,248	321.24
Malaysia						
Kuala Lumpur	1,405	—	270	15.06	295	83.88
Myanmar						
Yangon	4,107	—	510	3.62	4,965	172.02
Philippines						
Manila	10,686	D	113	2.69	545	66.21
Singapore						
Singapore	4,326	—	16	2.30	29	20.54
Thailand						
Bangkok	6,593	D	907	38.72	5,138	1,117.54
Vietnam						
HCM City	5,065	D	1,931	26.86	9,216	652.82

Note: Delta: Cities in deltaic locations tend to have higher coastal flood risk as a result of their tendency
to be at lower elevations and experience significant (natural and anthropogenic) subsidence.
Current city: situation in 2005; future city: future socio-economic situation with the 2070s' climate
change, natural subsidence/uplift, and human-induced subsidence).
Other ports included are Palembang, Surabaya, Ujang Padang, Davao, and Hai Phong.
Source: Nicholls et al. 2008.

floods, or erosion, and seek refuge in urban areas. The Asian Development
Bank (2009b) notes that there have been a number of speculative predictions
on human displacements at the global level despite many gaps in current
knowledge on climate change, migration, and the relationships among
these in Asia and the Pacific. It would be irresponsible to speculate on
future numbers of people likely to migrate.

CROSS-CUTTING RESPONSES

Urban Infrastructure

The rapid growth of the population and the economy is placing enormous
stress on existing urban infrastructure and services. Traffic congestion,

environmental degradation, and slums and squatter settlements are evidence that cities such as Bangkok, Jakarta, Manila, and Ho Chi Minh City have not managed to stay ahead of the growing demand for infrastructure and services. Infrastructure investment needs are immense, running into billions of dollars (see Table 1.29).

Table 1.29
Infrastructure Expenditure Needs (2006–10)

Country	Urban Sector (basic) ($ millions)	Urban Sector (basic + other) ($ millions)	Country	Urban Sector (basic) ($ millions)	Urban Sector (basic + other) ($ millions)
Cambodia	55.0	132	Philippines	1,043.7	2,504.9
Indonesia	1,998.7	4,772.9	Thailand	266.7	640.1
Lao PDR	26.4	63.4	Vietnam	455.4	1,093.0
Malaysia	279.3	670.3	Total	4,442.0	10,636.9
Myanmar	316.8	760.3			

Source: ADB 2008b, p. 41.

Southeast Asia needs to invest in a wide range of urban infrastructure. Urban areas need roads, water and power supplies, railway lines, ports, and airports to promote economic growth. Urban areas need to expand water supply and sanitation, education, and health facilities to reduce poverty and increase productivity. Urban areas need mass transit systems and improved solid waste management to improve the living environment. Adaptation to climate change will require investment in disaster preparedness.

One of the most visible infrastructure bottlenecks in Southeast Asia is urban transport. Bangkok, Jakarta, and Manila, but also Ho Chi Minh City and Phnom Penh, and even secondary cities, are notorious for their traffic congestion due to the rapid rise in various means of transport. Traffic congestion has economic, social, and environmental consequences. The economic and environmental costs of traffic congestion are immense, while the lack of affordable public transport has an impact on urban poverty.

In Hanoi the number of motorcycles increased from 56,648 to 1,076,581, and the number of private cars from 18,000 to more than 109,900, between 1981 and 2002 (Koh 2006, p. 165). Rapid motorization outstripped the expansion of the road networks in Bangkok, Jakarta, Manila, and Singapore. Due to a lack of convenient public transport modes, economic growth and increases in income lead to a rise in car ownership and road transport demand (see Table 1.30). As cities expand, the length of commuting trips increases, leading to more car dependence and road demand (see Table 1.31).

Many cities lack strategic planning and coordination capacity and a long-term public transport vision (APERC 2008, p. 1). At an early stage of development, cities need to assess future transport requirements so that investments in mass transit systems can be planned and high car dependence can be avoided. Once land use patterns have been fixed and residents have become dependent on private vehicles, major investments will be needed to redesign and rebuild the transport system, and to change people's behaviour to reduce car dependence (ADB 2005, p. 47).

Several cities in Southeast Asia have or are planning mass transit systems to reduce traffic congestion (see Table 1.32). However, independent government agencies and private companies often operate different parts

Table 1.30
Motor Car Ownership per 1,000 Population (1960–2000)

Year	Singapore	Kuala Lumpur	Bangkok	Jakarta	Manila	Surabaya
1960	39	46	14	n/a	n/a	n/a
1970	69	72	54	22	38	14
1980	64	86	71	38	55	20
1990	101	170	199	75	66	40
1995	116	209	249	103	74	n/a
2000	97	n/a	270	148	77	n/a

Source: Rimmer and Dick 2009, p. 238.

Table 1.31
Vehicles per Kilometre of Road in Selected Cities (2000)

City	Vehicles/km	City	Vehicles/km
Bangkok	1,332	Singapore	219
Jakarta	472	Chiang Mai	148
Metro Manila	435	Kuala Lumpur	113
Surabaya	422	Penang	93
Cebu	276		

Source: Rimmer and Dick 2009, p. 239.

Table 1.32
Mass Transit Systems in Southeast Asia

City	Mass Transit since	Length	City	Mass Transit since	Length
Bangkok	December 1999	47.3 km	Singapore	November 1987	147.7 km
Kuala Lumpur	December 1996	72.0 km	HCM City	Being planned	
Metro Manila	December 1984	45.6 km			

Source: <www.urbanrail.net5>.

of the public transport system, making coordination and integration of different modes of public transport difficult. As a result, even if a mass transit system exists, feeding the system through other modes of public transport is a problem.

Affordable mass transit systems provide the population with a wider choice of residential locations. If public transport is unavailable or expensive, low-income groups are forced to live close to their place of work, but such locations tend to be unaffordable. This forces many to live in slums and informal settlements near centres of employment. To prevent the development of informal settlements, governments need to set aside urban land for housing the urban poor and to connect these to centres of employment through inexpensive mass transit systems.

The Asia-Pacific Research Centre (APERC 2008, p. 50) evaluated the costs and benefits of mass rapid transit systems in Southeast Asia, estimating energy and CO_2 savings of such systems between 2005 and 2030. With an expanded MRT system, Bangkok could save 0.5 million tonnes of oil equivalent (Mtoe) or 17 per cent of its current gasoline consumption, and 1.2 million tonnes of CO_2 emissions (2 per cent of national transport CO_2 emissions). Manila could save 0.6 Mtoe or 19 per cent of its current gasoline consumption, and 1.5 million tonnes of CO_2 emissions (6 per cent of national transport CO_2 emissions).

As shown above, competitive cities also need "soft" infrastructure, including a reliable banking system, educational institutions, medical facilities, technological readiness, and business sophistication. Developing such infrastructure requires not only heavy investments, but also long-term planning. Institutional changes, in particular when they affect the distribution of power between national and local government, and between the public and the private sectors, are difficult to achieve.

Decentralization

Local governments need authority to manage urban areas better and to mobilize funds for development. However, Southeast Asian countries have generally relied on centralized forms of decision-making, with most national governments reluctant to give local governments more decision-making powers. They used to point to a lack of local management capacity, the opportunities for corruption, and the need to ensure the integrity of the nation state. What they allowed was some form of de-concentration (see Box 1.2) with a token role for local representatives, but this has changed.

The recent move towards decentralization in Cambodia, Indonesia, the Lao PDR, the Philippines, Thailand, and Vietnam (see Box 1.3) can be explained in different ways. It may have been a willingness to bring decision-making closer to the people, or a recognition that local needs and conditions need to be taken into account in decision-making, or a realization of the central government's inability to meet the growing demand for better cities and towns by the urban populations. Whatever the reason(s), devolution of powers to local government has occurred to various extents across Southeast Asia.

Decentralization has been welcomed as a step towards greater democracy and better governance, but experiences in Southeast Asia show that it is much easier to talk about decentralization than to implement it.

Box 1.2
Forms of Decentralization

Decentralization can take one or a combination of the following forms (White and Smoke 2005a, p. 6):

- De-concentration: sub-national governments act as agents of the national government ministries in the delivery of certain services without much or any authority over what and how they provide;
- Delegation: sub-national governments, rather than branches of the central government, are responsible for the delivery of certain services under the supervision of the central government;
- Devolution: (semi-)independent, elected sub-national governments are responsible for the delivery of public services and for imposing fees and taxes to finance the services.

Box 1.3
Decentralization Policies in Southeast Asia

Country	Policy
Cambodia	Hybrid case, with de-concentration to provinces and devolution to communes; commune system new and given greater emphasis, but provinces are more significant in terms of public expenditures.
Indonesia	Focus on substantial devolution to cities and districts, which replaced earlier emphasis on de-concentration to provinces; limited formal role at lowest levels; 2004 reforms increased the role of higher levels.
Philippines	Focus on devolution to subprovincial units, but provinces still play a significant role.
Thailand	Historical focus on de-concentration to provinces and districts, but 1997 framework shifts towards devolution to municipalities, districts, and sub-districts; implementation has been limited.
Vietnam	Focus mainly on de-concentration with stronger role for provinces, including regulatory control over sub-provincial levels; sub-national governments have been allocated rights over specific functions, approaching devolution.

Source: Smoke 2005a, p. 28.

Decentralization is uncharted territory for national and local governments. It is a process that takes time and is often not as rosy as initially thought.

Many factors determine the success of decentralization policies. National government must be committed to a sharing of powers with local government in a clear and transparent manner. Local government must have the legal powers, institutional capacity, human and financial resources, and political willingness to assume the new responsibilities, enforce laws, rules, and regulations, and adhere to the principles of good governance. Civil society (the media, NGOs, CBOs, etc.) must have the capacity and willingness to monitor the performance of local government and its partners, and to put pressure on local government to apply good governance principles.

National governments in Southeast Asia do not seem to have adopted decentralization policies wholeheartedly, as is evident from the substantial differences between *de jure* and de facto decentralization. Policies change often and there are frequent attempts by central governments to re-centralize decision-making. National governments tend to blame problems with decentralization on the lack of capacity of local actors, but policy incoherence appears to be a major problem.

Inconsistencies and discrepancies in the legal provisions of decentralization can pose serious problems (see Box 1.4). In the Philippines, decentralization was implemented in a compartmentalized way lacking coherence between different parts of the institutional framework (Guevara 2004, p. 2). In Indonesia, inconsistencies in the enabling legislation led to sustained uncertainty and even conflicts between different levels of government about their roles and responsibilities (Campos and Hellman 2005a, p. 250). Similar problems were observed in Thailand after decentralization was included in the 1997 Constitution (Wong 2007), and in Vietnam following decentralization as a part of public administration reform (Adam Fforde and Associates 2003).

Local governments are often assigned new tasks, but are unable to mobilize the resources to undertake those tasks (see Box 1.5). They remain dependent on tax sharing arrangements with, and transfers from, the national government. The Asian Development Bank (2008, p. xi) argues that local governments need greater control over tax policy and that they must be able to set rates and define the tax base, but must also administer their local tax systems better and reduce non-compliance.

Box 1.4
Conditions for Effective Decentralization of Expenditure Management

Conditions	Indonesia	Philippines	Thailand	Vietnam
Clear assignment of Responsibilities	low	medium	medium	medium
Matching of resources to responsibilities	low	medium	medium	medium
Matching of authority to responsibilities	medium	medium	low	low
Local capacity	medium	medium	low	medium
Local accountability	low	low	medium	low
National accountability	medium	low	medium	low

Source: Mountfield and Wong 2005a, p. 95.

Box 1.5
Sub-national Fiscal Structure

	Own-Source Revenues	Shared Taxes	Unconditional Transfers	Conditional Transfers	Informal Revenues
Cambodia	low	low	high[a]	n/a[b]	high
Indonesia	low	moderate	high	low	moderate
Philippines	moderate	moderate	high	low	moderate
Thailand	low	high	moderate	moderate	low
Vietnam	none	high	low	high	moderate

Note: "Low", "moderate", and "high" refer to the rough proportions of total sub-national revenues attributable to each revenue source relative to international experience.
a. Refers only to the commune level.
b. Most "provincial" agencies are de-concentrated arms of central ministries, so the term "transfer" does not apply.
Source: White and Smoke 2005a, p. 13.

Decentralization is expected to improve transparency and accountability, but often fails to do so. The benefits of decentralization are captured by the local elite, the rich and powerful, while the poor and other disadvantaged groups are not better off.

- In Indonesia decentralization did not empower the disadvantaged, but facilitated the rise of local patronage networks. Predatory interests effectively captured the process. Moreover, any abuse of power in a small town or village is less exposed by the media than such abuse in the capital city (Firman 2009, p. 336; Hadiz 2004).
- In Thailand, government officials at the provincial and local levels maintained de facto control over decision-making by elected councils, and local businessmen with interests in the construction sector tend to play a dominant role in the planning of infrastructure works. Decentralization also increased the powers of Members of Parliament in their provinces (Arghiros 2002; Wongpreedee 2007).

Decentralization increases problems of coordination and cooperation between local governments and between different levels of government. Most metropolitan regions cover different administrative entities and are fragmented sectorally with agencies in charge of transport, water, and power supplies. The administrative entities often have different functions: some are mainly residential, others are primarily commercial or industrial. This complicates the situation because investments may be needed in one part, but taxes are collected in another (OCED 2006, pp. 157–201). Decentralization generates "egoism" among local governments that only look inwards and think only about themselves (Firman 2009, p. 336; Firman 2010, p. 401).

There is a need to establish an additional layer of government at the regional level, but the idea would face strong opposition from the cities and towns concerned, and possibly also from the national government, as all of them would lose power. In the name of decentralization, national governments are more inclined to break up a large city into smaller municipalities to reduce its power. They fear the emergence of a strong local government that often belongs to the political opposition because its needs and priorities tend to be quite different from those of the country as a whole. The OECD (2006, p. 190) concludes that there is no simple governance model for metropolitan regions as the differences between models contain considerable trade-offs in terms of benefits and costs.

The problems experienced by local governments after decentralization are not an argument or an excuse to re-centralize power. Without decentralization there can be no advance in local governance; decentralization is a necessary first step (Arghiros 2002, p. 243). Making it work requires time and patience. Inconsistencies in the regulatory framework need to be removed. Some decision-making may need to be taking place at higher (intermediate) levels of government. Capacity development of local governments must be a critical part of any decentralization effort.

Privatization

Economic growth in Southeast Asia has led to the emergence of an urban middle class with good education, stable employment, and an adequate income. Enhanced education, better access to information, increased mobility, and heightened political awareness have made the urban middle class vocal and demanding. Their demand for quality public services is supported by a capacity and willingness to pay for these. If they find that the government cannot deliver, they turn to the private sector for the services.

This trend fits well with the global shift towards economic liberalization and privatization, which can be looked at from various perspectives. Some believe that the government is unsuited to delivering any services in an efficient manner because of its bureaucratic nature. Others stress that privatization fosters competition and gives consumers more choices. Osborne and Gaebler (1993, p. 35) argued that governments should concentrate on "steering" public affairs and leave the "rowing" to the private sector and civil society which are better equipped for such roles.

Privatization shifts the burden of raising capital for infrastructure investments from the government to the private sector. Local governments could issue bonds to finance urban infrastructure investments, but many have doubts about the credit worthiness of a local government. Many national governments are reluctant to allow sub-national entities to issue bonds because they would have to step in should a local government default. Privatization or public-private partnerships avoid the problem by leaving it to private companies to find the needed capital.

Public-private partnerships are often presented as the best of both worlds, but experiences in Southeast Asia show that they are difficult to conclude. The tollways of Bangkok are an example. It is difficult to estimate the long-term demand for the service on which the private sector can calculate its cash flow. Decisions by subsequent governments (e.g., opening new toll-free roads that compete with the tollway) may affect demand. Denying the private partner the agreed fee increases for political reasons can undermine the financial foundation of the project.

Public-private partnerships are criticized as "private management of public policy" because they lack transparency and accountability. This makes it difficult to assess if the government has brokered the best deal for the general public. The problem is not that the private sector seeks to make a profit, but that many local governments lack the capacity or political willingness to negotiate an outcome that is in the best public interest. Important decisions on public affairs are taken behind closed doors and ordinary citizens do not have proper access to these (OECD 2007, p. 13).

When it participates in a large infrastructure development project, the private sector will demand a say in its design to ensure that it can earn sufficient profit. As a result, public-private partnerships often operate the profitable lines of a mass transit system; they collect solid waste only in neighbourhoods that can afford to pay for the service. A private company will prepare an urban plan in exchange for valuable land, or build a mass transit system in exchange for the right to develop real estate along the railway lines.

Today the private sector across Southeast Asia fills gaps left by government to meet the demand for public services. Urban middle-class families in Jakarta, Manila, Bangkok, and elsewhere live in gated communities, guarded by private security firms rather than the police. They drink bottled water rather than tap water, drive on privately operated toll-roads rather than congested public roads, and enjoy a day at the private golf course rather than in poorly maintained public parks. They shop at private malls, cleaned and protected by private firms, rather than in dirty streets where they can be disturbed by beggars and are afraid of being mugged.

The urban middle-class households buy public services from the private sector because they have the money. The local government is left with limited resources to protect and maintain public spaces, tackle the problems of crime and pollution, and meet the needs of the urban poor. Political pressure to improve water supply, clean roads, ensure public safety, and build more parks is reduced because those in the best position to exert political pressure have already been looked after by the private sector.

At the other end of the socio-economic spectrum, the informal private sector develops its own urban areas. With one quarter to one third of the population living in informal settlements, the impact of the informal housing sector on urban development can be substantial. Its importance has led local governments to accommodate the informal sector in the formal urban fabric. In Bangkok the de facto occupation of sidewalks by informal vendors has been regularized on the condition that the vendors vacate the sidewalk at regular times to allow for cleaning. Closure of streets for food stalls during the evening is common in Thailand, Malaysia, and Singapore. The authorities in Bangkok recognize motorcycle-taxis as they provide public transport where other forms of transport are unfeasible.

Privatization by the formal and the informal sectors raises the question, "who decides on urban development?" As a result of economic globalization and an increasing reliance on market mechanisms to decide on investments and to supply public services, the number of decision-makers that take decisions affecting urban public affairs has become very large. Decisions that have an impact on urban development are now taken by private companies and civil society organizations at the local, national, and global levels.

GOOD URBAN GOVERNANCE

An important component of urban management is good governance. Governance is a complex concept that has been defined in many different ways. A relatively simple definition is "the quality of the relationship between the government and its citizens". This still abstract definition can be operationalized as: "the quality of the process by which decisions are taken that affect public affairs, as well as the quality of the implementation and outcome of these decisions".

The reference to "quality" implies that governance is a normative concept. Many different criteria have been proposed to measure the quality of governance, but there seems to be some consensus on the following criteria: inclusiveness, participation, transparency and accountability, equity, predictability, adherence to the rule of law, and subsidiarity. These criteria of good governance are related and reinforce one another. They offer different entry points into an assessment of good governance.

National and local governments are expected to take decisions related to public affairs, on behalf of the citizens whom they exist to serve and protect. They are accountable to the citizens for the decisions they have taken and for their implementation and outcomes. Globalization and privatization have weakened the role of government and increased the number of decision-makers, making transparency and accountability more difficult. Southeast Asia, with its open economies, has proven to be particularly vulnerable to decisions taken all over the world, as the 1997 financial crisis showed.

Urban Planning

Many urban areas in the region have become vast construction sites, experiencing constant change and development. Rural areas are urbanized; old buildings in historic centres are being demolished; new buildings are being constructed. There is a saying in Southeast Asia that someone who has not visited a neighbourhood for six months will surely get lost because the cityscape will have changed completely.

With the exception of Singapore, urban planning has a bad reputation in Southeast Asia. Many visitors to Bangkok ask the rhetorical question: What happened to urban planning here? Vorratnchaiphan and Villeneuve (2006, p. 347) write that in Thailand urban planning is an area in which cities and towns perform very poorly. Planning has almost no impact on how urban form and land use develop in Thailand. Cities and towns are self-organizing rather than planned, but in the self-organizing systems some have more influence than others. Private companies can develop shopping malls, offices, hotels, and new towns with disregard for urban plans and building regulations, while the urban poor are evicted from their unauthorized housing.

The lack of urban planning is not limited to free-market countries such as Thailand. In the socialist Lao People's Democratic Republic, private initiatives increasingly determine urban land uses. The transfer of state land to private ownership often occurs gradually on an informal basis, rather than by design, but it raises concerns that the private sector dominates the land market and could damage the wider public interest. Private investors often choose to ignore master plans and bypass planning guidance and controls (Rabé et al. 2007, pp. 28–30).

There is a disconnect between planners working in the traditional planning mode and the actual market-based mechanisms for urban development. Major decisions affecting public affairs at the local level are not taken by an (elected) local government. They are in the hands of a wide range of stakeholders at the local, national, regional, and global levels, with the local government often as the weakest player. Urban development becomes the result of negotiations over individual projects between private developers and the local government. Private sector developers often work hand-in-hand with local politicians and administrators to promote profits for the few rather than benefits for all.

Is ineffective urban planning the result of a lack of capacity, or a lack of political willingness to intervene? Is it a deliberate policy to leave urban development decisions to the market? The need for cities to compete in the global economy may have led to a shift in urban governance from managerialism to entrepreneurialism. According to OECD (2007, pp. 19–20, 30), managerialism is primarily concerned with the provision of services to citizens. Entrepreneurialism is concerned with pro-economic-growth strategies, a positive attitude towards the private sector and a willingness to collaborate with it, and city marketing to attract investors.

The repercussions of an entrepreneurialist urban agenda are that global capital increasingly determines the physical and social form of the city and that land use is determined on the basis of land value alone, not on the basis of social and environmental considerations (Hasan 2009, pp. 3–4). There is no attention paid to the broader picture, to public interest, to marginalized groups and to the local and global environment.

Public Leadership

Globalization, decentralization, and privatization have taken local governments into uncharted territory. With the central government unsure if it really wants to devolve powers, local governments cannot expect much guidance from higher authorities. They are, therefore, constantly on the lookout for good practices; that is, success stories about a local government that was able to solve a problem they have in common. Many local governments in Southeast Asia, alone or in partnership with the private sector or civil society, are trying out new approaches.

Good practices related to local government and good urban governance have emerged in Southeast Asia, and they address problems that many local governments face. Examples include Naga City in the Philippines, Tarakan and Yogyakarta in Indonesia, and Baan Mankong in Thailand (see Box 1.6). Good practices are often partnerships between a local government and one or more partner from among other local governments, the private sector, civil society, or urban poor communities.

Sceptics will argue that good practices cannot be replicated on a wider scale or applied in different circumstances, but although good practices cannot be cloned, valuable lessons can be drawn from experiences in other cities and towns. One condition that is usually highlighted is the need for strong leadership or a local champion. Mayors of the above mentioned towns are cited as persons without whom the good practice would not have developed.

Leaders must be able to overcome the inertia of the local administration and the opposition of vested interests that prefer the status quo, in order to make their city or town function better. The search is for leaders who can think laterally, innovate, and manage change. They reinvent local government so that it can make full use of its new responsibilities and become more effective after decentralization and privatization.

"We want a government of laws, not of men" [or women; YKS] is a quote attributed to John Adams. The call for, and the reliance on, leaders raise two questions: (a) Can a leader bring about structural changes that are sustainable after he or she leaves office? (b) Is a good practice, tested in one place, replicable without a leader ready to take risks to overcome

Box 1.6
Good Urban Practices

Country	City or Town	Good Practice
Philippines	Naga City	Naga City and fourteen surrounding towns formed the Metro Naga Development Council in a cooperative effort to complement limited resources and pool investment potentials and comparative advantages to promote economic development. It partners the private sector, enhances urban-rural linkages, and promotes participation, transparency, accountability, and predictability in managing public affairs (Mangahas, 2006, pp. 295–300) <metro.naga.gov.ph>.
Indonesia	Jogyakarta	Yogyakarta and two municipalities have set up a joint secretariat whose main objective is to ensure a balanced development of physical infrastructure in the region through coordination in planning, implementation, evaluation, and monitoring. The local governments have established this coordination mechanism, because they realize that urban infrastructure development and management can only perform well if it is managed as a system, regardless of administrative jurisdictions (Firman 2010).
Indonesia	Tarakan	After the decentralization of responsibilities to local government, the city of Tarakan adopted the "three pillars of development": human resources development, the rule of law and law enforcement, and economic development in the broad sense of development of the people's welfare. Singapore provided the inspiration for the initiative as it is an island-city like Tarakan. In addition, Tarakan includes environmental considerations in all its major decision-making (Sarosa 2006, pp. 173–78).
Thailand	200 cities	Baan Mankong supports community-based organizations in informal settlements to develop into city-wide networks that partner NGOs and academics to enable communities to negotiate better deals with landowners for the lease or purchase of land, with the aim of enhancing security of land tenure, developing basic infrastructure, and improving housing conditions for the urban poor <www.codi.or.th/housing>.

adversities? The answer to these questions is not clear and requires more study of good practices and the conditions that made them successful.

Inclusiveness

Good urban governance emphasizes the importance of inclusiveness, equity, participation, subsidiarity. It implies that all citizens, including the poor and other marginalized groups, have the right to:

- participate, directly or indirectly, in decision-making that affects their lives and livelihoods.
- be recognized for the contributions they make to development, even if these are made through the informal sector.
- share in the benefits of economic growth and development, including benefits such as access to basic infrastructure and services, and (land for) housing.

Good governance is critically important to avoid divided cities and towns. With advanced levels of privatization, an obstacle to inclusion for the poor are costs in terms of money and time, but even if there are no formal costs involved, exclusion is common and is often quite subtle. Language, appearance, or an informal settlement address stigmatizes rural migrants and denies them a service. The urban poor are also often targeted for harassment by law enforcement agents, treated with disrespect by those delivering public services, and asked for bribes before they can receive assistance to which they are entitled.

Some countries have formal barriers to inclusion and participation. In Vietnam, residential status determines an urban resident's right to access social assistance, the formal banking sector, employment in civil service, etc. In a resettlement programme in Ho Chi Minh City, households with only temporary urban registration were excluded from the benefits of the programme (Castiglioni et al. 2010, pp. 106–14). Other countries in Southeast Asia also have household registration systems that may deny residents certain rights outside the location where they are registered.

Good governance also relates to environmental sustainability, a particularly difficult issue in urban areas. Decision-makers must take account of the needs of future generations (Anand and Sen 2000) and must not compromise the ability of future generations to meet their needs when catering to the needs of present generations. This is becoming particularly urgent as the impact of climate change on the region could be devastating.

Inclusiveness also extends to the rural population. Cities and towns are in a position to contribute to improvements in agriculture productivity, a reduction of rural poverty, and the development of rural areas. Mechanisms that enable consultation, coordination, and cooperation between an urban local government and adjacent rural and urban areas are essential to expand the benefits of development to both sides.

The urban (and rural) poor are increasingly demanding their share of development. Growing sections of the urban population are exposed to new ideas as a result of ever more widely available information, universal education, and increasing organization. This leads to growing political awareness and empowerment of the urban poor who start challenging the inequalities in society. Because of the links between the urban poor and the rural poor, the demand for a fairer distribution of the benefits of economic growth and development becomes a national political issue.

Capacity Development

Local governments must be smart buyers and good urban managers to "steer" and reap the public benefits of globalization, decentralization, and privatization. They need staff with contract management experience, policy expertise, negotiation, bargaining and mediation skills, oversight and programme audit capabilities, and communication and political skills to manage programmes with third parties in a complex political environment (Van Slyke 2003, pp. 296–97). Large cities are hard-pressed to find such staff; for small cities and towns, it is nearly impossible.

Urban management capacity is lacking in most countries of Southeast Asia:

- In Cambodia the government has been unable to minimize the negative impact of rapid urbanization due to limited human, technical, and financial resources, leading to growing incidents of urban deficiencies and problems (Beng Hong 2006, p. 75).
- In Indonesia weakness in the institutional capacity, both at the national and local levels, is one of the major problems in the implementation of the new decentralization policy (Firman 2010).

- In the Lao People's Democratic Republic, the main constraints facing provincial and district-level land management authorities are a lack of staff, particularly staff trained in land management, the absence of a fully fledged network of district offices, and the lack of appropriate equipment and facilities required for their new tasks (Rabé et al. 2007, p. 33).
- In Thailand municipalities still have difficulty attracting and retaining a critical mass of high-quality, appropriately skilled staff. Many local governments want to increase the capability of their current staff rather than wait for an increase of staff or financial resources to recruit additional staff (Vorratnchaiphan and Villeneuve 2006, p. 346).
- In Vietnam local governments have a poor understanding of the nature of urbanization and lack the necessary skills to develop appropriate policies that are responsive to the development of a market economy (Nguyen 2006, p. 379).

The lack of expert staff is often used as an argument to turn back decentralization policies or to privatize public services. Capacity development is a critical requirement to make cities and towns more productive, inclusive, and sustainable. Capacity development in this respect includes both institutional development and human resources development. The needs for capacity development are enormous in particular as the decentralization of responsibilities for urban planning and management to local governments continues across Southeast Asia.

CONCLUSIONS

Urbanization is an inevitable process that occurs in tandem with economic development. The size, density, and diversity of an urban population lead to innovation, the division of labour, and economic growth. Urbanization has a positive social impact as it makes it easier to provide access to services such as education and health care. The impact of urbanization is, however, not only positive. The size and density of the population and of economic activities can lead to congestion, pollution, alienation, and crime. Moreover, urban poverty remains a serious problem and may increase as employment in agriculture declines.

A considerable portion of greenhouse gas emissions originates from urban areas, but not because they are "urban", but because urban areas are centres of economic activity and wealth. To mitigate the impact of climate change that will hit Southeast Asia particularly hard, urban residents will need to change the way they live and urban businesses will need to change the way they operate. If they do, urban areas can become the protectors rather than the destroyers of the environment.

Cities and towns in Southeast Asia face five major interdependent challenges: the promotion of economic growth and employment, the development of urban infrastructure and services, the reduction of poverty in urban (and rural) areas, the protection of the environment, and the mitigation of, and adaptation to, climate change. Urban areas will need to develop a culture that enhances urban living and improves urban sustainability while preserving those norms and values that are fundamental to the region.

Urbanization and urban development must be managed better, but this requires national policies and legal and institutional frameworks for decentralization that empower local governments to mobilize human and financial resources to improve urban infrastructure and services. It requires capacity development in urban management and good urban governance for elected and appointed officials in local government. At the same time national governments need to reaffirm their responsibility to ensure coordination and cooperation among the local governments, and also the redistribution of resources between more and less wealthy parts of the country.

Empowered local governments must promote productive, inclusive, and sustainable cities and towns. To achieve this, they need to support the private sector to generate economic growth and employment; assist the urban poor to improve their productivity and move out of poverty and help surrounding rural areas to reduce rural poverty and develop agriculture; strengthen partnerships with the private sector and civil society to protect the urban environment; reduce carbon emissions that damage the environment; and adapt to climate change. This is not an easy challenge, but cities and towns have the unique potential to achieve these goals.

References

Adam Fforde and Associates. *Decentralisation in Vietnam — Working Effectively at Provincial and Local Government Level — A Comparative Analysis of Long An and Quang Ngai Provinces*. Report prepared for the Australian Agency of International Development, 2003.

Airports Council International (ACI). *ACI World Airport Traffic Report 2008*. Geneva: Airports Council International, 2009.

Anand, Sudhir and Amartya Sen. "Human Development and Economic Sustainability". *World Development* 28, no. 12 (2000): 2029–49.

Arghiros, Daniel. "Political Reform and Civil Society at the Local Level: Thailand's Local Government Reforms". In *Reforming Thai Politics*, edited by Duncan McCargo. Copenhagen: Nordic Institute of Asian Studies, 2002.

Asia-Pacific Energy Research Centre (APERC). *Urban Transport Energy Use in the APEC Region: Benefits and Costs*. Tokyo: Institute of Energy Economics, 2008.

Asian Development Bank (ADB). *Connecting East Asia: A New Framework for Infrastructure*. Manila: Asian Development Bank, 2005.

———. *City Cluster Development: Towards an Urban-Led Development Strategy for Asia*. Manila: Asian Development Bank, 2008a.

———. *Managing Asian Cities: Sustainable and Inclusive Urban Solutions*. Manila: Asian Development Bank, 2008b.

———. *The Economics of Climate Change in Southeast Asia: A Regional Review*. Manila: Asian Development Bank, 2009a.

———. *Climate Change and Migration in Asia and the Pacific*. Manila: Asian Development Bank, 2009b.

Association of Southeast Asian Nations (ASEAN). *Third ASEAN State of the Environment Report 2006: Towards an Environmentally Sustainable ASEAN Community*. Jakarta: ASEAN Secretariat, 2006.

Bai, Xuemei and Hidefumi Imura. "A Comparative Study of Urban Environment in East Asia". *International Review for Environmental Strategies* 1, no. 1 (2000): 135–58.

Begg, Iain. "Cities and Competitiveness". *Urban Studies* 36, no. 5–6 (1999): 759–809.

Beijing Declaration Concerning Urban Culture. Adopted by the 2nd International Forum of Urban Planning and International Conference on Urban Culture, 11 June 2007, Beijing.

Beng Hong Socheat Khemro. "Cambodia". In *Urbanization and Sustainability in Asia: Case Studies of Good Practice*, edited by Brian Roberts and Trevor Kanaley. Manila: Asian Development Bank, 2006.

Benton-Short, Lisa, Marie Price, and Samantha Friedman. "Global Perspective on the Connections between Immigrants and World Cities". Occasional Papers Series. Washington DC: GW Centre for the Study of Globalization, George Washington University, 2004.

Brandon, Carter. "Cities and Health". *Environment Matters*, World Bank (Fall 1998): 44–47.

Bunjongjit, Naruemol and Xavier Oudin. "Small-Scale Industries and Institutional Framework in Thailand". Working Paper No. 81. Paris: Organization for Economic Cooperation and Development, 1992.

Campos, Jose Edgardo and Joel S. Hellman. "Governance Gone Local: Does Decentralization Improve Accountability?". In World Bank, *East Asia Decentralizes: Making Local Government Work*. Washington DC: World Bank, 2005*a*.

Castiglioni, Franck, Ludovic Dewaele, and Nguyen Quang Vinh. "Resettlement Issues of Informal Settlement Areas in Ho Chi Minh City: From Large-Scale Programmes to Micro-Projects". In *The Vietnamese City in Transition*, edited by Patrick Gubry et al. Singapore: Institute of Southeast Asian Studies, 2010.

Center for International Earth Science Information Network (CIESIN). "Low Elevation Coastal Zone (LECZ) Urban-Rural Estimates". In *Global Rural-Urban Mapping Project (GRUMP)*. New York: Columbia University, 2006 <http://sedac.ciesin.columbia.edu/gpw/lecz.jsp> (accessed 21 July 2010).

Chayovan, Napaporn, Peerasit Kamnuansilpa, and John Knodel. *Thailand Demographic and Health Survey 1987*. Bangkok: Institute for Population Studies, 1988.

Clawen, Anne. "Female Labour Migration to Bangkok: Transforming Rural-Urban Interactions and Social Networks through Globalisation". *Asia-Pacific Population Journal* 17, no. 3 (September 2002): 53–78.

Cohen, Barney. "Urban Growth in Developing Countries: A Review of Current Trends and a Caution Regarding Existing Forecasts". *World Development* 32, no. 1 (2004): 23–51.

Committee for Population, Family and Children [Vietnam] and ORC Macro. *Vietnam Demographic and Health Survey 2002*. Calverton: Committee for Population, Family and Children and ORC Macro, 2003.

Daniels, P.W. "Urban Challenges: the Formal and Informal Economies in Mega-Cities". *Cities* 21, no. 6 (2004): 501–11.

Davis, Benjamin, Paul Winters, Gero Carletto, Katia Covarrubias, Esteban J. Quiñones, Alberto Zezza, Kostas Stamoulis, Carlo Azzarri, and Stefania Digiuseppe. "A Cross-Country Comparison of Rural Income Generating Activities". *World Development* 38, no. 1 (2010): 48–63.

Department for International Development (DFID). "Non-Farm Income in Rural Areas". *Policy Planning and Implementation, Key Sheets*, No. 14 (2002).

Dutt, K. and N. Song. "Urbanization in Southeast Asia". In *The Asian City: Processes of Development, Characteristics and Planning*, edited by A.K. Dutt, F.J. Costa, S. Aggarwal, and A.G. Noble. Dordrecht: Kluwer, 1994.

Evers, Hans-Dieter and Rudiger Korff. *Southeast Asian Urbanism: The Meaning and Power of Social Space*. Singapore: Institute of Southeast Asian Studies, 2000.

FDI Intelligence. *The Shape of Things to Come: The FDI Outlook for 2009 and Performance Analysis for 2008*. London: *Financial Times*, 2009.

Firman, Tommy. "The Continuity and Change in Mega-Urbanization in Indonesia: A Survey of Jakarta–Bandung Region (JBR) Development". *Habitat International* 33 (2009): 327–39.

————. "Multi Local-Government under Indonesia's Decentralization Reform: The case of Kartamantul (The Greater Yogyakarta)". *Habitat International* 34, no. 4 (2010): 400–405.

Global Footprint Network. *Ecological Footprint and Bio-capacity 2006*, Global Footprint Network, 2009 <http://www.footprintnetwork.org/en/index.php/GFN/page/footprint_for_nations> (accessed 21 July 2010).

Global Urban Competitiveness Project (GUCP). *Global Urban Competitiveness Report 2007–2008*. Beijing: Chinese Academy of Social Sciences, 2008 <http://www.gucp.org/en/report.asp?bigclassid=2&smallclassid=20> (accessed 21 July 2010).

Gubry, Patrick et al. *The Vietnamese City in Transition*. Singapore: Institute of Southeast Asian Studies, 2010.

Guest, Philip. "Urbanization and Migration in Southeast Asia". In *Urbanization, Migration and Poverty in a Vietnamese Metropolis*, edited by Hy V. Luong. Singapore: NUS Press, 2009.

Guevara, Milwida M. "The Fiscal Decentralization Process in the Philippines: Lessons from Experience". Paper presented at the International Symposium on "Fiscal Decentralization in Asia Revisited", 20–21 February 2004, Tokyo.

Gultiano, Socorro and Wilhelm Flieger. "Urbanisation sans Development?". *Journal of Philippine Development*, No. 37, Vol. 20, no. 2 (1993): 264–88.

Gupta, Vikas. *Medical Tourism Market in Asia: Focus on Thailand, Malaysia, Singapore and India*. Vaishali: Koncept Analytics, 2008.

Hadiz, Vedi R. "Decentralization and Democracy in Indonesia: A Critique of Neo-Institutionalist Perspectives". *Development and Change* 35, no. 4 (2004): 697–718.

Hall, Kenneth. "Coastal Cities in an Age of Transition: Upstream-Downstream Networking and Societal Development in 15th- and 16th-Century Maritime Southeast Asia". Paper presented at the Small Cities Conference, "The Small City in the Global Context", 12–14 April 2007, Ball State University, Muncie.

Hasan, Arif. "The World Class City Concept and its Repercussions on Urban Planning for Cities in the Asia Pacific Region". Paper prepared for the *IAPS-CSDE Network Symposia on Culture, Space and Revitalization*. Istanbul, Turkey, 12–16 October 2009.

Hawksworth, John, Thomas Hoehn, and Anmol Tiwari. "Which are the Largest City Economies in the World and How Might this Change by 2025?". In *UK Economic Outlook* (November 2009). London: PricewaterhouseCoopers.

Healy, Andrew J. and Somchai Jitsuchon. "Finding the Poor in Thailand". *Journal of Asian Economics* 18 (2007): 739–59.

Henderson, Vernon. "The Effects of Urban Concentration on Economic Growth". Working Paper 7503. Cambridge: National Bureau of Economic Research, 2000.

International Labour Office (ILO). *Decent Work and the Informal Economy*. Geneva: International Labour Office, 2002*a*.

————. *Women and Men in the Informal Economy: A Statistical Picture*. Geneva: International Labour Office, 2002*b*.

————. *Labour and Social Trends in ASEAN 2007: Integration, Challenges and Opportunities*. Geneva: International Labour Office, 2007.

International Monetary Fund (IMF). *World Economic Outlook Database, April 2010 Edition*. Washington DC: International Monetary Fund < http://www.imf. org/external/pubs/ft/weo/2010/01/weodata/download.aspx> (accessed 21 July 2010).

Jacobs, Jane. *The Economy of Cities*. New York: Vintage Books, 1970.

Joint Monitoring Programme (JMP). *Progress on Sanitation and Drinking Water: 2010 Update*. Geneva: World Health Organization and UNICEF, 2010.

Jones, Gavin W. "Mega-cities in the Asia-Pacific Region". Paper delivered at the 10th Biennial Conference of the Australian Population Association: "Population and Globalisation: Australia in the 21st Century", Melbourne 28 November – 1 December 2000.

————. "Urbanization Trends in Asia: The Conceptual and Definitional Challenges". Paper prepared for the conference, "New Forms of Urbanisation: Conceptualising and Measuring Human Settlement in the Twenty-first Century", organized by the IUSSP Working Group on Urbanization, Bellagio, Italy, 11–15 March 2002.

————. "Comparative Dynamics of Six Mega-Urban Regions". In *Mega-Urban Regions in Pacific Asia: Urban Dynamics in a Global Era*, edited by Gavin W. Jones and Mike Douglass. Singapore: NUS Press, 2008.

————. "Changing Marriage Patterns in Asia". Working Paper Series, No. 131. Singapore: Asia Research Institute, 2010.

Jones, Gavin W. and Mike Douglass. "Introduction". In *Mega-Urban Regions in Pacific Asia: Urban Dynamics in a Global Era*, edited by Gavin W. Jones and Mike Douglass. Singapore: NUS Press, 2008.

———— (eds.). *Mega-Urban Regions in Pacific Asia: Urban Dynamics in a Global Era*. Singapore: NUS Press, 2008.

Kerkvliet, Benedict J.Tria and David G. Marr (eds.). *Beyond Hanoi: Local Government in Vietnam*. Singapore: Institute of Southeast Asian Studies, 2004.

Khan, Azizur Rahman. *Asian Experience on Growth, Employment and Poverty: An Overview with Special Reference to the Findings of Some Recent Case Studies*. Colombo: United Nations Development Programme and International Labour Office, 2007.

Koh, David W.H. *The Wards of Hanoi*. Singapore: Institute of Southeast Asian Studies, 2006.

Locke, Catherine, Nguyen Thi Ngan Hoa, and Nguyen Thi Thanh Tam. *The Institutional Context Influencing Rural-Urban Migration Choices and Strategies for*

Young Married Women and Men in Viet Nam. Norwich: Overseas Development Group, School of Development Studies, 2008.

Mahathir bin Mohamad. *The Malay Dilemma*. Singapore: Marshall Cavendish, 2008.

Malesky, Edmund J. "Push, Pull and, Reinforcing: The Channels of FDI Influence on Provincial Governance in Vietnam". In *Beyond Hanoi: Local Government in Vietnam*, edited by Benedict J. Tria Kerkvliet and David G. Marr. Singapore: Institute of Southeast Asian Studies, 2004.

Mangahas, Joel V. "The Philippines". In *Urbanization and Sustainability in Asia: Case Studies of Good Practice*, edited by Brian Roberts and Trevor Kanaley. Manila: Asian Development Bank, 2006.

Mason, Karen Oppenheim. "Family Change and Support of the Elderly in Asia: What Do We Know?". *Asia-Pacific Population Journal* 7, no. 3 (1992): 13–32.

MasterCard Worldwide. *Worldwide Centers of Commerce Index 2008*. Purchase: MasterCard Worldwide, 2008.

McCargo, Duncan, ed. *Reforming Thai Politics*. Copenhagen: Nordic Institute of Asian Studies, 2002.

McGranahan, Gordon, Deborah Balk, and Bridget Anderson. "Low-Coastal Zone Settlements". *Tiempo* 59 (April 2006): 23–26.

McGranahan, Gordon. "Urban Transitions and the Spatial Displacement of Environmental Burdens". In *Scaling Urban Environmental Challenges: From Local to Global and Back*, edited by Peter J. Marcotullio and Gordon McGranahan. London: Earthscan, 2007.

Moser, Sarah. "Putrajaya: Malaysia's New Federal Administrative Capital". *Cities* 27, no. 4 (2010): 285–97.

Mountfield, Edward and Christine P.W. Wong. "Public Expenditure on the Frontline: toward Effective Management by Sub-national Governments". In *East Asia Decentralizes: Making Local Government Work*. Washington, DC: World Bank, 2005a.

National Institute of Public Health (NIPH), National Institute of Statistics (Cambodia), and ORC Macro. *Cambodia Demographic and Health Survey 2005*. Phnom Penh and Calverton: National Institute of Public Health, National Institute of Statistics, and ORC Macro, 2006.

National Institute of Statistics (NIS), Directorate General for Health (Cambodia), and ORC Macro. *Cambodia Demographic and Health Survey 2000*. Phnom Penh and Calverton: National Institute of Statistics, Directorate General for Health, and ORC Macro, 2001.

National Research Council (NRC). *Cities Transformed: Demographic Change and Its Implications in the Developing World*, edited by M.R. Montgomery, R. Stren, B. Cohen, and H.E. Reed. Committee on Population, Division of Behavioral and Social Sciences and Education. Washington, DC: The National Academies Press, 2003.

National Statistical Office (NSO) [Philippines] and ORC Macro. *Philippines National Demographic and Health Survey 2003*. Manila and Calverton: National Statistical Office and ORC Macro, 2004.

Ness, Gayl D. and Prem P. Talwar. *Asian Urbanization in the New Millennium*. Kobe and Singapore: AUICK and Cavendish, 2005.

Newman, Peter. "The Environmental Impact of Cities". *Environment & Urbanization* 18, no. 2 (2006): 275–95.

Nguyen, To Lang. "Viet Nam". In *Urbanization and Sustainability in Asia: Case Studies of Good Practice*, edited by Brian Roberts and Trevor Kanaley. Manila: Asian Development Bank, 2006.

Nicholls, R. J. et al. "Ranking Port Cities with High Exposure and Vulnerability to Climate Extremes: Exposure Estimates". *OECD Environment Working Papers*, No. 1. Paris: Organization for Economic Cooperation and Development, 2008.

O'Meara, Molly. "Reinventing Cities for People and the Planet". *Worldwatch Paper* 147. Washington, DC: Worldwatch Institute, 1999.

Ooi, Giok Ling. *Housing in Southeast Asian Cities*. Southeast Asia Background Series No. 4. Singapore: Institute of Southeast Asian Studies, 2005.

Orbeta Jr., Aniceto C. *A Review of Research on Population-Related Issues: 1980–2002*, Discussion Paper Series, No. 2002-17. Makati City: Philippines Institute for Development Studies, 2002.

Organization for Economic Cooperation and Development (OECD). "International Symposium on Enhancing City Attractiveness for the Future", Nagoya, Japan, 2–3 June, 2005, Paris, Organization for Economic Cooperation and Development, 2005.

———. *Competitive Cities in the Global Economy*. OECD Territorial Reviews. Paris: Organization for Economic Cooperation and Development, 2006.

———. *Competitive Cities: A New Entrepreneurial Paradigm in Spatial Development*. OECD Territorial Reviews. Paris: Organization for Economic Cooperation and Development, 2007.

Osborne, David and Ted Gaebler. *Reinventing Government: How the Entrepreneurial Spirit is Transforming the Public Sector*. New York: Plume, 1993.

Peerenboom, Randall. "Show Me the Money: The Dominance of Wealth in Determining Rights Performance in Asia". *Duke Journal of Comparative and International Law* 15 (2005): 75–152.

Pejaranonda, Chintana, Sureerat Santipaporn, and Philip Guest. "Rural-Urban Migration in Thailand". In United Nations, *Trends, Patterns and Implications of Rural-Urban Migration in India, Nepal and Thailand. Asian Population Studies Series*, No. 138. New York: United Nations, 1995.

Prasad, Eswar S. "Rebalancing Growth in Asia". Working Paper 15169. Cambridge: National Bureau of Economic Research, 2009.

Rabé, Paul, Thenekham Thongbonh, and Vongdeuane Vongsiharath. "Study on Urban Land Management and Planning in Lao PDR". *Land Policy Study*, No. 10. Vientiane: 2007.

Ravillion, Martin, Shaohua Chen, and Prem Sangraula. "New Evidence on the Urbanisation of Global Poverty". World Bank Policy Research Working Paper, No. 4199. Washington, DC: World Bank, 2007.

Reid, Anthony. *Southeast Asia in the Age of Commerce 1450–1680. Volume Two: Expansion and Crisis*. Chiang Mai: Silkworm Books, 1993.

Rimmer, Peter J. and Howard Dick. *The City in Southeast Asia: Patterns, Processes and Policy*. Singapore: NUS Press, 2009.

Roberts, Brian and Trevor Kanaley, eds. *Urbanization and Sustainability in Asia: Case Studies of Good Practice*. Manila: Asian Development Bank, 2006.

Satrusayang, Cod. "Revolution in the Rice Field". *Bangkok Post*, 28 August 2010.

Satterthwaite, David. "The Implications of Population Growth and Urbanization for Climate Change". *Environment and Urbanization* 21, no. 2 (2009): 545–67.

Schwab, Klaus (ed.). *The Global Competitiveness Report 2009–2010*. Geneva: World Economic Forum, 2009.

Shiraishi, Takashi. "The Rise of New Urban Middle Classes in Southeast Asia: What is its National and Regional Significance?". *RIETI Discussion Paper Series*, 04-E-011. Tokyo: Research Institute of Economy, Trade & Industry, 2004.

Smoke, Paul. "The Rules of the Intergovernmental Game in East Asia: Decentralization Frameworks and Processes". In *East Asia Decentralizes: Making Local Government Work*. Washington, DC: World Bank, 2005*a*.

Statistics Indonesia (BPS) and Macro International. *Indonesia Demographic and Health Survey 2007*. Calverton: BPS and Macro International, 2008.

Suryadarma, Daniel, Wenefrida Widyanti, Asep Suryahadi, and Sudarno Sumarto. "From Access to Income: Regional and Ethnic Inequality in Indonesia". SMERU Working Paper. Jakarta: SMERU Research Institute, 2006.

Tacoli, Cecilia. "The Role of Small and Intermediate Urban Centres and Market Towns and the Value of Regional Approaches to Rural Poverty Reduction Policy". Paper prepared for the "OECD DAC POVNET Agriculture and Pro-Poor Growth Task Team Workshop", 17–18 June 2004, Helsinki.

Tey Nai Peng. "Trends and Patterns of Urbanization in Malaysia, 1970–2000". In *Asian Urbanization in the New Millennium*, edited by Gayl D. Ness and Prem P. Talwar. Kobe: AUICK, 2005.

Thompson, Eric C. *Unsettling Absences: Urbanism in Rural Malaysia*. Singapore: NUS Press, 2007.

Thrift, Nigel and Dean Forbes. *The Price of War: Urbanization in Vietnam 1954–1985*. Boston: Allen and Unwin, 1986.

Times Higher Education. *World University Rankings 2009: Top 200 World Universities* <http://www.timeshighereducation.co.uk/hybrid.asp?typeCode=438> (accessed 31 July 2010).

Tjiptoherijanto, Prijono and Eddy Hasmi. "Urbanization and Urban Growth in Indonesia". In *Asian Urbanization in the New Millennium*, edited by Gayl D. Ness and Prem P. Talwar. Kobe and Singapore: AUICK and Cavendish, 2005.

Tretheway, Michael and Ian Kincaid. "Competition between Airports in the new Millennium: What Works, What Doesn't Work and Why". Paper presented at the 8th Hamburg Aviation Conference: "Competition between Airports in the New Millennium", Hamburg, 2005.

Trinh Duy Luan, Nguyen Huu Minh, and Dang Nguyen Anh. "Urbanization and Urban Growth in Vietnam". In *Asian Urbanization in the New Millennium*, edited by Gayl D. Ness and Prem P. Talwar. Kobe and Singapore: AUICK and Cavendish, 2005.

UN-HABITAT. *State of the World's Cities 2008/2009: Harmonious Cities*. London: Earthscan, 2008.

———. *Urban Indicators Database*. Nairobi: UN-HABITAT, 2010 <http://www.unhabitat.org/stats/Default.aspx (accessed 21 July 2010).

United Nations. "Trends, Patterns and Implications of Rural-Urban Migration in India, Nepal and Thailand". *Asian Population Studies Series*, No. 138. New York: United Nations, 1995.

United Nations Centre for Human Settlements (UNCHS). *Population Distribution and Urbanization: A Review of Policy Options*. Nairobi: United Nations Centre for Human Settlements, 1985.

United Nations Development Programme (UNDP). *Human Development Report 2007/08: Fighting Climate Change: Human Solidarity in a Divided World*. New York, United Nations Development Programme, 2007.

United Nations Economic and Social Commission for Asia and the Pacific (UN ESCAP). *Statistical Yearbook for Asia and the Pacific 2008*. Bangkok: United Nations, 2008.

United Nations Population Division (UNPD). *World Population Prospects: The 2008 Revision Population Database*, New York, United Nations, 2009 <http://esa.un.org/unpd/wpp2008/index.htm> (accessed 21 July 2010).

———. *World Urbanisation Prospects: The 2003 Revision*. New York: United Nations, 2004.

———. *World Urbanisation Prospects: The 2009 Revision Population Database*. New York: United Nations, 2010 <http://esa.un.org/unpd/wup/index.htm> (accessed 21 July 2010).

United Nations Population Fund (UNFPA). *State of the World Population 2007: Unleashing the Potential of Urban Growth*. New York: United Nations Population Fund, 2007.

Van Slyke, David M. "The Mythology of Privatisation in Contracting for Social Services". *Public Administration Review* 63, no. 3 (2003): 296–315.

Vorratnchaiphan, Chamniern and David Villeneuve. "Thailand". In *Urbanization and Sustainability in Asia: Case Studies of Good Practice*, edited by Brian Roberts and Trevor Kanaley. Manila: Asian Development Bank, 2006.

White, Roland and Paul Smoke. "East Asia Decentralizes". In *East Asia Decentralizes: Making Local Government Work*. Washington, DC, World Bank, 2005a.

Wirth, Louis. "Urbanism as a Way of Life". *American Journal of Sociology* 44, no. 1 (1938): 1–24.

Wong, Jeff. *Thailand: Decentralization, or What Next*. Quezon City: Logolink-Southeast Asia, 2007.

Wongpreedee, Achakorn. "Decentralization and Its Effect on Provincial Political Power in Thailand". *Asian and African Area Studies* 6, no. 2 (2007): 454–70.

World Bank. *Vietnam Environment Monitor 2003: Water*. Washington, DC: World Bank, 2003a.

⸺. *Indonesia Environment Monitor 2003: Special Focus: Reducing Pollution*. Washington DC, World Bank, 2003b.

⸺. *East Asia Decentralises: Making Local Government Work*. Washington, DC: World Bank, 2005a.

⸺. *Lao PDR Environment Monitor*. Washington, DC: World Bank, 2005b.

⸺. *Philippines Environment Monitor 2006: Environmental Health*. Washington, DC: World Bank, 2007.

⸺. *World Development Report 2009: Reshaping Economic Geography*. Washington, DC: World Bank, 2009.

Worldwide Fund for Nature (WWF). *Mega-Stress for Mega-Cities: A Climate Vulnerability Ranking of Major Coastal Cities in Asia*. Gland: Worldwide Fund for Nature, 2009.

Cities as Engines of Development

2

ASEAN TRANSPORT POLICY, INFRASTRUCTURE DEVELOPMENT, AND TRADE FACILITATION

Anthony T.H. Chin

INTRODUCTION

One of the driving forces behind the formation of the Association of Southeast Asian Nations (ASEAN) in 1967 was to accelerate the economic growth of the region through cooperation. Economic growth was to be achieved through joint agreements such as the ASEAN Free Trade Area (AFTA) and, in recent times, through the formation of the ASEAN Economic Community (AEC), which aims to accomplish a single integrated regional market, plugged into the international economy. A central element of regional economic integration is the presence of efficient logistics and the availability and efficient management of transport infrastructure. The traditional understanding of logistics as moving inputs and products in production and warehousing has been superseded by the dynamism of the modern global supply chain. Logistics today begins at the stage of procurement of factors of production and ends at the point of consumption. It includes the planning, design, and support of the business operations of procurement, purchasing, real time inventory, warehousing, distribution, deployment of information technology, transportation, customer support, insurance, financial services, and management of human resources. The vital link in this whole chain is the availability of infrastructure and its efficient transportation management. Added to this is the flexibility and nimbleness of production centres as they relocate when costs escalate.

ASEAN economic indicators on trade and foreign direct investment (FDI) have been impressive. ASEAN's total merchandise trade reached US$1.53 trillion (ASEAN Merchandise Trade Statistics Database 2010) and its share of total global FDI inflow increased from 2.8 per cent to 3.6 per cent (VNS 2010). Trade requires the transportation of goods via the various modes of transportation, and having an efficient transportation network attracts foreign investors to locate production plants and offices in the region. Since trade and FDI are important contributors to economic growth and transport infrastructure, ASEAN had been cooperating closely through regional transport agreements and region-wide projects to ensure that the transport network is enhanced and poised for further growth in the region. As the world recovers from the global financial crisis (GFC), the forces of globalization and international connectivity require economies to be nimble and respond quickly to the urgent needs of foreign investors. Garment factories move from China to Bangladesh in very short periods of time when an alternative low-cost advantage presents itself. Underpinning macro considerations are micro-facilitators such as a qualified and competitive workforce, good physical and soft infrastructure, and good governance. This chapter assesses the performance of land transport strategies in ASEAN in light of the changing needs of the global supply chain. It also assesses the performance of rail and road transport (a crucial component in the entire transportation network) as a facilitator of trade. This is because the interconnectedness of the economy requires a multimodal transport system, including maritime and aviation transport. Transport infrastructure investments have often been an afterthought and coordinated into economic development plans. It is seldom integrated into the dynamics of a global supply chain, nor managed according to the hierarchy of customer and producer needs, especially with regard to regional and land use development. This chapter argues for a hierarchical logistic approach to incorporating transportation infrastructure investments in the economy in order to maximize its impact on the region. This approach takes into account the geography of ASEAN and land use.

GLOBALIZATION, TRADE, AND FINANCIAL CRISES

Trade drives economic growth in ASEAN. Globalization and increasing interdependence between ASEAN economies and the rest of the world subject ASEAN's growth to the volatility of the economies of major trading partners (ASEAN 2008). This highlights the role of efficient transport infrastructure and connectivity in managing the fluctuations of the economic cycle. Land transport infrastructure development is crucial to the realization of ASEAN's goal of economic integration. Additionally, physical connectivity through cross-border infrastructure development is crucial for enhanced regional cooperation and economic integration (Kuroda 2006). The acceleration to enhance physical connectivity includes resource sharing. To promote cross-border trade and investment, improve countries' competitiveness, and raise domestic output, it is important for ASEAN countries to be physically connected through various modes of transportation, such as roads and railways. Transport infrastructure thus consists of a network of links which allows for the production and exchange of goods and services. It can be categorized into hard infrastructure and soft infrastructure. The former refers to physical structures or facilities that support society and the economy, such as roads and railways. The latter refers to non-tangibles supporting the development and operation of hard infrastructure, such as policy, regulatory, and institutional frameworks; governance mechanisms; systems and customs procedures.

Economic (or business) cycles are becoming shorter and more frequent as a consequence of globalization. The occurrence of "bubbles" (Internet, housing, and food) is becoming more frequent. The Asian financial crisis (AFC) in 1997 and the recent GFC are cases in point. Shroff (1999) regards globalization as a process and not a state of being. It is a move or a series of moves towards what may be described as a global economy. It is best seen as a move away from national economies interacting with one another in a variety of ways, towards a fully integrated world economy. A financial crisis is characterized by currency crashes (Baldacci et al. 2002), and currency crashes result in a nominal depreciation of the currency of at least 25 per cent, accompanied by a 10 per cent increase in the rate of depreciation (Frankel and Rose 1996). ASEAN was caught in this situation during the AFC of 1997. Sach and Radelet (1998) pointed out that the Asian crisis was caused by a boom of international lending and capital inflow, followed by a massive outflow. This resulted in a drastic depreciation of the currencies of various Southeast Asian nations. Statistics showed that intra-ASEAN trade grew 279 per cent over the past ten years while extra-ASEAN trade increased 175 per cent. Both had shown sharp increases after the AFC. However, intra-ASEAN trade grew at a faster pace than extra-ASEAN trade.

ASEAN's total trade slowed down during the AFC, with total trade falling from US$698,641.9 million in 1997 to US$576,107.7 million in 1998, recording a fall of 18 per cent (see Figure 2.1). Total trade fell again in 2001, but, at US$690,990.7 million, was still much higher than during the AFC. Total ASEAN trade has been rising since. By 2008 the total trade of ASEAN reached US$1,710,371.7 million, a 197 per cent increase over the ten-year period from 1998.

Statistics from intra-ASEAN trade are a good indication of economic integration in the region. To some extent, it can show if transport policies are effective in deepening economic integration in ASEAN. The AFC caused intra-ASEAN trade to decrease from US$149,973.1 million in 1997, to US$120,917.8 million in 1998, recording a 19 per cent drop. Intra-ASEAN

Figure 2.1
ASEAN Trade Statistics, 1995–2008

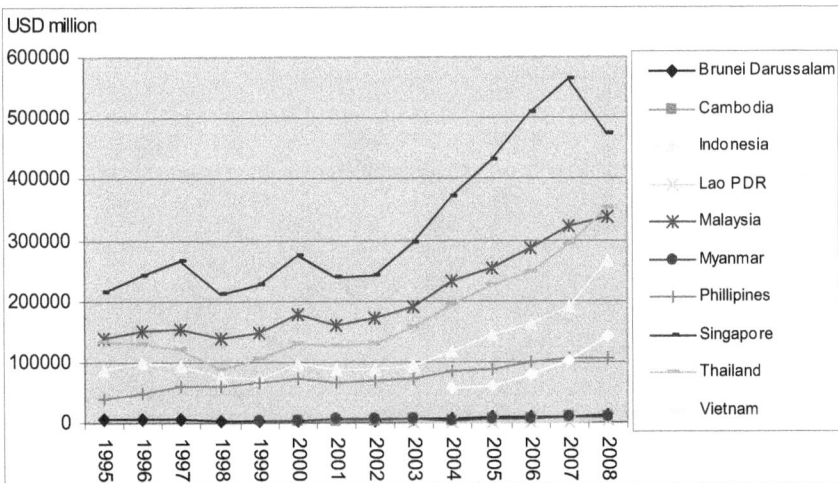

Source: ASEAN Statistical Yearbook 2008.

trade increased by 270 per cent from 1998 to 2008, post AFC (refer to Figure 2.2).

Figure 2.3 shows that extra-ASEAN trade fell from US$548,668.8 million in 1997 to US$455,189.9 million in 1998, recording a decrease of 17 per cent. The extra-ASEAN trade picked up from 1998 to 2008, growing by 175 per cent. This is perhaps due to the interconnectivity with other regional and global markets (see Figure 2.3). Figure 2.4 shows the relative importance of China in ASEAN's trade. In 2009 China had become the top trading partner of ASEAN, outside the ASEAN region. Comparing trade across other major trading partner and the European Union, China is emerging as ASEAN's top trading partner. In 2008 China's trade with ASEAN was only behind the European Union, Japan, and intra-ASEAN. China's share to total ASEAN trade was 11.3 per cent.

During the GFC, China-ASEAN trade totalled 1.6 per cent of ASEAN total trade. It reflects the rising economic status of China and its influence within the ASEAN region. Although the Singapore-Kunming Rail Link (SKRL) project which links the seven ASEAN countries with China is still under construction, ASEAN's general direction of improving connectivity

Figure 2.2
Intra-ASEAN Trade Statistics, 1995–2008

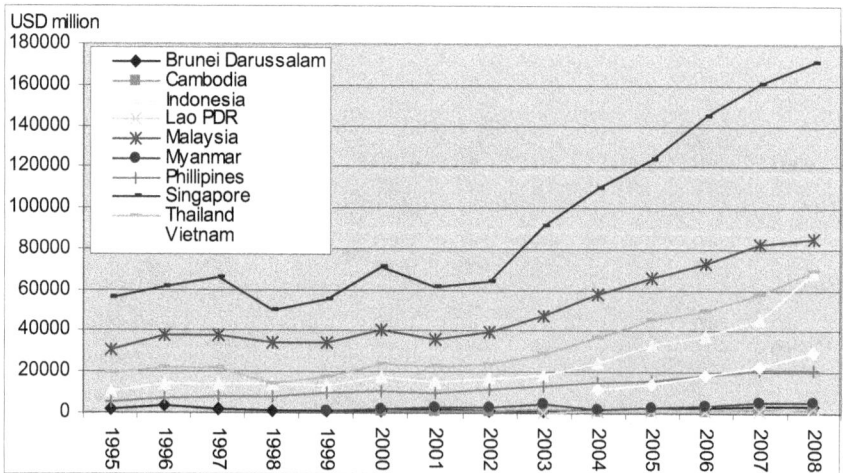

Source: ASEAN Statistical Yearbook 2008.

Figure 2.3
Extra-ASEAN Trade Statistics, 1995–2008

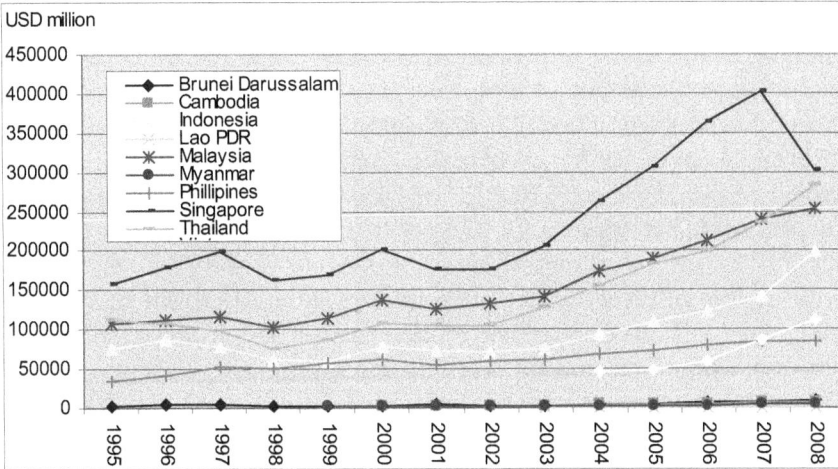

Source: ASEAN Statistical Yearbook 2008.

Figure 2.4
ASEAN Trade by Country, 1995–2008

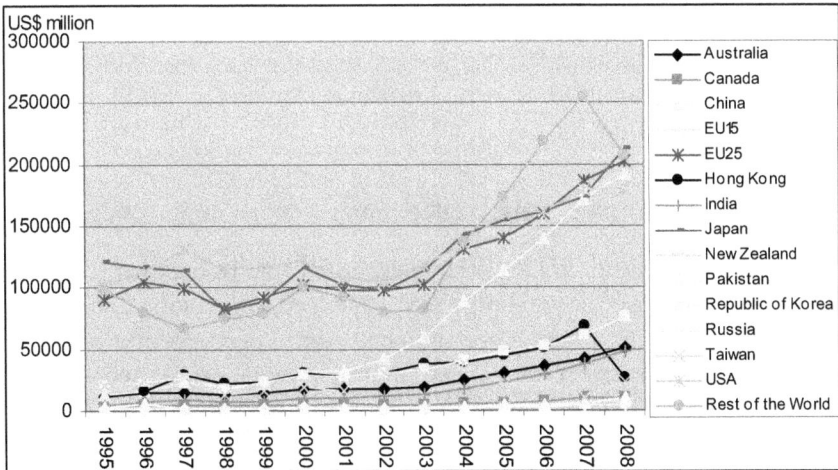

Source: ASEAN Trade Statistics Database.

with China is definitely on the right track. China offers immense potential for trade and market expansion. The scheduled completion of the SKRL in 2015 will further enhance trade relations between ASEAN and China.

ASEAN trade experienced a downturn during the GFC (ASEAN 2010) and total trade fell by 19 per cent from 2008 to 2009. The fall in total trade during the AFC was around 18 per cent. Even though the fall in total trade was about the same, the GFC was a "financial tsunami". This could be attributed to the resilience of ASEAN's economies. ASEAN's total merchandise trade fell from US$1,897.1 billion in 2008 to US$1,536.8 billion in 2009. However, this 19 per cent fall is less than the 22.6 per cent decline in worldwide trade.

FDI is seen as an indicator of a region's or country's potential. FDI inflows into ASEAN fell 32.6 per cent during the AFC from US$34,082.2 million in 1997, to US$22,959.8 million in 1998. FDI inflows fell to even lower levels in 2002 and did not start recovering until 2004 (see Figures 2.5a and 2.5b). Since then FDI inflows have increased rapidly, amounting to US$60,596.0 in 2008. Trade also picked up soon after the crisis and there was GDP growth. However, FDI also depends on the confidence level of investors. Investor confidence was shaken during the AFC and the uncertainty continued until 2004. Bhattacharyay (2008) has noticed that greater regional integration through enhanced physical connectivity supports trade and investment (including FDI) expansion. Following the AFC, ASEAN stepped up the completion of numerous land transport projects such as SKRL and the ASEAN Highway Network (AHN), and signed facilitation trade agreements. These measures added confidence to FDI flows. Figure 2.5b also shows that most of the FDI went to the ASEAN-5 countries, that is, Indonesia, Malaysia, the Philippines, Singapore, and Thailand.

TRANSPORT INFRASRUCTURE AND ECONOMIC GROWTH

Banister and Berechman (2001) have observed that transport investment can act as facilitators of economic growth and lead to development benefits. Historically there is a close correlation between the growth in demand for freight and passenger traffic, and economic growth. Similar conclusions have been found with respect to the wider economic benefits of transport infrastructure investments, a contemporary version of forward linkages of transport infrastructure (Lakshmanan 2010). Plummer and Chia (2009) have noted that through the implementation of "hard" and "soft" infrastructure

Figure 2.5a
Foreign Direct Investments Inflows into ASEAN, 2000–2008

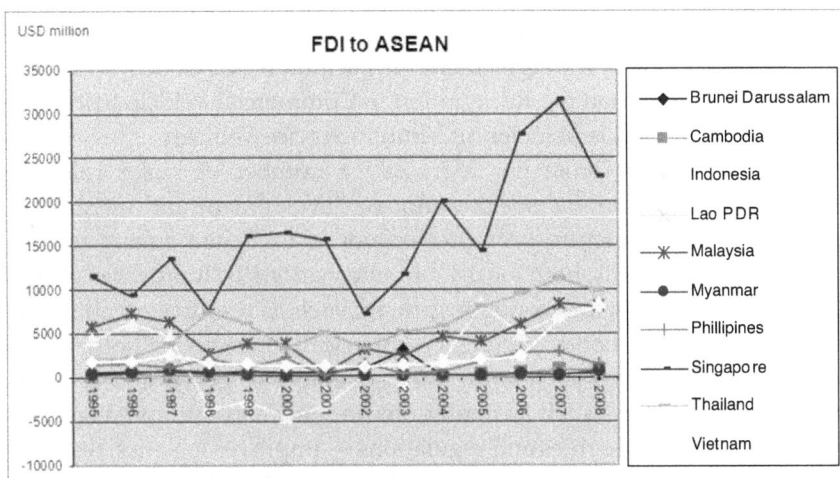

Figure 2.5b
Foreign Direct Investments Inflows into ASEAN, 2000–2008

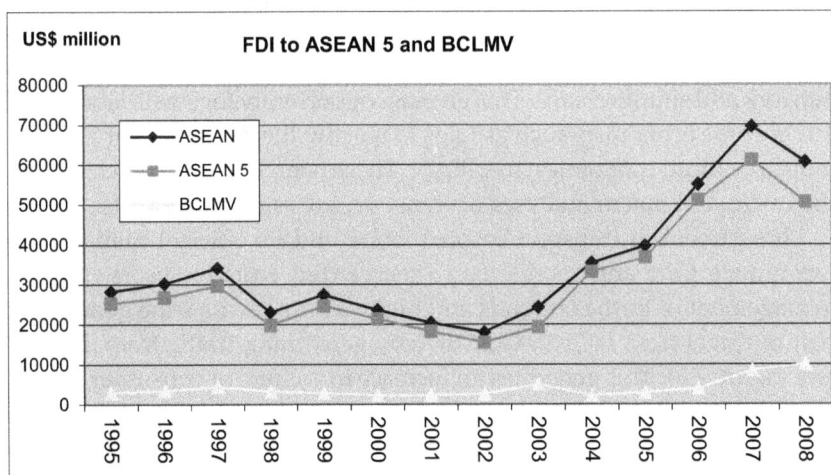

Source: ASEAN Secretariat — ASEAN FDI database as of 15 July 2009. From country submission based on the ASEAN AMS Balance of Payments data.

measures, there would be greater and deeper regional integration in infrastructure development, which aims to achieve an efficient, secure, and integrated transport network in ASEAN. The SKRL and AHN are examples of "hard" infrastructure. Examples of "soft" infrastructure include the ASEAN Framework Agreement on Facilitation of Goods in Transit, and the Agreement on the Recognition of Commercial Vehicle Inspection Certificates for Goods Vehicles and Public Service Vehicles.

Bhattacharyay (2008) has identified a number of major roles for infrastructure in regional socio-economic development and integration. First, basic infrastructure promotes economic exchange among various sectors of an economy, both locally and internationally. It provides greater access to key inputs for economic growth, such as resources, technology, and knowledge. Second, it enhances physical connectivity both within and among countries, facilitating the movement of goods and services. Soft infrastructure — such as modern technology and improved customs procedures and trade rules and regulations — improves logistics, resulting in reduced trade costs and the speedier movement of goods and services. Greater regional integration through enhanced physical connectivity supports trade and investment (including FDI) expansion, and financial market development.

Empirical evidence indicates that infrastructure spending can have a positive and statistically significant effect on long-run economic growth (World Bank 2002). It promotes efficient production, trade competitiveness, and trade flows, by allowing businesses to join the regional production network and supply chains. This gives an opportunity for small, landlocked, low-income economies such as Laos to narrow the development gap with more advanced economies in ASEAN. These benefits can be reflected from the micro and macro analyses of transport infrastructure effects.

Investment in transport infrastructure and its efficient management can reduce time and money cost (generalized cost) for users. Efficient management of traffic on roads and highways can reduce the generalized cost of travel from GC1 to GC2 thereby generating traffic from T1 to T2 (see Figure 2.6). This generates an increase in welfare or consumer surplus from CS1 to CS2 + CS3.

There is a time reduction due to improvement in speed due to the introduction of a green wave traffic lights system leading to cost savings. The demand function D represents the number of trip kilometres given different generalized costs (see Figure 2.6 and 2.7). The intersection of the

Figure 2.6
Consumer Benefits with Improvements in Traffic Management Schemes

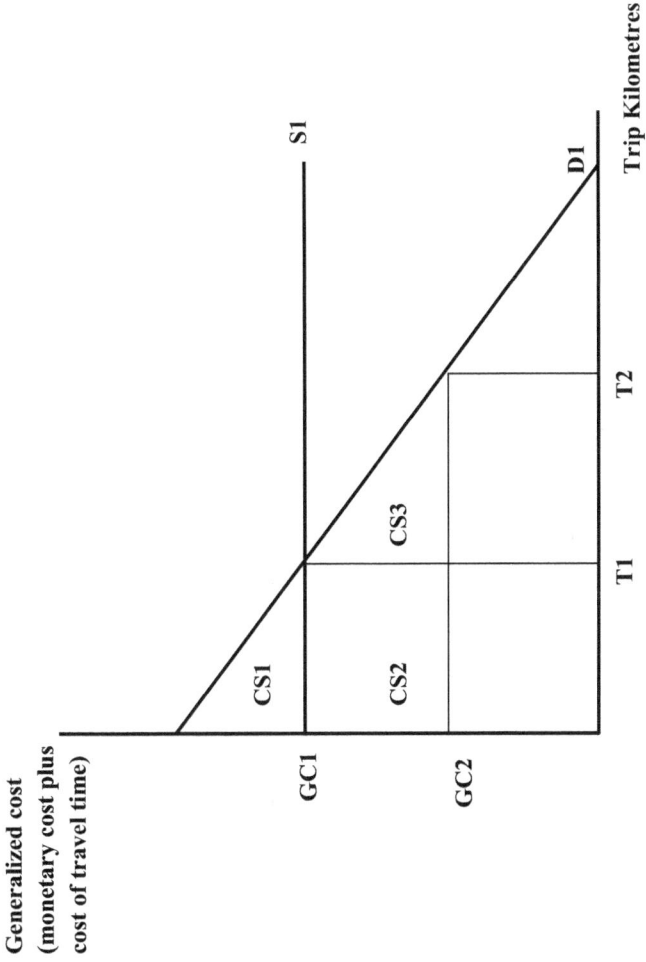

Generalized cost
(monetary cost plus
cost of travel time)

Figure 2.7
Consumer Benefits with Additional Infrastructure (S1 to S2)

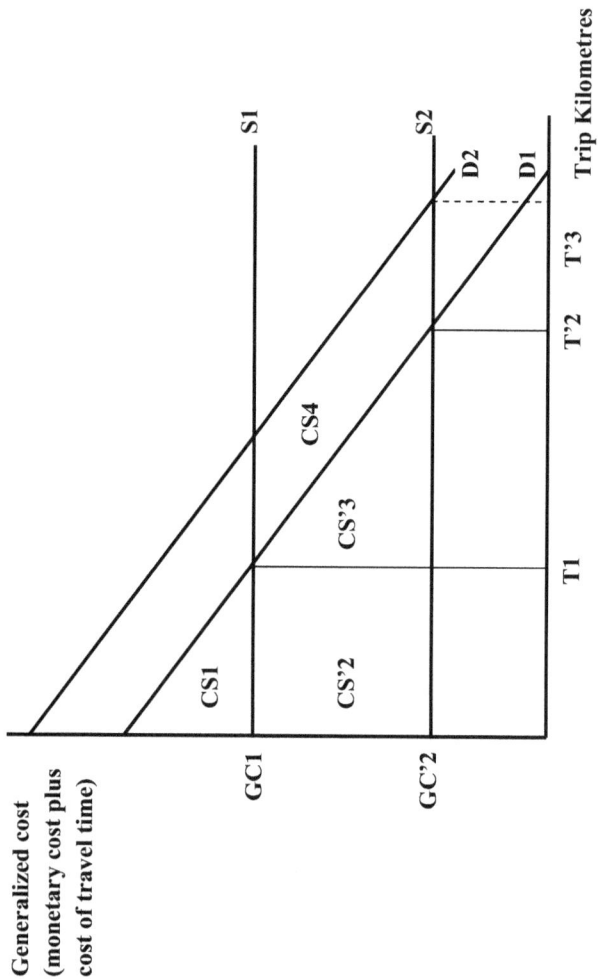

demand function and horizontal supply function (S1) gives the equilibrium trip kilometre (T1) before the infrastructure is built or improved. A highway widening investment programme from a four-lane to an eight-lane highway improves mobility as more capacity is created. The effect of an infrastructure improvement leads to a downward shift in the supply function from S1 to S2. This attracts new users and induces more trips and demand increases from D1 to D2, the number of trips increasing from T2 to T3 at GC2 (see Figure 2.7). User benefits increases further by CS4a + CS4b.

Wider Economic Benefits of Infrastructure Investments

Figure 2.8 suggests a probable impact of transport infrastructure on economic growth. This overall effect is based on the forward linkages created (Williamson 1974 and O'Brien 1983), where the market mechanisms will stimulate increases in output and income at least in the short run. Over time, dynamic development effects derived from the mechanisms will become visible as the market mechanisms develop over several phases. The improvements stimulate a variety of interconnected economy-wide processes that will in turn lead to increases in overall productivity and economic growth.

Phase 1 — Appropriate infrastructure development

This improvement in transport infrastructure is in the form of investments in highways, railways, or even the widening of roads. In addition, soft infrastructure such as the harmonization of standards and regulations can complement the hard infrastructure, bringing about faster and more efficient transportation.

Phase 2 — Efficiently priced and managed infrastructure

The improvement of transport infrastructure can help to reduce the total distance travelled from any origin to destination. The benefits of the reduction in travel distance are reflected in terms of lower cost for transportation and time savings through the efficient pricing of infrastructure usage and good traffic management. Road pricing and efficient tolls can reduce traffic congestion and the possibility of traffic accidents, thus providing greater reliability of transportation services for both goods and passengers.

Phase 3 — Improved accessibility lowers transportation cost, expands markets

The enhanced accessibility and physical connectivity within and between neighbouring countries expand markets, which can then reach a greater network, and they also link economies of cities and regions. This facilitates the trading of goods based on the country's comparative advantage, leading to specialization of production.

Phase 4 — Expansion in intraregional and interregional trade, competition increases

Opportunities for trade are enhanced with the transport infrastructure. Several channels of economic effects open up both in the product and factor markets. Export expansion will lead to higher levels of output, allowing higher sales to cover the fixed cost of operation. Increasing imports put competitive pressures on local prices. This pressure can remove monopoly rents and also improve efficiency in the markets. With the growth of interregional and cross-country trade, there has been an upsurge in intra-industry trade and the exchange of intermediate goods (see Figure 2.8). There are opportunities for adopting new technical knowledge associated with imports, and potential for knowledge and technology growth in the process of learning by doing and using.

Phases 5 & 6 — Consumption and production increase through innovation, knowledge transfers, and development of new technologies, and economic growth

With the cumulative effects of all the stages, production will expand. The transport infrastructure will ultimately lay the foundation for increasing total factor productivity and provide a supporting role for achieving sustainable economic growth.

ASEAN Land Transport Developments

Regional economic integration requires more than constructing roads and rail tracks. It must be accompanied by tariff reduction, removal of non-tariff barriers, reduction of obstacles to investment, and easing of restrictions on trade in services. Transport infrastructure is one of the key catalysts for the socio-economic development and international competitiveness that are

Figure 2.8
Economic Impact of Efficiently Managed Transport Infrastructure

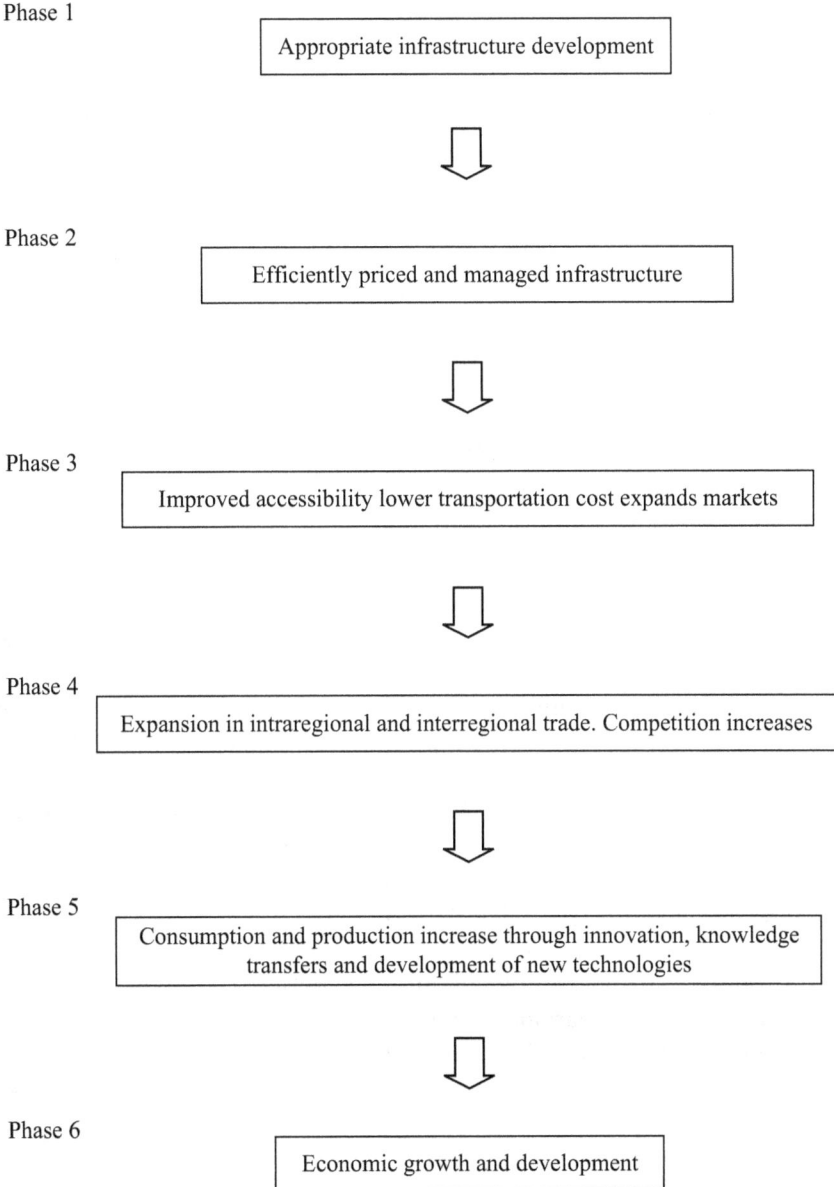

Phase 1

| Appropriate infrastructure development |

⇩

Phase 2

| Efficiently priced and managed infrastructure |

⇩

Phase 3

| Improved accessibility lower transportation cost expands markets |

⇩

Phase 4

| Expansion in intraregional and interregional trade. Competition increases |

⇩

Phase 5

| Consumption and production increase through innovation, knowledge transfers and development of new technologies |

⇩

Phase 6

| Economic growth and development |

essential for economic integration. Parallels are drawn to the "lifeblood and nervous system" of an integrated regional economy. It is of little use by itself, but when production of goods and services take place in different locations, an efficient transport network is very important in facilitating trade, capital, and other resource flows. ASEAN's land transport policy has focused on the creation of regional infrastructure (economic corridors) to help improve the connectivity in the region, thus achieving economic integration, that is, a transport corridor for facilitating regional economic development. The two transport corridors mooted under the AHN and the SKRL serve a very large region consisting of Cambodia, the Lao PDR, Myanmar, and Vietnam (CLMV). However, physical connectivity without harmonization of regulations, procedures, and standards, the presence of strong institutions, efficient management and good governance, will not have the desired maximum impact on regional economic integration.

ASEAN Highway Network (AHN)

This flagship project was signed at the Ministerial Understanding on the Development of the ASEAN Highway Network Project in Hanoi, Vietnam on 15–16 September 1999. The AHN is meant to be part of a "Trans-Asian Highway" passing through ASEAN member states, creating within ASEAN a denser network of intraregional highways. The AHN, which runs the length of 38,400 kilometres through all ten ASEAN countries, aims to be a complete highway network for ASEAN with compatible standards of design and road traffic safety. This project will strengthen existing ASEAN transportation systems and is a critical infrastructural support necessary for the closer integration of the ASEAN region as it will facilitate regional trade, investment, and tourism opportunities. A Ministerial Understanding signed in 1999 agreed on a timetable to develop the AHN according to acceptable standards (see Table 2.1):

- Phase 1 to be completed in 1999: network configuration and designation of national routes.
- Phase 2 to be completed in 2004: installation of road signs for all designated national routes and their upgrading to at least Class III standards. Building missing links in the national routes and designating cross-border points.

Table 2.1
ASEAN Highway Standards Classification

Highway Classification	Description	Pavement type
Primary	Access controlled motorway design speed (60–120 km/h) L: 100–120, R: 80–100, M: 60–80	Asphalt or cement concrete
Class I	4 or more lanes highway design speed (50–110 km/h) L: 80–110, R: 60–80, M: 50–70	Asphalt or cement concrete
Class II	2 lanes design speed (40–100 km/h) L: 80–100, R: 60–80, M: 40–60	Asphalt or cement concrete
Class III	2 lanes (narrow) design speed (40–80 km/h) L: 60–80, R: 50–70, M: 40–60	Double bituminous treatment

Notes: Abbreviations: L = Level terrain design speed (km/h); M = Mountainous terrain design speed (km/h); R = Rolling terrain design speed (km/h).
Source: <http://www.aseansec.org/ahnp_b.htm>.

- Phase 3 to be completed in 2020: upgrading to at least Class I of all designated national routes, although Class II standards would be acceptable for low-traffic non-arterial routes.

Basically, there are 4 classes of ASEAN highway standards, namely Primary, Class I, Class II, and Class III.

A significant length of the AHN had been completed by 2008 (97.4 per cent), but missing links remain and road quality has not been up to specification. About half of the AHN length still consist of "Class-III and below" roads, the lowest of road standards. About 14 per cent of the entire AHN in 2008 was still below Class III standards and these include some 2,069 kilometres of transit transport routes in the Lao PDR, Myanmar, and the Philippines. This is largely due to financing and implementation delays in the attempt to bring all designated routes to at least Class III by 2004.

The urgency is compounded by growth in intra-ASEAN trade figures. ASEAN remained the top country/region of destination for ASEAN exports from 1997 to 2008. Intra-ASEAN trade had been increasing until the Asian financial crisis (AFC) in 1998. Post AFC, trade had continued to pick up to pre-crisis levels.

Singapore-Kunming Rail Link (SKRL) Project

The objective of the SKRL is to create a vital link between the mainland's rail network from Singapore to Kunming in China, building on existing national networks spanning seven ASEAN countries and China. The main route of the rail link will connect Singapore-Malaysia-Thailand-Cambodia-Vietnam-China (Kunming). Besides the main route, spur lines link Thailand-Myanmar and Thailand-Laos. The project was first proposed at the Fifth ASEAN Summit in Bangkok in December 1995, and was included in the Hanoi Plan of Action in 1999 (the first six-year plan of action to implement the vision of an integrated ASEAN by 2020). The huge potential of benefits comes from enhanced physical connectivity between ASEAN and the rest of Asia. The SKRL also forms an important part of the Trans-Asian Railway network that will connect Asia with Europe through China.

The project has been hindered by a lack of funds and other technical issues in connecting the rail to major towns across the region. Thus far, the project is only operational between Singapore, Malaysia, and Thailand. The missing links are largely in Thailand and Cambodia, Thailand and Myanmar, and between Cambodia and Vietnam. Spur lines also need to be constructed within the Lao PDR to Vietnam and this requires substantial resources.

Furthermore, railway design standards and criteria differ across ASEAN member states, especially in the CLMV due to the historical background of the railway system of each member country. Harmonization of design standards for railways and also traffic control and signalling systems is necessary to ensure safe and efficient railway operations. This is a time-consuming and challenging task. It has to implement design standards concurrently on existing rail lines. Harmonization of traffic control and signalling systems is needed at both regional and domestic levels in each member country.

Enablers and Facilitators of Mobility

The key to maximizing the impact of roads and railways lies in the "softer side" which facilitates investments, mobility of labour and other resources, and cargo movement. While transport agreements serve to facilitate trade, this entails simplification and harmonization of rules of carriage and cross-border procedures, use of new technologies and other measures to address safety and security issues and other administrative impediments to trade (APEC 2002). Trade facilitation would result in lower transaction costs. Transaction costs are estimated at 7–10 per cent of the total value of trade (Leelawath 2007). A one per cent reduction in transaction cost would raise world income by US$40 billion (OECD 2003).

The ASEAN Framework Agreement on the Facilitation of Goods in Transit (AFAFGIT) was signed on 16 December 1998 in Hanoi, Vietnam. Transport agreements and projects were included in an attempt to enhance the economic integration of ASEAN member states and realize the goal of a single production base. The agreement aims to facilitate the transportation of goods in transit, simplify and harmonize transport, trade, and customs regulations and requirements to facilitate the movement of goods in transit, and establish an effective, efficient, integrated, and harmonized transit transport system in ASEAN (ASEANWEB 2003). This agreement consists of nine protocols:

- Protocol 1: Designation of Transit Transport Routes and Facilities (Signed on 8 Febuary 2007)
- Protocol 2: Designation of Frontier Posts
- Protocol 3: Types and Quantity of Road Vehicles (Signed on 15 September 1999)
- Protocol 4: Technical Requirements of Vehicles (Signed on 15 September 1999)
- Protocol 5: ASEAN Scheme of Compulsory Motor Vehicle Third-Party Liability Insurance (Signed on 8 April 2001)
- Protocol 6: Railways Border and Interchange Stations
- Protocol 7: Customs Transit System
- Protocol 8: Sanitary and Phytosanitary Measures (Signed on 27 October 2000)
- Protocol 9: Dangerous Goods (Signed on 20 September 2002)

Although the agreement was signed and adopted in 1998, there still remains outstanding protocols to be signed. Soesastro (2005) suggests that the implementation lags in transport and energy plans and projects are due to a lack of political will. Leelawath (2007) also lists various reasons for the implementation lags: poor coordination among government bodies, policy inconsistencies, financial constraints, development disparities, and complications in amending domestic rules and regulations.

The Agreement on Recognition of Commercial Vehicle Inspection Certificates for Goods Vehicles and Public Service Vehicles was signed on 10 September 1998 in Singapore. This agreement states that ASEAN member states agree to recognize the valid commercial vehicle inspection certificate with respect to goods vehicles and public service vehicles issued by the designated authorities or agencies of the member state, or by any person authorized or licensed by the member state (ASEANWEB 2010). The agreement — when implemented — would facilitate cross-border movement of commercial vehicles and, in turn, reduce delays and decrease the costs of trade. The agreement was ratified and came into force in November 2006, eight years after its adoption.

EVALUATION OF ASEAN TRANSPORT LOGISTICS PERFORMANCE

The short-term prospects of ASEAN land transport performance are not promising. AHN and SKRL face numerous challenges. The delay in the completion and full implementation of the projects will lead to costly lags in reaping the potential economic benefits of these projects and the development of the CLMV region. There are several reasons for this.

Heterogeneity of ASEAN countries

ASEAN is socially, culturally, economically, and politically diverse. Each country has different priorities and economic strategies are crafted with socio-political factors in mind. Furthermore, each of the countries in ASEAN are at different levels of development. The United Nations Development Programme (UNDP)'s Human Development Index (HDI) of 2010 classified Singapore, Brunei, and Malaysia as of high human development (HDI of 0.800 and above); the Philippines, Indonesia, Vietnam, Thailand are under medium human development (HDI between 0.500–0.799); Laos, Myanmar, and Cambodia are under low human development (HDI less than 0.500) (UNDP 2010).

Table 2.2 shows the ranking of ASEAN countries according to their level of infrastructure development. This demonstrates another aspect of heterogeneity among ASEAN member states. While there was an improvement in the ranking of each country between 1991 and 2005, there are also gaps in infrastructure availability across ASEAN member countries

Table 2.2
Ranking of ASEAN Countries According to the
Level of Infrastructure Development

Country	1991		2000		2005	
	Index	Rank	Index	Rank	Index	Rank
United States	25.96	1	22.95	1	20.66	1
Japan	16.28	5	18.65	4	18.58	2
Singapore	15.73	6	20.11	2	17.66	3
Malaysia	5.10	37	8.65	27	9.21	29
Thailand	4.17	43	5.48	38	5.89	42
Vietnam	0.91	92	1.85	75	3.27	61
Indonesia	2.23	69	2.74	63	3.21	62
Philippines	1.53	76	2.58	65	2.95	63
Lao PDR	0.55	99	1.19	84	0.87	92
Myanmar	0.97	90	0.79	91	0.76	95
Cambodia	0.45	100	0.66	93	0.55	98

Source: Bhattacharyay 2009.

(Bhattacharyay 2009). The gaps also seem to have widened, rather than narrowed, over time. Differences in the political environments could also hinder the pace of development.

Financial Constraints

Cross-border infrastructure projects are expensive. The lack of funds has slowed infrastructure development, exemplified by the missing links in the SKRL. Currently available cost estimates for the SKRL missing links in Cambodia, Lao PDR, Myanmar, Thailand, Vietnam and Kunming, China, indicate a requirement for some US$9.6 billion, even though these preliminary estimates are for only about 56 per cent of the missing rail track and does not yet involve the rolling stock, facilities and equipment necessary to run a proper rail service (Pushpanathan 2010).

To fill this gap, funding capacity depends on contributions from member countries. For example, Malaysia donated rail worth RM7.5 million to Cambodia in 2006 to connect a forty-eight-kilometre missing link from Poipet to Sisophon. However, this is not a sustainable way to drive projects and there are competing development priorities in the member countries themselves. Loans from international funding agencies are an alternative. In addition, ASEAN-6 could grant loans to relatively weaker

CLMV countries. ASEAN still lacks a concerted financing mechanism for these infrastructure projects.

On a positive note, the recent establishment of the ASEAN Infrastructure Fund (AIF) in May 2010 will boost progress of the projects in member countries, especially those hit hardest by the lack of funds. AIF will have an initial capital of $800 million, including contributions from ASEAN member countries and the Plus Three countries of China, Japan, and the Republic of Korea. The AIF is expected to facilitate the funding of projects more efficiently and provide more assurance and confidence to member countries participating in the infrastructure projects.

Lack of Complementary Measures

Land transport has always formed the spine in transportation networks. Land transport infrastructure such as road and rail remains crucial in the development of multimodal transport, that is, moving goods from production plants to seaport/airport and vice versa. Given the rapid growth in motorization in ASEAN over the last decade (doubling of vehicles in countries such as Cambodia, Indonesia, Myanmar, and Vietnam), the AHN and SKRL projects may help to relieve congestion in major ASEAN cities and reduce pressure on existing road infrastructure.

The immediate impact of the AHN and the SKRL is the reduction in transport costs and enhanced accessibility within ASEAN and beyond. Intra-ASEAN trade amounted to about US$369 billion in 2009. The share of intra-ASEAN trade has remained at 24 per cent over the last fifteen years. Extra-ASEAN trade is valued as US$1.15 trillion. Transport connectivity will be crucial for sustaining trade both within and outside ASEAN. Improved transport connectivity within ASEAN will help narrow the development gaps among and within ASEAN states by providing lower-income countries and landlocked regions and hinterlands access to markets, production networks, and industrial zones. In recent years, China has attracted large flows of FDI away from the ASEAN region. Labour costs in CLMV countries has been relatively lower than the coastal provinces of China. The combination of improved land transportation networks and improved quality labour force may attract global FDI to set up regional production networks and supply chains in ASEAN.

The strengthening of land transport connectivity by AHN and SKRL will complement air and maritime transportation of goods. But the intermodal connectivity and complementarities are far from adequate.

Even statistics are incomplete on countries such as Cambodia, Indonesia, the Lao PDR, Myanmar, Thailand, and Vietnam. The ASEAN Statistical Yearbook 2008 shows that the total length of road infrastructure had been increasing for all the ASEAN countries from 2000 to 2008. The increase of road infrastructure length can be interpreted as an improvement in the land transportation network. This trend of increase, to some extent, is due to the AHN project which pushes for the building of highways to connect ASEAN countries. Although the project has been troubled by the lack of funding from participating countries, a significant 97.4 per cent of the desired AHN length had been built by 2008, contributing to the length of road infrastructure (see Figure 2.9). No performance benchmarking exists.

Post-AFC, as the economies rebounded, on average showing growth of 5.4 per cent from 2000 to 2008, total vehicle registration rose in the same period, suggesting a strong positive correlation to GDP growth. Similar growth is recorded for goods vehicles. The rapid growth of motorization will require investments in road infrastructure if traffic congestion is to be avoided. While the AHN is intended to facilitate higher intercity mobility,

Figure 2.9
ASEAN Road Infrastructure, 2000–2008

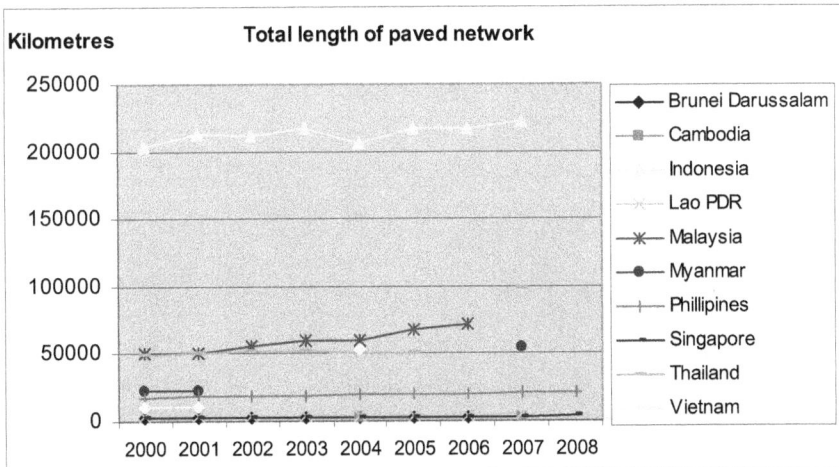

Source: Various sources from statistical yearbooks of various member countries; UNESCAP Statistical Indicators for Asia and the Pacific Compendium, November 2005; UNESCAP Asia-Pacific in Figures 2004.

linking land routes and enhancing intermodal transport, it may lead to higher urbanization and intracity traffic congestion. The insular nature of ASEAN means it will need efficient and effective road, maritime, and aviation connectivity.

Figure 2.10
ASEAN Road Fleet, 2000–2008

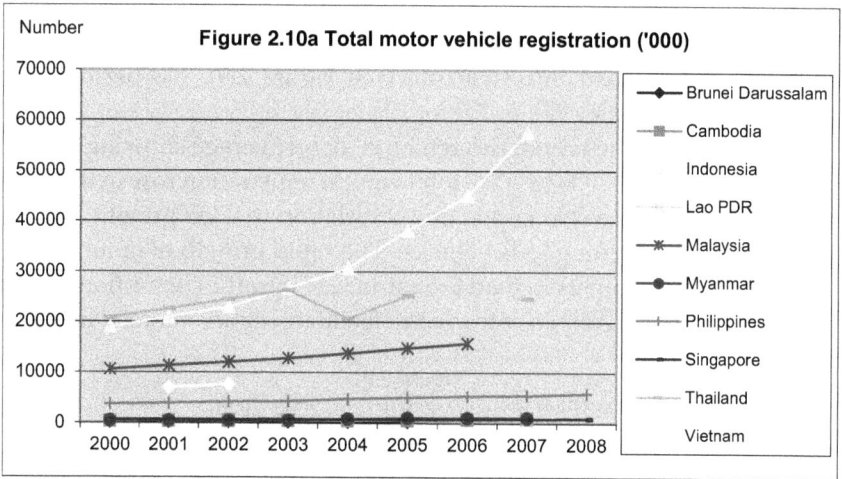

Number — Figure 2.10a Total motor vehicle registration ('000)

Legend: Brunei Darussalam, Cambodia, Indonesia, Lao PDR, Malaysia, Myanmar, Philippines, Singapore, Thailand, Vietnam

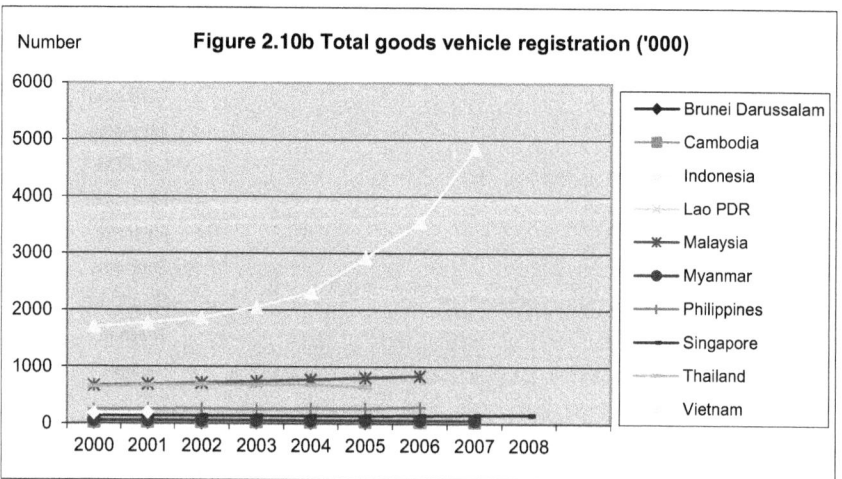

Number — Figure 2.10b Total goods vehicle registration ('000)

Legend: Brunei Darussalam, Cambodia, Indonesia, Lao PDR, Malaysia, Myanmar, Philippines, Singapore, Thailand, Vietnam

Source: ASEAN Statistical Yearbook 2008.

Cross-border rail service, in ASEAN are operational in the links between Singapore, Malaysia, and Thailand. Rail development has been slow and erratic. However, the remaining four countries involved in the SKRL projects have shown not much progress was made in extending the route length of railways from 2000 to 2008 (see Figure 2.11), the reason being that the SKRL project was hit by funding problems, thus hindering progress. Cambodia, for instance, had only secured US$40 million in the form of soft loans from the Asian Development Bank (ADB) in 2006. Additionally, Cambodia also received a donation of rails worth RM7.5 million from Malaysia to connect the forty-eight-km missing link from Poipet to Sisophon. But the connection work only took place in the first quarter of 2008. At the same time the statistics also show that countries not involved in the SKRL project (Indonesia and the Philippines) have actually increased their railways.

In terms of freight-kilometre, ASEAN countries that are participating in the SKRL project have shown a general increase in trend from 2000 to 2004. Due to the lack of information from ASEAN statistics, the trend cannot be deduced between 2004 and 2008. However, statistics show that the prospects the SKRL project will bring to ASEAN freight rail transportation are promising. There is more room for an upward trend for freight transportation through rail. As the SKRL project has only completed the links between Singapore, Malaysia, and Thailand, there is already an increasing trend in freight-kilometre. With the estimated completion date of the SKRL project in 2015, we can foresee that freight-kilometre can only have more potential to increase further in ASEAN.

TRANSPORT LOGISTICS PERFORMANCE

A worldwide survey of logistics operators (global freight forwarders and express carriers) on the "friendliness" of countries meeting the requirements of users, the trade environment and the demands of the global logistics environment gives some indication of the logistics performance of ASEAN countries (World Bank 2010) using the LPI (Logistics Performance Index). East Asia and the Pacific region, which includes ASEAN and the Asia-Pacific Economic Cooperation (APEC) countries, have performed as well as the Europe and Central Asia, and the Latin America and Caribbean regions. The performance of Asia-Pacific countries in six core logistics areas, the key components of the LPI, are commendable. ASEAN economies seem to

Figure 2.11
ASEAN Railways Statistics, 2000–2008

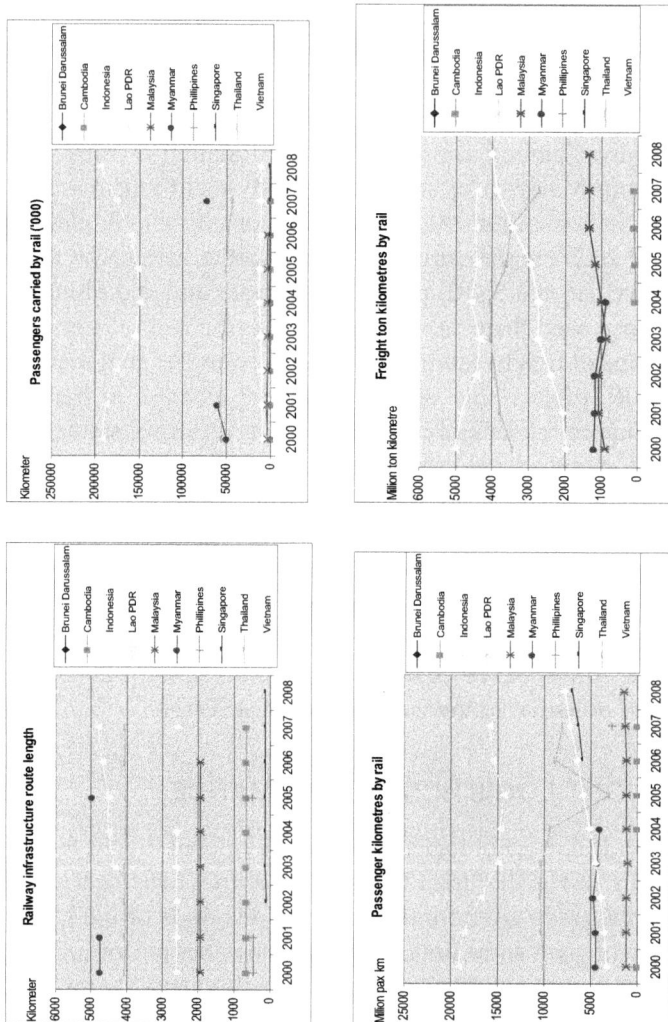

Source: Various sources from statistical yearbooks of various member countries; UNESCAP Statistical Indicators for Asia and the Pacific Compendium, November 2005; UNESCAP Asia-Pacific in Figures 2004.

perform better than the middle-income group in all areas. The reasonably good performance could be due to the transport strategies to improve logistics services from Singapore, Malaysia, and Thailand. Timeliness of deliveries implies that goods move with relative ease without significant delays. However, bottlenecks still exist because of lack of infrastructure quality and efficiency of border clearance. This is largely due to (1) financial constraints, (2) lack of coordination between governments, and (3) complication of domestic regulations in harmonizing and simplifying regulatory procedures such as customs procedures.

Table 2.3 shows the export and import lead times and costs of the Asia Pacific economies. Lead time is the transport time for export and imports from the point of origin to the port of loading or equivalent, or to the buyer's warehouse (LPI 2010). ASEAN economies are comparable to the high-income group for export median and best lead times. For costs of exports, ASEAN fares better than the high-income group. For imports, the best and median lead times are almost triple that of the high-income group, although the costs of imports are still lower. The low costs of imports and exports can be attributed to the transport strategies in place, as well as the relatively low cost of labour in ASEAN. Low costs of imports and exports increase the competitiveness of the ASEAN economies globally through increases in trade and FDI. However, the high lead times of import point to the fact that customs and border clearance needs improvement (LPI 2010). The clearance time with and without physical inspection and the rate of physical inspection are considerably higher than that of APEC and the high-income group. This could be attributed to the challenges faced by ASEAN in the implementation of harmonized border regulations and

Table 2.3
Export and Lead Times and Costs

Trade	Cost and delays	APEC	ASEAN	High Income
Exports	Best lead times (days)	1.9	2.0	1.7
	Median lead time (days)	2.8	2.8	2.7
	Cost in US$	849	651	980
Imports	Best lead times (days)	1.9	6.9	2.3
	Median lead time (days)	2.9	8.3	3.3
	Cost in US$	884	858	1024

Source: World Bank 2010.

procedures throughout the ASEAN economies, leading to longer clearance times and a higher rate of physical inspection.

STRATEGIES FOR MOVING AHEAD

Integrated Multimodal Transport Strategy

Transport networks and behaviour of users, be it passengers or freight, are very complex, especially when this involves trip chaining. Given the complexity of various modes of transport and routes planned, the integration of the network into land use plans and the coordination with other modes of transport are paramount, as is the constant monitoring of system performance. Businesses seek to utilize transport networks to minimize procurement and distribution costs. Cross-border impediments potentially discourage FDI and trade. The need for intermodal coordination in particular between seaport, highways, and dry ports to the hinterland is urgent. The urgency is exemplified by the insular nature of ASEAN. The complexities in ensuring smooth connectivity between port and cities requires not only efficient ports, but accessibility from factory to ports, sub-port to hub port, and port to distribution centres, and in some cases, port to rail and vice versa. The failure to improve intermodal connectivity will lead to possible trade diversion if and when the Eurasian land bridge, from Kunming in Yunnan to Kyaukpyu on the coast of Myanmar is realized. Using existing rail networks (by adding new ones and changing to the same gauge), the journey from Shenzhen through Myanmar and the Indian subcontinent through Turkey to Rotterdam will reduce the journey distance by 3,000 kilometres.

An integrated network entails a multimodal transport service which is well-coordinated throughout a network, either by one or multiple transport firms, which allow efficient transfers between modes. This includes the provision of seamless physical, scheduling, service, and tariff integration. The transport policy should include environmental, health, and social elements in particular to address the widening Gini coefficient which accompanies globalization.

One of the main benefits of an integrated transport network is the resulting efficiencies that it brings to users. This is in addition to the user benefits discussed in Figures 2.6 and 2.7. Efficiency measures of an integrated transport network relate resource inputs to intermediate or final outputs. They measure system performance and progress in terms of network integration. In addition to performance measures that are indicators of the transport network's effectiveness, there are other measures, such as the quality of service provided, costs saved, reliability, etc., which are indicators that depict a business owner's choice. There are three areas of efficiency measurements: Physical Transport Network Efficiency, Service Delivery Efficiency, and Environmental and Social Efficiency (UNESCAP 2007).

The presence of an efficient transport network aided the economic growth and industrialization of countries such as Singapore, Taiwan, the Republic of Korea, Indonesia, the Philippines, Malaysia, Thailand and the special administrative region of Hong Kong. Physical networks such as transport, information technology (IT), and communications form an infrastructure crucial for industrialization. These contribute directly to integrating economies on to the global stage. Barriers to investment, trade, and businesses were kept low in preference for growth seeking and market exposure. Foreign direct investments were prioritized and multinational corporations were encouraged to set up operations in industrial zones and commercial hubs through investment incentives and preferential tax treatment, taking advantage of cheap labour, abundant land, and growth potential. The next stage was to construct a reliable physical network where transport systems and communications complemented each other, thus ensuring investors the potential. Economic growth and development was rapid and growth was doubled.

However, this would not have been realized if non physical factors were not present. These include elements of business networks and *guanxi* (relationships) between countries, efficient management and governance, and a solid and established institutional foundation. Physical and non-physical networks that complement each other reap the benefits of globalization fully.

Development of Strategic Economic Clusters and Integrated Land Use and Transport Planning

The institutional framework and a road map for ASEAN integration have been set for 2015. In this respect, transport facilitation takes a multisector approach in creating a seamless movement of goods and people across borders and urban areas. However, the document seems like a cut-and-paste exercise from an official document and, at best, a collation of information obtained from the Internet. This chapter advocates the following:

1. Development of a road map which specifically develops capacities and capabilities in the transport sector in enhancing connectivity and market access, not only on a regional level, but more to enable urban and rural areas to take advantage of market access and trade facilitation. The Initiative for ASEAN Integration (IAI) should develop a set of benchmarks.

2. The set of benchmarks should evaluate whether the new coordinated simultaneous approach is more effective than the past parallel uncoordinated approach.

3. There is also a need to rediscover the competitive advantage of urban and rural areas. Cities will remain growth poles due to the phenomenal urbanization process, but most of this is at the expense of towns and rural areas. As globalization and urbanization continue to create and "feed" into megacities, this will lead to the eventual disappearance and demise of towns and villages if there is no reinvention. The current approach of "predict and provide" transport infrastructure is not sustainable. The paradigm shift ought to be creating accessibility based on integrated regional land use and transport planning. Cities should focus on development that is oriented towards public transport.

4. Cluster development suggests the development of urban and rural areas based on competitive clusters. This requires a decentralization of authority, administration and funding, capacity building, and a supportive legal framework in creating markets. The development and delivery of transport services must give careful consideration to the operating environment and this may require a review and reform of the sector. Figure 2.12 shows the role played by transport infrastructure as a facilitator and enabler of market access after an urban area has reinvented itself based on cluster strategy. The treatise is based on the following premise which is summarized in Figure 2.13. At best cluster development will slow the growth of megacities and redefine urban rural roles in ASEAN after 2015.

Rural-Urban and Intra-Urban Linkages

Figure 2.12 attempts to link the treatise on urban and suburban-rural development to the development of economic clusters. It proposes the following:

1. Identification of incidences of rural-urban and intra-urban linkages by assessing contemporary policies on promoting linkages and the

Figure 2.12
Relationship between Rural-urban, Inter-urban,
Interregional Linkage, and Integration

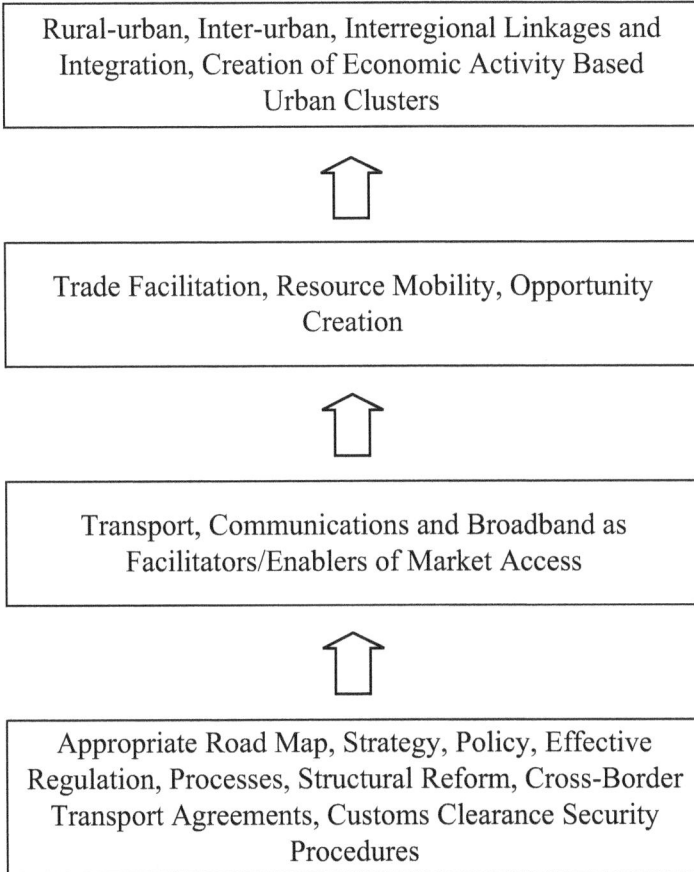

Rural-urban, Inter-urban, Interregional Linkages and
Integration, Creation of Economic Activity Based
Urban Clusters

⇧

Trade Facilitation, Resource Mobility, Opportunity
Creation

⇧

Transport, Communications and Broadband as
Facilitators/Enablers of Market Access

⇧

Appropriate Road Map, Strategy, Policy, Effective
Regulation, Processes, Structural Reform, Cross-Border
Transport Agreements, Customs Clearance Security
Procedures

impact on the Southeast Asian region, and drawing lessons to develop
positive links between rural and urban development; and

2. Identify opportunities and challenges in promoting rural-urban and
    intra-urban linkages and offer recommendations for regional/ASEAN
    cooperation and investing in transport infrastructure.

Figure 2.13
Cluster Development of Cities, Towns, and Villages Based on
Comparative/Competitive Advantage and Specialization

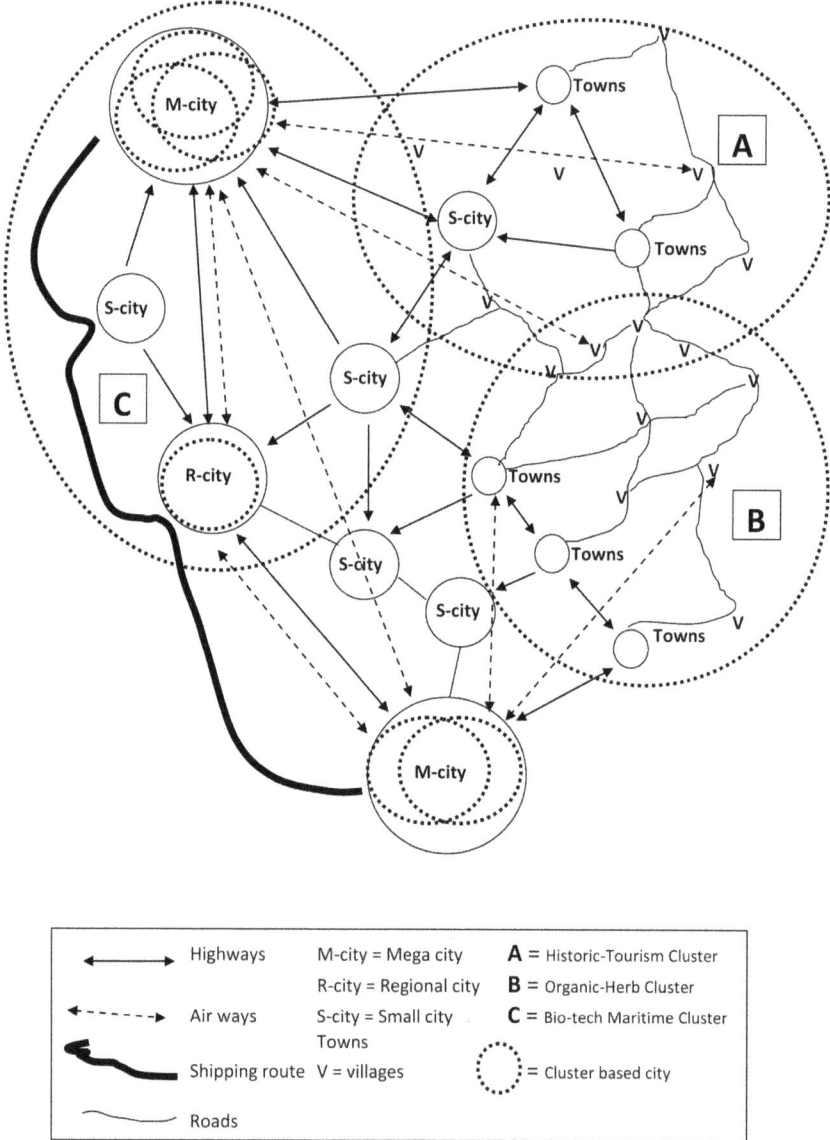

Highways	M-city = Mega city	**A** = Historic-Tourism Cluster
	R-city = Regional city	**B** = Organic-Herb Cluster
Air ways	S-city = Small city	**C** = Bio-tech Maritime Cluster
	Towns	
Shipping route	V = villages	= Cluster based city
Roads		

CONCLUSION

The growth of ASEAN economies is very much dependent on FDI and trade. The impact of multimodal transport development has been slow and this is exemplified by the slow completion of the AHN and SKRL. The lack of finance and harmonization of railway gauge and cross-border customs procedures and rules added further delay. Joint agreements on the economic integration of the ASEAN economies assume, among other things, the enhancement of the transportation network, such as the development of roads and railway lines. ASEAN seems to have performed on logistics comparable to middle-income and high-income country groups according to a World Bank report, but this is perhaps due to the excellent logistics infrastructure of Singapore, Malaysia, and Thailand. The availability of transport infrastructure and efficient supply management facilitate intra- and inter-ASEAN trade and attract FDI. However, much of this is still uncoordinated and not integrated into urban and regional land use plans. The competitiveness of ASEAN in the global supply chain is not enough in light of regional developments such as the Eurasian Highway and high speed rail connectivity in China. Transport infrastructure development must take into consideration: (a) strategic cluster development; (b) links between urban rural nodes, (c) development of an hierarchical logistic supply chain based on cluster development; (d) development of an appropriate institutional framework and (e) complementary macroeconomic stabilization and financial policies.

References

Abidin, M.Z. "Fiscal Policy Coordination in Asia: East Asian Infrastructure Investment Fund". ADBI Working Paper Series, 2010 <http://www.adbi. org/files/2010.07.30.wp232.fiscal.policy.coordination.asia.pdf>.

ASEAN. *ASEAN Statistical Yearbook 2008*. 2009 <http://archive.asean.org/ Publication-ASEAN-SYB-2008.pdf>.

———. "ASEAN Approves Setting up Infrastructure Fund". Towards ASEAN Community: From Vision to Action, 2010 <http://asean2010.vn/asean_en/ news/36/2DA89A/ASEAN-approves-setting-up-infrastructure-fund>.

———. External Trade Statistics. 2010. ASEAN Statistics, 2010 <http://www. aseansec.org/18137.htm>.

Baldacci, E., L. de Mello, and G. Inchauste. *Financial Crises, Poverty, and Income Distribution*. International Monetary Fund, Fiscal Affairs Department, 2002

International Monetary Fund <http://books.google.com/books?id=YPvKXG
VIUGwC&pg=PA10&dq=financial+crisis+definition&hl=en&ei=pmnkTPiJEM
eXccjYnKwM&sa=X&oi=book_result&ct=result&resnum=3&ved=0CDEQ6A
EwAg#v=onepage&q=financial%20crisis%20definition&f=false>.

Banister, D. and Y. Berechman. "Transport Investment and the Promotion of
Economic Growth". *Journal of Transport Geography*, 2010 <www.elsevier.com/
locate/jtrangeo>.

BERNAMA (Malaysian National News Agency). "More Funds Needed For
Singapore-Kunming Rail Link", 2006 <http://findarticles.com/p/news-
articles/bernama-malaysian-national-news-agency/mi_8082/is_20060826/
funds-needed-spore-kunming-rail/ai_n51534182/?tag=content;col1>.

———. "Work on missing link between Poipet-Sisophon to start in Q1: Chan"
<http://findarticles.com/p/news-articles/bernama-malaysian-national-
news-agency/mi_8082/is_20080117/work-missing-link-poipet-sisophon/
ai_n51572831/?tag=content;col1>.

Bhattacharyay, B. "Infrastructure and Regional Cooperation". Concept Paper
for ADB/ADBI Flagship Study, 2008 <http://www.adbi.org/research.
infrastructure.regional.cooperation/>.

———. "Infrastructure Development for ASEAN Economic Integration". ADBI
Working Paper Series, 2009 <http://www.adbi.org/files/2009.05.27.wp138.
infrastructure.dev.asean.economic.pdf>.

Cohen, J.P. "The Broader Effects of Transportation Infrastructure: Spatial
Econometrics and Productivity Approaches", 2008. Transportation Research
Part E 46 (2010): 317–26 <www.elsevier.com/locate/regec>.

Khan, S., F. Islam, and S. Ahmed. "The Asian Crisis: An Economic Analysis of
the Causes". *Journal of Developing Areas* 39, no. 1 (2005) <http://www.jstor.
org/stable/4192995>.

Lakshmanan, T.R. "The Broader Economic Consequences of Transport Infrastructure
Investments". *Journal of Transport Geography*, 2010 <www.elsevier.com/locate/
jtrangeo>.

Leelawath, W. "Trade Facilitation: Creating Efficiency in Asian Sub-regions".
Presentation to Expert Group Meeting on Promoting Trade between Asian
Subregions, 1–3 August 2007, Kunming, Yunnan Province of China <http://
www.unescap.org/tid/projects/protrade_s2watcharas.pdf>.

Mun, S. and S. Nakagawa. "Pricing and Investment of Cross-border Transport
Infrastructure". *Regional Science and Urban Economics* 40 (2010): 228–40 <http:
www.elsevier.com/locate/regec>.

Nathan, K.S. "Opinion: Potholes to Avoid on the Asean Highway". Institute of
Southeast Asian Studies <http://www.iseas.edu.sg/viewpoint/ksn8aug06.
pdf>.

Ojala, L., J.F. Arvis, M.A. Mustra, D. Saslavsky, and B. Shepherd. "Connecting to

Compete 2010: Trade logistics in the global economy". World Bank, International Trade Department. Washington, DC: World Bank, 2010 <http://siteresources. worldbank.org/INTTLF/Resources/LPI2010_for_web.pdf>.

Plummer, M.G. and S.Y. Chia. *Realizing the ASEAN Economic Community: A Comprehensive Assessment*. Singapore: Institute of Southeast Asian Studies, 2009.

Pushpanathan, S. "ASEAN Connectivity and the ASEAN Economic Community". *ASEAN Economic Community*, 2010 <http://www.aseansec.org/24808.htm>.

———. "East Asia Economic Integration: Role of Economic Corridors and the Emerging Architecture". 2010 <http://www.aseansec.org/25187.htm>.

Shepherd, B. and J.S. Wilson. "Trade Facilitation in ASEAN Member Countries: Measuring Progress and Assessing Priorities". *Journal of Asian Economics* 20 (2009): 367–83.

UNDP. Human Development Index, 2010 <http://hdr.undp.org/en/media/ HDR_2010_EN_Tables_reprint.pdf>.

UNESCAP. *Statistical Yearbook for Asia and the Pacific 2007*, 2007 <http://www. unescap.org/stat/data/syb2007/ESCAP-SYB2007.pdf>.

Welfens, P.J.J., C. Ryan, and S. Chirathivat. *EU-ASEAN: Facing Economic Globalisation*. Springer Verlag, 2009.

World Bank. *Connecting to Compete: Trade Logistics in the Global Economy*. Washington, DC, 2010, 50pp.

3

COMPETITIVE CITIES AND URBAN ECONOMIC DEVELOPMENT IN SOUTHEAST ASIA

Toh Mun Heng

INTRODUCTION

Cities are now the homes of more than half the population in the world. In fact, it is projected that more than 70 per cent of the world's population will be living in urban areas by 2030. Though most cities have higher economic growth, foreign investment, and labour productivity than the rest of the country, they are also more polluted, crime ridden, and socially disparate. Successful cities attract talented, young, highly-skilled workers, are centres of innovation and entrepreneurship, and are competitive locations for global and regional headquarters. The proximity of universities to research and production facilities means cities are where new products are developed and commercialized. It is reported that more than 80 per cent of patents are filed in cities. Empirical studies based on within-country information show a strong positive connection between density and productivity; transition to dense urban living seems to be part of the process of a country becoming richer over time (Glaeser and Gottlieb 2009).

Indeed, the rapidly rising degree of worldwide urbanization has led to the growing recognition that cities and their surrounding urban regions play a vital role in national economic competitiveness. A book co-authored by M. Weiss and H. Cisneros entitled, *Teamwork: How Cities and Suburbs Develop Metropolitan Economic Strategies to Innovate and Prosper in the Global Marketplace* asserts that cities and the metropolis — urban regions — are the fundamental building blocks of prosperity and quality of life, both for the nation and for families and communities.

However, one should not assume that cities do not falter. The OECD Territorial Reviews (2003) reports that cities such as Berlin, Fukuoka, Naples, and Pittsburgh perform below the national average for income, productivity, skills, and employment. There are also indications that mega-size cities — those with more than seven million people — such as Seoul, Mexico City, Istanbul, and Tokyo — have outgrown the economies of scale normally associated with cities. In a study of eight Asian cities,[1] it is reported that "urban development in Asia is largely driven by the concentration of local, national and increasingly, international profit-seeking enterprises in and around particular urban centres" and that "cities may concentrate wealth both in terms of new investment and high income residents but there is no automatic process by which this contributes to the costs of needed infrastructure and services". Furthermore, "an increase in the number of automobiles in Asian cities has created severe traffic problems and this in turn increases time taken in travel, stress and environment related diseases".

Nevertheless the negative findings can provide us with valuable pointers and they will not deter us from making effort to seek relevant answers and appropriate strategies for cities to grow and prosper. We notice the phenomena of concentration and dispersion of activities. Urbanization is a process of concentration of people at a location (which we will subsequently call city) emanating from rural areas. Meanwhile one also observes people moving away from areas of famine or disaster-struck districts to new places in search of better means of survival and safer habitats. One can recall the diasporas of Chinese immigrants to Southeast Asia, as well as other parts of the world, near the end of the nineteenth century; and the large-scale migration of Europeans to the United States of America. What are the fundamental reasons for such movements? Perhaps the main answer, though it may sound naive, is economic in nature. Other reasons can be subordinated to that. More often than not, all other rationales do not deviate from utility and well-being enhancement which fall in the domain of economics.[2]

The rationale for people to congregate — other than the fact that human beings are members of a sociable species — is to interact and engage in the activities of exchanging ideas, goods, and services. The locations where congregation take place will evolve into bazaars, towns, and cities, depending on the scale and intensity of the interaction. Technological advances in transport, communication, and production will facilitate the movement and congregation of people, knowledge, capital, as well as other paraphernalia (culture, religious practice, arts) that add value to the quality and comfort of living on planet Earth. For cities to grow and prosper, economists like to point to the fundamentals of competitiveness. To conduct a competitiveness analysis, it will be worth the while to understand basic global trends and the concept of competitiveness more intimately.

In the subsequent sections, the chapter will review some basic economic concepts and theories relating to urban economic development. In particular, the concepts of competitiveness, agglomeration economies, and industrial clustering will be useful for the purpose of discussing the development strategy pertaining to cities. Following that we discuss the possibility of exploiting the competitiveness framework in Southeast Asian cities in order to catalyse and stimulate economic development and growth of the country in which they are sited. Some concluding remarks and policy implications are included in the final section.

GLOBAL TRENDS

Before the role of a city can be understood, it is necessary to step back and understand the realities of this century's economy. Rypkema (2005) succinctly summarizes four such realities.

- First, the twenty-first century will be a globalized economy. This will affect every national economy, regardless of political or economic system.
- Second, the most significant impacts of the global economy will not be at the national or even provincial level. The biggest impacts will be local. Akio Morita, founder of the Sony Corporation in Japan, called this "Global Localisation". Management guru Michael Porter wrote in *The Competitive Advantage of Nations* that: "The process of creating

skills and the important influences on the rate of improvement and innovation are intensely local. Paradoxically, then, more open global competition makes the home base more, not less, important."

- Third, there will be a rapidly growing demand for products worldwide. But the manufacture of those products will require fewer and fewer people. Manpower employed in the manufacturing sector will diminish.
- Fourth, the areas of the economy that will grow, both in output and in employment are these: services; ideas; one-of-a-kind products, individually produced; culture; entertainment; communications; travel; education. For each of these growth areas, quality and authenticity will be major variables in consumer choice.

In recognition of the above realities, cities and their citizens to be successful would be wise to adopt five principles: globalization, localization, diversity, sustainability, and responsibility. Accepting globalization will allow a city the opportunity to identify which of its own characteristics can be competitive in the global marketplace and to establish measures that reduce the adverse impacts of a globalized economy. The definition of what "economic development" means needs to be localized. It must be specific and measurable. Many local economic development yardsticks in the twenty-first century will be qualitative rather than quantitative. Localization will always necessitate identifying assets (human, natural, physical, locational, functional, and cultural) that can be utilized to respond to globalization. Those assets must first be identified, then protected, and then enhanced. In his book, *Post-Capitalist Society*, business guru Peter Drucker writes, "Tomorrow's educated person will have to be prepared for life in a global world. He or she must become a 'citizen of the world' — in vision, horizon, and information. But he or she will also have to draw nourishment from his or her local roots and, in turn, enrich and nourish his or her own local culture."

Biologists were the first to understand the importance of diversity to a healthy ecological system. In the same vein, economic development analysts — based on the models of the ecologists — have noted that cities must have a diverse local economy in order to provide protection from the volatile patterns of demand in the marketplace. The nurturing and development of successful business ecosystems is desirable and pertinent because companies and individuals can use these as a common platform to co-create and deliver value to customers, partners, themselves, and the overall community. Excessive reliance on a single source of employment, production, and economic activity will leave cities inordinately vulnerable. With economic globalization as a given, successful economic development will specialize and customize to meet the needs of diverse markets rather than standardize and homogenize.

Sustainability is more broadly defined to recognize the importance of the functional sustainability of public infrastructure, the fiscal sustainability of a local government, the physical sustainability of the built environment, and the cultural sustainability of local traditions, customs, and skills, in addition to the appropriate pace of extraction of mineral resources to support economic development. The final principle is responsibility. Each city takes a large measure of responsibility for its own economic future. It needs leadership and cooperation with local government, the private sector, non-governmental organizations (NGOs), and individual citizens to define and pursue citywide and metropolitan economic development strategies.

COMPETITIVENESS

Recent years have seen a surge of academic and policy attention devoted to the notion of the "competitiveness" of nations, regions, and cities. It seems the only option to survive in the new global marketplace and the "new competition" being forged by the new information or knowledge driven economy is to be competitive. Competitiveness is a hot issue for many countries and companies. Policymakers at all levels have been swept up in this competitiveness fever.

Competitiveness is, on the whole, reasonably well understood and accepted as a meaningful concept at the level of the firm. For a firm, competitiveness is the ability to produce the right goods and services of the right quality, at the right price, at the right time. It means meeting customers' needs more efficiently and more effectively than other firms.

When we come to competitiveness at the national level, it is no longer that straightforward. Begg (2002) emphasizes that:

> it is important to appraise the different senses in which the term "competitiveness" is used. At one level it is equated, usually loosely, with the "performance" of an economy, an absolute measure. At another,

because it relates to competition, it implies a comparative element, with the implication that to be competitive, a city has to undercut its rivals or offer better value-for-money. In this sense, competitiveness is essentially about securing (or defending) market-share.

Meanwhile, Nobel laureate Paul Krugman (1996a and 1996b) has been highly critical of the current fashion of promoting competitiveness, arguing that it is nothing more than mercantilism in sheep's clothing and, thus, a threat to free trade. Simply put, Krugman's view is that competitiveness is an attribute of *companies*, not of cities, regions, countries, or continents. Others disagree. Michael Porter (1990), in his seminal study on competitive advantage, deplores the lack of attention to competitiveness in standard international trade theory and suggests that economic analysis is diminished by this lack. Porter goes on to assert his conviction that the national environment affects the competitive position of firms, and he observes that understanding the role of the nation "would yield some fundamental insights into how competitive advantage was created and sustained".

For a nation, the OECD defines competitiveness as "The degree to which a country can, under free and fair market conditions, produce goods and services which meet the test of international markets, while simultaneously maintaining and expanding the real incomes of its people over the long-term."[3] This could only be achieved under increased productivity.

A similar definition is adopted by the European Commission (1999), with competitiveness as "the ability to produce goods and services which meet the test of international markets, while at the same time maintaining high and sustainable levels of income or, more generally, the ability of regions to generate, while being exposed to external competition, relatively high income and employment levels".

At the aggregate level, and with the full employment of resources, competitiveness and productivity are essentially the same according to some economists. Again, Porter (1990) is forthright: "The only meaningful concept of competitiveness at the national level is national productivity." In response to the charge that competitiveness is mercantilism in disguise, Ciampi (1996) argues that competitiveness is not a "zero sum game". In other words, an increase in competitiveness in one country does not come at the expense of another. On the contrary, gains in productivity and efficiency in different countries can and must be integrated and mutually reinforcing. The same could be said of cities or regions within *and* between countries. It has to be emphasized, however, that this is true only when GDP growth is higher than productivity growth. Failing this, there is simply a redistribution of market shares with winners and losers, as well as labour saving and more unemployment — a "widening" of capacity, rather than a "deepening" of productivity.

Agglomeration and Urbanization

Agglomeration economies are, at their root, advantages that come from reducing transportation and transaction costs (Glaeser and Gottlieb 2009). Agglomeration economies are not restricted to intra-sectoral externalities. Geographic concentration offers many potential inter-industry spillover benefits, as documented, for example, in Jane Jacobs' seminal work on the benefits of urban diversity. The additional transport costs that may derive will be more than compensated by the cheaper functional linkages between the activities. For instance, a shopping mall provides space for co-location of many unrelated commercial activities. They substantially benefit from this clustering by sharing a common facility with many amenities (parking lots, public space) and having consumers combine multipurpose commercial trips into one (in addition to maximize the chances of impulse buying). Economic geography thus suggests a variety of possible gains from agglomeration, and economists have worked to identify how and when different intra-sectoral and inter-sectoral forces shape economic activity.

Manufacturers can reduce transport costs and shipping delays if they locate near their suppliers. They also benefit from the proximity of repair and other industrial services. Financial markets cluster in cities where domestic and international communication facilities are available and cheap. Manufacturers need access to banks and other financial institutions. They also need the city's communications to stay in touch with distant suppliers and markets, especially export markets. When the city in question is a national capital, manufacturers may locate there to gain ready access to government officials who control investment licences and incentives, import allocations, and a myriad of other policy and administrative devices that affect the profitability of the firm.

A theory that complements the theory of agglomeration economies is the theory of growth pole. The growth pole theory was introduced by French scholar François Perroux (1950). He believed that growth in an economy is derived from disequilibrium and domination, and thus occurs unevenly.[4] In this concept, "the pole" is referred to as an industrial group, namely the motor industry or key industry. By means of reinvestment and multiplier effects, it could accelerate regional economic growth. Initially the growth pole theory was designed for the study of industry. However, since the industrial park shares similar characteristics, this principle can be applied to various industries and economic zones as well.

Optimal City Size

While the concept of agglomeration economies is thought to be an important factor for the existence of a city, the history of cities shows certain regularities in size distribution of cities and towns with national economies. Urban and regional economists have tried to provide economic explanations for the existence of size distribution of cities. Losch (1940) argued that there exists an optimal city size because urban utility is affected by two opposite-scale effects. The positive effect is due to the agglomeration of economic activities. The negative effect is due to crowding, congestion, and environmental deterioration. Economic models formulated by Dixit (1973) and Henderson (1974) formally introduced the trade-off between these two scale effects, and the consequent inverted U-shape of the utility level as a function of the city size. In both models, urban production exhibits increasing returns to scale. The Dixit model assumes that residential areas exhibit scale diseconomies due to internalized traffic congestion, while the Henderson model takes account of land scarcity and its effect on urban production and housing.

Urban System — Competition among Cities

Several authors have noted the increase over the last fifteen years or so in competition among cities to gain investments and to promote themselves (see, for example, Harvey 1989; Butler-Jensen et al. 1997; and Cheshire and Gordon 1995). This upsurge in spatial competition can be explained in a variety of ways (Jensen-Butler 1997) and takes place across a wide range of policy areas, all of which point to facets of cities that affect performance and, arguably, competitiveness.

It is widely accepted that production — whether in services or in industry — is becoming more fragmented and footloose. Companies are able to choose more flexibly where they locate specific processes and can, consequently, select the locations that best suit each stage of production. This is especially true of the new, knowledge-based industries (OECD

1997*a*) in which the *agglomeration advantages* of cities come to the fore. The existence and importance of a global value chain and global production network are now thought to be key features of the international production and business models championed by multinational companies.

The urban system (cities) as a whole can also influence national competitiveness. Making effective use of urban assets requires that differences as well as complementarities of cities in the urban system be recognized, and that there are gains to be achieved from exploiting the characteristics that distinguish cities and give them their identity.

Lo and Yeung (1996) introduced the concept of a functional city system in their article on global restructuring and urban restructuring in Asia-Pacific economies. The two authors defined "a functional city system as a network of cities that are linked, often in a hierarchical manner based on a given economic or socio-political function at the global or regional level". In contrast to the conventional approach of the core-periphery model, they asserted that the functional city system may more accurately depict the present evolving relations between cities in dynamic and interdependent interaction in a changing, borderless global economy. Cities are no longer defined by population size, but rather by the operation of their externally linked functions. For example, Singapore serves as a hub of several functional networks, including imports and exports, telecommunications, international airlines, and international finance, thereby determining its extensive external linkages. In the present borderless economy, it is the acquisition and accumulation of functions that can determine the centrality and role of a city in the world economy.

COMPETITIVE CITIES IN SOUTHEAST ASIAN ECONOMIES

Cities in Southeast Asia are changing and evolving in tandem with international trends. A city may evolve from one that is simply serving the needs of the domestic economy to one that is serving the world economy. In becoming a world city, it will be characterized by being the location of major financial centres, headquarters of MNCs, international institutions, important manufacturing centres, and major transportation nodes. It is suggested that the most fundamental feature of a world city is its global service functions (King 1990).

Table 3.1 presents the basic socio-economic information of Southeast Asian economies and other Asian economies, listed in declining order of their GNI (gross national income) per capita. There is substantial

Table 3.1
Economic and Demographic Statistics of Asian Economies

	Total Population, 2009 (Million)	Projected Population in 2050 (Million)	Average Population Growth (2005–10)	Percent Urbanized	% Urban growth (2005–10)	Total Fertility Rate (TFR) 2009	GNI per capita (US$)
	1	2	3	4	5	6	7
Southeast Asia Economies							
Brunei Darussalam	0.4	0.7	1.9	75.0	2.5	2.1	50200
Singapore	4.7	5.2	2.5	100.0	2.5	1.3	47950
Malaysia	27.5	39.7	1.7	71.0	3.1	2.5	13230
Thailand	67.8	73.4	0.7	34.0	1.7	1.8	7880
Philippines	92.0	146.2	1.8	66.0	3.0	3.0	3710
Indonesia	230.0	288.1	1.2	53.0	3.4	2.1	3570
Vietnam	88.1	111.7	1.1	28.0	2.9	2.0	2530
Myanmar	50.0	63.4	0.9	33.0	2.9	2.3	2499
Lao People's Democratic Republic	6.3	10.7	1.8	32.0	5.8	3.4	2080
Cambodia	14.8	23.8	1.6	22.0	4.6	2.9	1720
Other Asian Economies							
Hong Kong SAR, China	7.0	8.6	0.5	100.0	0.5	1.0	43940
Japan	127.2	101.7	-0.1	67.0	0.2	1.3	34750
Korea, Republic of	48.3	44.1	0.4	82.0	0.7	1.2	24840
China	1345.8	1417.0	0.6	44.0	2.8	1.8	5420
India	1198.0	1613.8	1.4	30.0	2.4	2.7	2740

Source: UNFPA — State of the World Population 2009.

heterogeneity in the level of development among Southeast Asian economies. Countries such as Brunei and Singapore have a GNI per capita of more than US$47,000, in contrast to Myanmar, Cambodia, and the Lao PDR, which have a GNI per capita of less than US$2,500. While it is generally true that countries with a higher proportion of urbanized population enjoy higher GNI per capita, there are distinct anomalies. The degree of urbanization is quite similar for Thailand, the Lao PDR, Vietnam, and Myanmar, yet the GNI per capita for Thailand is three to four times that of the other countries. Nonetheless, we also note that Thailand has a megacity, Bangkok, with a population of seven million, contributing the bulk of the economic growth of the nation.

The mega-economies in Asia, such as China and India, are still experiencing relatively low urbanization rates. Industrialization and growth are expected to persist in these economies. Hence they are anticipated to be the key drivers of global economic growth in the next two decades. They will provide the much-needed growth impetus for the Southeast Asian economies. The new wave of growth propulsion emanating from the emerging Asian economies will provide the much-needed lift for the ageing economy of Japan and will also lead "old" newly industrializing economies (NIEs) to new opportunities for economic expansion.

The movement of (physical as well as human) international capital is expected to continue to rise in the next two decades, making countries and cities in the Asia-Pacific region even more tightly wedded in a web of economic interdependence, whose long-term consequences are profound (Lo and Yeung 1996). Capital mobility is one facet of the international division of labour and global production and value chain in which cities are perceived to play pivotal roles in an interconnected network of multinational firms and cities. The world of modern capitalism is both a worldwide net of corporations and a global network of cities. Against this background, cities in Southeast Asia will have to find their roles to serve the needs and aspiration of the residents of the country, and be worthy members of the system of cities.

Between 1990 and 2008, industrialization as measured by the share of value-added of industry in GDP, increased for all countries in Southeast Asia except for Singapore and the Philippines (See Figure 3.1). The latter two countries have experienced a large increase in the share of services value-added in GDP during the period. Cambodia, the Lao PDR, and Vietnam, which were late comers to the class of market economies, have

Figure 3.1
Southeast Asian Countries — Value-added Share (%) of Industry in GDP, 1990 and 2008

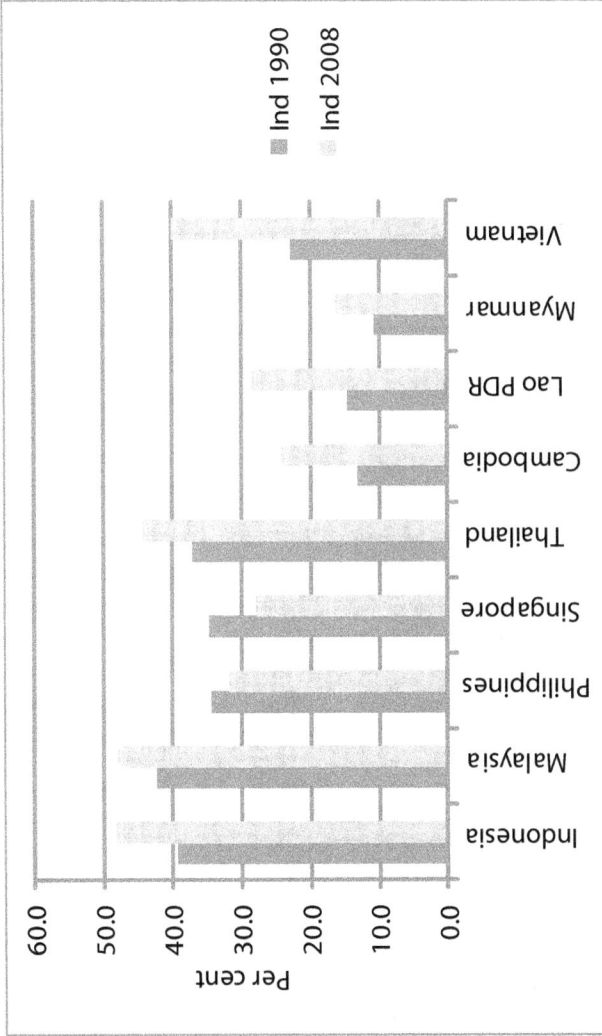

managed to double their share of industry in GDP during the eighteen years. The performance for Myanmar was less spectacular due to its difficult and uncertain domestic political situation.

In future, the cities of Southeast Asia will be important conduits for growth impulses emanating from global drivers in East Asia and other parts of the world and which are to be disseminated to the domestic economies. They will act as focal points or growth poles for localized and regional development. They will also have to collaborate with other cities. The growth of the megacities of Southeast Asia is often viewed as urban sprawl. However, this is changing. The emerging urban economies of Southeast Asia are no longer classical radial cities with urban cores, but hub-and-spoke cities that are beginning to transform themselves into loosely integrated, multi-nodal cities that merge into their hinterlands along the corridors of the main limited-access expressways.

The emphasis and expectation on agglomeration economies in Southeast Asian cities should not be exaggerated. The availability of an integrated transport system in a capital city will facilitate, but not guarantee, their realization and benefits. Concurrently, there is a need to provide accessibility and connectivity to cities and towns lower in the hierarchy of activities and functions. The demand for infrastructure and the role of government varies by city size. For example, cities of one million people or fewer may manage quite well with a road-based system that would be unsustainable for a city of ten million. Smaller cities get by with marginal increments to transport infrastructure, whereas megacities may require massive investment in new systems. In order to facilitate the identification of appropriate policy measures for cities of different sizes, Rimmer and Dick (2009) have proposed a simple fourfold typology of cities:

- Type A. Megacity with a full range of industries and business services; population of around ten million or more.
- Type B. Second large city which has achieved a minimum efficient size whereby domestic and foreign investment in broad-based, medium- and large-scale industries has become self-sustaining, but in which high-level business services are still underrepresented; population size around five million.
- Type C. City with some strong three-digit sectors, but with gaps in industrial structure according to two/three-digit International

Standard Industrial Classification (ISIC) categories and lacking many business services; population size around one to two million.

- Type D. Any other significant urban concentration, say around single-sector activities such as a port, mine, resource processing, or oil refining, but otherwise without much large or medium size manufacturing, and importing almost all business services; population size around 0.5 million.

We note that the classification is not strictly dependent on the size of the cities. The function and activities carried out in the city will also matter. Table 3.2 applies this categorization to the core Southeast Asian economies other than Singapore.

The capital cities of Indonesia, Malaysia, Thailand, and the Philippines are Type A cities providing a full spectrum of tertiary services: legal, medical, financial, educational, recreational, and international. Hanoi, the capital city of Vietnam, is classified as Type B, as there are some gaps in the level and scope of services and activities in Hanoi. In both Type A

Table 3.2
Categorization of Cities in Southeast Asia

Type	Indonesia	Malaysia	Philippines	Thailand	Vietnam
A	Jakarta (9.2)*	Kuala Lumpur (1.5)	Manila (11.7)	Bangkok (7.0)	—
B	Surabaya (2.5)				Ho Chi Minh City (6.1) Hanoi (2.8)
C	Bandung (2.4) Semarang (1.3) Medan (2.3) Makassar (1.2) Palembang (1.2)	Penang (1.0) Johor Baru (1.0)	Cebu (0.9) Davao (1.5)	Chiang Mai (1.0) Nakhon Ratchasima (0.2)	Da Nang (0.8) Haiphong (2.0)
D	Many	Many	Many	Many	Many

Notes: *Figures in parentheses represent projected population in 2010 measured in millions.
Source: Rimmer and Dick, 2009, Table 9.1 (p. 263). Population figures are projected for 2010 from the Population Division of the Department of Economic and Social Affairs of the United Nations Secretariat, World Population Prospects: The 2008 Revision and World Urbanization Prospects: The 2009 Revision at <http://esa.un.org/wup2009/unup>.

and Type B cities, rates of urbanization have slowed in tandem with lower population growth. However, urbanization rates are found to show signs of increasing in the Type C and Type D cities.

Our theoretical discussion has provided several pertinent concepts and ideas for the analysis and development of cities in Southeast Asia. Many of the Southeast Asian countries were formerly colonies of Western developed countries. Consequently many of the cities in Southeast Asia have been primarily administrative and cultural centres. Nonetheless, when colonies become independent sovereign states, the cities are often entrusted with the role of stimulating economic development and growth.

Cities allow agglomeration to happen, which will in turn facilitate economic growth. However, concurrent enabling factors are necessary to make growth possible. Regardless of which category a city is placed in, it needs to be competitive, or simply productive, to serve the needs of its residents. What are the basic ingredients for a city to be competitive? Abstracting from the various theories of city growth, a framework based on Michael Porter's diamond diagram, which encapsulated the main determinants for competitiveness, can be devised to help the formulation of strategies for economic growth and development. The diagram in Figure 3.2 is drawn with Porter's four locational factors (demand conditions, factors conditions, related and supporting industries, firm strategy and rivalry to other firms) as the domestic core. These four locational factors are complemented by four other factors: government; technology and communications; international contacts and trade; and social cohesion.

The presence of related and supporting industries is essential for agglomeration economies. The viability of enterprises in the city will depend on the business strategies adopted to leverage market demand and availability of factor inputs. The city will flourish when enterprises are performing well in an environment that is supported by pro-business public policies. In market-driven cities, land-use decisions are influenced as much by private developers as by government planners. A government can be an effective facilitator of economic activities by providing essential infrastructure such as power, utilities, roads, ports, and telecommunication networks. It can also encourage the use of technology and R&D for both product and process improvement in the economy through grants, fiscal rebates, and investment subsidy. In a globalized world, the profitability and viability of enterprises can be enhanced by selling abroad and procuring lower-cost material inputs from overseas. Active government participation

Figure 3.2
Competitive Framework for Cities

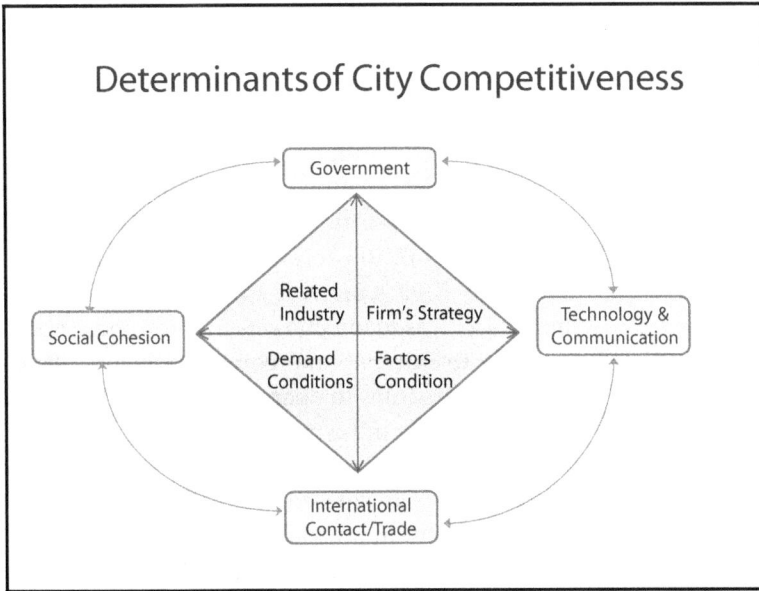

Determinants of City Competitiveness

in free trade agreements is also a means to enable cities to develop international contacts and expand market access in foreign countries. All the development efforts will come to nought, however, if citizens cannot identify with the aspirations of the city. There is a need for social cohesion so that the raw forces of competition will be tamed to improve the well-being of the citizens, and individuals are not rendered into callous digits, devoid of care and compassion by fellow human beings.

Government provision of infrastructure is essential. Although urban infrastructure can be provided in big cities at lower costs than the alternative of providing the same services in small, scattered towns, infrastructure is still the largest direct cost of urbanization. A study of cities and towns in India estimated that the capital cost of infrastructure provided for the manufacturing industry was $820 for every $1,000 of incremental value-added in manufacturing, or about $1,400 per employee in a city of one million. Only about a quarter of this is due to construction in the industrial area itself. The balance serves the residential areas and can generally be interpreted as the capital cost of supporting workers in the city. If the capital costs are amortized at 10 per cent a year and maintenance costs ($600 per employee) are added, it will appear that cities provide manufacturers with annual infrastructure services costing 13 per cent of the value-added.

Over the last forty years of compressed economic growth, government policy has had a large influence on industrial and spatial development in the NIEs, such as Singapore and the Republic of Korea. The governments of these countries selected strategic industries and developed industrial estates for them, and employed administrative and financial (fiscal) assistance extensively to support those industries. In the case of Singapore, the government has relied heavily on foreign capital to jump-start its industrialization programme. MNCs are able to bring along technology, management know-how, as well as ready markets for the goods produced. The "immediate" exposure to international competition has played an important part in fostering companies to operate efficiently, and learning and absorbing best practices in the industries quickly.

Meanwhile, other cities in Southeast Asia, following in the footsteps of the NIEs, are also making significant progress in catalysing domestic growth, and are slowly but surely mimicking and adopting policies and measures to be world cities in the coming years. Kuala Lumpur has aspired to be a centre for Islamic banking and is making headway by leveraging its religious and cultural similarities with business communities in the Middle East economies. Bangkok, the capital city of Thailand, has been the growth pole and main driver of industrialization in Thailand. It is no exaggeration, as some economists will assert, that the economic development of Bangkok is essentially the development of Thailand, which has been able to attract foreign investments from the developed economies in the West, as well as those in East Asia.

In particular, auto makers from Japan, Europe, and the United States are attracted to Thailand to set up plants to produce for the Southeast Asian market. Leveraging the free trade agreements among ASEAN countries (AFTA), a production network for auto and auto parts has been put in place in the CLMV region (Cambodia, Lao PDR, Myanmar, and Vietnam), with Bangkok as a focal point. In this network, cities in the CLMV countries are given the opportunity to establish economic linkages to the outside world, though these are still limited in scale and scope. Factories and plants in Phnom Penh (Cambodia) and Vientiane (Lao PDR) are able to provide parts, components, and other paraphernalia (embroidery) for cars.

Vietnam is not left out of this endeavour. Hyundai, a Korean automobile manufacturer, has transferred its automobile engine production technology to its Vietnamese partner, the Vietnam Motor Industry Corporation. Consequently, an automobile factory, producing Hyundai buses and trucks, was inaugurated in northern Bac Giang province in March 2006. Worthy of note is that AFTA has helped to promote complementarities among automakers' operations in the region, generate agglomeration economies, and strengthen the competitiveness of the ASEAN auto industry.

With scarce natural resources and a small domestic market, NIEs such as the Republic of Korea and Singapore, have inevitably been tied closely with overseas markets. Because of this overseas orientation, the cities' contacts with the outside world have proved to be an important attribute in attracting central decision-making functions of various industries. Starting with the large corporations that led the Republic of Korea's overseas trade over the decades, other related industries and supporting services are clustered in Seoul and enjoy close contacts with government agencies and other key decision-making bodies.

Much the same can be said of Singapore. Singapore has relied heavily on a cluster-based industry development approach to jump-start and to maintain its industrialization drive and economic growth over the last fifty years. The clustering of industries in a geographically proximate location enables agglomeration economies to materialize. The building of an industrial estate in Jurong provided the foundation for industrialization. The same strategy is applied in the development of the petrochemical sector located on offshore Jurong Island reclaimed from the almalgamation of five islets. This has helped Singapore retain its importance as the world's third-largest oil refinery. More recently, the same approach has been used to develop the biomedical sciences (BMS) sector as a new growth engine and to inject new activities into the manufacturing sector.

Development Strategy — Outline

Theories, trends, and the current status of development in Southeast Asian cities and countries have generated much thought on possible suggestions for public policies and economic growth. We venture to propose an outline of an effective economic strategy to develop Southeast Asian cities. Weiss (2001) indicates the need to focus on two key elements. The first is investing in fundamental assets and activities that will help fuel productivity and innovation. Among these are:

- transportation and infrastructure
- education and workforce development
- research and technology
- venture capital and other forms of business financing
- services and amenities
- economic development incentives
- trade promotion and market expansion
- business and employment attraction and retention
- entrepreneurial culture and business-friendly institutions
- regional coordination and civic leadership
- taxation and regulatory policy
- environmental preservation and restoration
- community and family development
- quality of life

The second key element in the economic strategy is promoting modern and dynamic industry networks that accelerate the pace of innovation and growth. Such broad-based groups of interconnected firms and organizations, also called *industry clusters*, are best able to capitalize fully on the mix of specialization and diversity in the region's firms and assets, and to foster a climate of innovation in business processes, technology, and the design and production of goods and services that can enhance global competitiveness and generate substantial growth in jobs and incomes. Singapore has used this approach and attained many successful outcomes.

Fundamental assets and key dynamic industry networks will vary from city to city, and region to region. One size definitely does not fit all. Every region must find the right mix and most important assets that work best in its particular circumstances for generating innovation and prosperity.

CONCLUDING REMARKS AND POLICY IMPLICATIONS

What are the characteristics of a competitive city? Making it clear that the focus at the urban level may differ significantly from the national level, Kresl (1995) cites six attributes which he considers signal a competitive urban economy:

- The jobs created should be high-skill, high-income jobs
- Production should evolve towards environmentally benign goods and services

- Production should be concentrated in goods and services with desirable characteristics, such as high income elasticity of demand
- The rate of economic growth should be appropriate to achieve full employment without generating the negative aspects of overstressed markets
- The city should specialize in activities that will enable it to gain control over its future, that is, to choose among alternative futures rather than passively accepting its lot
- The city should be able to enhance its position in the urban hierarchy (Kresl 1995, p. 51)

We have discussed some economic concepts and theories that may be useful for the formulation and implementation of development plans and industry planning in cities and urban areas. The possible positive role of government in city development cannot be downplayed. Governments can have a role in boosting the competitiveness of cities. As the various contributions to an OECD publication (1997) make clear, the role of governments is undoubtedly shifting from direct provision to an enabling one. Where public intervention is most successful, this tends to be attributable to effective infrastructure, policies which enhance the quality of labour, and the promotion of appropriate specialization and economic linkages.

The individual city's government and private sector entities can do a great deal to enhance the city's competitiveness and to enable it to achieve the most desirable economic future possible. The main scope for action by urban policymakers is to stick to the basics: "investment in infrastructure and human capital, promotion of smaller firms, ensuring an adequate complement of business and financial service providers, articulation of a well-thought-out and clearly expressed strategic plan, effective governance, and a supportive regulatory environment" (Kresl 1995).

There is also a need to recognize that intangible assets — knowledge and the ability to use it being central — are vital ingredients in the competitiveness of a "new" activity, notably IT-related industries. In this regard, the propensity to innovate is important in generating advances, and small firms are one of the obvious mechanisms that promote innovation. However, diffusion of knowledge, especially towards established firms whose growth provides volumes of employment and value added, also contribute to the desired outcome. Changes in the business environment have to be achieved to accommodate the information-driven economy (Drake 1997). This requires much more of a partnership approach between government and increasingly nimble private-sector agents.

In the discussion of Southeast Asian cities, we note that large primate cities are not necessarily harmful for economic development. Even megacities such as Bangkok, Jakarta, and Manila are still capable of generating increasing returns to urban size and high rates of growth of income and employment. Megacities of Southeast Asia are at a stage when it has become urgent for them to invest in transportation infrastructure to cope with rising populations and economic and business activities. People movers such as the rail and metro system are believed to be able to enhance accessibility of consumers, enable multiplier effects on demand and business transaction, and have a consequential positive impact on employment generation and the well-being of residents. On the other hand, Type-B, C and D cities would benefit more from empowered urban governments with better access to a local tax base, than from an ad hoc revision of grants or soft loans for transport and communications infrastructure (Rimmer and Dick 2009).

Cities do compete with one another. They do so internationally, nationally, and regionally. Equally, cities cooperate through specialization and exchange of goods and services, and as components in an urban system that increasingly transcends national borders. Cooperation is also evident in the articulation of common problems such as social exclusion or environmental degradation, sharing of experience, and the establishment of policy networks. The twinning of cities and specific city-to-city exchanges in terms of cultural activities and economic cooperation are an expression of the desire for mutual understanding, and for finding solutions to problems encountered jointly.

A case in point is the formation of SIJORI (Singapore-Johor-Riau), later known as the Indonesia-Malaysia-Singapore Growth Triangle (IMS-GT) in 1994. The vertices of the triangle are the cities in each subregion. The SIJORI Growth Triangle is a partnership arrangement between Singapore, Johor (in Malaysia), and Batam (in the Riau Province of Indonesia) that combines the competitive strengths of the three areas to make the subregion more attractive to regional and international investors. More specifically, it links the infrastructure, capital, and expertise of Singapore with the natural and labour resources of Johor and Riau. The "triangle of growth" jived well with Singapore's regionalization efforts of the 1980s and 1990s, to relocate systematically labour-intensive and land-intensive industries to neighbouring countries or regions. Singapore government-linked companies partnered private Indonesian enterprise to develop the Batam Industrial Park (Batamindo), an industrial estate on Batam Island, and to take advantage of its status as a duty-free export processing zone

(EPZ) and of the business generated when industries move over from Singapore. The status and importance of Batam was not diminished despite the onset of the Asian financial crisis in 1997. In fact, it has become an icon for Indonesia to muster ASEAN and international support for trade and investments to jump-start the economic recovery after the crisis. Batam became an autonomous or self-governing city in 1999, and was granted Free Trade Zone status in 2007.[5]

The single-minded pursuance of competitiveness for a city is acceptable, but may not be desirable for a nation. Developing a competitive society (nation) is a more sophisticated undertaking than just maximizing business efficiency. A competitive society is a society that has found a dynamic equilibrium between wealth creation on one side and social cohesion on the other. It does not necessarily mean economic efficiency at all costs in all areas. Each country's competitiveness depends on its ability to balance the economy of globality, which may generate revenues and technology, and the economy of proximity, which mainly generates employment and social cohesion.

Notes

1. Satterthwaite 2008. The cities included are Manila, Beijing, Hanoi, Phnom Penh, Chiang Mai, Surabaya, Pune, and Karachi.
2. A more in-depth discussion about why cities exist can be found in Glaeser and Gottlieb 2009.
3. <http://stats.oecd.org/glossary>.
4. See Parr 1999. Other terms have been used to describe "growth pole", including dynamic industry, export-based industry, propulsive industry, lead firm, innovative super-profit, and economic driver.
5. The signing of the Framework Agreement between Singapore and Indonesia on Economic Cooperation on the islands of Batam, Bintan and Karimun (BBK) was done on 25 June 2006 and signifies another notch higher in cross-country economic cooperation. A key feature of the agreement is that Singapore will assist the development of the three islands as a Special Economic Zone (SEZ). For further discussion on the IMS growth triangle, see Toh and Ng 2009.

References

Begg I. *Urban Competitiveness: Policies for Dynamic Cities*. Bristol: Policy Press, 2002.

Ciampi C.A. "Enhancing European Competitiveness". Banca Nazionale di Lavoro, *Quarterly Review* 197 (1996): 143–64.

Dixit, A. "The Optimum Factory Town". *Bell Journal of Economic Management Science* 4 (1973): 637–51.

Drake K. "Industrial Competitiveness in the Knowledge-based Economy: The New Role of Government". In *Industrial Competitiveness in the Knowledge-based Economy: The New Role of Governments*. Paris: OECD, 1997.

European Commission. "Report on the Competitiveness of the EU". DGIII. Mimeographed. 1997.

Glaeser, E. and J. Gottlieb. "The Wealth of Cities: Agglomeration Economies and Spatial Equilibrium in the United States". *Journal of Economic Literature* 47, no. 4 (2009): 983–1028.

Gordon, I.R. and P.C. Cheshire. "Locational Advantage and the Lessons of Territorial Competition in Europe". Paper prepared for the international workshop on "Theories of Regional Development: Lessons for Policies of Regional Economic Renewal and Growth", Uddevalla, Sweden, 14–16 June 1998.

Henderson, J.V. "The Sizes and Types of Cities". *American Economic Review* 64 (1974): 640–56.

Jensen-Butler, C. "Competition between Cities, Urban Performance and the Role of Urban Policy: A Theoretical Framework". In *European Cities in Competition*, edited by C. Jensen-Butler, A. Shachar, and J. van Weesep. Aldershot: Avebury, 1997.

Jensen-Butler, C., A. Schacher, and J. van Weesep (eds.). *European Cities in Competition* Aldershot: Avebury, 1997.

King, A.D. *Global Cities: Post Imperialism and the Internationalization of London.* London: Routledge, 1990.

Kresl, P. "The Determinants of Urban Competitiveness". In *North American Cities and the Global Economy: Challenges and Opportunities*, edited by P. Kresl and G. Gappert. London: Sage, 1995.

Krugman P. "Making Sense of the Competitiveness Debate". *Oxford Review of Economic Policy* 12 (1996*a*): 17–25.

———. "Urban Concentration: The Role of Increasing Returns and Transport Costs". *International Regional Science Review* 19 (1996*b*): 5–48.

Lo Fu-Chen and Yeung Yue-Man. "Global Restructuring and Emerging Urban Corridors in Pacific Asia". In *Emerging World Cities in Pacific Asia*. New York: United Nations University Press, 2009.

Losch, A. *The Economics of Location.* New Haven: Yale University Press, 1940 (Translated from German in 1954 by W.H. Woglom).

Markusen, A. "Interaction between Regional and Industrial Policies: Evidence from Four Countries". *International Regional Science Review* 19 (1996): 49–78.

Marshall, Alfred. *Principles of Economics.* London: Macmillan, 1890.

OECD. *Industrial Competitiveness.* Paris: OECD, 1996.

————. *Industrial Competitiveness in the Knowledge-based Economy: The New Role of Governments*. Paris: OECD, 1997a.

————. *Industrial Competitiveness: Benchmarking Business Environments*. Paris: OECD, 1997b.

Parr, John B. "Growth Pole Strategies in Regional Economic Planning: A Retrospective View. Part 1: Origins and Advocacy". *Urban Studies* 36, no. 7 (1999): 1195–215.

Perroux, François. "Economic space: Theory and applications". *Quarterly Journal of Economics* 64 (1950): 90–97.

Porter, M.E. *The Competitive Advantage of Nations*. London: Macmillan, 1990.

————. "Competitive Advantage, Agglomeration Economies and Regional Policy". *International Regional Science Review* 19 (1996): 85–90.

Rimmer, Peter J. and Howard Dick. *The City in Southeast Asia: Patterns, Processes and Policy*. Singapore: NUS University Press, 2009.

Rypkema, D.D. "Globalization, Urban Heritage, and the 21st Century Economy". *Global Urban Development* 1, no. 1 (2005): 1–8.

Satterthwaite, D. "Understanding Asian Cities: A Synthesis of the Findings from Eight Asian Cities". *Global Urban Development* 4, no. 2 (Nov 2008): 1–24.

Toh, M.H and Ng K.K. "The Batam, Bintan, Karimum Special Economic Zone: Revitalizing Domestic Industrialization and Linking Global Value Chain". In *Plugging into Production Networks: Industrialization Strategy in Less Developed Southeast Asian Countries*, edited by I. Kuroiwa. Japan and Singapore: IDE-JETRO and Institute of Southeast Asian Studies.

Weiss, M.A. "Productive Cities and Metropolitan Economic Strategy". Paper presented to the United Nations International Forum on Urban Poverty (IFUP), Fourth International Conference, Marrakech, Morocco, 16–19 October 2001.

4

PUBLIC-PRIVATE PARTNERSHIPS AND URBAN INFRASTRUCTURE DEVELOPMENT IN SOUTHEAST ASIA

Nutavoot Pongsiri

In Southeast Asian countries, urban areas have been developed with rapid economic growth and expansion of population. The economies of the Association of Southeast Asian Nations (ASEAN) experienced an average growth rate of 5.9 per cent between 2003 and 2008 (ASEAN Secretariat 2009). The total population of the region in 2008 was about 580 million and was projected to rise to 650 million by 2020, with more than half living in urban areas (United Nations 2007). The urban population in the region has been steadily increasing from 31.6 per cent of the total population in 1990, to about 47 per cent in 2008 (ASEAN Secretariat 2009). However, due to the rising population in major cities, the development of urban infrastructure and public services such as sewage systems, wastewater treatment facilities, and public transportation networks, has been inadequate and these services have become less effective, causing serious problems to the quality of life of residents, and obstructing sustainable growth of the ASEAN countries.

Since the introduction of decentralization efforts in several ASEAN countries in the 1990s, many local governments have been responsible for the delivery of urban services. However, their financial and administrative autonomy remains a challenging issue. The ability of local governments to raise revenue and provide adequate services continues to deteriorate as city populations grow, while their administrations are still trapped in bureaucratic traditions and lack capable staff.

Facing budgetary constraints and recognizing their inability to provide infrastructure services efficiently, governments in many countries have been rapidly adopting neoliberal approaches and a market-based economy. This has led to radical changes in the characteristics and respective roles of the public and private sectors. Coping with the new market economy requires governments to reduce the size of the public sector and give a greater role to a more dynamic private sector under public-private partnership schemes.

The purpose of this chapter is to identify issues and challenges in the area of public-private partnerships for infrastructure provision and finance at the urban and national levels in Southeast Asia. More thought will be given to discussing essential features of the regulatory and legal frameworks required to support public and private sectors to deliver urban infrastructure services effectively.

PRIVATE PARTICIPATION IN URBAN INFRASTRUCTURE DEVELOPMENT IN ASEAN — SOME LESSONS LEARNED

Public-private partnerships (PPPs) are arrangements between government and private sector entities for the purpose of providing public infrastructure, community facilities, and related services. PPP infrastructure development can take place at a regional level on a large scale, such as a cross-country tunnel construction, or on a small scale at an urban area such as city waste water treatment and sewage rehabilitation. The partnership arrangements can provide a broad umbrella to shelter and protect public interest while bringing investment potential and added value from the private sector.

Governments in the ASEAN countries have used the public-private partnership mechanism extensively, partly because they suffer from budgetary constraints, and partly because they lack technical expertise and resources to secure financing. This unfolds in the critical case of urban infrastructure development, where in exchange for a building licence, the private investor promises to build public infrastructure such as roads and sewer systems that the local government cannot effectively accomplish. In addition, decentralization has significantly empowered and given autonomy to local governments to control and supervise their private partners' performance by utilizing or manipulating the permit or licensing system. Therefore, the success or failure of urban development relies to some extent on whether the private investor's rights, as derived from government licences and permits, are secure in order for the investors to continue to invest at adequate levels to support urban infrastructure development projects.

Some success stories of PPPs in ASEAN countries are in urban water supply and distribution. Traditionally the public sector has been responsible for the management of water services, but in recent times it has been argued that it lacks the capability that is needed to provide efficient services at a time of increasing demand. The provision of water by many municipal governments has been marred by inefficiencies, especially due to low coverage, high non-revenue water (NRW) levels, intermittent supplies, and poor water quality. Greater involvement of the private sector in water supply and distribution, through innovative approaches such as PPPs, has become one of the solutions. Examples include the private sector participation in urban water supply through the concessions in metropolitan Manila and Jakarta, which have been in place for almost a decade, serving a total population of twenty million people.

In Manila two concessions were awarded in 1997 to cover two areas. The Western concession, operated by Benpres-Suez, was the larger and covered most developed portions of the city, with a total population of about seven million people. The smaller Eastern concession, operated by Ayala-United Utilities, covered about four million residents. Even though the implementation of the two concessions faced major difficulties from the beginning due to the Asian financial crisis, access to piped water in Manila expanded significantly during the decade. From 1997 to 2006, the zone coverage significantly expanded from 67 per cent to 86 per cent for the Western concession, and from 49 per cent to 94 per cent for the Eastern concession (Philippe 2009) whereas the average water coverage for the national urban area grew moderately from 46 per cent to 58 per cent. An estimated four million people gained access to piped water in Manila during the period 1997–2006.

Access to piped water in Jakarta was initially even lower. Before the two concessions — to Suez for the Western zone and to Thames Water for the Eastern zone — were awarded in 1998, water supply covered, on average, 30 per cent of the population. Many city dwellers obtained water from private wells. Between 1998 and 2005, the two concessionaires added 210,000 water connections to the system, providing access for an additional 1.7 million people. Access to piped water in Jakarta's Western zone went up from 32 per cent to 50 per cent, and from 57 per cent to 67 per cent in the Eastern zone (Philippe 2009) whereas national urban water coverage stagnated at a low 30 per cent in the same period. However, it was difficult to expand access to water supply in Jakarta any further. Many households were unwilling to pay a connection fee plus periodic bills, because they had already invested in pumping equipment and were not paying any extraction charge for the water they were getting from their wells.

The performance of PPPs in water supply and distribution in Indonesia and the Philippines has demonstrated achievable success, with more expansion of coverage, improved operational efficiency, and better quality of service. Despite some problems, the concessionaires have obtained very encouraging results. They have successfully retendered and are now gaining considerable success in the area of high non-revenue water (NRW) management.

It is vital for a successful PPP to have an effective procurement and financing strategy in place, including regulatory frameworks that identify roles and responsibilities for the local governments and the private partners at the outset. There are some lessons to be learned from the PPP urban infrastructure development projects in countries such as Malaysia and Thailand indicating failures — mainly because of the lack of adequate guarantees for long-term investment return, and the impact of political intervention at the local governmental level.

PPP Failures Caused by Economic Risks and Inadequate Financial Guarantees

Examining experience in more detail shows that there are a number of features that raise the risk profile of urban infrastructure development for private investors. An urban sewage rehabilitation project illustrates some of the PPP pitfalls caused by economic risks and inadequate financial guarantees. In Malaysia the provision of sewage services was privatized to Indah Water Konsortium (IWK) in 1993. The project arose from concerns over the local governments' weak technical and financial capability in the face of poorly maintained facilities, and rising demand for better sewage services. An unsolicited proposal was brought to the central government and approved rapidly in 1994. This Malaysia example is interesting because the sanitation programme provides a core urban infrastructure service, but is managed at the national level.

There are 144 local authorities in the country and IWK has taken over the management and provision of sewage services for eighty-four of the local authorities (Abidin 2004). Investments and the level of service improved dramatically in the immediate term. As the demand for effective sanitation increased, IWK turned to other private companies to build waste water management systems. However, even before the economic crisis in 1997, IWK faced problems with revenue collection because many consumers refused to pay the imposed rates (Annex 2006). Consumers felt that the tariffs charged were too high. They perceived that the price of a public utility had increased, following the transfer of the service from the government to the private sector.

The tariff structure originally stipulated in the agreements was then suspended without compensation for the private investors, and a new tariff structure was established in 1997. In addition, IWK discovered that the rehabilitation required more investment than anticipated. As a result, the government felt obliged to provide substantial financial support to IWK, including a long-term, soft loan package. In conclusion, although the government succeeded in attracting private involvement, the structure of guarantees provided and the underestimated risks involved in the project were such that both the capital mobilized and the physical achievements of the projects were much less than originally expected.

PPP Failures Caused by Undue Political Intervention

Experience in ASEAN countries has revealed that the PPP success can be hampered significantly by undue political intervention in the policymaking process. For example, politicians made promises to support the development of a particular project, but then continued lobbying against the development of a similar project backed by the opposing politicians. Such political competition may produce unhealthy results for the economic functioning of a city.

A prime example is the transport sector in Bangkok (Valentine 2008). There are two rail systems currently operating in the city. The first one, owned by the Bangkok Metropolitan Authority (BMA), is the BTS Sky-train which began operation in 1999 under a PPP concession of the Build-Operate-Transfer (BOT) model, managed by the Bangkok Mass Transit System (BTS) Public Company. The second one is the underground electric mass rapid transit system called the MRT (Mass Rapid Transit), which is operated by the Mass Rapid Transit Authority (MRTA), a state-owned enterprise under the supervision of the Ministry of Transportation.

The local government authority is authorized to operate the BTS Sky-train within the central Bangkok area, whereas the MRTA is authorized to operate the underground MRT systems within the Greater Bangkok area and the nearby provinces. In 2008 the BTS and its expansion plans were linked to local politicians who were in fierce competition with their political opponents in the central government, who favoured the MRT system. These opponents considered that the best way to promote the extensions for the MRT concessions was to prohibit the extensions for the BTS network.

This political tension caused an extremely slow expansion of both the MRT and BTS systems that serve the residents of Bangkok. It has obviously led to negative implications for the city's infrastructure development in terms of mobilizing finance and accelerating private participation in project investments.

REGULATORY AND LEGAL FRAMEWORKS TO SUPPORT PRIVATE PARTICIPATION IN INFRASTRUCTURE DEVELOPMENT

The infrastructure needed by developing countries to support their economic activities are mainly those related to transportation, energy, water, and, most recently, telecommunications. However, high capital investment costs and the lack of technology can impede infrastructure development. Many developing countries cannot afford such development without it affecting other economic activities. Considerable attention has been paid to the development of regulations for the promotion of private involvement in public infrastructure services, with a view to encouraging private firms to participate and, thereby, mobilize private capital into public work projects.

Improvement of programme performance, cost efficiencies, better service provision, and the appropriate allocation of risks and accountabilities, have been identified as factors that can open avenues for public-private partnership in design, construction, operation, maintenance, and financing of infrastructure through management and lease contracts, concessions, and divestitures. There are some enabling factors of regulation that are essential for private investment in infrastructure development. These include the setting up of a regulatory framework and institutions at the outset; sound regulations to protect private sector investment; contractual safeguards against potentially disputable matters; and governance and accountability frameworks.

Institutional and Regulatory Setting

Regulation is a key element to maintaining competitive market discipline on public infrastructure services. While many governments in developing countries have already signed their first demonstration public-private partnership contracts, most have not yet designed the legal and regulatory framework for monitoring the performance of private contractors and ensuring contractual compliance. Experience in these countries confirms the importance of putting a sound regulatory framework in place before implementing public-private partnership programmes (IP3 2000).

A regulatory system should be established as soon as possible to define clear rules for financial performance, provide practical experience to staff responsible for their implementation, and provide assurance to the private sector that the regulatory system includes protection from expropriation, arbitration of commercial disputes, and respect for contract agreements. In turn, the regulatory system will increase benefits to the government by achieving better and more informed decision-making and improved performance, and by raising efficiency and accountability (World Bank 1994).

Investment Protection

Investor security is critically important. Regulation is also useful to protect the interests of private investors by preventing direct or indirect expropriation of investment capital. For example, regulation in public-private partnerships can act as a buffer against political interference from governmental bodies in pricing decisions. This buffer function is particularly important as government objectives — for political or social reasons — may act as a disincentive to investment and, indeed, may not even be in the consumer interest (World Bank 1994). In developing countries with limited history of private participation, investors with doubts about the safety of their investments will either require very high returns, or not invest. The only way for these countries to be successful in attracting private capital is to establish a regulatory regime that reduces this risk and protects private-sector investment.

Contractual Safeguards

The financial and other resources of private and state enterprises are always limited. Projects developed as public-private partnerships are mostly based on risk sharing and a security package of interrelated contracts between the two parties (IP3 2000). Consequently many developing and emerging market economies require effective models on how best to design and establish legal frameworks for contract compliance and performance monitoring of public-private partnerships.

On the one hand, the private sector needs a great deal of certainty and protection against unforeseeable changes, as the economic and financial costs of poorly designed, drafted, and negotiated agreements can be tremendous, and can jeopardize entire public-private partnership programmes. The establishment of a transparent and sound regulatory framework is a necessary precursor to private sector participation in a public-private partnership. On the other hand, governments need regulation to ensure that essential partnerships operate efficiently and optimize the resources available to them in line with broader policy objectives, ranging from social policy to a policy for environmental protection (World Bank 1994, pp. 57–59).

However, over-regulation and contractual safeguards can restrain economic growth and hinder the private sector's ability to remain competitive in the market (Lundqvist 1988).

Governance and Accountability Framework

Private investors will keep away and will seek a more hospitable place to invest if regulation is unlimited in scope, unclear in operation, inclined towards micromanagement, and lacks good governance. The regulatory regime must be limited, transparent, fair, and consistent, and the government must always keep its promises. Private investors are cautious not only of expropriation, but also of many small regulatory actions that together constitute incremental expropriation, taking away the private partner's option of legitimate recovery of costs and profits proportional to the risks undertaken. Private investors must be convinced that the government, as a prudent partner, will commit to good governance to protect private investments, and will not use regulation as a direct or indirect mechanism for "administration expropriation". Even if public-private partnerships appear to reduce costs, they cannot be defined as a success if their regulation results in the need for more government oversight and expensive monitoring (Sparer 1999).

Public-private partnerships also involve sharing or transferring a measure of responsibility and control of operations. This may cause shifts in accountability arrangements, creating new responsibility hierarchies and reporting requirements for public-sector managers. While governments have been largely preoccupied with political accountability through the electoral process, public-private partnerships open new channels of accountability. In arrangements where the government still retains ultimate or partial accountability, government partners must ensure the respective accountability of their partners through the use of sound formal agreements (Pongsiri 2002).

There are also new accountability demands on private participants in a partnership as they are required to disclose information about partnership-related activities, including expenditures to their partners and the public. Problems that arise as a result of shifts in accountabilities can be avoided if appropriate arrangements are put in place towards clear governing regulations. From a government's viewpoint, a well-defined regulatory framework is essential if the private partners ideologically and financially oppose seeing themselves as having additional accountabilities to the public interest (Hassan 1996; Colton et al. 1997).

REGULATORY AND LEGAL CONSIDERATIONS AT A NATIONAL-URBAN PPP SETTING

PPPs bring multiple benefits to the stakeholders involved. However, there are operational, political, and financial risks that are borne by local governments and the private companies involved in urban development PPPs. Therefore, central governments and local authorities need to ensure that a regulatory and legal framework shall be made available to permit, facilitate, and secure private investment in public work projects.

Although the concept of public-private partnerships is becoming increasingly common as a means of delivering urban infrastructure services, the level of private sector involvement is not yet sufficient in ASEAN countries. More importantly, a well-defined regulatory framework for partnerships is more an idea than a reality at present. What most public and private organizations have found is that the implementation of a regulatory framework in their partnership has created a number of issues that are in need of clarification. Some issues and challenges at the national-urban PPP setting that need to be addressed to provide sustainable participation by the private sector are discussed below.

Overlapping Regulations and Unclear Roles at the Urban PPP Setting

Urban PPPs are a commercial transaction between an urban local government and a private party, whereby the private organization performs an urban function for, or on behalf of, the local government. The private sector, acquiring managerial work or using urban property for its own commercial purposes, assumes substantial financial, technical, and operational risks, and receives a financial benefit in respect of the project. Several PPP projects have clearly demonstrated how effective combinations of private and public financing and enterprise can strengthen urban service provision significantly and improve the well-being of people in urban areas, cities, and towns. Some other benefits to an urban local government are transfers of technology, employment benefits, and capacity building.

Urban authorities are important in the creation or enhancement of this enabling environment for PPPs in cities and towns. In many countries these authorities have significant governmental autonomy under Private Participation in Public Infrastructure Development Acts or similar regulations. They can enter into PPP contracts without needing consent from the central government as long as the costs of the contract can be covered by the urban budget. This means that local authorities must have their own resources and taxation authority, and the ability to formulate, negotiate, award, implement, supervise, and monitor PPP projects. Effective decentralization is therefore a precondition for PPP development at the urban level.

Although urban local officials in general do not have the power to influence positive changes in the country's investment climate, they need adequate clarity on their roles and authority levels, not just to sign contracts, but also to undertake all the other tasks related to maintaining the public-private partnership. These include financial and legal frameworks and other areas of public administration. However, in some countries there is confusion and inconsistencies in the regulatory frameworks of the central government that inhibit urban government actions to attract capital investment.

One of the biggest challenges facing urban officials is the legacy of complex and interlinked regulations that often involve inherent confusion and duplication. For example, in Thailand the frameworks underpinning PPP activities are derived from the Act on Private Participation in State Undertaking B.E. 2535 (1992). However, the institutional regulatory framework for infrastructure provision and management is a fragmented hierarchy where many different bodies across several sectors have assumed various responsibilities of regulation (Valentine 2008). Certain PPP projects at an urban level are covered by their own regulations because the 1992 Act does not prescribe the methodology for project valuation or procurement methods. It also does not provide a methodology for sharing the risks and burdens with the private sector when projects are not commercially viable. The regulation thus becomes less effective and lends itself to frequent clarification and interpretation on several aspects (Susangarn 2007).

Many countries have adopted special arbitration mechanisms at an urban level to solve technical, contractual, and labour disputes. The arbitration panels can include members of the public and the private sectors, with supporting guidelines for conflict resolution. This minimizes difficulties and tensions that sometimes arise. If there are no special arbitration mechanisms, urban authorities themselves need to perform the roles of different regulatory authorities, including judicial bodies, when disputes arise. In some contracts involving international partners, there can be special clauses for court jurisdiction which can be outside the host country. This is sometimes favoured by foreign investors, who are unfamiliar with, or are distrustful of, local judicial objectivity and processes. As such, urban officials need to understand the implications of these clauses in potential contracts and agreements.

Comprehensive and Consistent Regulatory Framework at the National PPP Setting

At the national level, there must be legal, regulatory, and administrative processes that uphold and respect foreign investors. A comprehensive and consistent framework of PPP regulation is very important as it provides a reference point for the main actors in the partnership. There is also a real need for consistency in national PPP policies over the long term, regardless of changes that may occur in political regime.

In Thailand all PPP projects are governed by the Act on Private Participation in State Undertaking B.E. 2535 (1992), which was intended to provide appropriate scrutiny processes for large PPP projects, to ensure that projects are viable and that contracts are carried out through proper procedures. At the time of its enactment, it had been designed to prevent corruption in granting rights to private investors for the operation or use of state properties, rather than to delineate the necessary components of a sound regulatory and institutional framework for PPP projects. As a result, the 1992 Act has provided governmental authorities with inadequate content and an unclear governing framework (Susangarn 2007). There is need for an amendment to provide a broader definition of the PPP concept and a more streamlined process for implementing PPP projects.

A central feature of PPPs is the contractual arrangement. These contracts are often highly technical, cumbersome, and have significant legal, financial, and technical implications. The regulatory framework enforced by the central government thus requires a comprehensive guideline for procurement, regulation of prices, and conditions of arbitration, including the handling of labour disputes. Other related contractual issues that may have an impact on the contracting of private parties at the national level are exchange rates, ability to transfer profits, taxation, labour laws, and insurance. In some countries, the level of decentralization provides urban officials with adequate authority over the PPP, but these officials lack sufficient understanding. Confusion over authority, functions, and decision-making within the local government and among several relevant central government agencies can make the design, procurement, and implementation of PPP projects difficult.

It is necessary for the central government to enforce a clear regulation on when and how urban or local governments need consultation with existing regulatory authorities at the national level, and how the central government should take part in contractual matters, such as issues related to pricing and dispute resolution. Good examples for Southeast Asia are South Africa, which has a national framework of laws, regulation, and administrative processes guiding urban governments on the use of PPPs (PPP Manual, South Africa 2004), and Germany, which has a unit for the coordination of PPP design and management in the country (PPP Coordination Unit,

Germany 2006). The primary goal of the PPP Coordination Unit is to establish a regulatory framework for public authorities (at the national and urban levels), related to the application of a range of PPP instruments to implement national and urban development strategies; deliver support for PPP projects' market development; and provide consulting services to local authorities.

Legal provisions and procedures related to private sector participation in Southeast Asian countries are complex, numerous, scattered over many different instruments, and have no fixed time frame for completion (ESCAP 2006). To address these problems, several governments have established specialized units and devised suitable legal instruments to reduce the level of uncertainty surrounding public-private partnership projects and increase investor confidence. The Build Operate Transfer Centre (BOTC) in the Philippines and the National Committee for the Acceleration of Infrastructure Provision Policy (KKPPI) in Indonesia were established to serve as catalysts for the promotion and implementation of private sector participation projects.

With a national PPP Regulation and Coordination Unit in place, there is still a need for the central government to support capacity development for local authorities to manage the PPP process and to have a better understanding of the nature of PPP agreements. Governments in South Africa and Germany, as well as many others countries, maintain websites that clearly demonstrate national frameworks to guide PPP development. Other initiatives include associations and institutions created by central and local governments in and outside the state to discuss, evaluate, and in some cases, promote more active participation by the private sector. It is most advantageous to combine the PPP experience at the central government level with local government knowledge of the needs and priorities of its constituency. When borrowing is involved, the central government should be consulted as subsequent future liabilities concern the whole nation.

CONCLUSION

Like for other developing countries, the fiscal pressures on local governments in ASEAN are becoming more intense, and the prospect of shifting investment responsibility to private infrastructure providers has played a significant role in the increasing acceptance of private-sector involvement in urban infrastructure development. Such partnerships enhance the strengths of both the public and private sectors in pursuing urban infrastructure service delivery. However, the public sector still maintains an obligation to act in the public interest in the delivery of public goods, whilst private firms expect binding agreements and regulations to prevent administration expropriation and to secure long-term maximization of profits. As a result, public-private partnerships are still subject to extensive and complicated bodies of legal doctrine and to legal enforcement mechanisms.

Most developing countries still do not have the regulatory and surveillance machinery in place at both the national and urban levels to ensure effectiveness, fairness, and openness of their public-private partnership schemes. They have embraced the PPP concept at the national level as a key strategy in overcoming some of the infrastructure backlog at the urban level. For some countries, the decentralization of PPP implementation may lead to confusion and inconsistencies in the frameworks of national government that inhibit urban authority action and hurt private sector interest. From the perspective of international investors, countries perceived to have inconsistent regulatory and legal frameworks are considered unattractive to capital investment. The regulatory framework needs to be consistent and harmonized in order to reduce confusion resulting from interpretation of sub-national governments that can affect PPP transactions.

Note

An earlier version of this chapter appeared in the *International Public Management Review Journal* 12, no. 1 (2011).

References

Abidin, Z. "Water Resources Management in Malaysia — The Way Forward". Opening Remarks to the Conference on Asian Water 2004, Kuala Lumpur, Malaysia, April 2004.
ASEAN Secretariat. "Fourth ASEAN State of the Environment Report", 2009.
Annex, P.C. "Urban Infrastructure Finance from Private Operators: What Have We Learned from Recent Experience?" World Bank Policy Research Working Paper 4045, November 2006.
Colton, R., K.B. Frisof, and E.R. King. "Lessons for the Health-Care Industry from America's Experience with Public Utilities". *Journal of Public Health Policy* 18 (1997): 389–400.

ESCAP. "Review of Developments in Transport in Asia and the Pacific". United Nations Economic and Social Commission for Asia and the Pacific (UNESCAP) — Document E/ESCAP/MCT/SGO/6, Busan, 6–8 November 2006.

Hassan, M.M. "Let's End the Non-Profit Charade". *New England Journal of Medicine* 334 (1996): 1055–57.

IP3. "Structuring and Negotiating Legal Agreements for Public-Private Partnership Projects". Washington, DC: Institute for Public-Private Partnerships (IP3), April 2000) <http://www.ip3.org/legal2000.htm> (accessed 16 September 2006).

Lanjekar, P. "Public Private Partnerships and Urban Water Security: Issues and Prospects in Mumbai, India", *Ritsumeikan Journal of Asia Pacific Studies* 27 (2010): 167–76.

Levinsohn, D. and D. Reardon. "Municipal PPP Projects in South Africa: Obstacles and Opportunities". Washington, DC: Institute for Public-Private Partnerships (IP3), 2007.

Lundqvist, L. "Privatisation: Towards a Concept for Comparative Policy Analysis". *Journal of Public Policy* 8, no. 1 (1988): 1–19.

Philippe, M. "Public-Private Partnerships for Urban Water Utility: A Review of Experiences in Development Countries". *Trends and Policy Option No. 8*. Washington, DC: World Bank, 2009.

Pongsiri, N. "Regulation and Public-Private Partnerships". *International Journal of Public Sector Management* 15, no. 6 (2002): 487–95.

PPP Coordination Unit. "Public-Private Partnerships Task Force". Germany, 2006 <http://www.ppp-bund.de/en/fragen.htm> (accessed 22 August 2007).

PPP Manual, South Africa. Notes issued in terms of the Public Finance Management Act. National Treasury PPP Practice, South Africa, 2004 <http://www.ppp.gov.za/Documents/Manual/Main%20Intro+Contents.pdf> (accessed 16 March 2007).

Sparer, M.S. "Myths and Misunderstandings: Health Policy, the Devolution Revolution, and the Push for Privatisation". *American Behavioural Scientist* 43 (1999): 138–54.

Susangarn, C. "Public-Private Partnership in Thailand: Past Experiences and Future Prospects". Paper presented at the Asia-Pacific Ministerial Conference on PPPs in Infrastructure, Republic of Korea, October 2007.

United Nations. "World Urbanization Prospects: The 2007 Revision Population Database". Department of Economic and Social Affairs of the United Nations Secretariat, 2007 <http://esa.un.org/undp> (accessed 19 May 2009).

Valentine, J. "Public-Private Partnerships in Infrastructure: Best Practices from the International Experience and Applications for Thailand". National Economic and Social Development Board (NESDB), Bangkok, Thailand, 2008.

World Bank. "World Development Report: Infrastructure for Development". Washington, DC: Oxford University Press, 1994.

5

REGIONAL COOPERATION AND THE CHANGING URBAN LANDSCAPE OF SOUTHEAST ASIA

Myo Thant

This chapter discusses how urban development in Southeast Asia has and is being shaped and affected by regional cooperation. The initial reaction of some may be bewilderment or a retort that regional cooperation in Southeast Asia has always been limited, and its impact on urban development is even more so. The chapter argues against both these perspectives and, in the first part, discusses how regional cooperation in the colonial era had profound and long-lasting impacts on the urban sector. The second part of the chapter argues that trade-facilitation-focused regional cooperation is today changing the urban landscape of Southeast Asia through the reduction of transaction costs, risks, and uncertainty. The chapter notes that while primate cities will still continue to grow, there will be significant activity among the secondary cities and smaller towns of the region. The final part discusses the motive forces that will take the emerging urban landscape further, as well as the challenges faced. Policy-induced regional cooperation will change urban patterns, but further development depends on economic growth and the ability to take advantage of market forces. While all of Southeast Asia is considered, the focus is on mainland Southeast Asia, which includes Thailand as well as the newer members of ASEAN — Cambodia, Laos, Myanmar, and Vietnam — which are primarily thought of in terms of their ability to "catch up" with older members. The chapter argues that their reputation as laggards may become inappropriate in a very short time.

COLONIAL ERA REGIONAL COOPERATION[1]

The evolution of Southeast Asian urbanization has been depicted by Dutt and others as consisting of four phases: (i) indigenous urbanization, (ii) colonial urbanization, (iii) extended pre-industrial urbanization, and (iv) industrial city urbanization (Dutt 1994). The focus of many studies has been on colonial urbanization and, in particular, the location of major cities in coastal areas or at river mouths to support trading activities and, later, to facilitate the export of raw materials from the colonized countries. Urban development, therefore, took place within the context of a global economy which was effectively controlled by a few European countries and prominent business concerns within these countries. Burma, for example, was progressively incorporated into the British Empire between 1825 and 1885 and became the rice granary of the empire. What is less discussed is that integration at the global level was replicated at a regional level by cooperation of a sort. Burma was administered as part of British India, a region with which most of Burma had only limited historical ties, aside from Buddhism. Laos, Cambodia, and Vietnam, which had become French colonies about the same time, found themselves in a similar situation. Collectively they were part of the French empire, but at the regional level they were governed from Hanoi, even though ties — between Laos and Cambodia on one side and Vietnam on the other — had not been particularly close historically.

Colonial era regional cooperation had both direct and indirect impacts on the urban structure of countries. Direct impacts include the creation of towns with areas which represented a facsimile of the home country (church, living quarters, club), massive secretariats and security buildings, and parks and monuments which commemorated colonial heroes. Smaller specialized towns were also developed such as the mining or oil town

(Yenangyaung in Burma), summer capitals (Maymyo in Burma, and Dalat in Vietnam), and garrison towns (Fort Hertz in Burma). It is, however, arguably the unobserved or indirect effects of colonial era regional cooperation that had the most impact on the urban landscape. Urban and, in general, economic development was essentially neglected in those regions of the colony which were not essential for the running of the colonial enterprise. In those areas where colonial enterprises were important, the urban landscape was changed by new trade patterns. Although the locus of the Burmese population had been in the centre of the country, close to the Irrawaddy River, for over a millennium, the rapid growth of the rice export industry led to the development of numerous towns and cities in its delta, which specialized on one aspect or another of the rice industry. Rangoon itself, which was only a large village in the eighteenth century and was less well known than its neighbouring towns of Syriam and Dalla, became the most important city of Burma (Andrus 1947).

Colonialism was also accompanied by the introduction of new transport technology needed for colonial administration as well as economic activity. Coastal and riverine steamships made travel to distant destinations easier and cheaper and, perhaps more importantly — by freeing ships from their reliance on monsoon winds and the direction of the flow of water — permitted all-season travel with much reduced uncertainty, particularly in the newly inhabited delta. Newly cut canals facilitated travel while the telegraph system made communication easier. However, the transport innovation that had the single biggest impact on the urban landscape was the railway system which, in Burma, was installed in 1877, some years before it was set up in Japan. Rail transport which was faster and cheaper than riverine travel ensured the gradual death of numerous towns along the Irrawaddy.[2]

Colonial era regional cooperation, combined with modern transport, also facilitated the movement of cheap labour between Burma and India. The colonial government subsidized the annual transport of up to a million labourers from India each year to be employed as coolies in the rice trade. The vast majority returned to India after the harvest, but a few stayed behind in Burma and over the years the accumulation of Indian/foreign labour became sizeable. Such local government as was allowed under colonialism protested against the free flow of labour, but to little avail. Thus the 1941 census showed that the Burmese were a minority in the capital city of Rangoon, which was spatially segregated between Europeans,

Anglo-Burmese, Indians, Chinese, and Burmese. Furthermore, the Burmese generally occupied the lowest positions on the economic totem pole except in areas which required strong literacy skills (printing, machinery), or were based on traditional crafts and native culture.

MODERN REGIONAL COOPERATION

In the past two decades urban development in mainland Southeast Asia has been subjected to two major forces of change. First came the fundamental shift in development strategy from a planned economy to one of reliance on the market mechanism. By 1993 Cambodia, the Lao People's Democratic Republic, Myanmar, and Vietnam had all embraced the market mechanism. The new development paradigm emphasized export promotion, welcomed foreign investment, and promoted tourism. This shift led to the rapid development of some towns which had initial advantages (ports, proximity to government policymakers, human capital), or towns where a particular industry was rapidly emerging, for example, the coffee industry and the resurrection of rice exports in Vietnam, or Luang Prabang as a key tourist destination in the Lao People's Democratic Republic. The second big force was regional economic cooperation, starting with the Greater Mekong Subregion programme in 1992.

Regional cooperation in the post-independence era is more obvious than colonial-era regional cooperation which, for many, was involuntary. Nevertheless an impartial observer is likely to comment that regional cooperation in Southeast Asia has been limited to ASEAN, and that ASEAN (as in other sectors) has not had much impact on urban development. This chapter argues that such a conclusion is unwarranted, although perhaps understandable, in light of the slow growth of ASEAN. Its main economic instruments for promoting regional cooperation has been the ASEAN Preferential Trading Arrangement (1977) and the ASEAN Free Trade Area (AFTA), which is based on the Common Effective Preferential Tariff (CEPT). However, CEPT use has been limited by high administrative costs of acquiring preferences, the low margin of tariff preference between CEPT and most favoured nation, the lack of private sector awareness, and the lack of a robust dispute settlement mechanism. Aside from the limited effectiveness of the CEPT, its spatial impact and effect on the urban landscape are diluted by the fact that preferences are countrywide rather than for specific areas.

Trade-liberalization-based regional cooperation such as that represented by AFTA is, however, not the only type of regional cooperation utilized by Southeast Asian countries. Since the early nineties, regional cooperation based on trade facilitation has gathered strength and may well be the means through which deeper regional integration can be achieved, given that discriminatory tariffs influence only a small area of regional trade. Trade-facilitation-based regional cooperation consists of two chief instruments: (i) growth triangles and (ii) economic corridors. Since both have been discussed extensively elsewhere, the present discussion is limited to how they influence urban development (Thant 1998).[3]

Growth Triangles

The term "growth triangle" came into common use after the then Deputy Prime Minister of Singapore Goh Chok Tong used it in December 1989 to describe the subregional economic cooperation involving Singapore, southern Johor in Malaysia, and Batam Island in Indonesia. In their most basic form, growth triangles exploit complementarities between geographically contiguous areas of different countries to gain a competitive edge in export promotion (Thant 1998). Growth triangles differ from trade-liberalization-based regional cooperation in several ways:

1. they encompass only parts of a country;
2. they are extra-regionally oriented;
3. they do not have common harmonized policies, but instead facilitate trade through the removal of non-tariff barriers, transport impediments, and uncertainty;
4. they benefit the border areas of participating countries directly; and
5. they can serve as demonstration areas for the implementation of a bold and innovative policy which can be easily terminated in case of problems.

Impatience with the slow progress of ASEAN economic integration, threats from trading blocs from other parts of the world, and the prospect of being able to achieve cooperation at a fraction of the cost of trade liberalization led to a "golden age" of growth triangles (1989–98) during which the following growth triangles were created: (i) Singapore-Johor-Riau (SIJORI); (ii) Indonesia-Malaysia-Thailand growth triangle (IMT-GT); and

(iii) Brunei-Indonesia-Malaysia-Philippines East ASEAN Growth Area (BIMP-EAGA). The Greater Mekong Subregion (GMS) Programme, consisting of six countries, was created within the same time period. Although its size and population made it different from the other triangles, the spatial element was highlighted by the inclusion of only Yunnan province from the People's Republic of China (PRC) within the grouping.

Aside from the GMS, about which there will be further discussion, the SIJORI seems to be the most successful triangle to date. Two major impacts on the urban landscape can be seen. First the de facto expansion of factory space, as well as the improved quality of life through access to leisure space, has had an indirect but not inconsiderable impact on Singapore's growth and prosperity. Second, the landscape of Batam and Bintan has been transformed as they have become large industrial estates, as well as leisure centres, which have attracted thousands of workers from other parts of Indonesia. Batam became an autonomous self-governing city in 1999 and gained Free Trade Zone status in 2007.

IMT-GT and BIMP-EAGA, both of which started out with great enthusiasm from both the public and private sectors, were severely affected by the 1997 Asian financial crisis, political problems, and civil unrest, and even natural problems, such as the 2004 tsunami and earthquakes in Sumatra. Two developments, however, suggest that substantial progress is possible in the longer term. First, both have received strong political ownership at the highest levels and are included on the agenda of the ASEAN Summit meeting. Second, there has been re-engagement with the Asian Development Bank (ADB) which played a key role in preparing the initial master plans.[4] Progress on cooperation could be reflected in urban development of port cities such as Songkhla, Georgetown, and Manado as well as provincial towns such as Medan and Hat Yai. Given the improvement in physical infrastructure over the past decade, some border towns on both sides of the Thai-Malay border of the IMT-GT could also see rapid growth.

Economic Corridors

The 1997 Asian financial crisis completely disrupted the momentum of the growth triangles which had, in some cases, even expanded beyond their original geographical boundaries as new areas clamoured for inclusion.

The economic corridor concept, which was unveiled for the first time at the Eighth Greater Mekong Subregion Ministerial Meeting in October 1998, was a direct outcome of the attempt to jump-start the stalled progress of the growth triangles. In light of the subsequent loose use of the term, it is useful to see how the idea of the economic corridor was originally conceived.

Economic corridors are defined as mechanisms for linking production, trade, and infrastructure within a specific geographic region where there is a clear economic rationale for such linkages. An economic corridor consists of many elements among which are defined location, physical infrastructure, including transport systems, economic activities, and policies and institutions ("software") that can make cross-border cooperation feasible. The importance of having a spatial focus was recognized from the very beginning and justified by the need to focus scarce resources in areas with the highest economic potential, and where the leveraging of private sector investment is most likely to succeed. Nodes or nodal points were recognized as critical components of corridors since they are required to anchor corridors and provide the focus for investment. Several types of nodes were identified: general industrial estates, export processing zones, commercial and recreational complexes, and multimodal communications nodes, such as road, rail, air, and sea connections (Thant 1999).

The Eighth GMS Ministerial Meeting in 1998 discussed five possible corridors, several of which were based on precolonial historical routes:

1. Kunming-Mandalay-Yangon;
2. Kunming-Lao PDR-Bangkok;
3. Kunming-Hanoi-Haiphong;
4. the East-West Economic Corridor (EWEC); and
5. the Yangon-Bangkok-Phonh Penh-Ho Chi Minh city rail corridor.

The six GMS countries endorsed the corridor concept and gave priority to the EWEC, a 1,450 km route which would connect the Indian Ocean with the South China Sea by a road corridor linking Mawlamyine, Mae Sot, Phitsanulok, Khon Kaen, Savanakhet, Mukdahan, Lao Bao, Hue, and Da Nang (ADB 2001). Subsequent discussions among the six countries produced agreement on a set of six corridors and this would largely remained unchanged until 2007, when four more corridors were added, thereby arguably diluting the entire concept. The corridors that were agreed on were:

1. the East-West Economic Corridor (EWEC);
2. the North-South Corridor between Kunming and Bangkok via the Lao People's Democratic Republic;
3. the North-South Corridor between Kunming and Bangkok via Myanmar (Tachileik);
4. the North-South Corridor between Kunming and Hanoi/Haiphong;
5. the Southern Corridor between Bangkok and Vietnam via Cambodia (Bavet/Moc Bai); and
6. the Southern Corridor between Bangkok and Vietnam (Quy Nhon).

Since the initial agreement on these corridors, the GMS landscape for cooperation has become more complicated, but potentially more rewarding through the addition of more spatial development initiatives, many of which were initiated by the countries themselves and are not restricted to road transport. These include the following:

1. The Singapore-Kunming railway by way of Cambodia and Vietnam. Rehabilitation of war-ravaged Cambodian rails is ongoing. An alternate route which is shorter (4,444 km vs. 5,441 km) and passes through Myanmar exists although about 250 km of track needs to be laid by Thailand and Myanmar. A feasibility study for this route was completed in 2007.
2. Mekong river navigation. The original GMS plans did not include riverine travel even though travelling (up) the Mekong River to China had been a dream of colonial explorers. The omission is even more surprising given the cost effectiveness of riverine transport, the existence of an extensive network which is accessible to low-income groups, the existence of an international organization looking after the Mekong development that had managed to survive the Indo-China conflict, and the importance of river traffic for millions in the region. The People's Republic of China (PRC), Lao People's Democratic Republic, Myanmar, and Thailand signed the Commercial Navigation Agreement for the Upper Mekong in April 2000, thereby making possible a 780 km trip between Simao in the PRC and Luang Prabang in the Lao People's Democratic Republic. Trade has increased despite environmental concerns and low water levels. Trade between Thailand and China has increased to such an extent that the Thai Government is investing in a new 1.55 billion baht container port at Chiang Saen. More recently the Cambodia–Vietnam Waterway Transport agreement

signed in December 2009 allows freedom of navigation on the lower Mekong, and covers sixty-five ports in the two countries on the Mekong and major tributaries.

3. The Quadrangle Economic Cooperation initiative established in 2000 between Yunnan, Northern Thailand, Myanmar, and the Lao People's Democratic Republic. Activities are more along the lines of sharing information and contacts, such as trade fairs, periodical publication, and field trips. Rapid development at its northern apex of Jinghong and the southern apex of Chiang Rai and the existence of multimodal transport systems (road, shipping, and air) give this mini corridor great potential.

4. The Development Triangle created in 2002 between Cambodia, the Lao People's Democratic Republic, and Vietnam. The triangle covers an area of 111,000 square kilometres and ten provinces in the three countries, and focuses on mining, hydroelectricity, agro forestry, and trade. The area has only four million people, but is rich in natural resources.

5. The Ayeyarwady-Chao Phya-Mekong Cooperation Scheme (ACMECS) consisting of all members of the GMS, except the PRC. The first summit was held in November 2003 in Bagan, Myanmar, and the countries agreed to cooperate on trade and investment, agriculture, industry, transport, tourism, human resource development, and public health.

6. The unilateral expansion of the GMS by the PRC to include the Guangxi Zhungang Autonomous region in 2003. Subsequently the PRC and Vietnam announced an agreement in May 2004 to develop "two economic corridors and the Tonkin Gulf economy belt" (An 2005). The first corridor would stretch from Kunming to Haiphong and cover nineteen million people in an 80,000 km^2 area. The second corridor would be between Nanning and Quay Ninh and include twenty million people in a 60,000 km^2 area while the belt would stretch from ten coastal localities in Vietnam to Hong Kong and Macau. The first Pan Beibu Gulf Economic Cooperation forum was held in July 2006.

Implications for Urban Development

The urban landscape of mainland Southeast Asia will be confronted in the near future by two forces simultaneously: rapid growth from urbanization levels, which are still low, and regional economic cooperation. The development of major corridors, as well as other programmes which have been initiated by GMS members, have important implications for the urban landscape of mainland Southeast Asia. The relationship between regional cooperation and space has been made tighter by the corridor concept. In some cases corridors make possible year-long physical connectivity between areas which had hitherto not been possible. Vehicle operating costs are also reduced by improved physical infrastructure. In all cases, door-to-door travel time and uncertainty regarding travel times are reduced and the overall cost of transport is further reduced as well. The catchment areas of urban centres are also expanded. Economic opportunities for those urban centres specifically included in the individual corridors have increased. Corridor development will have a reciprocal relationship with different types of urban areas among which the following is a sample of what is likely:[5]

1. seaports (Danang, Mawlamyine, Can Tho, Vung Tau);
2. transport junctions (Khon Kaen, Phitsanulok, Chiang Rai);
3. border town pairs (Mae Sot-Myawaddy, Mukdahan-Savanakhet, Bavet-Moc Bai, etc.);
4. major tourist destinations (Hue, Mawlamyine); and
5. end points of corridors (Kunming, Quy Nhon).

Corridor development affects urban areas in at least four noteworthy respects. First, there is greatly reduced uncertainty as to which urban areas are most likely to grow. Political decisions and agreements, technical considerations of transport networks, and geographical proximity together provide visible road signs. Second, most urban areas affected are not national capitals and are of intermediate size. Third, a large number of urban areas, particularly in Thailand, are in the interior of their respective countries and generally have developed less than coastal areas and/or the primate city. The development of the interior is de facto economic decentralization, even if the absolute importance of the major city of each country is unlikely to diminish. Fourth, the improved connectivity made possible through corridor development has changed the relationship between urban areas within a country, as well as across borders. Distance between urban centres has been reduced and urban areas are closer to one another, with both an enhanced probability of competition as well as cooperation.

Taken as a whole, the system of economic corridors, which will be largely completed by 2012, will have changed the urban landscape of mainland Southeast Asia into a new community in which roles, functions, and relationships will be defined by governments, or emerge through market forces.

PROSPECTS

The urban landscape of mainland Southeast Asia is being dramatically altered, but how much good can come of this and where the motive force for further progress will come from require some consideration. Both the new economic geography (agglomeration) and literature on path dependency ("history matters") stress that agglomeration economies, once started, are not easily stopped and can lead to a concentration of growth and wealth in a few isolated urban areas. Similarly Rigg has noted that there is an intersection of space, economy, society, and politics, and not all will benefit from the new urban order (Rigg and Wittayapak 2009). There is clearly room and rationale for policymakers to become more involved in the urban development beyond the usual concerns of urban management such as finance, administration, and municipal facilities, or newer ones such as "green" growth.

The issue of motive force is no less important and there are substantial grounds for optimism. The first can be simply called the "China factor" although there are various sub-strands. Chinese Government aid on generous terms is one factor, as is investment from Guangxi and Yunnan, frequently for raw materials and hydropower generation and distribution. The overriding factor however is the China ASEAN Free Trade Area (CAFTA), which was established in early 2010 and, with 1.9 billion people, is the world's largest free trade area. The newer members of ASEAN will be subject to CAFTA provisions by 2015, but initiatives to use mainland Southeast Asia as a springboard for production to the rest of ASEAN, or to re-export back to China, have started in earnest. Urban centres in the Jinghong-Chiang Rai area, as well as the "two corridors one belt" area between Vietnam and the PRC, are most likely to benefit from these developments. One advantage of the CAFTA-driven regional cooperation is that it is less likely to be dependent on global value chains and intra-industry trade for which countries such as Myanmar, the Lao People's Democratic Republic, and Cambodia may not yet be ready, except at the lowest technological levels, given their systemwide shortcomings in trade logistics.

Other factors which, on balance, suggest sustained growth of intermediate-size urban centres in mainland Southeast Asia include:

1. Thai Government policy which is expected to remain more or less constant on the issue of connectivity and establishing Thailand as a transportation hub for the GMS, despite changes in the government;
2. continued support from the ADB and its co-financiers, given the extent of their previous investment in the GMS;
3. continued development and popularity of Special Economic Zones, which are frequently located near urban areas for better access to labour and logistics, and would benefit greatly from the arrival of "sunset" industries from other parts of ASEAN; and
4. ability to tap into global value chains which are currently key drivers of global trade and investment.

Great potential for urban development through regional cooperation exists in Myanmar. In general, investment in regional cooperation in Myanmar has been extremely limited compared with that in other GMS countries because of its having no access to concessional assistance from multilateral and bilateral development organizations. The country has, however, made substantial investments with its own resources and invested heavily in bridges, transport, and road networks. Noteworthy is the Mawlamyine road and rail bridge which is the longest in Southeast Asia; it connects the two parts of the country and intersects with the western terminus of the EWEC (*New Light of Myanmar* 2005). Mawlamyine, which has slowly declined since the end of the rice and timber trade from its status as the third-largest city in Myanmar, could see a rapid renaissance, given its location, access to labour, and good (or greatly improved) transport services.

Other urban areas within Myanmar that could benefit greatly are Kyaing Tong (on the North-South corridor), Dawei where there has been a great deal of interest in a deep seaport that would allow the shipment of Thai goods to India, and towns along the Myanmar route of the Singapore-Kunming railroad. Kyaukphyu and Bokpyin, which are also being considered as deep seaports, could also benefit. Towns along a "new Burma road" between China, Myanmar, and India could also benefit substantially from trade-facilitation-based regional cooperation.

Challenges

It is only fair to ask what issues pose a threat to the above scenario. Six challenges stand out:

1. Conflict over negative externalities, which can run from smuggling of animal parts and trafficking of human beings to pandemics. To date, countries have jointly addressed these issues although none, with the exception of the SARS and Avian flu pandemics, has threatened whole nations on a long-term basis. The issue of the multiple uses of the head waters of the Mekong and the impact on downstream countries is a potential source of conflict.

2. Conflict over border town activities. One of the hallmarks of mainland Southeast Asian urban development is the rapid growth of small border villages into semi-lawless boom towns that provide sexual services, gambling, and drugs to citizens from the other country. Mongla in the Wa Special Autonomous Zone in Myanmar was, as late as 1989, a village which served as a regional headquarters of the Burma Communist Party. In the middle of the decade this town attracted over a thousand visitors a day from across the border in China for services not available and proscribed in China (Williams 2003). Similar towns exist on the Thai-Cambodian and the Laos-PRC borders. The activities may be legally curtailed over time, but their replacement as a source of investment and employment may not be easy.

3. Quasi-extraterritoriality of foreign investors, leasing of land for long periods without transparency, and eviction of the original tenants without much compensation, create resistance to further cooperation. At present the issue seems to be the most serious in the Lao People's Democratic Republic, where land rights are being used as collateral to fund investment from Thailand and Vietnam, as well as China (Nyiri 2009).

4. Lack of institutions to regulate cross-border migration. Since the early nineties cross-border migration from neighbouring countries to Thailand has increased almost unabated, and increased connectivity through corridors will most likely strengthen this trend. At present foreign labour is estimated to be 5–10 per cent of the labour force, although it is highly concentrated in fishing, garments, construction, domestic service, and the rice industry. The labour force, which is estimated at about 1.5 million, is to a great extent illegal in both the country of origin (left without documents) and in the destination (not registered and/or no work permit). Numerous studies have highlighted worker abuse manifested by workers being paid less than the official minimum wage, forced overtime, poor work conditions, and harassment by local officials (Arnold and Hewison 2006). The system benefits Thailand in

that its industries remain globally competitive and firm owners make large profits from the cheap labour. However, the arrangement also benefits the origin country, which receives remittances and is able to alleviate its unemployment problem. The arrangement is least beneficial for individual workers. Termination of this system by either one of the governments involved could have spatial consequences since many of the industries that are heavily migrant dependent are geographically clustered (garments and fisheries).

5. Appropriate institutions to complement the work of economic corridors. Institutions are important at the interface of transport and land use because they are the rules by which decisions are made (Stough 2004). However, the long experience of the Cross Border Transport Agreement (CBTA), which provides a framework for the smooth flow of goods and services across the six GMS countries, shows that designing, agreeing on, ratifying, and implementing agreements can be a costly and time-consuming activity requiring deep financial and technical resources. At the end of 2009, three countries were observing the CBTA, but this comes only after ten years of negotiation (Yushu Feng 2010). The need for an institution that ensures the smooth functioning and development of each economic corridor was recognized early on and an "EWEC Commission" that would develop the corridor, as well as ensure equitable distribution of benefits and costs, was proposed (ADB 2001). Some movement in this direction can be seen in the convening of corridor meetings and a "Governor's Forum", although its effectiveness might be limited by its large membership and the lack of financial and technical resources. Effective institutions must also have fair representation within each country, as well as across countries. It is essential that the needs and preferences of the private sector be addressed by such institutions.

6. Limited local capacity to take advantage of new economic opportunities. Regional cooperation leads to de facto decentralization which itself can take many guises (Yap 2010). However, whatever form it takes, it is a further demand on the already limited capacity for urban management at the local level. In the Lao People's Democratic Republic, the contribution from the government has been generally reactive. No comprehensive policy strategies for components of the many regional cooperation programmes exist, leaving the country vulnerable to being exploited by stronger partners that have already formulated and implemented clear plans and strategies (Mabitt 2006).

Sok Chenda has noted the existence of both institutional and capacity constraints in Cambodia, but these are equally applicable to many other GMS countries. Capacity constraints include the limited authority of local government, lack of strategy, lack of ability to implement key facilities, as well as inward-looking orientation, short time horizons, and overlapping demands (Sok Chenda 2009). Unless national capacities are improved, countries will not be able to implement complementary policies and investments, and thereby take full advantage of the new opportunities provided by regional cooperation. Decentralization may also lead to new identities, or the resurrection of older ones, and to conflicts between the political centre and other regions of the country (Burnell 2006).[6]

CONCLUSIONS

Over the past twenty years urban areas in mainland Southeast Asia have been subjected to successive rounds of change. First came change as a result of the adoption of the market economy. Second came regional cooperation, and later economic corridors that explicitly combine economic liberalization, cooperation, and notions of economic space. The fourth wave is increasing economic cooperation with the PRC through economic and transport corridors, CAFTA, and more general economic interaction between the two areas.

Regional economic cooperation has had an impact on the urban landscape of Southeast Asia since at least as early as colonial times. Trade-facilitation-focused regional cooperation, rather than the trade liberalization type exemplified by ASEAN and CEPT, is shaping the urban landscape in mainland Southeast Asia by lowering transaction costs and reducing risk and uncertainty. Growth triangles and economic corridors, which were introduced in the early and latter part of the nineties respectively, will, through their tight relationship between trade and investment on one side, and geography and location on the other, shape urban landscapes. The full impacts of these forces will be felt after 2015 when the GMS is fully connected by corridors and CAFTA provisions apply to all ASEAN countries, including the four mainland Southeast Asian countries that are currently exempt.

The urban landscape will change, leading to a de facto decentralization of urban activities, although urban centres will not gain equally. Urban centres located in the Jinghong-Chiang Rai subcorridor and the "two corridors, one belt" region between the PRC and Vietnam are likely to benefit the most, as is the eastern part of the EWEC. Further development is likely, given the "China factor", Thailand's strong interest in acting as a hub for the region, and continued expansion of SEZs. The emerging urban landscape, while not preventing further significant increases in the sizes of primate and megacities, will nonetheless create a more balanced pattern of human settlement and diffuse economic development more evenly within countries.

Challenges, however, exist and include tensions relating to negative externalities, perceived or real extraterritoriality rights, migrant labour issues, and the lack of appropriate institutions to sustain regional cooperation. A major challenge will be in promoting local level capacity of small to medium-sized urban settlements and their private sectors to tap market opportunities successfully and harness the challenges unleashed by increasing regional economic cooperation. ASEAN can play a multifaceted role in the urban evolution of mainland Southeast Asia. The most obvious role is that of accelerating regional cooperation through both trade facilitation and trade liberalization.

The further pursuit of regional integration and connectivity should include addressing proactively the linkages from regional integration on the one hand and urban issues, including changes in settlement patterns, on the other. The Master Plan on ASEAN Connectivity that was adopted at the 17th ASEAN Summit in October 2010 covers much ground and is useful in drawing attention to seven key strategies needed to enhance physical connectivity, as well as the need to find the financing for these strategies and projects. ASEAN may play a leading role in three key areas: (i) generation and dissemination of relevant knowledge and ideas, particularly between policymakers and academics; (ii) development of sister cities such as border towns or cities that share common issues, for example, cooperation between Mawlamyine, Dawei, Ranong, and Penang which face the Indian Ocean and have links with one another; and (iii) mobilization of the very large amount of financial resources that will be required for urban development in the region.

Notes

This chapter was completed before the rapid political changes that took place in Myanmar in late 2011.
1.   A complete study of Southeast Asian urbanization should note that urban

development predates colonialism not by two or three centuries, but by millennia. At least a dozen major walled cities based on irrigated agriculture, trade, and salt production have been identified in Myanmar alone. The larger ones such as Beikthano (second century BC – fourth century AD) and Halin (second century – ninth century AD), have been excavated, but others still retain their secrets. The situation in present-day Cambodia and southern Vietnam is probably analogous.

2. This can be seen clearly by comparing the John Crawford map of 1825 with maps drawn one hundred years later.
3. Other mechanisms for promoting ASEAN connectivity, such as the eASEAN Framework Agreement, ASEAN ICT Master Plan, and ASEAN Power grid also exist but their impacts may be largely spatially neutral.
4. The BIMP-EAGA programme resumed ties with the ADB in 2001, while IMT-GT resumed ties in 2006. ADB's role as honest neutral broker between different factions and countries is arguably a more critical function than that of its traditional financier role, since the cooperating countries are relatively open to international financial markets and the private sector is well established.
5. The PRC has gone the furthest among the GMS countries in specifying the link between regional cooperation and urban development. Kunming has been identified as a "regional international economic center". Yuxi is seen as an "economic corridor development sub center" while Geiju, Kaiyuan, Mengi, Pu'er City, and Jinghong are identified as important corridor cities (Xu Lei 2009).
6. The case of Thailand comes readily to mind. Bangkok is a middle-class city whose interests are not in alignment with the hinterland according to some (Webster and Maneepong 2009). The high level of per capita income in Bangkok is, however, seen in a more positive light by others (Oizumi 2010).

References

An, Dinh Van. "Vietnam-China Economic Relations: Progress and Problems". Paper presented at the conference on "New Opportunity for the Furtherance of Regional Economic Integration", 24–25 November 2005, Nanning, People's Republic of China.

Andrus, J. Russell. *Burmese Economic Life*. California: Stanford University Press, 1947.

Arnold, Dennis and K. Hewison. "Exploitation in Global Supply Chains: Burmese Migrant Workers in Mae Sot, Thailand". In *Transnational Migration for Work*, edited by Kevin Hewison and Ken Young. London: Routledge Curzon, 2006.

Asian Development Bank. *Pre-investment Study for the Greater Mekong Subregion, East-West Economic Corridor*, vols. I–VI. Manila, Philippines, 2001.

Bunnel, Tim et al. "Global City Frontiers: Singapore's Hinterland and the Contested Socio-political Geographies of Bintan". *International Journal of Urban and Regional Research* 301 (March 2006).

Dutt, A.K. et al., eds. *The Asian City: Processes of Development, Characteristics and Planning*. The Netherlands: Kluwer, 1994.

Feng, Yushu. *Implementation of GMS Cross-Border Transport Agreement*. Presentation at Asian Development Bank Transport Forum, Manila, 27 May 2010.

Moore, Elizabeth H. *Early Landscapes of Myanmar*. Bangkok: Bangkok Printing, 2007.

New Light of Myanmar. "Thanlwin Bridge (Mawlamyine), Longest and Largest in Myanmar, Emerge to Serve Interest of State and Region", 6 February 2005.

Nyiri, Pal. "Foreign Concessions: The Past and Future of a Form of Shared Sovereignty". Paper presented at conference on Extraterritoriality. Amsterdam Free University, Amsterdam, 19 November 2009.

Oizumi, Keiichiro. "The Changing Face of Cities in Asia's Emerging Economies — Rising Competitiveness and Expanding Markets". *Pacific Business and Industries* 10, no. 37 (2010).

Rigg, J. and C. Wittayapak. "Spatial Integration and Human Transformations in the Greater Mekong Subregion". In *Reshaping Economic Geography in East Asia*, edited by Y. Huang and A.M. Bocchi. Washington, DC: World Bank, 2009.

Roberts, Brian and Trevor Kanaley, eds. *Urbanisation and Sustainability in Asia: Case Studies of Good Practice*. Manila, Asian Development Bank, 2006.

Sok Chenda. *The Strategic Role of Corridor Towns: Opportunities and Challenges. Institution and Capacity Building*. Fifth Greater Mekong Subregion Development Dialogue, Manila, Philippines, 30 November 2009.

Stough, Roger R. "Institutions, Land Use and Transportation". In *Handbook of Transport Geography and Spatial Systems*. Elsevier, Amsterdam, 2004.

Thant, Myo, et al. *Growth Triangles in Asia: A New Approach to Regional Economic Cooperation*, 2nd ed. New York: Oxford University Press, 1998.

Thant, Myo. "The Development of Economic Corridors in the Greater Mekong Subregion". In *Private Sector Perspective in the Greater Mekong Subregion*. New York: United Nations, 2000.

Webster, Douglas and Chutatip Maneepong. "Bangkok Global Actor in a Misaligned National Governance Framework". *City* 13, no. 1 (2009).

Williams, Joan. "Mong La: Burma's City of Lights". *The Irrawaddy* 2, no. 1 (2003).

Xu, Lei. *Infrastructure Investments*. Fifth Greater Mekong Subregion Development Dialogue, Manila, Philippines, 30 November 2009.

Yap, Kioe Sheng. *Promoting Productive, Inclusive and Sustainable Cities and Towns in Southeast Asia*. Singapore, 2010.

Inclusive Cities

6

ADDRESSING URBAN POVERTY IN ASEAN
Diversity of Conditions and Responses, Unity of Purpose

Anna Maria M. Gonzales

URBANIZATION AND POVERTY IN ASEAN

The steady urbanization of Southeast Asian nations is generally viewed as a positive development in the economic history of the region. Cities are recognized as epicentres of economic growth and contribute significantly to national incomes. Because of their ability to earn more in absolute terms, urban populations are generally perceived to be better off than their rural counterparts.

All over Asia, poverty incidence is still much higher in rural areas than in urban areas. National governments will therefore tend to address rural poverty in national policy and plans, given resource limitations. It is often said that although poverty seems more visible and geographically concentrated in cities, the poor who choose to stay in urban areas are much better off than their rural counterparts. Despite having very low cash incomes, the poor in urban areas are expected to have, at the very least, more access to social services in the cities.

Because poverty has often been associated with rural areas in Southeast Asia, urban poverty issues have largely been relegated to the background in the regional policy discourse. Regional level efforts that deal with economic development as a means to address poverty often focus on investments in infrastructure and agricultural productivity in rural areas. Urban development is then largely left to market forces or private sector decisions. Moreover, rural poverty is seen as more urgent and compelling and therefore more resources and time are poured into addressing it.

However, with the rise of urban populations and, with it, an increase of urban poverty incidence, addressing urban poverty issues alongside rural poverty issues may no longer be delayed. An estimated 41.8 per cent of Southeast Asia's total population or, almost 245 million people, live in urban areas. In 1950 the urban population represented only 15.4 per cent of the total population. By 2025, the urban population of the region is expected to increase to 49.7 per cent of the total population (Yap 2010).

The rise of urban populations is expected to put pressure on the existing infrastructure and social services in cities. The informality of infrastructure and services provision in cities, as evidenced by informal settlements in rapidly expanding urban centres, is a concern of national governments. Civil society organizations and community-based non-government organizations regard informal settlements as solutions rather than problems.

The urban development concerns of national governments are often focused on large-scale urban infrastructure projects such as roads, bridges, and transport facilities. The conventional route for governments wishing to increase investments in urban areas is to facilitate the participation of the private sector in the provision of utilities. While the infrastructure and economic projects help create wealth for urban areas, such endeavours, if not accompanied by social safety nets targeted at the very poor, bypass or displace urban dwellers in informal settlements.

Because poor urban dwellers provide the labour force in cities, it is imperative that measures, programmes, and policies target their well-being and enable them to live with dignity in urban areas. Urban development policies and plans are therefore not complete without policies that address urban poverty.

Defining Urban Poverty in ASEAN

Income, or the lack thereof, has traditionally been the means by which poverty is measured. For global comparison, the United Nations initially used US$1 a day and presently US$1.25 a day (2005 PPP) as the international poverty line. Table 6.1 shows that recent data on this poverty line for Southeast Asia are available only for six out of ten ASEAN countries and even those are for different years. Based on these data (which exclude Indonesia, the largest country of ASEAN), there are about forty-seven million people living on less than US$1.25 a day in urban and rural areas. How many of these are urban poor is, however, not known.

In order to measure rural and urban poverty separately, it is necessary to take into account the differences in the costs of the basket of basic goods and services that determines the poverty line in urban and rural areas. Moreover, the basket of basic goods and services also differs between urban and rural areas; items such as housing and transport have a very different weight for rural and urban residents. In addition, the urban poor are often a very heterogeneous population: some have regular employment, a very low income, but certain employment benefits, while others have an irregular income and no benefits. Measuring and comparing urban and rural poverty is therefore fraught with problems.

On the other hand, the rural-urban distinction is becoming less relevant. The poor in Southeast Asia often migrate back and forth between urban and rural areas, and many poor households derive their income from both urban and rural sources.

Development agencies such as UN-HABITAT, UNESCAP, and the World Bank, however, have also started to recognize that poverty is not just about money, but is rather a three-dimensional condition, that is, people

Table 6.1
Poverty Line for Southeast Asia

	% of population <$1.25 a day	Year	Population (million)	Year	Population on <$1.25 a day (million)
Cambodia	40.2	2004	13.9	2005	5.6
Lao PDR	44.0	2002	5.4	2000	2.4
Malaysia	2.0	2004	25.6	2005	0.5
Philippines	22.6	2006	85.5	2005	19.3
Thailand	2.0	2004	65.9	2005	1.3
Vietnam	21.5	2006	84.0	2005	18.1
Total					47.2

Source: UNESCAP, 2010.

are poor because of two other factors in addition to the lack of income. The two other factors that keep people in poverty are their lack of access to basic infrastructure services, such as clean water and sanitation, and their lack of access to power and decision-making processes.

The primary direction and goals of urban poverty reduction, therefore, revolve around effectively analysing and simultaneously addressing the three dimensions of poverty, that is, the lack of income, lack of access to basic infrastructure services, such as clean water and sanitation, and lack of access to power and decision-making processes. Further rendering the poor vulnerable is the lack of space and land for accommodating them in urban areas. The poor in cities have to resort to living in slums and inadequate housing. This limits the possibility of security of tenure for a large portion of the urban population, and in many cases they face the continuing threat of eviction.

The faces of urban poverty differ from country to country and, in many cases, from city to city. The variety of cultures and histories of the countries that make up ASEAN contribute to this situation. The following factors may make it difficult to come up with a common view, especially with the aim of formulating a regional policy on urban poverty:

1. Differences in definitions of "urban" across countries;
2. National political and policy frameworks;
3. Levels of economic development and diversity of economic bases; and
4. Cultural and living practices of people and their communities.

The combination of an area's resource base, ecology, history, socio-cultural networks, as well as the rate and primary drivers of urbanization determine the nature and causes, magnitude, and impact of urban poverty in different localities. With the exception of Singapore, however, urban poverty is a reality that ASEAN countries have to face, although the impetus to deal with it could be clouded over by the seemingly more urgent task of dealing with rural poverty in member countries.

General Poverty Reduction Principles

According to the World Bank's Poverty Reduction Strategy Paper (PRSP) initiative, five core principles should be the basis for the development and implementation of poverty reduction strategies:

1. Country-driven, but involving broad-based participation by civil society and the private sector in all operational steps;
2. Results-oriented: focusing on outcomes that will benefit the poor;
3. Comprehensive in recognizing the multidimensional nature of poverty;
4. Partnership-oriented — involving the coordinated participation of development partners (bilateral, multi-lateral and non-governmental);
5. Based on a long-term perspective for poverty reduction (Lindahl 2005).

These five core principles are best used as indicators to test programme strategies aimed at reducing poverty in urban areas.

Housing and Community Development: Enabling Strategies for the Urban Poor

When one speaks of urban poverty or urban development issues, the issue of housing takes centre stage. For the poor to survive and lead meaningful lives in urban areas, they must have a minimum standard of dignified living. It is also in settlements and community development that the three dimensions of poverty could be addressed in an integrated manner.

Housing interventions in Asia are undertaken by both government and NGOs, with the latter taking approaches that also ensure people's empowerment and participation. In this connection, UN-HABITAT and UNESCAP (2008) identified seven enabling strategies when working with housing for the poor:

1. Investing in building partnerships;
2. Providing basic services through partnerships;
3. Supporting community savings and credit;
4. Developing community leadership;
5. Softening rules and regulations;
6. Working from locally rooted information;
7. Creating space for dialogue.

The first four strategies could be seen as embodying long-term goals, or as values that a sustainable city possesses. Partnerships rely on continuing efforts and are constantly renewed, renegotiated, and strengthened over time. The same is true for savings and credit programmes, which need to be nurtured continuously to be relevant to their users. Community leadership is constantly developed and renewed as the urban population continuously shifts and is therefore in need of new blood and new ideas. The last two strategies could be seen as tools that enable the poor to work towards these long-term goals.

The fifth strategy, however, is best seen as an interim step, and is something that has to be used with caution, especially considering the geohazards present in the region. While there are benefits for the poor to have more flexible standards, there are also risks involved as urban areas are densely populated and full of hazards. This particular strategy is therefore best applicable to those areas with plenty of space for urban development, but may not work for areas with high densities of population and economic activity.

In the face of climate change and the realities of environmental degradation, it would be hazardous and unjust to subject the poor to downgraded standards of development. In recognizing the possible long-term negative effects of the fifth strategy, we may be able to cut through a vicious cycle that keeps the poor apart from the rest of the Southeast Asian city, and, with some luck, come upon more sustainable solutions to providing space for the urban poor in the city.

Empowerment Principles and Poverty Reduction

There are four elements involved in poverty reduction: information, inclusion and participation, accountability, and local organizational capacity (Narayan 2002, p. xix). These elements enable poor people to develop their own capabilities, increase their assets, and move out of poverty.

Empowerment is key to poverty reduction because history has shown that most governments do not have the capacity to provide completely all the resources required to enable people to rise from poverty. The other half of poverty reduction rests on capacitating the poor and enabling them to have their voices heard in what is collectively called civil society, as well as to participate in governance.

That said, the state has a role in providing the environment to increase inclusion and decrease inequality within an overall policy that improves governance and encourages both public and private actors to develop partnerships and institutions that reach the poor, and eventually bring them out of poverty.

RECOMMENDATIONS FOR URBAN POVERTY REDUCTION IN ASEAN

A Policy Framework for Urban Poverty Reduction in ASEAN: People before Projects

Countries in ASEAN should develop policy frameworks for urban poverty reduction and, in doing so, they need to take into account two principles: urban poverty reduction policies should aim at making the urban poor productive participants in the urban economy, and urban development should not occur at the expense of the urban poor.

Populations move in search of better employment and income opportunities and better access to essential services. Populations across ASEAN move not only from rural to urban areas, but also across national borders. Whatever their destination, many migrants still perform low-productivity jobs and still have limited access to essential services. They therefore do not escape from poverty. ASEAN member nations must strive to adopt policies that will enable people to become more productive urban dwellers. Cities that strive to be engines of development require a wide diversity of people who constitute the labour force necessary for the wide variety of economic activities in urban areas.

Across ASEAN and, for that matter, all over the world, "urban" and city planning is associated with physical infrastructure. There is a tendency to focus on infrastructure development and improvement as the primary function of city governments. This focus on infrastructure can have the effect of exacerbating the conditions of the poor in urban areas and rendering them vulnerable by current practices of resettlement and, consequently, the destruction of their social networks. Current practices in resettlement tend to send the poor outside the city, far away from employment opportunities and other services, thus making them even poorer.

The Framework for the ASEAN Plan of Action on Rural Development and Poverty Eradication (2004–10) highlights regional priorities leading towards inclusive policies for the rural and urban poor. This framework recalls objectives of the ASEAN Ministers on Rural Development and Poverty Eradication (established in 1997), calling for "innovative and holistic strategies to facilitate access of the rural and urban poor to public utilities and facilities", and for "a conducive environment for income-generation and employment opportunities for the poor". Elements of empowerment can be found in the framework's sections on employment and income generation, and on partnerships and local participation.

However, the focus of the framework is largely on rural development, and more attention is needed for urban poverty reduction.

ASEAN can strive to put together a framework for inclusive cities that is sensitive to local conditions and culture, as an example for the global community. It can either build on the existing framework for poverty reduction, or complement it with a policy framework that addresses urban poverty reduction separately. An effective policy framework for urban poverty reduction should include the following components.

Addressing the Three Dimensions of Poverty

Because every service in the city has a price, people's access to essential infrastructure and services in the city requires that they have adequate income. For people to engage in income-generating activities, they must have good health and education. They must also have access to services such as market information and credit. In order to be assured of inclusion in the delivery of essential services, they must be able to participate in decision-making. Thus the relationship of the three dimensions is circular, in the sense that participation in decision-making also requires access to services, as well as time to spend on participation without loss of income. Consequently poverty reduction requires a comprehensive approach that simultaneously reduces poverty of income, poverty of access, and poverty of power.

A Framework for Inclusive Cities: Incorporating the Poor's Needs in All Aspects of Urban Development

Since the Cities Summit organized by the United Nations in 1996, several issues (ISTED 2008, p. 16) have been consistently mentioned as critical to effective urban development. When dealing with these issues, it is important that the "viewpoints of the poor" are incorporated to ensure that their needs are considered in overall urban development.

Urban data/Mapping

For the sake of urban planning, decision-makers have to have access to reliable data and information on the city concerned, and the information needs to be spatially comprehended, in view of the complexity and density of economic activities, and land uses in urban areas. Many cities do not have reliable data, and even where they exist, the data do not always reflect the true conditions of the urban population, especially of the poor. Geographic information systems (GIS) can ensure that data on the urban poor are incorporated in maps in a timely manner.

There are at least two ways through which information on the poor can be included in urban data. One is through community mapping, where neighbourhoods of informal settlers are asked to participate in completing information on the location of homes and basic services in their localities, as well as in providing socio-economic data on income, occupations, and other such information. Another way is by assigning addresses to the houses of the poor in the city. This will contribute much to the city's ability to monitor its inhabitants' welfare and ensure that urban services such as water and electricity are distributed where they are needed most. Such data also enable cities to determine the impact of health programmes as well as to plan education campaigns.

Urban governance

The recognition of the role of cities in development has drawn attention to the importance of decentralization and urban governance. The localization of decision-making renders it easier for city managers to reach out to all their constituents, including the poor. Urban governance that emphasizes community participation enables cities to address one dimension of urban poverty, that is, the lack of access to decision-making and power. By breaking down the city into neighbourhoods, or by establishing mechanisms for local participation through people's councils, people's voices may be incorporated into planning processes (ISTED 2008, p. 3).

Urban finance

Cities require adequate financing to support their needs. Water supply and sanitation, transport, housing, waste collection and disposal, and environmental protection can ensure decent living conditions, but require investment and operating funds. Cities rely on national transfers, local revenue collection, borrowing, and public-private partnerships to mobilize the necessary funds. How can the poor be assured of their place to live in the city, given the limitation of funds? UN-HABITAT presents five strategies (2008, *Quick Guide* 5, p. 22) to ensure that housing finance reaches the poor. These are:

- Community-based self-finance;
- Simplifying the formal sector;
- Channelling loans through community savings groups;
- Using intermediate institutions to bridge formal and informal finance; and
- Cost reduction strategies through design, internal cross subsidies, and incremental building.

Similar strategies are needed to ensure that the poor have access to other urban benefits.

Participatory urban development planning tools

Approaches such as the City Development Strategy (CDS) aim to provide balanced city development based on increased participation by all sections of the population. Urban development objectives are determined through a process of joint evaluation of strengths and weaknesses, opportunities of, and threats to the city. While the CDS is not comprehensive, it nevertheless has three strong points:

- CDS makes it easier to link local decision-makers' vision of the city with its economic, environmental, and poverty reduction objectives;
- CDS enables cities to choose their priorities for action and investment;
- CDS encourages the participation of local organizations and stakeholders (ISTED 2008, p. 78).

Participatory processes in community and housing development have been very instrumental in creating security of land tenure for the poor in cities and in providing them with opportunities to exercise their power as residents of cities.

Land and housing

It is estimated that about 30–50 per cent of Asia's urban residents lack legal tenure documents that entitle them to occupy their land (UN HABITAT/ UNESCO 2008, *Quick Guide* 3, p. 2). It is said that some 72.5 million people in Southeast Asia live in informal settlements, mainly in Indonesia (twenty-eight million) and in the Philippines (twenty-three million). Slum dwellers often lack security of land tenure and access to basic infrastructure such as adequate water supply and sanitation. Moreover, there are currently fewer and fewer opportunities for the poor to settle on unused land in urban areas.

To make conditions worse for poor communities, private landowners and government agencies evict poor people from large areas to free up land for commercial and infrastructure projects. Evictions may be effective in clearing land for other uses, but this approach only worsens the poverty situation in cities and creates more problems than it seeks to solve. The poor lose their livelihood and their social support systems when they are forced to move far away from where they used to live. Governments must understand that evictions result in increased poverty.

When a significant portion of urban households are excluded from legal shelter, the prospects of a city's economic development decreases because without adequate shelter, access to safe water, and sanitation, the urban poor cannot become productive urban residents. Below are a number of strategies from UN-HABITAT (2008, *Quick Guide* 3, pp. 19–33) to make land more accessible to the poor:

- Planning for higher densities, multi-storey dwellings and lessening sprawl;
- Planning for pedestrians and not cars, creating space for efficient, liveable, and affordable housing;
- Land use regulations that consider the needs of the poor, not impose unrealistic standards that make land expensive and inaccessible to the majority of the population;
- Better land information for all;
- Better land taxation systems;
- Land sharing for various income levels;
- Land readjustment;
- Cross subsidy schemes;
- Regularization of existing slums;
- Support for community initiatives.

Principles of self-help and participation in the physical work that go into shelter construction make it possible for the poor to build houses for much less than if they have to rely on government agencies or the private sector to provide them with the same amount of space.

Sustainable cities (urban ecology) resilience against disasters

The urban population continues to increase, while land does not expand. This situation often forces the urban poor to develop their settlements in areas that are unsuitable for habitation. Most Southeast Asian cities are located in coastal areas, many of which are under threat of rising sea levels, and therefore may no longer be developed with self-built housing. It may also no longer be possible to expand urban areas as forestland and other naturally wild areas need to be conserved to stave off the effects of global warming.

Cities that are vulnerable to flooding need to conserve their wetlands, flood plains, and riverbanks and, in doing so, will severely limit areas that could be developed for self-help housing. It is unfortunate that in their search for security of tenure and protection from eviction, communities will ultimately be "evicted" by natural forces. It is therefore imperative for urban development thinkers to find ways to integrate the poor into what is considered the safe havens of those who have the resources.

While self-help and participation are critical in development, they do not necessarily mean that people have to build their houses themselves. The question to be asked is: Is it possible for urban poor communities to collaborate with local government, and private business with corporate social responsibility programmes, to create affordable liveable spaces? Planners should give more attention to the development of integrated communities with a mix of incomes.

ASEAN-wide Poverty Assessment

Reducing poverty in ASEAN requires a good understanding of its scope and nature, and this can be achieved through the development of a comparable database of poverty incidence in the ASEAN member countries. The ASEAN Socio-Cultural Community Blueprint, adopted in February 2009 at the 14th ASEAN Summit in Thailand, emphasizes poverty alleviation as a key measure. In support of ASEAN members' efforts to meet the Millennium Development Goals (MDG) target of eradicating extreme poverty and hunger, one of the priority actions listed in the blueprint states that ASEAN will "work towards the establishment of an ASEAN data bank on poverty incidence and poverty reduction programme, which can be shared among Member States".

Such a database needs to take into account the cultural diversity of ASEAN nations. ASEAN members may agree to conduct a region-wide poverty assessment that will determine minimum economic, social, political, and cultural goods needed to maintain an acceptable way of life in that particular society.

The following categories of indicators are useful for urban poverty assessments (Hentschel and Seshagiri 2000, p. 4):

- Income and consumption indicators (poverty rate, that is, percentage of population not able to finance a basic basket of goods,[1] and extreme poverty rate, that is, the percentage of population not able to finance a basic basket of goods with their total income).
- Health and education outcome indicators (under-five malnutrition rate, infant mortality rate and under-five mortality rate, maternal mortality rate, life expectancy of the city population, incidence of specific diseases, literacy rate of the population, years of schooling of different age groups).
- Access and service satisfaction indicators (access to water and sanitation, electricity, garbage collection, schooling, health centres and hospitals, public or private transport, social programmes such as nutrition, child care, social assistance, and microfinance).
- Non-income deprivation indicators (unemployment, violence rate in cities, child labour, discrimination in workplace).

The poverty assessment must also consider the gender dimension, taking into account that in many cities, women are the worst off.

Emerging Issues: Natural and Built Environments, Food Security, and Urban Life

Aside from strengthening links between local government and communities, there is also a need to develop programmes that strengthen the links between rural and urban areas, and between the natural and built environments. As populations move more easily between rural and urban areas, the divisions between the two are increasingly blurring. Moreover, it is difficult to separate food production, human capital, and wealth creation, that is, the sustainability of life in urban areas, from the larger ecosystem. Cities are, after all, still located in space, and depend much on the health of the environment for water supply, air quality, and food supply.

While urban life is not associated with food production, it is now widely recognized that food security and therefore urban agriculture may play an important part in a sustainable urban future. If poor dwellers are able to grow their own food, there will be less reliance on cash to enable them to put food on the table. An urban food security programme, which either enables urban dwellers to grow food within the city, or strengthen links between food production areas and the city, will resolve one aspect of urban poverty, that is, that of food supply. After all, "ensuring adequate access to food at all times for ASEAN people" is a stated priority in the ASEAN Socio-Cultural Community Blueprint.

Note

1. "Basket of goods" refers to the minimum of goods essential for the survival of a household: food, clothing, water, transport, housing, etc.

References

ASEAN. "Framework for the ASEAN Plan of Action on Rural Development and Poverty Eradication (2004–2010)" <http://www.asean.org/9162.htm> (accessed November 2010).

ASEAN Secretariat. *ASEAN Socio-Cultural Community Blueprint*. Jakarta, 2009.

Hentschel, Jesko and Radha Seshagiri. *The City Poverty Assessment: A Primer*. World Bank, Washington, DC, 2000.

ISTED (Institut des Sciences et des Techniques de l'Equipement et de l'Environnement pour le Développement). *Emerging Cities: Keys to Understanding and Acting*, 2008.

League of Cities of the Philippines. The City Development Strategy Toolkit for Philippine Cities, 2004.

Lindahl, Claes. *Wealth of the Poor: Eliminating Poverty through Market and Private Sector Development*. Sida Studies no. 14 (2005).

Narayan, Deepa (ed.). *Empowerment and Poverty Reduction: A Sourcebook*. Washington, DC: World Bank, 2002.

United Nations Economic and Social Commission for Asia and the Pacific (UNESCAP). "Urban Poverty and the Working Poor: Facing the Challenges of Urbanization and Urban Poverty in Asia and the Pacific". Item 6 of the provisional agenda of the Committee on Poverty Reduction of Fourth session, 12–14 December 2007, Bangkok.

United Nations Human Settlements Program and United Nations Economic (UN-HABITAT) and Social Commission for Asia and the Pacific (UNESCAP). *Housing the Poor in Asian Cities, Quick Guides 1-7*, 2008.

Veneracion, Cynthia C. *Capability Building for Urban Slum Upgrading: Views from Five Communities in Quezon City*. Quezon City, Philippines: Institute of Philippine Culture (IPC), Ateneo de Manila University, 2008.

Yap Kioe Sheng. *Promoting Productive, Inclusive and Sustainable Cities and Towns in Southeast Asia*. Overview Paper presented at the 2nd Regional Workshop on Urbanisation in Southeast Asian Countries, Singapore, March 2010.

7

THE HDB COMMUNITY
A Work in Progress

Tan Ern Ser

INTRODUCTION

Any foreign visitor to Singapore, on leaving Changi Airport and commuting several kilometres on most roads, would not fail to notice that public housing is one of the most recognizable and ubiquitous features covering much of the island republic. Indeed, official figures indicate that 83.2 per cent of Singapore residents, comprising citizens and those granted permanent residency, live in flats built by the Housing and Development Board (HDB), a government statutory body, while most of the rest reside in private condominium apartments or landed properties (Department of Statistics 2010, p. 7).

Moreover, notwithstanding the "public housing" label, an overwhelming 97 per cent of HDB dwellers live in "sold", as opposed to "rental", properties. Some 77 per cent of the "sold" units are of the larger flat type, ranging from four-room to executive apartments (HDB 2010a, p. 14). These figures are the outcome respectively of the government's home ownership policy, as well as a manifestation of residential and social mobility, which has contributed to the emergence of a visually homogeneous middle-class society in housing terms.

IS COMMUNITY POSSIBLE AND ALIVE IN THE HDB ESTATE?

This highly successful housing programme began in the 1960s to handle the massive resettlement of the population from kampongs or villages and overcrowded inner-city neighbourhoods with poor utilities and sanitation amenities. A consequence of this programme was the rupturing of old neighbourly ties and community, real or imagined. Not surprisingly, providing citizens with a roof over their heads has turned out to be not the HDB's only mission. It also aims at community building, a process which corresponds to nation building in post-independence Singapore.

Wong and her colleagues (1997, p. 443) observed that "the HDB's housing philosophy has evolved from the emphasis of the early 1960's on providing basic shelter to the present emphasis on providing a total living environment and supporting community development within the housing estates". They also noted that "the concepts of neighbourhood and precinct planning, the provision of common spaces such as void decks, playgrounds and segmented corridors, have been introduced in order to encourage social interaction among residents who share common facilities", and that "HDB area officers are being trained in community relations and extensive co-operation is given to grass-roots organizations and voluntary agencies to help nurture a community spirit among the residents" (Wong et al. 1997, p. 444).

But community building involving the grafting of people from diverse locations into an urban context can be rather challenging, though not impossible. Wong and her colleagues (1997, p. 444) pointed out that the popular perception is that community existed only in the "idyllic" village or small town, while the urban context, characterized by "the size, density and heterogeneity of the city [which] give rise to a generally impersonal competitive environment", spells the demise of community. Such a view is obviously untenable, given the weight of the evidence. They countered that "sociologists and urban anthropologists have long found the persistence of primary ties, informal groups and well-organized neighbourhoods" in the urban environment (Wong et al. 1997, p. 444).

Somewhat similarly, Chua (1997, p. 439) argued that while "the generalized sense of community as in the village is no longer possible", it is "now replaced by much more personalized sentiments localized at a particular void deck or in one's routine routes". In other words, community is not quite dead, but merely reduced in scope and sphere of activities in the modernist, urban environment.

A MULTIDIMENSIONAL HDB SOCIAL LANDSCAPE

Thus far, we have been speaking in fairly broad terms about the HDB social landscape. Let us now take a closer look at the characteristics of the residents within HDB neighbourhoods. As noted earlier, the HDB has a mission to provide affordable housing to citizens, regardless of their race and class, and to facilitate home ownership. This has served to "homogenize" Singapore visually, as well as, to a significant extent, making it a showcase of Singapore — as a middle-class society.

However, as we zoom in on where the people are, we will notice that the HDB population is rather heterogeneous in composition. But this heterogeneity could be reconfigured by the people themselves, through a self-selection process, and thereby transformed into segregated, homogeneous groupings within distinct geographical boundaries. Such a possibility prompted the HDB to prevent consciously the formation of ethnic enclaves via the "ethnic quota" policy, and of class enclaves by locating mixed flat types within the same neighbourhood, precinct, and even apartment block.

The HDB neighbourhood is clearly a multidimensional social landscape. Apart from being multiracial and multi-class, it is also multi-religious and multigenerational. With the stepping up of immigration in recent years, it has become more multinational as well.

Obviously the HDB estates and towns are not all multidimensional to the same degree. For instance, in a comparison of HDB towns in 2008, the Central Area was found to have the lowest median household income of S$2,979 (S$1=US$0.75), while Punggol had the highest median income of S$6,569, and Bukit Timah came a close second with $$6,560 (HDB 2010a, p. 52).

Overall it can be seen that a large proportion of HDB dwellers live in middle-income housing, defined as "four-room or large flat type". The size of the middle class, using flat type as a crude indicator, has grown considerably over the last twenty years, increasing from 41.3 per cent in 1987, to 77.0 per cent in 2008 (Table 7.1).

Table 7.2, focusing on education level, also shows a significant increase in the number of HDB dwellers aged fifteen years or older who have attained polytechnic or university qualifications, with this figure rising from 19.9 per cent in 1998 to 31.4 per cent in 2008. The proportion with "no qualification" or "primary qualification" remains somewhat high at 30.5 per cent, though this is lower than the 37.7 per cent figure a decade ago.

Table 7.1
HDB Residents by Flat Type (%)

Flat Type	HDB Residents			
	1987		2008	
	%	cum. %	%	cum. %
1-room	6.3		1.2	
2-room	7.0		2.2	
3-room	45.4		19.6	
4-room	29.0		41.0	
5-room	9.9	41.3	26.7	77.0
Executive	1.6		9.3	
HUDC	0.8		—	
Total	100.0		100.0	

Source: HDB 2010a.

Table 7.2
HDB Residents by Education Level (%)

Education Level	HDB Residents			
	1998		2008	
	%	cum. %	%	cum. %
No qualification	11.8	37.7	8.2	30.5
Primary	25.9		22.3	
Secondary	35.4		32.9	
Upper Secondary	6.9		4.5	
Polytechnic	10.7	19.9	15.3	31.4
University	9.2		16.1	
Others	0.1		0.7	
Total	100.0		100.0	

Source: HDB 2010a.

Using occupation as an indicator, however, suggests a somewhat modest increase in the proportion of HDB dwellers in middle-class jobs classified as "professionals" or "associate professionals and technicians". At the same time, it could be observed that the proportion of "cleaners and unskilled workers" has climbed slightly from 8.1 per cent in 1998 to 10.7 per cent in 2008, the consequence of a greying population (Table 7.3).

In regard to household income, the indications for 2008 are that 20 per cent have household incomes of $8,000 or higher, while 25 per cent earned below $2,000. The latter figure suggests that one out of every four HDB households earned less than half of the median household income. Moreover, 8.5 per cent do not have any earned income (Table 7.4).

There is also some intersection between age and class, using income as a crude indicator. Table 7.5 shows that elderly households are more likely to be living in rental one-room or two-room flats, compared with non-elderly households: 14.6 per cent and 2.9 per cent respectively. Correspondingly, 57.9 per cent of elderly households are found in the below-S$2,000 household income bracket, compared with 16.6 per cent in the case of non-elderly households (Table 7.6). Indeed, slightly more than a third of elderly households have no earned income.

Another correlation is that between race and class — again using income as a crude indicator. Table 7.7 shows that 70.2 per cent of Malay households earned less than S$5,000 on average, compared with 58.4 per

Table 7.3
HDB Residents by Occupation (%)

Occupation	HDB Residents			
	1998		2008	
	%	cum. %	%	cum. %
Legislators, Senior Officials, and Managers	10.9		10.7	
Professionals	8.5	29.5	11.9	34.5
Associate Professionals and Technicians	21.0		22.6	
Clerical Workers	13.6		12.8	
Service and Sales Workers	12.7		12.6	
Production Workers	21.2		15.0	
Cleaners and Labourers	8.1		10.7	
Others	4.0		3.7	
Total	100.0		100.0	

Source: HDB 2010a.

Table 7.4
Monthly Household Income of HDB Residents (%)

| Monthly Household Income (S$) | HDB Residents | | | |
| | 2003 | | 2008 | |
	%	cum. %	%	cum. %
No earned income	10.2		8.5	
Below 1,000	7.5	30.1	4.4	24.8
1,000–1,999	12.4		11.9	
2,000–2,999	17.8		12.3	
3,000–3,999	15.8		12.9	
4,000–4,999	9.3		10.1	
5,000–5,999	7.1		8.6	
6,000–6,999	6.3		6.2	
7,000–7,999	4.1		5.3	
8,000–8,999	2.0		4.4	
9,000–9,999	2.6	9.7	3.1	19.9
10,000 & above	5.1		12.4	
Total	100.0		100.0	

Source: HDB 2010a.

cent for the Chinese, and 61.9 per cent for the Indians. The same pattern, though less contrasting, may also be discerned with regard to the proportion of households earning less than S$2,000 on average: among the Chinese, 24.3 per cent; Malays, 27.7 per cent; and Indians, 25.3 per cent.

The last diversity to be highlighted here is that of nationality. Unfortunately, I do not have the figures on the nationalities of HDB dwellers. As an approximation, I shall refer to the Census 2010 data. What is interesting is the significant presence of residents hailing from East Asia (China, Hong Kong, and Macau), South Asia (India, Pakistan, Bangladesh, and Sri Lanka), other Southeast Asian countries (particularly Indonesia), Europe, North America, and Australia and New Zealand. Nearly one in four Singapore residents were born outside the country (Table 7.8). The majority of these originated from Malaysia.

Table 7.5
Flat Type by Elderly and Non-Elderly Households, 2008 (%)

Flat Type	Elderly Households		Non-Elderly Households	
	%	cum. %	%	cum. %
1-room	7.0	14.6	0.8	2.9
2-room	7.6		2.1	
3-room	40.3		21.3	
4-room	30.2		39.3	
5-room	12.3	14.9	27.5	36.6
Executive	2.6		9.1	
Total	100.0		100.0	

Source: HDB 2010a.

Table 7.6
Monthly Household Income (S$) from Work by Elderly and
Non-elderly Households, 2008 (%)

Monthly Household Income (S$)	Elderly Households		Non-Elderly Households	
	%	cum. %	%	cum. %
No earned income	36.3	57.9	2.4	16.6
Below 1,000	7.4		3.0	
1,000–1,999	14.2		11.2	
2,000–2,999	9.5		13.2	
3,000–3,999	9.5		13.9	
4,000–4,999	5.3		11.2	
5,000–5,999	4.4		9.2	
6,000–6,999	3.7		6.7	
7,000–7,999	2.7		5.8	
8,000–8,999	2.1		4.7	
9,000–9,999	1.5		3.5	
10,000 & above	3.4		15.2	
Total	100.0		100.0	

Source: HDB 2010a.

Table 7.7
Monthly Household Income from Work of Ethnic Groups, 2008 (%)

Monthly Household Income (S$)	Chinese Households		Malay Households		Indian Households	
	%	cum. %	%	cum. %	%	cum. %
No earned income	8.8		6.6		8.1	
Below 1,000	4.2		5.3		4.9	
1,000–1,999	11.3	58.4	15.8	70.2	12.3	61.9
2,000–2,999	11.8		15.2		12.5	
3,000–3,999	12.6		14.9		13.5	
4,000–4,999	9.7		12.4		10.6	
5,000–5,999	8.5		8.8		8.8	
6,000–6,999	6.1		7.4		5.6	
7,000–7,999	5.4		4.1		5.4	
8,000–8,999	4.6		3.2		4.1	
9,000–9,999	3.4		1.7		2.2	
10,000 & above	13.7		4.6		12.2	
Total	100.0		100.0			

Source: HDB 2010a.

Table 7.8
Resident Population by Place of Birth, 2010

Place of Birth	Proportion (%)
Singapore	77.2
Malaysia	10.2
China, Hong Kong, Macau	4.6
South Asia	3.3
Indonesia	1.4
Other Asian countries	2.4
Europe	0.4
North America	0.2
Australia and New Zealand	0.1
Others	0.1
Total	100.0

Source: DOS 2010.

DOES DIVERSITY SPELL SOCIAL TENSIONS AND CONFLICT?

I have described above the multidimensional diversity of the population of the HDB estates. A critical question to ask is whether or not this diversity spells social tensions and conflict involving opposing values and interests; apparent harmony, but characterized by an absence of social ties and networks; or the emergence of community with the development and accumulation of social capital?

Data from my (Tan 2004, pp. 36–37) 2001 survey indicate that, among Singaporeans, 85 per cent had "friends from lower income groups", while 11 per cent said that they did not. Slightly less impressive were the figures on having "friends from higher income groups". Seventy-seven per cent had "friends from higher income groups", compared with 18 per cent who did not. A high proportion of Singaporeans (47 per cent), and 60 per cent of those who placed themselves in the "lower class", also indicated that "successful people in Singapore tend to look down on the less successful ones".

With regard to inter-ethnic relations, 21 per cent of Singaporeans indicated that they did not "have close friends of a different race". It was also shown that older people are less likely to "have close friends of a different race", compared with younger people. In addition, Singaporeans with lower education have fewer "close friends of a different race" than those with higher education. This is also true for the majority Chinese compared with their counterparts in the minority ethnic categories (Tan 2004, pp. 38–39). A more recent survey (Tan and Koh 2010) indicates that 23 per cent of Singaporeans agreed that they "don't have much in common with Singaporeans of other races".

The same recent survey also casts some light on the challenges confronting citizen-foreigner integration. It shows that two thirds of Singaporeans felt that the "policy to attract more foreign talent will weaken Singaporeans' feeling of one nation, one people". The proportion with a "negative" inclination towards foreign talent was highest among those in the smaller house type or with low income, declining from 72 per cent among those living in one- to three-room HDB flats, to 49 per cent among those residing in private properties.

Singaporeans are somewhat more accommodating on immigration when they factor in the economic imperative. Specifically, two thirds of Singaporeans in the survey agreed that the "Government is right to increase the number of foreigners working in Singapore if our economy needs it."

However, the proportion who disagreed was again highest among those living in the smaller house type or with low income, declining from 45 per cent among the one- to three-roomers, to 24 per cent among those residing in private properties.

Within the HDB estates, a somewhat similar pattern can also be observed. The proportion of HDB residents who perceived that the foreigners in their midst are integrating well is 44.3 per cent, compared with 25.9 per cent who thought otherwise. Like the findings from the national survey reported above, HDB residents with higher education, living in larger house types, and younger in age are more likely to perceive foreigners in a positive light (HDB 2010b, p. 66).

Despite some of the "negative" figures highlighted above, I would argue that, given what we know of Singapore over the last forty years, it would not be justifiable to suggest that the country is characterized by, or prone to, class, ethnic, religious, or citizen-migrant conflict. If anything, the "positive" figures outweigh the "negative" ones.

Nevertheless my intention here is to suggest that the diversity could potentially be a source of social tensions or conflict. For instance, a 25 per cent "negative" figure with respect to how Singaporeans feel about migrants in Singapore, while a statistical minority, can be significant, given that it reflects the views of almost 800,000 people, the size of three major HDB towns combined (HDB 2010a, p. 15). This explains why the state emphasizes integration even with the much taken-for-granted prevalence of harmony and stability in Singapore. It should be noted that integration is more than just about the absence of conflict, or even the presence of harmony. It seeks to promote understanding, acceptance, connection, and collaboration across social divides.

ORIENTATIONS OF HDB RESIDENTS

Apart from examining the social characteristics of HDB residents, another dimension that may have a bearing on community building in the HDB estates is that of residential orientations. This term "captures" how residents relate to their estate, including the extent to which their daily routines are conducted within its boundaries. It influences the probability of their developing a sense of belonging, ownership, commitment, and rootedness, and thereby contributing to community building.

I would hypothesize that the following types of residential orientations, in terms of commitment and time spent in activities, are found in the HDB estate.

Probably the least committed would be the subtenants and rental tenants since they are in transition, whether short term or long term. However, this orientation does not render them visually invisible, if they are non-Singaporeans and likely to congregate with their fellow nationals in neighbourhood facilities, such as basketball courts or shopping malls.

I am not sure how best to characterize foreign domestic workers. They spend the most time in the estate, and are likely to form networks among fellow domestic workers from other households in the neighbourhood, but can they be deemed to be contributing to community building? In the broad sense, the answer would be affirmative.

Elderly persons, housewives, and young children also spend much of their time in the estate, and have probably established their own social networks through their daily routines: for instance, mothers sending their young children to kindergarten or school, housewives shopping in a nearby wet market, elderly persons chatting at the void deck on the ground floor, elderly men having a drink with friends at a coffee shop, or young children using the playground.

The ones who probably spend the least time in the estate due to study or work responsibilities are the young and older adults. However, given their educational and occupational profile, there is a good chance they have the qualities and, potentially, the commitment, to provide leadership in the community-building process.

SOCIAL CAPITAL IN THE HDB ESTATE

Now that I have discussed the factors that impact on social distance between social categories, and the residential orientations that could enhance social participation, let me move on to consider the data on social capital, a measure which indicates not only the reduction of social distance, but, more importantly, the degree of connectedness and collaboration. Enhancing social capital could in turn help to create a caring, vibrant community populated by residents possessing a strong sense of ownership, belongingness, and identity, and having the capacity to produce a secure living environment and good quality of life in a society characterized by growing complexity, diversity, heterogeneity, and risks.

Social capital is by now a well-established concept in sociological literature. I quote here the rather comprehensive definition used in the report on the HDB Sample Household Survey 2008 (HDB 2010b, p. 14):

Social capital refers to the accumulation of people's trust, confidence and shared relationships with each other in both formal and informal settings. It has both an individual and collective dimension... At the individual level, it refers to the resources available to a person, through his networks of relationships with informal groups (e.g., family, relatives, neighbours, colleagues) and formal institutions (e.g., community and government agencies)... which can facilitate and enable the pursuit of his objectives... At the community level, social capital refers to the collective strength of individuals' social networks, along with related attributes, which facilitates (and enables) the pursuit of collective or shared objectives.

The HDB Sample Household Survey 2008 found that on a scale of 0 ("Not at All") to 10 ("Completely"), HDB residents have mean social capital scores of above 6 (Table 7.9). If we conceive of social capital scores as indicators of social health, or the extent to which community is taking shape — and there are strong empirical bases for doing so — then we have good reason to be optimistic that the HDB estate is becoming more of a community over the years. However, family and kinship ties, in terms of trust and reciprocity, remain stronger and more extensive than that of neighbourly ties (Tables 7.10 and 7.11). Another positive sign for social integration is that 77 per cent of HDB residents are interacting across ethnic and/or nationality lines (Table 7.12).

CONCLUDING REMARKS

The findings I have mobilized above indicate that while social divides are present within the diversity that characterizes the HDB estate, they do not have to lead to social conflict; rather, the social distance could

Table 7.9
Social Capital Scores of HDB Residents

Component of Social Capital	Mean Score
Trust in informal and generalized networks	6.4
Reciprocity in informal and generalized networks	6.6
Confidence in institutions	6.8
Average size of informal networks	61 persons

Source: HDB 2010b.

Table 7.10
Norms of Trust in Informal and Generalized Networks

Network	Mean Score
Family members	9.0
Relatives	7.2
Friends who are not neighbours	6.3
Friends who are neighbours	6.1
Neighbours in general	4.9
Overall score	6.4

Source: HDB 2010*b*.

Table 7.11
Size of Informal Networks

Network	Mean Number of People
Family members	7
Relatives	17
Friends who are not neighbours	24
Friends who are neighbours	6
Neighbours in general	10
Overall score	61

Source: HDB 2010*b*.

Table 7.12
Interaction with Neighbours across Ethnic and Nationality Lines

Type of Interaction	Proportion (%)
Interacted across ethnic lines	60.3
Interacted across nationality lines	2.0
Interacted across both ethnic and nationality lines	14.7
No interaction across ethnic and/or nationality lines	23.0

Source: HDB 2010*b*.

be bridged or narrowed through the development of social capital and thereby of community.

The data also suggest that community-building policies and programmes, aided by infrastructural designs and town planning that facilitate social interactions, together with relentless nation-building efforts, have been largely successful in transforming the HDB estate into more than just a decent physical shelter in a high-density urban environment.

In terms of methodology, the use of social capital measures to "capture" the extent of community building is a step in the right direction in that they serve as valid and convenient indicators for conducting comparative and trend analysis.

I will conclude by making several other observations that have a bearing on community building in Singapore.

First, if the desire is to build community from the ground up, it makes sense to encourage those with the capacity for leadership to step forward. The capacity for leadership is already present among those with higher education, but they may not have the time due to work and familial responsibilities. Perhaps a practical approach is to customize the time commitment required to match individual schedules. This facilitates participation from a larger talent pool, and the possibility that involvement produces its own momentum for further involvement.

Second, allowing for voice and civic participation would strengthen sense of ownership and belongingness, and, in turn, community. Given the rise in the education level of the population, we would expect the capacity and propensity for civic participation to expand as well. A possible consequence of civic participation is that HDB residents would see themselves less as customers to be served, but more as stakeholders with a responsibility to serve the community.

Third, strengthening the sense of security among citizens would enhance their acceptance of the migrants and foreigners in their midst, thereby contributing to social integration.

Fourth, even as Singapore emphasizes self-reliance as a value, it is important to emphasize mutual support within a caring community as a counterbalance. A community is established on networks of interdependency, rather than on a collection of self-sufficient individuals.

References

Chua, Beng Huat. "Modernism and the Vernacular: Transformation of Public Spaces and Social Life in Singapore". Reprinted from *Journal of Architectural and Planning Research* 51, no. 1 (1991): 36–45. In *Understanding Singapore Society*, edited by J.H. Ong, C.K. Tong, and E.S. Tan. Singapore: Times Academic, 1997.

Department of Statistics (DOS). "Population Trends 2010". Singapore: DOS, 2010.

Housing and Development Board (HDB). "Public Housing in Singapore: Residents' Profile, Housing Satisfaction and Preferences". HDB Sample Household Survey 2008. Singapore: HDB, 2010*a*.

———. "Public Housing in Singapore: Well-Being of Communities, Families, and the Elderly". HDB Sample Household Survey 2008. Singapore: HDB, 2010*b*.

Tan, Ern Ser. *Does Class Matter? Social Stratification and Orientations in Singapore.* Singapore: World Scientific, 2004.

Tan, Ern Ser and Gillian Koh. *Citizens and the Nations: Findings from NOS4 Survey.* Singapore: Institute of Policy Studies, 2010.

Wong, Aline, G.L. Ooi, and Rennis Ponniah. "Dimensions of HDB Community". Reprinted from *Housing a Nation: 25 Years of Public Housing in Singapore*, pp. 455–94. In *Understanding Singapore Society*, edited by J.H. Ong, C.K. Tong, and E.S. Tan. Singapore: Times Academic Press, 1985.

8

RURAL-URBAN AND INTRA-URBAN LINKAGES IN SOUTHEAST ASIA
Old Field, New Dynamics

Chuthatip Maneepong

The topic of rural-urban dynamics in ASEAN is hardly new; in fact, it has been a mainstay of both academic and public policy debate in the region for at least six decades. What is new is that the context has changed dramatically over the last ten to twenty years. This chapter revisits ASEAN's rural–urban dynamics from such a perspective. What is new in terms of the context of rural–urban dynamics can be summarized as follows:

1. The growth of peri-urban areas: The rise of manufacturing in several countries in Southeast Asia has led to the growth of peri-urban areas, which are an important destination for rural migrants.
2. Increase in cross-border trade under the ASEAN Free Trade Area: Urban, peri-urban, and rural areas are increasingly affected by external forces such as the increase in cross-border trade. While there can be winners or losers, the impact of cross-border trade is generally unfavourable for rural areas.

3. Increase in connectivity: Rural and urban areas are much better connected in communication and transportation terms as a result of the rise of low-cost powerful communications and transportation systems. Cellular phones are now ubiquitous in ASEAN countries; information circulates at speeds unthought of ten years ago, with 3G networks likely to become widely accessible, thereby further increasing communication potential between rural and urban areas, including among urban migrants and the rural poor. Transport is similarly becoming less expensive, including travel by low-cost airlines serving smaller centres. This means that migration is less jarring, while information on most markets, for example, for urban labour and farm prices, is much more efficient.

4. The rise of regional migration: While labour mobility is relatively more restricted than the flow of goods in ASEAN, the reality is that residents of ASEAN increasingly consider, and often act on, regional labour options for the sake of higher standards of living, or as refugees. Cross-border migration for employment is becoming widespread throughout the region; for example, Cambodians staff tourist facilities in Koh Chang, Thailand. Thus rural-urban linkages may be between a rural area in one country and an urban one in another — complementing traditional rural-urban linkages which tend to be with the nearest large city in the same country.

5. The rise of new rural industries: Global demand is creating new industries in rural areas of Southeast Asia, as epitomized by ecotourism.

6. Cross-border dynamics: The price differentials in factor resources among ASEAN countries influence the nature of cross-border economies, whether between Singapore and Batam in Indonesia, or between Mae Sot in Thailand and Myawaddy in Myanmar. These areas often have significant rural-urban linkages, but the linkages go beyond national borders.

RURAL–URBAN DYNAMICS IN AN EMERGING URBAN-DOMINATED SOUTHEAST ASIA

The remarkable urbanization in Southeast Asia, from 15.4 per cent of the population in 1950, to 48.2 per cent of the region's total population in 2010, is the product of high rates of rural-urban migration and the reclassification of selected rural areas as urban, in addition to natural increase in urban populations. It indicates the significant social and economic role and function of urban areas (Yap 2010). Henderson (2000) conducted a study of 80–100 countries over the period 1960–95, which showed that national urban concentration increases as economic output and household incomes rise. For example, the urban population growth rate of Cambodia from 2010 to 2015 is projected to grow approximately 5.0 per cent annually as its average annual GDP growth rate (in 2009 US dollars) increased to 9.3 per cent; its GNI per capita was projected to reach US$2,018 in 2009 (UNDP 2008; World Bank 2010).

The statistics on urban and rural poverty in East Asia indicate that the percentage of urban poor increased from 18.96 per cent to 20.28 per cent of the total population between 1993 and 2002. Given the increasing share of urban population in East Asia, this means that urban areas contributed significantly to poverty reduction in East Asia. An analysis of 208 household surveys (1992–2004) from 87 countries representing 92 per cent of the population of the developing world corroborates this finding; it indicates that urbanization contributed significantly to reducing absolute income poverty in East Asia (Ravallion, Chen, and Sangraula 2007).

The World Bank's yearly World Development Report entitled, *Reshaping Economic Geography*, in 2009 notes that without industrialization and urbanization, countries cannot generate economic growth. The foregoing raises the policy debate as to whether urbanization should be accorded higher priority than rural development, and whether rural and urban development should be treated as separated domains from a policy perspective. In fact, the current practice of governments is to separate rural and urban planning into independent administrative streams. When any settlement reaches the status of municipality (or equivalent), it is administratively separated from its rural hinterland. On the other hand, others argue that the rural–urban divide is artificial and developmental policy should be spatially unitary.

Paudyal (2006) and Krongkaew (2003) found that urban-rural disparities contribute significantly to income inequality. The national Gini-coefficient ranges from 0.318 to 0.498 among Southeast Asian countries, with much of the inequity being the product of urban-rural disparities. Compared with low-income countries, middle-income countries such as Malaysia, Thailand, and the Philippines display significantly greater income or consumption disparity.

In addition, during the 1980s and 1990s, rural people in selected countries of Southeast Asia had limited access to services, such as piped water on premises and electricity, and low levels of adult literacy (Panel on Urban Population Dynamics 2003). For example, in the Lao PDR the rate of adult literacy among rural people was found to be 50.6 per cent, and that among urban people was 79.1 per cent (Paudyal 2006). These socio-economic data reflect the weakness of the rural sector in terms of its self-reliance.

On the other hand, some argue that urban areas in Southeast Asia (unlike First World countries such as Japan and South Korea) face diseconomies of scale associated with urban primacy because there are so few urban centres (Clawen 2002; Yap 2010). For example, Thailand with only one real metropolitan centre (Bangkok), is denied the opportunity to utilize technologies such as high speed rail, connecting a network of cities.

Rural regions function not only as sources of labour supply for urban areas, but also as international labour reserves. The result is international migration from rural areas from one country to another's urban areas, as exemplified by the millions of rural Indonesians migrating to fill urban jobs in Malaysia (Douglass 1998) and over a million rural Myanmar workers in Thai urban areas, in both the border towns and greater Bangkok (Maneepong 2006). However, these international migrant workers receive limited social welfare, security, and other protection.

These emerging challenges raise concerns about the sustainability of development and competitiveness of Southeast Asia in the long term. This chapter discusses these two issues by assessing contemporary policies promoting urban-rural linkages and their impacts on the Southeast Asian region. The author then draws on the lessons learned to suggest how to promote positive linkages between rural and urban areas. In the last section of the chapter, the author identifies emerging opportunities and challenges in promoting rural-urban and intra-urban linkages, and makes recommendations for ASEAN cooperation in this area.

FRAMEWORKS OF RURAL-URBAN AND INTRA-URBAN LINKAGES IN SOUTHEAST ASIA

Douglass (1998), Ruddle (1979), and Tacoli (2004) highlight the socio-economic roles and functions of rural towns, or small and intermediate urban centres, as components of a continuous regional, national, and international landscape, interrelated with urban or metropolitan areas through an array of flows of people, finance, production inputs, consumer goods, waste materials, technology, information, and decision-making. Rural and urban economies are not separate entities, but linked with each other, and are hence affected by policies applied to either realm. On the one hand, cities generate pollution from households, industry, and service activities; they discharge untreated waste into natural waterways that flow through rural areas; and industries and fossil-fuelled vehicles release greenhouse gases that obviously do not stop at urban boundaries, but lead to global warming (Newman 2006; Maneepong 2004). Thus collaboration between urban and rural areas is highly desirable to mitigate unintended impacts of economic growth on the environment, and the longer-term sustainability of development in both rural and urban areas. In addition, citizen participation and democratization in both urban and rural areas have the potential to promote inclusive and participatory decision making (UNDP 2000).

Economic and Social Benefit and Resilience from Rural-Urban Development

According to Rondinelli et al. (1983), inadequately articulated and integrated settlement systems are responsible for less-than-expected diffusion of the benefits of regional growth pole strategies in rural-urban development programmes, especially programmes that targeted secondary urban centres. This weakness is thought to cause economic agglomeration in regional cities without adequate compensating flows outwards, and drain capital, labour, and raw materials from rural hinterlands. Growth poles do not generate sufficient industrial linkages into rural hinterlands because there are missing links in the structure of social production. Local capital and technological innovation failed to develop adequately, thus causing economic dependency (Polenske 1988). Thus, achievement in promoting rural development and stemming rural to urban migration has been limited (Douglass 1998).

Migration from rural to urban areas contributes significantly to the availability of an inexpensive labour force in urban areas, especially of unskilled and semi-skilled labour. This increased the competitiveness of many Southeast Asian cities by lowering the cost of manufacturing during the 1970s–1980s (Begg 1999). Migrant remittances are a source of investment in rural areas, especially international migrant remittances. For example, the average annual earnings of foreign workers in Japan from Malaysia, Indonesia, and the Philippines was US$18,688.75 in 2004 (ADB 2006). Remittances are considered to be a significant factor in rural poverty reduction, and to have significant implications for agricultural production. The migrants' investment in rural development and assets is also a means to increase their own social safety net (Webster 2002; Department for International Development 2002; Tacoli 2008). Clawen (2002) considers migration a form of social remittance. For example, Thai migrant women who have been introduced to modern, urban attitudes, skills, identities and practices, use their education and technology to introduce new lifestyles and businesses in rural areas when they return.

Environmental Sustainability from a Rural-Urban Development Perspective

Drakakis-Smith (1995) and Tacoli (2008) raise the issue of sustainability of rural-urban development programmes, such as programmes targeting secondary urban centres that result from industrial decentralization. The reason is that most Third World countries have limited knowledge and information about environmental degradation and tend to consider environmental quality as a secondary priority as their first priority is the more pressing problem of economic growth. In addition, without central government support, local government agencies have limited revenue and capacity to monitor and address the environmental impacts of the activities of enterprises and to deal with the influx of unregistered migrants.

Governance and Citizen Participation in Rural-Urban Development

The flows of information between rural and urban areas, made possible by the astounding growth of low-cost telecommunications, websites, and other media, have dramatically increased the exchange of ideas and resources and the interaction and participation by the rural population in effective decision-making. Now rural migrants can find a job within a couple of days before or after their arrival in an urban centre. The information flows between the northeast and the industrial central and eastern regions of Thailand serving the enormous number of rural migrants are high (Webster 2002). Low-cost airlines and extremely low-cost rail tariffs in countries such as Thailand are making physical movement among regions easier and more affordable and are making migration, at least in this sense, a less jarring experience. However, the UNDP (2000) notes that the voices of the rural poor have not been much heard in national development, which favours urban development.

ASSESSMENT OF CURRENT POLICIES ON RURAL-URBAN LINKAGES

An assessment of current policies promoting rural-urban linkages illustrates the level of achievement in support of a more dispersed and balanced pattern of spatial development and rural development. It also identifies positive links between rural and urban development.

Rural Industrialization: Cottage Industry Programmes (OTOP Programmes)

The remarkable success of the OVOP (One Village One Product) Programme in Oita Prefecture, Japan, in 2001 inspired many similar programmes in developed and developing countries, such as the One-District-One-Industry programme in Malaysia, the One-Town-One-Product Programme in the Philippines, and the One-Tambon-One-Product programme in Thailand. These programmes promote cottage industries, targeting rural people to generate domestic consumption through exports of non-agricultural products. They try to maximize backward linkages to the agricultural sector for local raw materials and local skills and talents. This bottom-up movement is based on three principles: (1) think globally, act locally; (2) self-reliance and creativity; and (3) fostering human resource development (Maneepong 2009).

In 2004 the Philippines gave priority to the One-Town-One-Product Programme as a mainstream development strategy in the medium-term plan to promote micro, small, and medium-sized enterprises. Significant national and local government inputs included credit, technology, marketing, and the promotion of public-private partnerships. At present the small-scale OTOP fruit growers in Mindanao make regular shipments to Belgium. An established linkage with a private transport corporation facilitates forty-eight-hour shipments from Mindanao to Manila. Region 12, which ranks first in fresh fruits and processed products, attracts the most investment and generates the most export sales. It has created 3,305 new jobs and sustained 2,332 jobs (Cutarn 2008). However, to sustain this remarkable achievement, Cutarn (2008) highlights the collaboration of key stakeholders and visionary leadership in the application of the movement.

Ecotourism Programmes

In 1999, UNDP recognized ecotourism as a new measure for poverty reduction that can benefit rural communities with social, economic, and environmental changes. This emerging programme provides alternative recreational activities for domestic and international tourists from urban areas. Successful ecotourism programmes also promote natural and cultural conservation through the awareness of and participation by indigenous communities and the appreciation of visitors (Lao National Tourism Administration 2005).

In the Lao PDR, 46 per cent of revenue from international tourists (but only US$18 million out of US$54 million in 2004) arises from natural and cultural tourism, of which ecotourism is a subsector. The outstanding pilot programme of Nam Ha in Luang Numtha Province was initiated by the Lao National Tourism Administration with the support of New Zealand and UNESCO. It is replicated in four other regional cities and is a collaboration with Vietnam and Cambodia. Twenty National Protected Areas (NPAs) have been designated to promote ecotourism. These areas are rich in biodiversity and are populated by ethnic communities that are the nation's poorest.

There are a number of challenges in promoting ecotourism, which include striking the right balance between tourism development and natural protection, coordination among government agencies to enable better accessibility and basic infrastructure investment, capacity building for host communities, access to the tourism market, plus updated and accurate databases for planning, management, and marketing (Lao National Tourism Administration 2005).

Intragovernmental Cooperation in Peri-urban Areas

Cooperation between the central and local levels of government is necessary for successful investment in environmental facilities in peri-urban areas. This cooperation facilitates economies of scale. In Thailand cooperation between local governments, enabled by SAHAKAAN or the Federation of Municipalities, has been recognized in the Municipality Act since 1953.

More recently, the Decentralisation Act of 1999 has provided the opportunity for every type of local authority to cooperate horizontally with others. However, despite these legal opportunities, horizontal cooperation among local governments has been rare (DOLA and JICA 2002).

Some successful projects have resulted from strong informal partnerships, when combined with financial and technical support from the national government. For example, the Banbu solid waste disposal scheme in Songkhla Province, Thailand, which was a partnership of two municipalities and three (rural) Tambon Administrative Organizations (TAOs), was successful by utilizing an operational committee to manage the task of solid waste disposal in the extended urban area. The scheme received significant external inputs as the Ministry of Science and Technology provided funding to purchase appropriate technology (DOLA and JICA 2002). Successful partnerships among local governments have been limited to specific projects, and not as a part of overall planning and investment programming (Maneepong and Webster 2008).

Border Town Development

Interest in the development of Asian cross-border zones has burgeoned since the late 1980s and early 1990s after the Cold War period. Border town development has been promoted as a mechanism for economic decentralization away from metropolitan regions, and as a stimulus for cross-border cooperation with neighbouring countries. A number of cross-border oriented regional economic cooperation programmes has been established (Maneepong et al. 2004).

Mae Sot district, on the main border with Myanmar, is one of the most important border areas in Tak province, Thailand. Over the period 1993–2000, the industrialization of Mae Sot was remarkable due to its increasing number of factories, employment, and capital (Department of Industrial Works 2009). The industrial sector of Tak Province, which includes the border town of Mae Sot, boasted a 40 per cent share of gross provincial product during the Thai economic boom (1993–97) although it decreased to about a 35 per cent share of gross provincial product between 2000 and 2007, after the Asian economic crisis (NESDB 2000; NESDB 2009). It became the destination for relocated garment industries and other labour-intensive activities availing themselves of access to inexpensive foreign labour (TDRI 1991; NESDB 1998; International Development Centre of Japan et al. 2001). About half of all the factories in Tak Province are located in

Mae Sot District. In 2000 the output of its 218 factories was US$29 million and the factories employed 14,793 workers.

The availability of inexpensive Myanmar migrant labour attracted a number of non-indigenous and mainly labour-intensive industries to Mae Sot. In 2002 there were about 20,000 migrant workers and their number increased to 26,889 workers in 2005. These workers took about 85 per cent of the available industrial jobs in Mae Sot (Maneepong 2003; Kudo 2007). It was estimated that by employing migrant labour rather than Thai labour, Thai businesses could reduce labour costs by up to US$308 million annually (*Krungthep Business News* 2005). In other words, local economic development benefits were realized, but not, in the most part, by the local population.

Kudo (2007) interviewed about a hundred Myanmar workers in Mae Sot and discovered significant nominal wage differences between working in the garment industry in Yangon, Myanmar and in Mae Sot. In 2004 earnings were about US$20 per month in Yangon and about US$94 per month in Mae Sot, a differential of 4.7:1. Furthermore, helped by the low cost of living in Mae Sot, plus free on-site accommodation and subsidized prices for meals, 79 per cent of interviewees said that they remitted money to their hometowns.

At the community level, many factories are acknowledged as sources of local employment and as purchasers of various raw materials from nearby villages. However, some of the industries do not have much community awareness and often disrupt communities with noise, water pollution, and traffic problems. Government officers claim that they have received many complaints from residents (Maneepong 2004). The environmental impacts of fast-growing large and medium-sized factories in both rural and urban areas such as Mae Sot are severe because of excessive pollution, inadequate environmental infrastructure, and poor monitoring (Asian Engineering Consultant Corp. et al. 1998). Due to limited resources, local government agencies depend on technical support and financial subsidies from the central government. Without appropriate levels of funding and other technical assistance, they face major difficulties in trying to deal with environmental degradation.

All Southeast Asian countries, including Thailand, have implemented migration policies that aim to reduce their overall dependence on migrant labour and to protect and promote local employment. Moreover, in the long term, migrant labour retards the upgrading of technology and industrial development because entrepreneurs often tend to focus their business development on a low-production-cost strategy (Martin 2002; Chalamwong 2005). In addition, the registration of Myanmar migrant workers does not guarantee their social and health welfare because at present the Government of Thailand has not implemented health care measures and other rights for migrant workers. As a result of this lack of government concern, there has been a number of labour abuse cases (Asian Human Rights Commission 2003).

In sum, linkages between rural-urban and intra-urban development contribute to some positive impacts. For example, local economic development programmes, such as OTOP rural industrialization programmes, are associated with such linkages. Rural livelihood diversification, such as in ecotourism programmes, results from economic linkages with urban areas. Nevertheless, there are concerns regarding negative impacts from such urban-rural linkages, particularly in regard to environmental quality, local rural benefits, and human rights. The limited capacity of local government agencies, especially in rural and peri-urban areas, is a major challenge.

EMERGING OPPORTUNITIES AND CHALLENGES

New roles for urban areas in Southeast Asia are increasing the economic share of the service sector, but they also emphasize the importance of clean and green city programmes, especially for tourism, and the need for urban energy efficiency and conservation. These emerging urban development issues need strong support from, and linkages with, rural development.

After the 1997 Asian financial crisis, low-cost airlines made tourism to secondary towns significantly more affordable for domestic and international tourists. Southeast Asia has seen an increasing number of tourists visiting natural and cultural attractions in rural areas and secondary towns. This was made possible by the existence of twenty-one low-cost airlines in Southeast Asia and new routes to major destinations such as Angkor Wat, Siem Reap in Cambodia, Luang Prabang in Laos, and Bali in Indonesia.

The average annual growth of tourism in Laos from 1990 to 2004 exceeded 27 per cent. By 2013 the Laotian Government aims to attract one million stay-overnight tourists and two million day trippers per annum. Based on this projection, about US$500 million revenue per annum will be achievable (Lao National Tourism Administration 2005).

A major increase in the number of low-cost airline passengers has been noted. At the Budget Terminal of the Singapore Changi International Airport, the number of passengers on Tiger Airways and Cebu Pacific Airlines increased significantly from 1.4 million in 2006 to two million in 2007. A survey of customers' perceptions of low-cost airlines in Europe and Asia shows that the market for low-cost airlines is predominantly the leisure markets (O' Connell et al. 2005). By 2015 ASEAN, China, Japan, and South Korea, under the "ASEAN+3" agreement, will implement an open skies policy that will liberalize air transport services fully (Zhang 2009).

To compete for tourism with other cities, each city needs to improve its physical, social, and cultural environment significantly. The promotion of clean and green cities will benefit tourists and create a higher quality of life for local residents. In addition, it will mitigate environmental impacts on peri-urban and rural areas downstream. Many cities now allocate funds for clean and green cities programmes. The vision of Kuala Lumpur is to become a world class city by 2020. It is based on the concept of the sustainable city, which balances physical, economic, social, and environmental development. A key development strategy is to protect and enhance the environment by improving urban services for drainage, sewage, public transportation, solid waste management, and green spaces (Kuala Lumpur City Hall 2008).

However, in lower-income countries with limited resources, municipalities face a challenge in giving priority to investment for urban environmental improvement and development, including low-cost housing. Even Phnom Penh, which is significantly poorer than cities such as Kuala Lumpur and Bangkok, aims to develop a sustainable city with residents and visitors experiencing good quality water, soil, and air; and well-managed solid and liquid waste disposal. However, higher priority is being given to poverty reduction, security, and public order rather than to environmental initiatives (Phnom Penh Municipality 2010).

Tariff reduction under the ASEAN Free Trade Area (AFTA) should facilitate larger-scale, higher value-added production. While this would benefit urban areas and upgrade manufacturing, it may have a negative impact on low-cost labour. Lower tariff barriers will result in a realignment of winners and losers in the agricultural areas of ASEAN.

In some countries, local raw materials will not be able to compete with higher quality or more competitively priced raw materials, including agricultural produce, from neighbouring countries. The UNDP (2000) has expressed concern about the impacts of such trade liberalization and globalization, fearing that it could increase inequalities between metropolitan and rural regions, and between the rich and the poor. Without tariff barriers to imports and larger-scale export opportunities, low-cost, unskilled domestic labourers from rural areas in labour-intensive industries in peri-urban areas and secondary towns may lose their jobs, or earn less because of the new intra-ASEAN division of labour, including firm relocation.

This may lower remittances and cause an increase in rural poverty as factories in some peri-urban areas become uncompetitive, and the unemployed turn to the urban informal sector. In other areas, where industry is expanding, rural areas may experience different impacts, such as the loss of their agricultural land for urbanization and high-value industries, new towns, and industrial estates. The result may be low agricultural production. There are many examples of these trade-related dynamics affecting peri-urban and rural areas in ASEAN, creating winners and losers: Vietnam's manufacturing sector is growing quickly, creating new opportunities for rural workers, while Cambodia's garment industry has struggled with the opposite effects. The share of employment in manufacturing in Thailand has not increased since 1998, removing potential ladders of opportunities for rural workers.

CONCLUSIONS AND RECOMMENDATIONS FOR REGIONAL/ASEAN COOPERATION

Rural-urban and intra-urban linkages cannot be effectively promoted on the basis of separate management of development of urban and rural areas. The interrelation and inter-impacts between the two areas are strong, and increasingly made more complex through external regional and global forces acting on interrelated urban and rural systems, primarily through labour. The weakness of current rural-urban and intra-urban linkages discussed earlier call for a non-conventional, human-centred, and a non-urban-biased approach. More local benefits and a needs-oriented development approach should be considered for rural areas. With the limited economic power and marginal resources of rural areas, the cluster development of a subregional approach, such as the subregional products of OTOP, are more promising for improving rural-urban linkages.

Top Priorities for Better Integrating Rural-Urban and Peri-urban Areas Development

Promote cooperation and coordination

Areas of cooperation and coordination between local governments include land use, coordination of infrastructure investments to link urban and rural areas better (including roads, airports for low-cost airlines, affordable Internet infrastructure), and enhancing the responsibility of urban areas for environmental deterioration of rural areas, including clean-up when accidents occur.

Support human resource development and social welfare

To increase ASEAN economic competitiveness, key factors are skill development and improvements in social welfare. Although the quantitative gap in terms of education between rural and urban areas is narrowing in most ASEAN countries, there are still very wide quality gaps, which are perhaps increasing (for example, quality of teachers, access to high-speed Internet). As trade is liberalized and the economies, particularly the urban economies, of ASEAN countries grow, the lower quality of education in rural areas puts people at a disadvantage.

Government incentives and subsidies to skill development and improvements in social welfare should be carefully customized for rural areas. Often rural skill training does not look to the future or take into account opportunities in readily accessible urban and peri-urban areas, but train people for local economies that may be in decline. In addition, mechanisms need to be developed to facilitate the local registration of migrants to cities. This would help increase local government revenues and legitimize migrants' involvement in local government (Maneepong and Webster 2008).

Build the capacity of local government agencies and other stakeholders

Building capacity in local government agencies, non-governmental organizations, and community-based organizations should be a key element in supporting effective rural development and linkages with urban areas. Financial management and revenue generation should be targets of capacity building in the rural and peri-urban areas (Maneepong and Webster 2008). Key development sectors that should be the focus of local capacity building are local economic development, environmental management, local finance, information management, etc.

International private sector involvement

Multinational companies (MNCs) are a key driver of development in peri-urban areas. Private firms operating on a global scale need to become involved in local planning and management processes. These multinational firms have significant knowledge, access to technology (such as environmental technologies), as well as deep financial resources. As such, they should be invited to contribute to the development of peri-urban areas and share their experience and resources with local governments. In particular, the environmental and management skills of these firms could be useful. Often cooperation is in the interest of both parties, as MNCs do not want bad publicity resulting from their behaviour, but want local governments to deliver real services in return for the taxes they pay. Most contacts by MNCs with local governments is mediated by the industrial parks; or they deal directly with the national government on issues such as industrial incentives, taxation and tariffs, bypassing local governments (Maneepong and Webster 2008).

Latest communication technology

Over the last decade it has been increasingly recognized that accessible and affordable communications systems, serving both rural and urban populations, can be a powerful driver of social and economic change in ASEAN countries, and drive rural-urban linkages. In essence, infrastructure investment needs to shift from roads (which accounted for most of the hard rural development investment in the past in Southeast Asia) to communications infrastructure (Webster et al. 2003). The new norm is 3G broadband access. In Thailand Chulalongkorn University researchers indicate that the low-income population of Thailand can increase their incomes by 22 per cent by 2015 as a result of the financial and educational services they receive through 3G-enabled devices (Smith 2010).

Areas for Regional Cooperation

Facilitate labour mobility in ASEAN

ASEAN needs to come up with a mechanism to facilitate freer flows of accredited skilled labour. ASEAN can learn much from the European Union in this regard.

Clusters and networking of regional, subregional, and intercity cooperation

Various programmes to create intra-ASEAN learning networks, such as sister cities, clusters of ecotourism provinces, and cottage industries which are the mainstay of OTOP type activities, should be promoted to enhance economic collaboration, information exchange, sharing of good practices, and technology transfer. Regional universities and domestic institutes of higher education that are outward-looking can play a role in supporting such activities. The ASEAN University Network (AUN) is one such entry point.

Besides supporting formal business associations, governments should recognize informal networks formed by local stakeholders that enable the strengthening of information-pooling systems, enact rules, and design measurement devices that ensure uniformity of interpretation of such information and also narrow the scope for non-tariff barriers to trade (Parrilli 2007). Again, rural areas are often cut off from the advantages of intraregional economic integration because their products do not conform to region-wide standards. The fact that production units are smaller in rural areas makes it more difficult to standardize products from information and capital perspectives.

References

Arnold, D. "The Situation of Burmese Migrant Workers in Mae Sot, Thailand". Working Papers Series. No. 71. Hong Kong: City University of Hong Kong, 2004.

Asian Development Bank (ADB). *Workers' Remittance Flows in Southeast Asia*. Manila: ADB, 2006.

Asian Engineering Consultants Corp. Ltd & Pro En Consultants Co. Ltd. *Feasibility Study on Urban Infrastructure Development in Border Towns: Mae Sot Municipality, Tak Province* (in Thai). Public Works Department, Ministry of Interior, Bangkok, 1998.

BBC News. "Jakarta Bans Beggars and Buskers". <http://news.bbc.co.uk/go/pr/fr/-/2/hi/asia-pacific/6989211.stm> (accessed 9 September 2007).

Begg, I. "Cities and Competitiveness". *Urban Studies* 36, nos. 5–6 (1999): 759–809.

Bunjongjit, N. and Oudin, X. *Small-Scale Industries and Institutional Framework in Thailand*. Paris: Organization for Economic Cooperation and Development, Development Centre (Research programme on Governance and Entrepreneurship), 1992.

Chalamwong, Y. "Government Policies on International Migration: Illegal Workers in Thailand". In *International Migration in Southeast Asia*, edited by A. Ananta and E.N. Arifin. Singapore: Institute of Southeast Asian Studies, 2004.

Chen, M. A. "Rethinking the Informal Economy: Linkages with the Formal Economy and the Formal Regulatory Environment". DESA Working Paper No. 46, United Nations, Department of Economic and Social Affairs (DESA), 2007) <http://www.un.org/esa/desa/papers> (accessed 29 January 2009).

Clawen, A. "Female Labour Migration to Bangkok: Transforming Rural-Urban Interactions and Social Networks through Globalization". *Asia-Pacific Population Journal* 17, no. 3 (2002): 53–78.

Clement, N.C. "The Changing Economics of International Borders and Border Regions". In *Borders and Border Regions in Europe and North America*, edited by P. Ganster, A. Sweedler, J. Scott, and W.-D. Eberwein. San Diego: San Diego State University Press and Institute for Regional Studies of the Californias, 1997.

Cutarn, R.E. *Sustainable Local Development through One Town One Product (OTOP): The Case of Mindanao*. Japan: Graduate School of Policy Science, Ritsumeikan University, 2008.

Department of Industrial Works. *Factory Directory in Selected Border Towns From 1993 to 2008* (in Thai). Bangkok: Department of Industrial Works, 2009.

Department of International Development (DFID). "Non-Farm Income in Rural Areas". Key Sheets, No. 14, 2002.

Drakakis-Smith, D. "Third World Cities: Sustainable Urban Development 1". *Urban Studies* 32, nos. 4–5 (1995): 659–77.

Douglass, M. "A Reciprocal Network Strategy for Reciprocal Rural-Urban Linkages: An Agenda for Policy Research with References to Indonesia". *Third World Planning Review* 20, no. 1 (1998).

Faier, R. "Filipina Migrants in Japan Rural and Their Professions of Love". *American Ethnologist* 34, no. 1 (2007): 148–62.

Forsyth, T. "Shut Up or Shut Down: How a Thai Medical Agency was Closed After it Questioned Worker Safety at a Factory Owned by Thailand's Largest Employer". *Asia Inc.* (April 1994): 30–37.

Glassman, J. and Sneddon, C. "Chiang Mai and Khon Kaen as Growth Poles: Regional Industrial Development in Thailand and Its Implications for Urban

Sustainability". *The ANNALS of the American Academy of Political and Social Science* 590 (2003): 93–114.

Hapsari, I.M. and C. Mangunsong. *Determinants of AFTA Members' Trade Flows and Potential for Trade Diversion*. Asia-Pacific Research and Training Network on Trade Working Paper Series, No. 21, November 2006.

Henderson, V. *The Effects of Urban Concentration on Economic Growth*. Working Paper 7503. Cambridge: National Bureau of Economic Research, 2000.

Howard, R.W. "Khaosan Road: An Evolving Backpacker Tourist Enclave Being Partially Reclaimed by the Locals". *International Journal of Tourism Research* 7 (2005): 357–74.

Infineum. *What is REACH?* 2009 <http://www.infineum.com/pages/whatisreach.aspx> (accessed 28 February 2010).

International Development Centre of Japan, International, Pacific Consultants International, and KRI International. *The Study on the Integrated Regional Development Plan for the Northeastern Border Region in the Kingdom of Thailand and the Study on the Integrated Regional Development Plan for Savannakhet and Khammouan Region in the Lao P.D.R. (Final Report)*. Bangkok: Japan International Cooperation Agency, Committee for Planning and Cooperation, Lao PDR and Office of the National Economic and Social Development Board, the Kingdom of Thailand, 2001.

Lao National Tourism Administration. *Lao National Tourism Administration Ecotourism Strategy*. Vientiane: Lao National Tourism Administration, 2005.

Lazim, R.B. "Malaysia (1), Country Report". In *Rural Life Improvement in Asia*, edited by D.A. Cruz. Report of the APO Seminar on Rural Life Improvement for Community Development, held in Japan, 22–26 April 2002. Tokyo: Asian Productivity Organization, 2003.

Khai, N.Q. "Towards A Sustainable Rural Development Policy for Vietnam". Paper presented at the Conference on Sustainable Development in Vietnam, held at the Adele H. Stamp Student Union Bldg., University of Maryland, College Park, Maryland, 13 November 2003.

Krongkaew, M. "Income Distribution and Sustainable Economic Development in East Asia: A Comparative Analysis". Paper presented at the Annual Meeting of the East Asian Development Network (EADN), organized by the Singapore Institute of International Affairs (SIIA), in Singapore, 10–11 October 2003.

Krungthep Business News. "Academia Claim that Government Economic Policy is the Main Cause of the Problem of Illegal Migrant Workers". 2005. <http://board.dserver.org/m/midnightuniv>.

Kuala Lumpur City Hall. "Draft Kuala Lumpur 2010 City Plan" <http://klcityplan2020.dbkl.gov.my/eis/index.php?page_id=402> (accessed 24 February 2010).

Kudo, T. "Border Industry in Myanmar: Turning the Periphery into the Center of Growth". Institute of Developing Economies (IDE) Discussion Paper. Chiba: Japan External Trade Organization (JETRO), 2007.

Maneepong, C. "Dynamics of Industrial Development in Border Towns: Case Studies of Thailand". Unpublished PhD thesis, University of New South Wales, 2003.

———. "Rural and Urban Linkages". In *Development Economics* (an undergraduate textbook in Thai), edited by O. Srisaowaluk. School of Economics, Nonthaburi: Sukhothai Thammathirat Open University, 2004.

———. "Regional Policy Thinking and Industrial Development in Thai Border Towns". *Labour and Management in Development* 16, no. 4 (2006): 1–29.

———. "Is OTOP a New Local Economic Sector? A Case Study of Phra Nakhon Si Ayutthaya Province". Paper presented at Western Conference of the Association for Asian Studies (WCAAS), at University of Arizona, Tucson, AZ., the United States, 23–24 October 2009.

Maneepong, C. and D. Webster. "Governance Responses to Emerging Peri-Urbanization Issues at the Global–Local Nexus: Ayutthaya, Thailand". *International Development Planning Review* 30, no. 2 (2008): 133–54.

Maneepong, C. and C.T. Wu. "Comparative Borderland Development in Thailand". *ASEAN Economic Bulletin* 21, no. 2 (August 2004): 135–66.

Martin, P. "Thailand: Improving the Management of Foreign Workers". Paper presented at the National Tripartite Seminar on the Future of Migration Policy Management in Thailand, organized by ILO, IOM, and Ministry of Labour and Social Welfare, at the United Nations Conference Centre in Bangkok, 14–15 May 2002.

MEAs Intelligence Unit. "Kumphangsaen Goes for EU Exporting Market". *Thasethakit*, 2447, from 26–29 July 2009.

National Economic and Social Development Board. *The Seventh National Economic and Social Development Plan*. Bangkok: NESDB, 1982.

———. *Development Guidelines on Border Economy* (in Thai). Bangkok: NESDB, 1998.

———. "Gross Provincial Products [in Thai]" <http://www.nesdb.go.th> (accessed 2009).

Newman, P. "The Environmental Impact of Cities". *Environment & Urbanization* 18, no. 2 (2006): 275–95.

O' Connell, J.F. and G. William. "Passengers' Perceptions of Low Cost Airlines and Full Service Carriers: A Case Study Involving Ryanair, Aer Lingus, Air Asia and Malaysia Airlines". *Journal of Air Transport Management* 11 (2005): 259–72.

Paudyal, D.P. "From the Peasant Charter to the ICARRD: An Overview of the Current Trends and Emerging Issues in Rural Development in the Asia-Pacific Region". *Asia-Pacific Journal of Rural Development* 16, no. 1 (2006): 1–60.

Phnom Penh Municipality. "Vision and On-going projects" <http://www.phnompenh.gov.kh/english/message_governor.htm> (accessed 24 February 2010).

Polenske, K.R. "Growth Pole Theory and Strategy Reconsidered: Domination, Linkages, and Distribution". In *Regional Economic Development: Essays in*

Honour of Francois Perroux, edited by B. Higgins and D.J. Savoie. Boston: Unwin Hyman, 1988.

Parrilli, Mario Davide. *SME Cluster Development: A Dynamic View of Survival Cluster in Developing Countries*. Basingstoke: Palgrave Macmillan, 2007.

Provincial Chamber of Commerce of Tak. *Problems of Myanmar Migrant Labour in Tak Province from 1999 to 2000*, Vol. 2 (in Thai). Tak: Provincial Chamber of Commerce of Tak, 2000.

Rondinelli, D. *Decentralising Urban Development Programs, A Framework for Analyzing Policy*. Washington, DC: Office of Housing and Urban Programs, U.S. Agency of International Development, 1990.

Rondinelli, D. and G.S. Cheema. "Implementing Decentralization Policies: An Introduction". In *Decentralization and Development: Policy Implementation in Developing Countries*, edited by G.S. Cheema and D. Rondinelli. Thousand Oaks: Sage, 1983.

Ruddle, K. and D.A. Rondinelli. "Urban Functions in Rural Development: Integrating Spatial Systems for Equitable Growth". *Journal of Economic Development* 4, no. 1 (1979): 91–116.

Satien, S. *Chiang Mai Province and Its Emerging Development Problems*. Chiang Mai: Faculty of Economics, Chiang Mai University, 1992.

Sabran, D.S. "Malaysia (2), Country Report". In *Rural Life Improvement in Asia*, edited by D.A. Cruz. Report of the APO Seminar on Rural Life Improvement for Community Development, held in Japan, 22–26 April 2002. Tokyo: Asian Productivity Organization, 2003.

Smith, C.W. "Decision Time for Thailand's Communication Future". *Bangkok Post*, Telecommuncations, 27 July 2010, p. B2.

Song, H.S. *Language Policy in Korea for Immigrants through International Marriage*. Second Language Studies Department, University of Hawaii, 2006.

Tacoli, C. "The Role of Small and Intermediate Urban Centres and Market Towns and the Value of Regional Approaches to Rural Poverty Reduction Policy". Paper presented at the OECD DAC POVNET Agriculture and Pro-poor Growth Task Team Workshop, Helsinki, 17–18 June 2004.

———. "Linkages between Rural and Urban Development in Africa and Asia". Paper presented at the United Nations Expert Group Meeting on Population Distribution, Urbanization, Internal Migration and Development, at the Population Division, Department of Economic and Social Affairs, United Nations Secretariat, New York, 21–23 January 2008.

Thailand Development Research Institute (TDRI). *National Urban Development Policy Framework*. Bangkok: National Economic and Social Development Board, 1991.

Thant, M., M. Tang, and H. Kakazu. *Growth Triangles in Asia: A New Approach to Regional Economic Cooperation*, 2nd ed. New York: Oxford University Press, 1998.

van Grunsven, L., S.-Y. Wong, and W.B. Kim. "State, Investment and Territory: Regional Economic Zones and Emerging Industrial Landscapes". In *The Asian Pacific Rim and Globalization (Enterprise, governance and territoriality)*, edited by R. le Heron and S.O. Park. Avebury, Aldershot, 1995.

UBM Asia. "Renewable Energy Asia" 2010 <http://www.entechpollutec-asia.com/blue/index.php> (accessed 26 February 2006).

UNDP. *Rural-Urban Linkages: An Emerging Policy Priority*. New York: Bureau for Development Policy, UNDP, 2000.

Warr, P. "Agriculture in Thailand". In *Agriculture in Times of Crisis*, edited by G. Hooke, P. Warr, B. Shaw, A. Fforde, and C. Brassard. Canberra: Australian Agency for International Development, 1999.

Webster, D. *Achieving Sustainable Urbanization in the Ayutthaya Extended Urban Region: Issues and Possible Strategic Thrusts*. Manila: Planning for Sustainable Urbanization Project, Asian Development Bank, 2002.

Webster, D. and N. Tapananont. *Enhancing Rural-Urban Linkages in Thailand*. Manila: Planning for Sustainable Urbanization Project, Asian Development Bank, 2003.

Wu, C.-T. "Cross-border Development in Asia and Europe". *GeoJournal* 44, no. 3 (1998): 189–201.

Yap, K.S. "Promoting Productive, Inclusive and Sustainable Cities and Towns in Southeast Asia: Overview Paper". Paper presented at the 3rd CLC-ASC Regional Workshop on Urbanization in Southeast Asian Countries in Singapore, 1 July 2010.

Yimprasert, J.L. "The Life of Football Factory Workers in Thailand". Bangkok: Thailand Labour Campaign, 2006.

Zhang, A. *Low-Cost Carriers in Asia: Deregulation, Regional Liberalization and Secondary Airports*. Vancouver: School of Business, University of British Columbia, 2009.

Cities and the Environment

9

CLIMATE CHANGE AND SOUTHEAST ASIAN URBANIZATION
Mitigation and Adaptation Considerations

Victor R. Savage

Two major global processes dominating the twenty-first century are expanding urbanization and climate change. These combined events are likely to have colossal impacts on human activities globally and in Southeast Asia. Rapid urbanization has made cities the norm of human living worldwide. Globally the world's urban population lives in 408 cities of over one million people and twenty megacities of over ten million people; of the 408 cities, 377 cities are in the developing world, and Asia has 67 per cent (377 cities) of the global total (Flavin 2007, p. xxiii). Despite the fact that cities cover less than 1 per cent of the world's surface area, they accommodate over 50 per cent of the world's population, use 75 per cent of the world's energy, account for 78 per cent of carbon emissions, and are responsible for 75 per cent of greenhouse gases (Brown 2001, p. 188; World Wide Fund for Nature (WWF) 2009, p. 8).

There is a plethora of literature on global climate change which does not need repeating here (Flannery 2006; Dawson and Spannagle 2009; Touffut 2009; Posner and Weisbach 2010). Another endorsement of climate change is the recent idea of "planetary boundaries", which are meant to define "the safe operating space for humanity with respect to the Earth system and are associated with the planet's biophysical subsystems or processes" (Rockström et al. 2009, p. 472). Based on nine Earth-system processes (climate change, rate of biodiversity loss — terrestrial and marine — interference with the nitrogen and phosphorous cycles, stratospheric ozone depletion, ocean acidification, global freshwater use, change in land use, chemical pollution, and atmospheric aerosol loading), this study found that three of the nine Earth-system processes, namely climate change, rate of biodiversity loss, and interference with the nitrogen cycles, "have already transgressed their boundaries" (Rockström et al. 2009, p. 473). Given these twin issues, this chapter aims to assess the adaptive and mitigation challenges Southeast Asian cities face with respect to climate change. Specifically, the chapter explores the urban policy options regionally and nationally.

While the impact of climate change has clearly affected the whole Southeast Asian region (see Figure 9.1), its impact in urban areas can be viewed under two themes: (1) the direct impact of climate change on urban environments, which include typhoons and tropical cyclones, sea level rises, and heavy and sustained rainfalls; and (2) the indirect impact of climate change — essentially the impact of climate change affecting the contributing hinterlands of urban areas. Based on selected cities in the region, Table 9.1 demonstrates the varied impacts of climate change in specific cities. Not all cities are exposed to all the impacts of climate change, although Manila would seem the most vulnerable in the region. Both the direct and indirect (food and water security) impacts of climate change can also be seen as translations of the intra-urban and extra-urban impacts of climate change. When measuring the impact with respect to the city's population exposure, economic activities, and its national economic significance, Jakarta becomes the most climate change–sensitive city in the region, with Manila and Bangkok (all megacities) also having high sensitivity (see Table 9.2).

In dealing with the impacts of climate change on the urban environments in Southeast Asia, there are several blanket variables that need to be considered in terms of the impacts and adaptive issues:

Figure 9.1
Climate Change Vulnerability in Southeast Asia

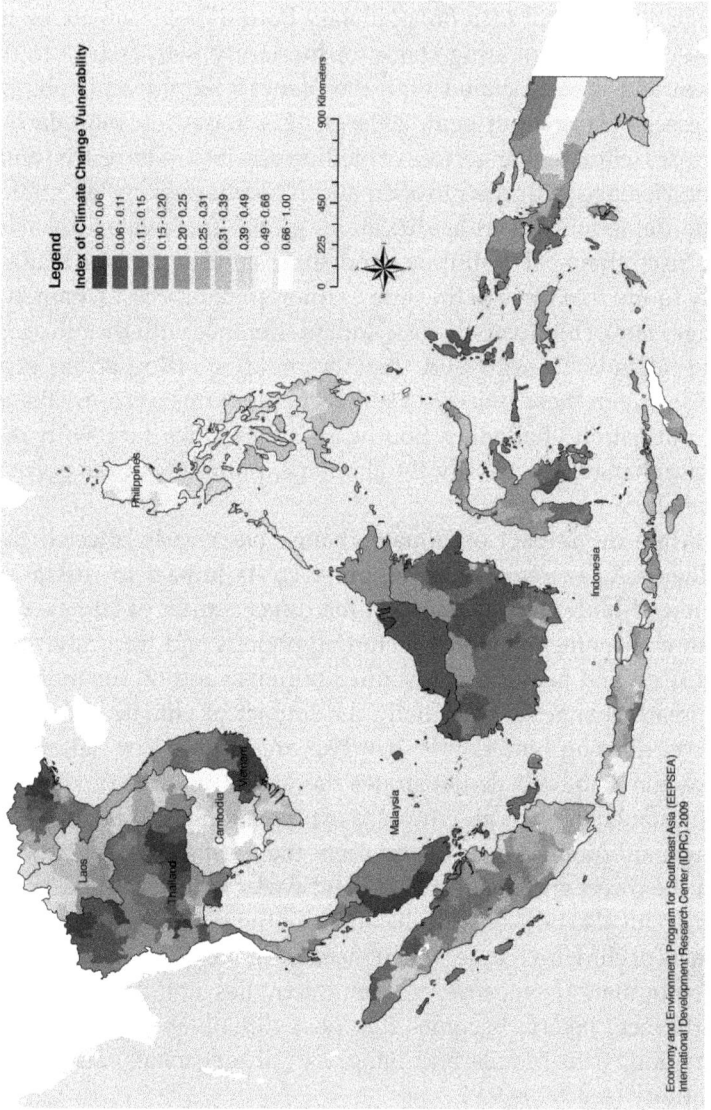

Source: International Development Research Centre, 2009, "Climate Matters in SEA", Economy and Environment Program for Southeast Asia.

Table 9.1
Impact of Climate Change on Selected Cities in Southeast Asia

City	Population (million)	Land area (km²)	Typhoons/ tropical cyclones	Floods	Water scarcity	Sea level rise	Food insecurity
Bandar Seri Begawan, Brunei Darussalam	27,000 Census: 2002	100.36		✓	✓	✓	
Bangkok, Thailand	11.97 Census: 2008	7,761		✓	✓	✓	✓
Ho Chi Minh City, Vietnam	7.1 Census: 2009	2,092	✓	✓	✓	✓	
Jakarta, Indonesia	8.792 Census: 2007	740.28		✓	✓	✓	✓
Kuala Lumpur, Malaysia	1.6 Census: 2009	243.65		✓	✓		
Manila, the Philippines	11.56 Census: 2007	638.55	✓	✓	✓	✓	✓
Phnom Penh, Cambodia	2.0 Census: 2009	290		✓	✓		✓
Singapore	4.9 Census: 2009	710			✓	✓	
Vientiane, Lao PDR	0.2 Census: 2005	not available		✓	✓		✓
Yangon, Myanmar	5.5 Census: 2009	598.75	✓	✓	✓	✓	✓

Table 9.2
Exposure and Sensitivity of Selected Cities in Southeast Asia to Climate Change Impacts

City	Exposure[1]	Sensitivity[2]
Jakarta	6	10
Manila	9	7
Phnom Penh	4	6
Ho Chi Minh	8	6
Bangkok	5	7
Kuala Lumpur	3	5
Singapore	4	6

Notes:
[1] Exposure here refers to city's exposure to typhoons, storm surges, droughts, floods.
[2] Sensitivity based on population, GDP, relative importance of urban economy to national economy.
Source: World Wide Fund for Nature: Mega-Stress for Mega Cities: A Climate Vulnerability Ranking of Major Coastal Cities in Asia, 2009, pp. 4–5.

(1) the demographic profile of countries and the degree of urbanization in the state; (2) the population sizes of cities/towns, which could range from 10,000 to one million, or five million to over ten million; (3) the rates of population growth in urban areas and the nature of the growth (natural increase, in-migration, or both); (4) the urban quality of life and living in cities (per capita incomes) and the poverty levels; and (5) the current state of urban infrastructure and proportion of residents benefiting from it. Based on varied criteria, the WWF has shown that various cities in the region are more vulnerable to climate change impacts than other cities. The most vulnerable are Jakarta and Manila and the least vulnerable are Kuala Lumpur and Singapore (see Table 9.3).

ADAPTATION AND MITIGATION

The common response to the challenges of climate change remains focused on two options: adaptation and mitigation, and both must go hand in hand as a system; "we need to do both, on a very large scale" (Stern 2009, p. 59).

In many ways Southeast Asian communities have a long tradition of coping with environmental hazards (droughts, earthquakes, floods) and

Table 9.3
Overall Vulnerability of Climate Change for
Selected Southeast Asian Cities

City	
Jakarta	8
Manila	8
Phnom Penh	7
Ho Chi Minh	6
Bangkok	5
Kuala Lumpur	4
Singapore	4

Source: World Wide Fund for Nature: Mega-Stress for
Mega Cities: A Climate Vulnerability Ranking of
Major Coastal Cities in Asia, 2009, p. 4.

thus over the centuries have developed adaptive mechanisms. Communities in the region have been so used to adjusting to natural hazards that such natural disasters are no more regarded as "abnormal situations but as quite the reverse, as a constant feature of life" (Bankoff 2007, p. 108). The opposite side of this thinking is that this prolonged history of adaptation to environmental hazards might lull the region's peoples and communities into having a resigned, fatalistic outlook, with little interest in believing that governments and communities need to prepare for an environmental catastrophe that cannot be handled at the local level alone. The onslaught of climate change–induced environmental challenges might however pose a more continuous series of problems that communities and governments might be less able to cope with, adapt to, or mitigate against, if early steps, plans, and policies are not currently worked out.

Mitigation Challenges: What Can Southeast Asian States Do?

Mitigation is defined as "human actions that prevent greenhouse gases from entering the atmosphere or to actions that remove greenhouse gases from the atmosphere" (Dawson and Spannagle 2009, p. 278). Mitigation is about cutting back greenhouse gas emissions or what Brand (2009, p. 12) calls "avoiding the unmanageable". While mitigation is a long-term solution to reducing global warming, it can mainly be addressed by countries with technological prowess, a strong research and development culture, and well-established climate research centres. To put it starkly, Brand (2009,

p. 20) argues that no amount of environmentally green grass-roots groups will meet the climate change challenge; it requires government intervention.

Thus one can conclude that developing countries are unable to deal with mitigation issues because stabilizing CO_2 rates at 450 ppm or 550 ppm are issues too large financially and technically complex. Based on the equation that 11 tonnes of carbon dioxide equals 3 tonnes of carbon, the global emission of carbon dioxide in 2025 will exceed 38 billion tonnes, or over 10 billion tonnes of carbon (Romm 2007, p. 62). Over the last few decades, 60 per cent of carbon dioxide remained in the atmosphere while the other 40 per cent was absorbed by several "sinks" — the ocean, soils, and vegetation, which essentially means these sinks remove carbon from the global ecosystem. In Southeast Asia, the only significant global contributor to carbon dioxide is Indonesia, and it lies with her forests. Other less significant contributors are countries involved in the oil industry, oil refining, and petrochemical industries: Brunei, Singapore, Malaysia, and Indonesia and, probably, Myanmar; Timor Leste and the Philippines could be added to this list.

Given the rising oil prices and dwindling reserves, many Southeast Asian countries will be forced to look at alternative energy sources because they will have few options available. The prospects for alternative energy are mixed, and with the poverty in the region, firewood and charcoal remain important energy sources for the poor. Countries in the region are certainly investing in non-fossil fuels and alternative energy sources. The region is the biggest contributor to biofuels and synfuels based on oil palm (Indonesia, Malaysia, and Thailand) and jatropa (see Table 9.4). Many ASEAN countries are even considering nuclear energy to supplement their energy demands. Indonesia has indicated building a nuclear energy plant in Sulawesi (Gorontalo); Thailand is projecting one by 2021; Vietnam plans to build its first nuclear plant by 2020 (Caballero-Anthony and Sofiah 2009, p. 58); and Malaysia announced in May 2010 its intention to go nuclear as well by 2020. The worry for any nuclear plant is disposing its waste, the dangers of leakages due to a lack of safety standards, economic viability, corruption, and problems arising from natural disasters.

The important winner of the Copenhagen conference and dialogue was not any country or bloc of countries, but rather the forests. The tropical forest serves as a carbon sink which absorbs a billion tonnes of carbon annually (Romm 2007, p. 71) and the importance of conserving tropical forests will be a major step in mitigating climate change for tropical developing countries. Southeast Asia has 203 million hectares of forestlands,

Table 9.4
Biofuels Policies in Selected Southeast Asian Countries

Country	Targets for 1st-Generation Biofuels and Plans for 2nd-Generation Biofuels	Economic Measures
Indonesia	Domestic biofuels utilization: 2% of energy mix by 2010, 3% by 2010, and 5% by 2025	Diesel: subsidies (at the same level as fossil fuels)
Malaysia	No target identified. Promotion of jatropha, nipa, etc.	Diesel: plans to subsidize prices for blended diesel
Philippines	No target identified. Studies and pilot projects for jatropha	Ethanol and diesel: tax exemptions and priority in financing
Thailand	Plan to replace 20% of vehicle fuel consumption with biofuels and natural gas by 2012. Utilization of cassava	Ethanol: price incentives through tax exemptions

Source: Yan, J. and T. Lin (2009) "Biofuels in Asia", Applied Energy (86): S1–S10.

representing 5.1 per cent of the world's total forest (ADB 2009, p. 107). It would seem that the developed countries have finally bought former Malaysian Prime Minister Dr Mahathir's economic views on forests (Tay 2009) through the establishment of the UN-sponsored scheme, Reducing Emissions from Deforestation and Degradation (REDD), in developing countries. Under REDD the developed world's governments and investors would pay developing countries not to cut down forests, thereby offering developing countries an alternative source of income (ADB 2009, p. 130). Given that in Indonesia, the Philippines, Thailand, and Vietnam, 75 per cent of greenhouse gases are emitted due to deforestation, the conservation of forests will be instrumental in reducing carbon emissions from these countries. The translation of the REDD programme in Southeast Asia is interesting because it has involved indigenous peoples' rights and use of forest resources. In November 2008, the Southeast Asia Indigenous Peoples Regional Consultation on REDD was launched, with indigenous peoples from Myanmar, Cambodia, Indonesia, Malaysia, the Philippines, Thailand, and Vietnam involved (ADB 2009, p. 130).

Adaptation: National and Regional Perspectives

Dawson and Spannagle (2009, p. 1) define adaptation as a reference "to all responses, adjustments or actions by humans and natural systems to accommodate and/or reduce their vulnerability to the impacts of climate change". Or put in simple terms, it means "managing the unavoidable" (Brand 2009, p. 12). As it stands, the United Nations Framework Convention on Climate Change (UNFCCC) in 2007 revised the costs of adaptation upwards: by 2030 the annual costs of climate adaptation would be between US$49 billion and US$171 billion (Anjali 2009). The challenge for Southeast Asian countries preparing for adaptation measures is the hope for better, scientific-quality precision projections, both spatially and temporally in climate change impacts: say from several hundred kilometres to just tens of kilometres, and from a timescale of centuries to a decade or less (Heffernan 2010, p. 860). The IPCC 2007 Report alludes to high-resolution (50 km) circulation models, which is a marked improvement from the first-generation general circulation models (Armatte 2009, p. 68).

In my view, adaptation comes in four ways: (1) recognition of the magnitude, extent, scale, and speed of climate change impacts on cities; (2) radical change in lifestyle, living standards, and methods of livelihood; (3) economic changes and the technological ramifications; (4) the infrastructural adjustments in designing ecocities and the relational issues between cities, their hinterlands, and their ecological footprints. The urban adaptations to climate change vary from the individual household response to government macro-adaptive mechanisms and processes and reflect both an immediate reactive to more long-term anticipatory responses (see Table 9.7).

Given the poverty of many countries in the region and the still unclear impacts of climate change for urban areas specifically, governments in the region seem unlikely to take on proactive adaptive mechanisms. The WWF report on climate change in Asia clearly demonstrates that different cities in the region have varied capacities for coping with, and adapting to, climate change impacts (see Table 9.5). The richer cities with better infrastructure and good governance such as Singapore, Kuala Lumpur, and Ho Chi Minh City, have better adaptive capacities than cities such as Phnom Penh, Jakarta, and Manila (see Table 9.5). There are other features that one can identify with respect to adaptation, such as: (1) it takes place at the local and regional levels; (2) is concerned with the human-societal aspects of climate change impacts and not the scientific issues of greenhouse gas emissions; (3) is about prevention of climate change impacts, but not a cure to global warming or the stabilization and reduction of greenhouse gases.

The rather bleak record of national policies on adaptation preparation on climate change speaks for itself: it demonstrates either that governments

Table 9.5
Inverse Adaptive Capacity in
Selected Southeast Asian Cities

City	
Jakarta	7
Manila	7
Phnom Penh	10
Ho Chi Minh	3
Bangkok	4
Kuala Lumpur	3
Singapore	1

Source: World Wide Fund for Nature: Mega-Stress for
Mega Cities: A Climate Vulnerability Ranking of
Major Coastal Cities in Asia, 2009, p. 5.

in Southeast Asia are unperturbed about climate change, or that the governments are ignorant about the extent and impacts of climate change on society (see Table 9.6). Furthermore, Yuen and Kong (2009, p. 8) note that none of the twenty-eight planning schools in Southeast Asia offers a teaching course in climate change. These examples demonstrate that the region is far from prepared in handling climate change adaptive responses.

Despite all the different classifications of climate change adaptive responses, this chapter would like to advocate four major adaptive responses for Southeast Asian governments to consider seriously in tackling the impact of climate change on its urban environments. These are: (1) technological adaptive mechanisms; (2) behavioural adaptive mechanisms, such as changes in our food, recreational choices and, more important, our change in civic and public responsive behaviour; (3) managerial adaptive systems with regard to changing crop patterns or the choice of crops in agricultural systems; and (4) policy issues in adaptation, such as initiating new planning regulations with regard to lower energy building technologies.

Technological and technical eco-friendly adaptations

The history of human development in the region has also been a study of the history of ingenious forms of human adaptations to varied environmental

Table 9.6
Coverage on Adaptation Policies and Measures in the National Communication Documents of Selected Southeast Asian Countries

Country	Total No. of Pages	No. of Pages on Impacts and Vulnerability	No. of Pages on Adaptation
Cambodia	63	10	2
Indonesia	116	10	3
Lao PDR	97	2 lines	1 line
Malaysia	131	30	7
Singapore	75	5	1 line
Thailand	100	15	2.5
Philippines	107	20	12
Vietnam	135	17	4

Source: Francisco, Herminia (2008) "The economics of and institutions for adaptation to climate change impacts: A regional outlook for Southeast Asia", Institute of Southeast Asian Studies Regional Outlook Forum, Session III, "The Economics of Environmental Disaster: The Socio-Cultural Impact", Singapore: Institute of Southeast Asian Studies.

challenges through folk technology and indigenous techniques. When industrialization created vast negative environmental problems, some environmentalists introduced the concept of "industrial ecology", defined by industrial ecologist Graedel as "to enable technology to provide the goods and services that people want and need without depleting resources and without generating impacts on the planet more severe than the planet can accommodate" (Stoll 2008, p. 157).

However, others have noted its limitations as seen in the huge use of energy for recycling materials that could be costly, and have pointed out that industrial ecology "won't save growth" (Stoll 2008, p. 159). In some areas, such as "green architecture", the recycling of waste can be of benefit. The fifteen-storey IBM building in Kuala Lumpur by Yeang is an example of how vegetation planted on the exterior of the building captures water and helps reduce energy needed for air conditioning (Lee 2007, p. 19). What we need now is another industrial revolution of green technology (green cars, air conditioning, office and home appliances, etc.) to boost economies in a sustainable manner.

Given that cities are relatively small spatial entities, they do not attract much scientific attention in the new climate scenarios because global climate change tends to cover larger spatial areas with extensive climatic impacts. One wonders how urban areas will feature in the more sophisticated integrated earth system models that will combine three models: integrated assessment models, climate models, and impact models (Moss et al. 2010, p. 754). The future research on climate change towards "regional-scale climate scenarios and projection methods, especially for impact and adaptation assessment" (see Moss et al. 2010, p. 749), and the projections for future models towards "higher spatial and temporal resolution and improved representation of extreme events" (Moss et al. 2010, p. 750) augur well for the region and urban locations. It is for national governments to utilize the new technologies for their urban populations and translate domestically the new methods to handle specific adaptive measures for their urban environments.

In many Southeast Asian cities, there is a wide disparity of wealth between the squatters and slum dwellers on the one hand and the nouveau riche living in gated communities on the other. The urban poor require infrastructural support in order to adapt to climate change. In Thailand the Community Organizations Development Institute (CODI) launched a huge campaign in 2003 to develop good housing, infrastructure, and secure land tenure for 300,000 households in 2,000 poor communities in 200 Thai cities within five years. By September 2006, 450 community upgrading projects were under way, covering 750 communities in 170 towns and cities, involving more than 45,500 households (Perlman and Sheehan 2007, p. 180). In 2006 UN-HABITAT found that Thailand was on track to meet the Millennium Development Goal of improving the lives of slum dwellers; their numbers had fallen 18.8 per cent a year (Perlman and Sheehan 2007, p. 180). Singapore is another good example of how slum and squatter settlements were replaced with public housing, which in turn created a clean and green city (Savage 2010, pp. 225–29).

Given the general prognosis that climate change is likely to increase precipitation in equatorial regions and drought conditions in other tropical areas (Flannery 2006), Southeast Asian governments need to put the right infrastructure in place in cities to ensure that their urban populations are safeguarded against such extreme climatic conditions. In equatorial situated Singapore, the recent deluge of rainfall on two occasions in July 2010 led to major floods in prime residential areas and the city state's iconic retail highway, Orchard Road — with high economic losses to people and businesses, and an embarrassment to the government.

The lessons for Singapore and other high rainfall–prone cities in the region is that the city's water drainage system must be large enough to handle increasing intense periods of high precipitation or else cities in future are likely to face devastating urban floods that will cripple urban economies, incur major economic losses, and worse still, lead to human casualties. Unlike rural and natural landscapes where rainfall is absorbed by the soil bed and vegetation, in urban built-up areas, rainfall run-off is magnified and intensified because it is collected over large built-up areas and then funnelled into urban drains.

As climate change intensifies in the next two decades, the environmental impacts are likely to be greater because the gestation intervals between major typhoons and heavy downpours are likely to be shortened and many cities will be unable to cope with constant and intense precipitation or typhoons. Governments in Southeast Asia must realize the enormous benefits in spending money on flood management — the Kyoto example shows that a dollar spent on flood management will mitigate flooding 1,300 times better than a dollar spent on Kyoto city per se (Lombørg 2008, p. 86).

The lack of water is one of three major climate change issues for the twenty-first century. The 2009–10 drought in mainland Southeast Asia and the Philippines has led governments to try an array of adaptive systems, such as constructing more water wells, purchasing thousands of irrigation pumps, and employing cloud seeding operations in the hardest hit northern provinces.

Desalination seems to be a growing industry in arresting water deficiency in countries and cities. The International Desalination Association states that there are now 12,300 desalination plants operating in 155 countries, with a collective capacity to produce 47 million cubic metres of water a day (Barlow 2008, p. 26). Saudi Arabia has 2,000 desalination plants accounting for one quarter of the world's desalinated water production (Barlow 2008, p. 26), but such high energy methods for producing drinkable water are only affordable to oil-rich countries. Despite its high energy consumption, global desalination is likely to grow 25 per cent annually (Barlow 2008, p. 27).

Yet Barlow (2008, pp. 27–28) severely questions whether desalination is the answer to quenching the thirst of global populations. She lists three major impediments in desalination processes: (1) the high energy use is a burden to local power grids (no problem for oil-producing countries such as Saudi Arabia); (2) the plants generate lethal by-products of brine mixed with chemicals and heavy metals, and, to prevent salt erosion, for every litre of desalted water, a litre of poison is pumped back into the sea (current desalination plants worldwide produce 20 billion litres of waste daily [Barlow 2008, p. 27]); (3) water fed into the desalination plants may contain contaminants (viruses, bacteria, algal toxins, shellfish poisons) that are not filtered out by the reverse osmosis process. Since developing countries discharge 90 per cent of their waste into the sea, it is not hard to imagine the quality of water used in desalination plants (Barlow 2008, p. 28).

Besides desalination, there are indeed lessons which other Southeast Asian states can learn from the Singapore management of water resources. Given Singapore's dependence on water imports from Malaysia (Johor) and the rather turbulent political relations with Malaysia, especially during the Mahathir years, the Singapore Government must have seen that there was political and economic necessity to try and provide better water security for the city state. Hence over the last four decades, the Ministry of Environment and Water Resources (MEWR), the Public Utilities Board (PUB), and the universities (the National University of Singapore and Nanyang Technological University) have invested huge financial resources and human expertise in various water conversion, conservation, and generating systems: desalinisation, water capture (storing run-off water from roads), recycling (NEWater), increasing reservoir capacities (Singapore River barrage), water conservation programmes (price controls), expanding the water catchment area to over 50 per cent of the city state land area, and underground water storage systems. Specifically, the recycling of water (NEWater) currently provides 15 per cent of consumption needs and will have covered 30 per cent by 2011 (ADB 2009, p. 100; WWF 2009, p. 32).

The city state is becoming a "global hydrohub" and magnet for water technology companies and exporting private sector water experts and technology worldwide. The government is also making huge investments in R & D in water technology — for example, the Environment and Water Industry Development Council in February 2007 announced setting aside US$330 million to fund world-class water research and train researchers in water solutions for the private sector (Barlow 2008, p. 72). Due to the government's financial support and user-friendly environment for water R & D, many companies are using the city state as their test bed for water technologies. Major companies relocating in Singapore are the

American engineering and consulting company, Black & Veatch, and the German company, Siemens Water Technologies. Singapore water treatment companies have also mushroomed, such as Sembcorp, Dayen, Darco, EcoWater, Salcon, and Hyflux, which developed Singapore's recycled water, NEWater, the technology of which is being exported to Australia, India, Thailand, the Middle East, and China (Barlow 2008, p. 73).

Singapore has certainly been able to reduce its water footprint considerably and it seems confident that by 2061 (the end date of the last water agreement for Malaysian water supplies), it will be self-sufficient in water. One important contribution to the island state's water self-sufficiency is its recycling water system. Senior Minister Goh Chok Tong proudly announced in May 2010 that by 2020 reclaimed water will meet 40 per cent of Singapore's water needs, up from the current 30 per cent (122 million gallons a day) it contributes (Chew 2010, p. 1). By 2020 Singapore will have five NEWater plants in Changi, Ulu Pandan, Kranji, Seletar, and Bedok, producing some 197 million gallons a day (Chew 2010, p. 1). Clearly water technologies are one promising area of green technology and green business for the Southeast Asian region. Singapore's desalinization project through reverse osmosis on seawater produces 136 million litres of water a day (ADB 2009, p. 100; WWF 2009, p. 32). This concern with water has also rubbed off on to the private sector and hence Singapore has some successful private sector companies engaged in water systems, the most well known of which are Hyflux and Sembcorp, which are involved in water systems in the Middle East, North Africa, and China (Zhangjiagang in Jiangsu Province). Globally the water market is said to be US$400 billion annually, but Maude Barlow (2008, pp. 90–91) estimates that when one adds up all the types of water companies (from domestic bottled water to high-tech water systems) involved, one can conservatively say it is a trillion-dollar industry annually.

Many capital cities in Southeast Asia, due to their coastal location, face the full brunt of sea level rises. Singapore as an island city state is the most vulnerable. Over the decades, the Singapore Government has been expanding the republic's land area through costly land reclamation schemes — with over 20 per cent of the state's land area now reflecting reclaimed land. With sea water rises expected this century to be between 0.5 to 1.5 metres (Dawson and Spannagle 2009, p. 106), the reclaimed land in Singapore is now likely to be threatened. Recent studies indicate that the costs of protecting Singapore's coast will be between US$0.3m to

US$5.7m by 2050, and US$0.9m and US$16.8m by 2100. The city state has
a few options, including building sea walls, sea dykes like in Holland, or
erecting other coastal hard and soft defence systems against coastal erosion,
storm surges, and higher water levels. There are a whole range of adaptive
strategies available for cities in coastal areas to adopt in combating rising
sea levels (see Table 9.7).

Behavioural adaptive mechanisms

Reduction of energy and water consumption, which is necessary in adapting
to climate change, can only be done if individuals and families take steps to
change their domestic consumption behaviour patterns. But with modern
living and the array of modern appliances, the domestic consumption
of energy is increasing. Because of the increasing heat waves and hotter
climates, air conditioning in the region is becoming pervasive at home, in
the workplace, and for recreational activities. Affluent cities such as Bandar
Seri Begawan, Kuala Lumpur, Bangkok, Jakarta, Ho Chi Minh City, and
Singapore, are likely to see increasing domestic consumerism, energy usage,
and CO_2 emissions, which are likely to add to global warming.

Without behavioural changes it would be difficult to tackle climate
change impacts on urban areas. Certainly the idea that environmental issues
can only be solved at the macro governmental levels need changing and

Table 9.7
Technologies for Adaptation in Coastal Zones

Protection	Retreat	Accommodation
Hard Structures: dykes, sea-walls, tidal barriers, breakwaters	Establishing set-back zones Relocating threatened buildings	Early warning and evacuation systems
Soft Structures: dunes or wetland restoration, beach nourishment	Phasing out development in exposed areas	New agricultural practices New building codes
Indigenous Options: walls of wood, stone, afforestation	Creating upland barriers Rolling easements	Improved drainage Desalination system

Source: UNFCC (2006).

revising. One pertinent example of how public behaviour can contribute to producing environmental friendly urban systems is Japan. Anyone visiting Tokyo, a city of twenty-six million people, will be amazed at the civic behaviour of Tokyo residents in keeping their city clean — everyone dutifully uses recycle bins for their litter, and no one litters. Southeast Asia's urban governments need to engage in public education to inculcate responsible environmental civic behaviour because no amount of money, technology, and draconian laws can be as effective in maintaining and sustaining urban environments and reducing carbon emissions.

Of all the countries in the region, Singapore is perhaps the archetypal example of a country with a government constantly trying to develop civic responsibility and engineer public behaviour through strict laws, effective legal enforcements, and periodic public campaigns, to the point that it has become known as the "nanny state" (Lee 2000, p. 211). The general economic argument, however, for changing environmental behaviour is to allow states to go through the economic development life cycle. Proponents of this argument view economic growth as good for the environment. They assert that the empirical evidence of improvements in the quality of life in economically driven, capitalistic, developed countries over the last two decades shows that when services overtake manufacturing, environmental improvements take place. These "environmental contrarians" argue that environmental problems will be solved with more development based on three primary assertions: (1) the environment in Western countries is in better shape than it was decades ago; (2) environmental regulation costs more than it is worth; (3) continued growth, free markets, and technological progress will solve the remaining problems (see Ayres 1999, pp. 139–41). Once societies reach the developed status, they become post-material and post-modern societies, and automatically green behaviour and environmental consciousness take over. But unfortunately this post-material argument has not stopped the United States, Europe, Australia, and Japan from still maintaining high energy consumption levels and adding to carbon dioxide emissions. The recent subprime crisis in the United States and the current national debt crisis in Europe have also undermined confidence in the capitalistic-driven economic development trajectories of current developed countries.

There is growing literature on how environmental-friendly behaviour exists amongst many tribal and indigenous communities, and since the region still has many of these communities, governments could tap into these cultural traditions (Eisler 2008). In analysing Asian traditional thought and Buddhism, Peterson (2001) contends that the secret of indigenous sustainable living lies in the "relational self" where everything is "interdependent and relative". The question is whether such indigenous, environmental-friendly behaviour can be translated to modern urban communities. For McCallum (2008), communities need to develop "ecological intelligence" that would govern their behaviour. All these views require radical changes in our mindset, behaviour, economic systems, and societal obligations.

Ultimately when people cannot make specific adaptations within their locale, they choose to migrate: environmental and climate change refugees are likely to grow in numbers in the decades ahead and are likely to drift into cities (see Table 9.8). The tragedy is that cities have become the focus of environmental refugees. ASEAN needs to develop regional social and political capital amongst its urban communities and states to ensure greater interactions between peoples and communities, not only for resource governance, but increasingly for climate change management and adaptation. The regional social capital was clearly underscored when Vietnam and Thailand came to the aid of the Philippines during the rice crisis in 2008. Thus the environment and space Southeast Asians operate in has to move from dominance to partnership, from confrontation to dialogue, and from assertiveness to cooperation. As we become an urban species, we need to ensure that we are able to coexist with the natural ecosystems; indeed the urban and nature relationship has become more symbiotic.

Table 9.8
Types of Human Systems' Adaptation to Climate Change

Sector	Reactive	Anticipatory
Private	Moving home Changing insurance premiums Buying air conditioning systems	Changing architecture of buildings Buying hazard insurance Devising new customer products
Public	Offering compensation or subsidies Enforcing building codes Beach nourishment	Installing early warning systems Establishing new building codes Constructing dykes

Source: UNFCC (2006).

The Millennium Ecosystem Assessment (2005, p. vii) begins its report by underscoring the importance of the diversity of dynamic ecosystems around the world and emphasizing that peoples are "integral parts" of ecosystems, driving change in ecosystems which in turn cause "changes in human well-being". The assessment lists ten ecosystem types, including the "urban", and eight major services that ecosystems provide to human communities (Millennium Ecosystem Assessment 2005, p. ix) (see Table 9.9). The better prepared governments and ASEAN are meeting climate change challenges, the more effective the region will be in adapting to changing environmental scenarios and natural hazards in the near future. The key operative management system for the region is for grass roots "dialogue" and governmental "cooperation" based on a regional "common-pool" resource ideology.

Managerial adaptive systems

The IPCC 2007 Report notes that the tackling of impacts of, and responses to, climate change should not be seen as a problem of knowledge, but rather as a problem of management and decision making (Armatte 2009, p. 68). Self-reliance and developing regional resilience should be the first proactive steps needed to combat the region's climate change challenges. As Lovelock (2009, p. 91) prescribes, "Gaia, like God, helps those who help themselves". National governments and ASEAN need to be in the driver's seat of their own national and regional destinies and not wait or rely solely on international aid and capacity building assistance.

The economic damage of flooding from sea level rises can be enormous, especially for cities that have more tangible wealth, more goods, and better infrastructure. The recent example of Katrina on New Orleans is a case in point: the city suffered major economic losses put at between US$81 billion (Lombørg 2008, p. 76) and more than US$100 billion (Romm 2007, p. 28). Yet, in poor Cuba, the proactive evacuation system led to zero deaths when Katrina hit the island, thereby demonstrating the importance of good managerial systems. In the Southeast Asian region, the poor system for managing hazards in Myanmar led to enormous human casualties (140,000 people killed) arising from Cyclone Nargis.

Interestingly, one of the important lessons that governments and researchers learnt from the devastating 2004 Indian Ocean Tsunami was the importance of natural coastal ecosystems; those areas with natural

Table 9.9
Global Assessment of Ecosystem Types in Selected Southeast Asian Areas

Ecosystem Types	Sub-Global Assessment					
	Tropical Forest Margins (Central Sumatra; Tenasserim Coast, Myanmar)	Papua New Guinea	Laguna Lake Basin, Philippines	Downstream Mekong Wetlands, Vietnam	Arafura and Timor Seas	Indonesia
Coastal		✓		✓	✓	✓
Cultivated	✓	✓	✓	✓		
Forest			✓	✓		
Inland Water			✓			
Island		✓			✓	✓
Marine		✓			✓	✓
GLOBAL ASSESSMENT OF ECOSYSTEM SERVICES IN SELECTED SOUTHEAST ASIAN AREAS						
Food	✓	✓	✓	✓	✓	✓
Water	✓	✓	✓	✓	✓	✓
Fuel and Energy		✓	✓	✓		
Biodiversity-related	✓	✓	✓	✓	✓	
Carbon Sequestration	✓	✓	✓	✓		
Fibre and Timber	✓	✓		✓		
Run-off Regulation	✓	✓		✓		
Cultural Spiritual Amenity		✓	✓	✓		
Others	✓	✓		✓	✓	

Source: Millennium Ecosystem Assessment (2005) Our Human Planet: Summary for Decision Makers. Washington: Island Press, pp. vii–x.

coastal ecosystems were least damaged by the tsunami. The purpose of preserving natural coastal ecosystems is to let these serve as buffers against coastal erosion and to minimize wave energy action from storm surges. Cities in the region will need to prepare themselves for sea level rises and increasing floods. According to Lomborg's (2008, p. 69) estimate, 180 of the world's 192 nations will spend less than 0.1 per cent of GDP on coastal protection for sea level rises.

Specifically, the restoration of mangrove forests has been a key adaptive feature for coastal cities such as Bangkok, Manila, and Jakarta. However, mangrove forest restoration is not an easily implementable matter because such coastal forest areas have been replaced by economically lucrative prawn farms and aquaculture in coastal areas surrounding Ho Chi Minh City, Bangkok, Jakarta, Singapore, and Manila. Martinez-Alier (2005) provides case studies of how governments in Thailand, Indonesia, the Philippines, and Malaysia have awarded private concessions to lucrative shrimp farming, leading to the eradication of swamp forest despite laws protecting valuable mangrove ecosystems. The rapid development of shrimp farms has led to mangrove forest in Thailand shrinking from 370,000 hectares in 1961, to 170,000 hectares by 1996 (Fahn 2004, p. 178). In Bang Khunthian, Bangkok's only seaside district, over 483 hectares of mangrove have been removed over the last thirty years (Asian Development Bank 2009, p. 26). In the Philippines, aquaculture was responsible of clearing 388,000 hectares of mangrove forests since 1968, and in Malaysia, 20 per cent of available mangroves were slated for aquaculture development (Martinez-Alier 2005, p. 86). Governments in the region must decide whether shrimp farming is more important — for economic development — or whether mangroves are more valuable as they preserve coastal ecosystems, maintain local cultures, and provide a defence for storm surges.

The Food and Agriculture Organization (FAO) predicts climate change will affect the availability, variability, and annual distribution of freshwater resources. As agriculture uses about 70 per cent of all water withdrawal, the FAO has cautioned that water scarcity will significantly affect agriculture, inland fisheries, and aquaculture, thus causing food insecurity. If lack of food security and water resources are major negative outcomes of climate change, in the near future, governments in the region might be able to focus on adaptive mechanisms to avert such problems in the short term. Globally the 2007–8 food crisis caused riots in more than sixty countries and set off land grabbing in Africa and Southeast Asia.

Several governments around the world have taken steps to secure more reliable food supplies by leasing, renting, and buying farm areas in food producing countries (see Table 9.10). Food dependent countries such as Singapore, the Philippines, and Brunei have made and are making pacts with food exporting countries such as Thailand and Vietnam to secure food supplies. The regional umbrella of ASEAN has certainly helped to ensure that intra-ASEAN food security amongst states is predicated on regional cooperation.

Table 9.10
Countries Making Farm Deals for Food Security

Country	Farm Deals from other Food Producing Countries
China	Leasing land from Australia, Brazil, Burma, Russia, and Uganda
India	Croplands in Paraguay and Uruguay
Libya	Leasing 250,000 acres in Ukraine for oil
Saudi Arabia	Looking for farmland in Egypt, Pakistan, South Africa, Sudan, Thailand, Turkey, and Ukraine
South Korea	Land deals in Madagascar, Russia, and Sudan

Source: Brown, Lester R. (2009) "Could Food Shortages Bring Down Civilization?" Scientific American, May, 300(5):44.

Climate change this century will provide pluses and minuses for agricultural production around the world. Decades ago there was recognition that climate change would change the geography of world food suppliers and industrial activities (Idso 1974; Cooper 1978). In his thought-provoking article in Foreign Affairs, Cooper (1978) argued that climate change and global warming would improve current marginal crop production areas in even subarctic regions and make them productive agricultural areas by lengthening the growing season with a one degree Celsius increase in temperature. The net result would be that the Soviet Union (Russia), Canada, Alaska, and the Scandinavian countries reap benefits in agricultural production (Cooper 1978, p. 505).

Climate change is already affecting rainfall patterns in the region, with impacts on national agricultural production. The 2009–10 drought in the

Philippines has damaged or destroyed nearly 162,000 hectares or 400,000 acres of farmland, costing farmers an estimated 2.84 billion pesos or US$61 million (Conde 2010, p. 3). Despite careful water controls, the Philippine Government had no choice but to import 2.2 million tonnes of rice due to the 2010 drought. At the urban level, the Angat dam, which supplies water for both farms and 97 per cent of Metro Manila's potable water needs, is being reserved for urban use (Olchondra 2010, p. A3).

At the regional level, in 1980 ASEAN put in place the ASEAN Food Security Reserve Board (AFSRB), which manages emergency rice reserves and provides food security for member countries. The rice reserves were 50,000 tonnes when ASEAN had five members, but with ten members now, the rice reserve stocks have increased to 87,000 tonnes (ASEAN 2001, p. 2), which is still low if a major food crisis takes place in the region. Given the environmental challenges from climate change, food security in ASEAN is likely to be tested more frequently in the coming decades. As it stands currently, both Myanmar and Thailand are targets of richer, food-deficit countries in terms of securing their food supplies: China has leased lands from Myanmar, and Saudi Arabia has eyes on Thailand's farm lands. Such land deals can be politically sensitive issues as we have seen in March 2009 when the Malagasy president was ousted from office because of leasing farm lands to a South Korean *chaebol*.

Another major societal impact arising from climate change is the spread and management of tropical diseases. Lomborg (2008, p. 45) estimates that it would cost the world community US$13 billion to reduce malaria by 50 per cent globally, protect 90 per cent of newborns, and cut death of children under five years by 72 per cent. In cities, both the lack of water and an excess of water can have dire consequences for human health. Stagnant water is the breeding ground for mosquitoes and other parasites that will endanger human health and lives, while water scarcity and drought can generate unhygienic environmental conditions for urban residents. Cities might need to look at alternative methods of flushing toilets if there is water scarcity. It is the urban developed environments that provide the best breeding zones for mosquitoes if there are no natural checks to their population growth. Many tropical diseases (malaria, dengue fever, filariasis, etc.) are not only related to the tropical environment, but are products of poor urban development (lack of roads, water drainage) (Nicolai 2000). Therefore, sound urban development can be a buffer against tropical diseases.

Policy oriented adaptive mechanisms

Given the importance of national development trajectories, governments should view their overall long-term developmental programmes as national adaptations to climate change impacts. One of the problems in government circles and the public arena is the lack of awareness of the impacts of climate change in various sectors: economic, health, food security, water resources, energy use, agricultural production, flood control, drought conditions, biodiversity, and seawater rises. Before countries and communities can commit to tackling climate change issues, the region needs public policies that are geared to providing all communities with a holistic, honest, and fairly accurate picture of climate change challenges.

At the macro level, the largest challenge to societies and urban communities is to evaluate whether the current capitalist driver of economic growth is sustainable. The Southeast Asian countries in the throes of development and modernization must realize that "adaptation must be part of development" and that "development is the most important form of adaptation" (Stern 2009, p. 14). Until and unless there is a major restructuring of international and national economic systems, future development trajectories are likely to remain bounded to capitalism. Rigg (1997, p. 286) argues that despite the capitalistic-driven development in Southeast Asia of the last fifty years, national discourses on development have distracted attention from real failures and inconsistencies, widening human and regional disparities, cronyism and corruption, exclusion of communities from national development, and endemic poverty. The Asian Development Bank's 2009 *Climate Change Report* notes that in 2005, ninety-three million (18.8 per cent) of Southeast Asians lived below the US$1.25-a-day poverty line, while the Population Reference Bureau (2005) records that 44 per cent (221 million) lived with less than US$2 a day. The poorest countries in the region are Timor-Leste, Cambodia, the Lao PDR, Myanmar, and Vietnam. They will have the greatest difficulties adopting and implementing adaptation programmes.

Since food and water security are major challenges for urban communities in the region, the question is what kind of trade-offs should governments embark on. The thirst for energy has led to vast investments in hydroelectric power in Thailand, the Philippines, Indonesia, Vietnam and, in particular, the Mekong region (Diokno and Nguyen 2006). But is this a sensible pathway? Hydroelectric power might be a cheap and clean source of electricity, but it creates forest losses, has biodiversity impacts, leads to displacement of communities, and can generate impacts on water supplies and agriculture. In prolonged dry months, dams can provide little energy relief and affect irrigation supplies. The main impact of food, livestock, and natural resource consumption amongst urban dwellers is that we create a "water footprint", not so much in the actual water we drink, but the "virtual water" we consume in products (Dayrit 2009, p. 26).

To find eco-friendly adaptive systems and increase agricultural productivity, governments need to take national policy decisions with regard to implementing varied new agricultural developments: organic farming, sustainable agriculture, and genetically modified (GM) foods. GM foods are likely to be the panacea for food insecurity in the twenty-first century, especially for countries facing food problems. In 2009 the world's GM seed market was worth US$10.5 billion and the crops grown worth US$130 billion (*The Economist* 2010, p. 14). Clearly, as populations drift to cities and climate change provides more varied and unpredictable weather conditions, agricultural adaptation becomes a key immediate area for scientific research and development. *The Economist* (2010, p. 14) in its editorial expressed it best when it noted: "From soil management to weather forecasts to the preservation, study and use of agricultural biodiversity, there are many ways to improve the agricultural systems on which the world's food supply depends, and make them more resilient as well as more profitable. A farm is not just a clever crop; it is an ecosystem managed with intelligence. GM crops have a great role to play in that development, but they are only a part of the whole."

REFLECTIONS

In summing up this chapter, I would like to conclude on a broader academic canvas. In my view the global dialogue on climate change requires trying to find common ground on four intersecting issues.

Firstly, we now need to move away from Snow's (1961) dismal prognosis of the culture wars, the clash between the natural sciences and the humanities/social sciences, in order to understand climate change impacts on societies. The scientific community would like to advocate the importance of science in Stephen Gould's concept of "scientific magisterium", and certainly it is not hard to accept Garte's (2008) reasoned defence of the importance of science to human welfare, health, and living standards. As human beings we cannot live in isolation of our biosphere. The chaos theory (the science of complexity) informs us that we cannot predict the future states of complex systems. Even the science behind understanding the complex processes of climate change seems currently inadequate and is probably the cause for so many doubts, misinformation, unwillingness to act, and psychological defence mechanisms (Garvey 2008, pp. 143–46).

This need for dialogue and interrelationship between the natural sciences and social sciences is best underscored by Hulme (2008, p. 10) when he notes: "climate is an idea which encapsulates the immersion of the physical with the cultural, in which local and global dynamics interweave and where the memory of the past meets the possibilities of the future". The relationship between history and science is best demonstrated in the Diamond and Robinson edited book, *Natural Experiments of History*, where they try to bring both historians and scientists closer in research. To the natural scientists, the message is to study "historical phenomena scientifically", and to the historians, it is to overcome their reluctance in "embracing scientific methods as the basis for making inferences" (Mahoney 2010, p. 1578). As humanity's response to climate change lies in complex decision-making processes rather than uncovering its scientific underpinnings, climate change thus delves into broader philosophical issues about human morality and the issues of manageable, politically desirable, and generally expedient ways of dealing with its challenges. Garvey (2008, pp. 114–18) argues that any morally adequate proposal for climate change mitigation and adaptation requires states and communities to take into account four criteria: historical responsibilities; present capacities; sustainability; and procedural fairness.

Secondly, we need to bridge the environmental and economic divide and specifically address environmentally sustainable ways in dealing with consumerism, capitalism, the growth fetish, and the whole industrial production process. To judge from the debates, the proponents on both sides (for capitalism and for environmentalism) seem to be in opposing camps with few compromises and no solutions in sight. The environmental economists who provide solutions, such as the polluter pay, cap and trade, and carbon credit systems to handle climate change emissions, do not and will not address the long-term global problems. Sociologists have attempted to bridge this gap through the concept of "ecological modernization" by explaining how economic development can be made compatible with environmental sustainability, such as employing green technology, soft energy paths, alternative technologies, and green de-industrialization

(Hajer 1995; Korhonen 2005; Sutton 2004, pp. 145–52). Given the way economic issues are so intertwined with climate change processes, we might do better to address global forums on climate change with economic calculations and cooperation in mind than by looking purely at the global environmental impacts.

Victor's (2009, p. 344) recommendations for negotiators at Copenhagen were that "they should junk the toolbox of environmental diplomacy and recognize global warming for the problem of economic cooperation that it is". Thomas Sterner (2009) argues that the distinction between rich and poor people over ecosystem common-pool resources should not be disaggregated and measured differently since taste changes over time or income. The fundamental economic measure of ecosystem resources should not be based on preferences by rich or poor people, but based on the notion that such ecosystem resources are getting scarcer from a supply side — land and water will rise in price if they become scarcer in future due to climate change.

The most forceful endorsement of creating new politics and economics to address climate change challenges comes from the thought-provoking book by Nordhaus and Shellenberger, *Break Through* (2009, p. 235), which provides an optimistic argument for not separating nature and markets, but for starting to think of "creating natures and markets to serve the kind of world we want and the kind of species we want to become". The authors chastise environmentalists for arguing for a "return to some Edenic past" and pursuing a politics of essentialism, when in fact we should be elevating ourselves into "pragmatic politics" and asking ourselves what "new environments can we imagine and create?" (Nordhaus and Shellenberger 2009, p. 239).

Thirdly, the political perspective based on the nation state as the unit of analysis versus the global common-pool Gaian perspective are equally at odds with each other. The climate change meetings in Kyoto and Copenhagen demonstrate the power of the nation state in defining the territorial and spatial jurisdiction of the earth, dividing Mother Nature into political spheres and bifurcating ecosystems in national economic domains. It is thus no wonder that of the 250 international environmental treaties, only fifteen to twenty have broad global sponsorship, the rest are bilateral and regional agreements (Speth 2005, p. 78).

Unfortunately while countries want all the benefits of economic globalization, they do not want any responsibilities or adhere to international laws. Essentially all the states want free rider status to global environmental issues. Each country wants to keep to its pattern of unilateralism in climate change issues, and when they need it, subscribe to "a la carte multilateralism" (Speth 2005, p. 110). The power relationships of states seeking national advantage over climate change negotiations will certainly undermine any holistic solution for the global community of organisms and human beings. Progress on climate change would require Gaian mindsets, international perspectives, and global common-pool initiatives, which at international forums are in short supply. So long as nationalism and state territorial concerns remain the stakeholders' interests in climate change negotiations, no global solution is likely to arise in the near future, and all negotiations will become piecemeal, politically convenient, and economically expedient, short-term, adaptive solutions.

In other words, we need to transform egocentric environmental ethical thinking to ecocentric ethical thinking; the first concept is focused on individual or national good, the latter is grounded in the cosmos, the whole environment (Merchant 2005, pp. 64–79). Developing countries such as India, however, have modified the global commons position by advocating the principle of "common but differentiated responsibility", which they feel is a fairer representation of global responsibility (Pachauri 2009, p. 1054).

Fourthly, as cities become the norm of human living, the conflict over resources, food, water, and energy is being played out between urban biosphere peoples and the ecosystem peoples in "rural" and non-urban hinterlands. The main nexus of climate change enquiry is the future of the city and its urban inhabitants: are they sustainable entities? In his masterly study of *The Production of Space*, Henri Lefebvre (2009) argues that past civilizations and cities were organized on a greater integration of cosmic "naturalness" and "organic" human-nature relationships than the social spaces of global cities today. Current urban spaces emphasize technological domination, capitalistic spaces (commodities and money), and the social spaces of production (production of labour; networks, and exchanges), which in turn create a production of urban space that transcends biomorphic and natural space.

The question confronting societies today is how we should connect urban spaces to "agro-pastoral" space and ensure the "symbiotic relationship with that rural space over which (if often with much difficulty) it holds sway" (Lefebvre 2009, pp. 234–35). Hence, over the last two decades, various attempts have been made to redefine the city as the garden city, sustainable city, green city, and ecocity. Based on human historical records, few cities have survived as hallmarks of civilizations over a thousand years. Climate change, especially prolonged drought, has nailed civilizations into oblivious cemeteries. If civilization is the "grandfather, the patriarch of world history", according to Braudel (2002, p. 65), then the cities of the world are the custodians of civilization and human history. Until we find the right prescriptions to keep cities sustainable within the rising challenges of climate change, human civilization as we know it in the twenty-first century is likely to be severely socially undermined, spatially circumscribed, and culturally moribund. We need to change the equation between urban areas and their hinterlands so that ecological footprints are minimized and the urban-hinterland equation is a seamless harmonious ecosystem of environmental sustainability.

Despite the doomsday scenario by Rees (2003) and Martin (2007) on the demise of the human species this century, there are others who seem optimistic. Sachs (2008, p. 112) in his book, *Common Wealth,* states categorically that "climate change is a solvable problem", and Nordhaus and Shellenberger (2009, p. 151) are positive that human societies "can overcome ecological crisis". The issue here is that we might have the science and technology to solve the problem, but do we have the global mindset, the "ecocentric environmental ethics" (Merchant 2005), and the political will to ensure climate change is solvable?

References

ADB (Asian Development Bank). Report by ADB on Economics of Climate Change in Southeast Asia: Report and Multimedia Toolkit, 2009.

Anjali, N. "Cost of Climate Change Underestimated". *Nature* 461, no. 3 (2009).

Armatte, Michel. "Building Scenarios: How Climate Change Became an Economic Question". In *Changing Climate, Changing Economy*, edited by Jean-Philippe Touffut. Cheltenham: Elgar, 2009.

ASEAN. "ASEAN Briefing Paper on Food, Agriculture and Forestry". Jakarta: ASEAN Committee on Culture and Information, 2001.

Au, Jeremy Yong. "Stamford Canal Review 'Top Priority'". *Straits Times,* 20 July 2010, p. 1.

Ayres, Robert U. *Turning Point: The End of the Growth Paradise.* London: Earthscan, 1999.

Bankoff, Greg. "Storms in History: Water, Hazard and Society in the Philippines

1565–1930". In *A World of Water: Rain, Rivers and Seas in Southeast Asian Histories*, edited by Peter Boomgaard. Singapore: NUS Press Singapore, 2007.

Barlow, Maude. *Blue Covenant: The Global Water Crisis and the Coming Battle for the Right to Water*. Melbourne: Black, 2008.

Brand, Stewart. *Whole Earth Discipline: An Ecopragmatist Manifesto*. New York: Viking, 2009.

Braudel, Fernand. *The Perspective of the World: Civilization and Capitalism 15th–18th Century, Volume 3*. London: Phoenix, 2002.

———. "Could Food Shortages Bring Down Civilization?" *Scientific American* 300, no. 5 (May 2009): 44.

———. *Eco-Economy: Building an Economy for the Earth*. New York: Norton, 2001.

Brown, Lester. *Eco-Economy: Building an Economy for the Earth*. London: Norton, 2001.

Caballero-Anthony, Mely and Safiah Jamil. "The Rush for Nuclear Energy in Southeast Asia: Promises and Pitfalls". In *Strategic Currents: Emerging Trends in Southeast Asia*, edited by Yang Razali Kassim. Singapore: S. Rajaratnam School of International Studies, 2009.

Chew, Cassandra. "Newater to Meet 40% of S'pore's Needs". *Straits Times*, 4 May 2010.

Conde, Carlos H. "Months After Typhoons, Torn by Drought". The Global Edition of the *New York Times*, 20–21 February 2010, p. 3.

Cooper, C.F. "What Might Man-induced Climate Change Mean?" *Foreign Affairs* 56, no. 3 (1978): 500–20.

Dawson, Brian and Matt Spannagle. *The Complete Guide to Climate Change*. London: Routledge, 2009.

Dayrit, F.M. "Sustain Water to Sustain Society". In *Agenda for Hope: Ideas on Building a Nation*, edited by F.M. Dayrit. Manila: Ateneo de Manila University Loyola Schools, 2009.

Diokno, Maria Serena I. and Nguyen van Chinh, eds. *The Mekong Arranged & Rearranged*. Chiang Mai: Mekong, 2006.

Eisler, Riane. *The Real Wealth of Nations*. San Francisco: Berrett-Koehler, 2008.

FAO. "Climate Change, Water and Food Security". FAO event, 26–28 February 2008 <www.fao.org/foodclimate/expert/em2/narrative-em2/en>.

Fahn, James David. *A Land on Fire: The Environmental Consequences of the Southeast Asian Boom*. Chiang Mai: Silkworm Books, 2004.

Flannery, Tim. *The Weather Makers: How Man is Changing the Climate and What it Means for Life on Earth*. New York: Grovve, 2006.

Flavin, Christopher. "Preface". In *2007 State of the World: Our Urban Future*, edited by Linda Starke. New York: Norton, 2007.

Francisco, H. "The Economics of and Institutions for Adaptation to Climate Change Impacts: A Regional Outlook for Southeast Asia". Institute of Southeast Asian Studies Regional Outlook Forum, Session 3, on "The Economics of

Environmental Disaster: The Socio-Cultural Impact". Singapore: Institute of Southeast Asian Studies, 2008.

Garte, Seymour. *Where We Stand: A Surprising Look at the Real State of Our Planet.* New York: American Management Association, 2008.

Garvey, James. *The Ethics of Climate Change: Right and Wrong in a Warming World.* New York: Continuum, 2008.

Hajer, M.A. *The Politics of Environmental Discourse: Ecological Modernization and the Policy Process.* New York: Oxford University Press, 1995.

Heffernan, O. "'Climategate' Scientist Speaks Out". *Nature* 463 (2010): 860.

Hulme, M. "Geographical Work at the Boundaries of Climate Change". Transactions of The Institute of British Geographers 33 (2008): 5–11.

Idso, S.B. "Climatic Effects of Increased Industrial Activity upon the World's Established Agro-ecosystems". *Agro-Ecosystems* 1, no. 1 (1974): 7–17.

IPCC (Intergovernmental Panel on Climate Change). "Climate Change 2007: The Physical Science Basis. Summary for Policymakers". Geneva: IPCC Secretariat, 2007.

Korhonen, J. "Reconsidering the Economics Logic of Ecological Modernization". *Environment and Planning A* 40 (2005): 1331–46.

Lee, Kai N. "An Urbanizing World". In *2007 State of the World: Our Urban Future.* New York: Norton, 2007.

Lee Kuan Yew. *From Third World to First: The Singapore Story: 1965–2000.* Memoirs of Lee Kuan Yew. Singapore: Singapore Press Holdings, 2000.

Lefebvre, Henri. *The Production of Space,* translated by Donald Nicholson-Smith. Oxford: Blackwell, 2009.

Lombørg, B. *Cool It: The Skeptical Environmentalist's Guide to Global Warming.* New York: Vintage Books, 2008.

Lovelock, J. *The Vanishing Face of Gaia.* New York: Basic Books, 2009.

Mahoney, J. "History as a Laboratory". *Science* 327 (5973) (2010): 1578–79.

Martin, James. *The Meaning of the 21st Century: A Vital Blueprint for Ensuring our Future.* New York: Riverhead Books, 2007.

Martinez-Alier, Joan. *The Environmentalism of the Poor: A Study of Ecological Conflicts and Valuation.* New Delhi: Oxford University Press, 2005.

McCallum, I. *Ecological Intelligence: Rediscovering Ourselves in Nature.* Golden, CO: Fulcrum, 2008.

Merchant, Carolyn. *Radical Ecology: The Search for a Livable World.* New York: Routledge, 2005.

Millennium Ecosystem Assessment Team. *Our Human Planet: Summary for Decision Makers* Washington: Island, 2005.

Moss, R.H., J.A. Edmonds, K.A. Hibbard, M.R. Manning, S.K. Rose, D.P. van Vuuren, and T.R. Carter, "The Next Generation of Scenarios for Climate Change Research and Assessment". *Nature* 463 (2010): 747–56.

Nicolaï, Henri. "Health and Tropical Geography". *Belgeo* 1-2-3-4 (2000): 103–13.

Nordhaus, T. and M. Shellenberger. *Break Through: Why We Can't Leave Saving the Planet to Environmentalists*. New York: Mariner Books, 2009.

Olchondra, R.T. "Water Released to Prepare Farms for Rains". *Philippine Daily Inquirer*, 29 May 2010, A3.

Pachuari, R.K. "India Pushes for Common Responsibility". *Nature* 461 (2009): 1054.

Perlman, Janice E. and Molly O'Meara Sheehan. "Fighting Poverty and Environmental Injustice in Cities". In The Worldwatch Institute, *2007 State of the World: Our Urban Future*. New York: Norton, 2007.

Peterson, A. *Being Human: Ethics, Environment, and Our Place in the World*. Berkeley: University of Californnia Press, 2001.

Population Reference Bureau. *2009 World Population Data Sheet*. Washington, DC, 2009.

Posner, E.A. and D. Weisbach. *Climate Change Justice*. Princeton: Princeton University Press, 2010.

Rees, Martin. *Our Final Century: Will the Human Race Survive the 21st Century?* London: Heineman, 2003.

Rigg, Jonathan. *Southeast Asia: The Human Landscape of Modernization and Development*. London: Routledge, 1997.

Rockström, J., W. Steffen, K. Noone, A. Persson, F.S. Chapin III, E.F. Lambin, and T.M. Lenton. "A Safe Operating Space for Humanity". *Nature* 461 (2009): 472–75.

Romm, Joseph. *Hell and High Water*. New York: Harper Perennial, 2007.

Sachs, Jeffrey. *Common Wealth: Economics for a Crowded Planet*. New York: Penguin, 2008.

Savage, Victor R. "Sustaining Cities with Climate Change: Is There a Future for Human Livelihoods?" In *World Cities: Achieving Liveability and Vibrancy*, edited by Ooi Giok Ling and Belinda Yuen. Singapore: World Scientific, 2010.

Snow, C.P. *The Two Cultures and the Scientific Revolution*. Cambridge: Cambridge University Press, 1961.

Spash, C.L. *Greenhouse Economics: Value and Ethics*. London: Routledge, 2002.

Speth, James Gustave. *Red Sky in the Morning*. New Haven: Yale University Press, 2005.

Stern, N. *A Blueprint for a Safer Planet: How to Manage Climate Change and Create a New Era of Progress and Prosperity*. London: Bodley Head, 2009.

Sterner, Thomas. "In Defence of Sensible Economics". In *Changing Climate, Changing Economy*, edited by J.P. Touffut. Cheltenham: Elgar, 2009.

Stoll, S. *The Great Delusion*. New York: Hill and Wang, 2008.

Sutton, Philip W. *Nature, Environnment and Society*. New York: Palgrave Macmillan, 2004.

Tay, Simon. "Institutional Challenges for Environmental Cooperation". In *Critical States: Environmental Challenges to Development in Monsoon Southeast Asia*, edited by Louis Lebel, Anond Snidvongs, Chen-Tung Arther Chen and Rajesh Daniel. Kuala Lumpur: Strategic Information and Research Development Centre, 2009.

The Economist. "Attack of the Really Quite Likeable Tomatoes". *The Economist* 394 (2010): 14.

Touffut, J.P. (ed.). *Changing Climate, Changing Economy.* Cheltenham: Edward Elgar, 2009.

UNFCC (United Nations Framework for Climate Change Convention). "Technologies for Adaptation to Climate Change". Adaptation, Technology and Science Programme of the UNFCC Secretariat, 2006.

Vaughan, Victoria. "100 mm: Expect Floods If This Much Rain Falls in an Hour". *Straits Times,* 22 July 2010, p. A8.

Victor, D. "Plan B for Copenhagen". *Nature* 461 (2009): 342–44.

WWF (World Wide Fund for Nature). *Mega-Stress for Mega Cities: A Climate Vulnerability Ranking of Major Coastal Cities in Asia.* 2009.

Yan, J. and T. Lin. "Biofuels in Asia". *Applied Energy* 86 (2009): S1–10.

Yuen, Belinda and Leon Kong. "Climate Change and Urban Planning in Southeast Asia". *Surveys and Perspectives Integrating Environment and Society* (2)3, 2009 <http://sapiens.revues.org/index881.html> (accessed 22 January 2010).

10

URBAN GREEN SPACES AND LIVEABILITY IN SOUTHEAST ASIA

Tan Peng Ting

While there are diverse definitions of liveability, few would disagree that green spaces are an important contributor to liveability in urban places. In a paper published in 1987, two officers from the Department of Environmental Management of the United Nations Environment Programme (UNEP) agreed that "there is consensus in the view that the quality of urban life depends largely on the amount and quality of green space within it or close to it" (Olembo and Rham 1987). The former mayor of Bogota, Colombia, Enrique Penalosa, went as far as to expound that "parks and other pedestrian places are essential to a city's happiness" (PPS 2003).

Indeed, many studies have shown the multiple benefits of urban green spaces for the social, environmental, and economic well-being of urban communities. The well-being of these three spheres is essential for building a liveable city. In addition, good governance and integrated planning are necessary as they facilitate programmes and policies that ensure the health and well-being of the three spheres.

Liveability is defined as the suitability to live in a place and is often associated with the city's environmental quality, health, and quality of life (Mamas and Komalasari 2008). Beyond basic needs such as sanitation and water, there are social, economic, and environmental health needs. The provision of urban green spaces is a prime example of how policy programmes can effectively augment the social, environmental, and economic liveability of a city. This chapter will explore how urban green spaces are increasingly being recognized as an important source of fulfilment of social, environmental, and economic needs in Southeast Asian cities.

ROLE OF URBAN GREENERY

The terms "urban greenery" or "urban green spaces" include everything in cities that has vegetation, also collectively known as "green infrastructure" (Gairola and Noresah 2010). It includes horticultural parks, streetscapes, green areas, and open spaces, as well as forests and other natural habitats of urban biodiversity such as riverine and coastal parks. Such a broad definition is necessary as a city's geography and history shape its urban greenscape differently. Some recent developments in horticultural parks have further blurred the divide by attempting to "recreate naturalistic landscapes … characterized by informal design, favourable maintenance to wildlife and a preference for native vegetation" (Tzoulas and James 2004). A common denominator in all is the role of these green spaces and parks as a type of urban open space.

UN-HABITAT's *State of the World's Cities 2008/2009* reported that urban residents who are suffering from overcrowding, noise, air pollution, and lack of green spaces and communal meeting places such as parks also suffer from increased stress levels and declined mental well-being as a result (UN-HABITAT 2008, p. 128). While the availability of urban green spaces is only one of many urban issues, it is well positioned to address many other urban issues and improve the living conditions in urban areas. Urban greenery as a form of urban open space plays an important role in the city, not only by improving environmental quality, but also contributing to the economy, its people's physical and psychological health, social cohesion, and community building. Some benefits of urban parks (Lerner and Poole 1999; Chiesura 2004; Fuller and Gaston 2009; Gairola and Noresah 2010; Emmanuel 2009) include the ability to:

1. attract investment, residents, businesses, tourists, and economic activity
2. provide leisure and recreation space and a high quality of life

3. improve social and psychological well-being
4. revitalize a community and promote social interactions
5. provide a centrepiece for neighbourhood renewal
6. provide ecosystem services such as air and water purification
7. stablize microclimate and reduce the urban heat island effect
8. ensure biodiversity conservation

As Laquian (2008, p. 19) highlighted, "forests, green areas, parks and open space act as the lungs of the city" and have to be included in urban plans to achieve sustainable and inclusive urban development. Efforts to improve environmental quality, such as providing for urban greenery, are important components of city development strategies that should be "integrated directly into city planning processes rather than added on at the end" (UN-HABITAT 2008, p. 192). However, for cities in many developing countries, including those in Southeast Asia, green spaces do not receive high priority, while urbanization and associated economic growth are also often associated with deforestation (Olembo and Rham 1987; Douglass et al. 2008). The first two authors continued to lament that "new Third World urban areas are commonly treeless, even when they have taken over previously forested areas", and municipal governments "practically never provide for future green space" in physical planning.

Status of Urban Greenery in Southeast Asia

> Fortunately, some Third World cities have done well in maintaining or even enhancing their green space. Among them Singapore has perhaps the best record, but other cities in Southeast Asia … could also be mentioned. One cannot fail to notice, however, that this seems possible only when the standard of living and education has risen significantly.
> — Olembo and Rham (1987)

Despite the report being written more than two decades ago in 1987, Singapore was already known for being a "Garden City", with its tree planting efforts beginning almost two decades earlier in 1971. Since then, there has been a further increase in recognition of the importance of urban green spaces in Southeast Asian cities. In 2009 four ASEAN capitals — Jakarta, Manila, Vientiane, and Bangkok — adopted a "Cool ASEAN, Green Capitals Initiative" declaration aimed at "improving the urban landscape of Southeast Asia's major cities to cope with the impact of climate change" (*Bangkok Post*, 2009). One of the strategies covered in the declaration includes the expansion of urban green spaces.

Perhaps as Olembo and Rham (1987) suggested, this increase in green spaces could be due to the rise in standards of living and education. Prominent Singaporean architect William Lim (1990) agrees with Olembo and Rham in his 1986 speech on the subject of "Livable Urban Spaces in Singapore". He stated that "the basic needs of food, health, education, shelter and employment having been met, increasing emphasis and attention is now being given to improving the quality of life and to the providing of leisure facilities" (Lim 1990, p. 175). Maslow's hierarchy of needs theory would explain the increasing phenomenon of capital cities in the region now placing more emphasis on urban green spaces as the population attains higher levels of education and standard of living and the city state also attracting more global talents. On the flip side, the newly emerging cities in rapidly urbanizing Southeast Asia are adhering to Maslow's hierarchy and neglecting the importance of urban greenery.

At the same time, with increasing environmental awareness and global concerns about climate change, there is a growing trend for small cities and large towns in the region to circumvent the progression described above. More "new" cities are now also giving urban greenery emphasis in early stages of their city development. Many of the winners of the ASEAN Environmentally Sustainable Cities (ESC) Award, such as Palembang in Indonesia and Puerto Princesa in the Philippines, are relatively small, growing cities, yet they have set goals to increase greenery in the city. In fact, cities dependent on tourism dollars or those that realize the economic potential of the city's greenery would likely find greater incentives to protect their greenery in the process of urbanization. Indeed, Singapore in its early years of industrialization and urbanization, similarly recognized this economic incentive in enhancing its urban greenery to attract foreign investments (*Straits Times*, 7 May 2009).

> To woo investors from developed countries, we had … to show investors that this was a well-organised place. Coming from the airport into town, they would pass by lush greenery, and when they visited me in the Istana, they would see well-maintained lawns and shrubs. Without [my] having to tell anything they would understand this is a country where the administration works, where there is a system.
>
> — Singapore Minister Mentor Lee Kuan Yew
> (*Straits Times*, 7 May 2009)

Despite this, Douglass et al. (2008, p. 292) reported that "Southeast Asian mega-urban regions have among the least amount of green/public space per capita of all city regions of similar size in the world". Table 10.1 provides a summary of the estimated green space per capita in selected Southeast Asian capital cities. It shows that many of the cities do not meet the international minimum standard of nine square metres of urban green space per capita as recommended by the World Health Organization (Kuchelmeister 1998). Furthermore, not much has changed since Kuchelmeister (1998) observed that there is a dearth of data on green spaces in many developing Southeast Asian cities. The differing definitions of green spaces across cities also cause difficulty in the precise cross-comparisons of the data. Some include private green spaces, such as golf courses, and others include street plantings, while yet other figures include strictly parkland only.

The more-developed cities of Kuala Lumpur and Singapore continue to perform well in terms of increasing the city's green spaces since

Table 10.1
Estimated Green Space per Capita in Selected Southeast Asian Capital Cities

	City	Country	Estimated Urban Green Spaces (m²/per capita) (year)	References
Below International Standard	Bangkok	Thailand	1.00 (1997) 0.47 (2002) 3.30 (2008) 3.49 (2010)	Kuchelmeister (1998) Douglass et al. (2008) BMA (2010) BMA (2010)
	Ho Chi Minh City	Vietnam	1.00 (2003) 0.70 (2009)	Douglass et al. (2008) Vietnews (2009)
	Jakarta DKI	Indonesia	0.22 (1986) 1.27 (2002) 1.62 (2010)	Kuchelmeister (1998) Douglass et al. (2008) Jakarta Globe (2010)
	Metro Manila	Philippines	4.50 (2007)	Siemens (2011)
Above International Standard	Kuala Lumpur	Malaysia	2.25 (1997) 7.00 (2005) 12.00 (2010)	Kuchelmeister (1998) CHKL (2008) PEMANDU (2010)
	Singapore	Singapore	22.00 (2003) 19.44 (2010)	NParks (2003) NParks (2010)

Kuchelmeister's 1998 report. An emerging city such as Ho Chi Minh City, struggled with losing half of its urban greenery between 1998 and 2009 (*Vietnews*, 2009) in the process of rapid urbanization. Megacities such as Bangkok, Jakarta, and Manila are working towards increasing the cities' green spaces through various initiatives. However, the region's performance cannot be judged purely by these estimates as proportional green space figures are determined also by a city's population, geography, and size (Fuller and Gaston 2009). The following section details some of the plans and initiatives by the cities.

Singapore

The city state began implementing its vision of a Garden City as early as three years after its independence, with the launch of the "Keep Singapore Clean" campaign in 1968. The campaign took on an additional dimension with the launch of "Tree Planting Day" in 1971. This grew into a tradition which symbolized "the government's vision for Singapore to be transformed into a tropical garden city — both clean and green" (Tan 2009, p. 6). It was the vision of then Prime Minister Lee Kuan Yew who wanted Singapore to become a garden city to soften the harshness of the high-density urban environment (Kwang, Fernandez, and Tan 1998).

Even as the city began its rapid industrialization and urbanization[1] programmes in the 1960s, there was a clear vision at the top that a "clean and green environment [was] necessary to provide a good quality of life" (Tan 2009, p. 5). Lee also believed that "well-kept trees and gardens were a subtle way of convincing potential investors in the early and crucial years that Singapore was an efficient and effective place" (Koh 2000, p. 40). This belief was translated into policies that spanned more than forty years for implementing the "transformation of Singapore into a clean and green city" — a "declared objective of the government" in Parliament in 1968 (Koh 2000, p. 40).

The strong policy of greening the city has allowed green spaces to be reserved in plans and enforced through development control guidelines. It also enabled the government to invest heavily in environmental infrastructure in its early days of development, such as spending over S$400 million on cleaning up the polluted Singapore River over ten years from 1977 to 1987 (Tan 2009). Two decades later, the government continues to make heavy investments on green spaces by giving up prime land in the reclaimed Marina Bay area for the ninety-four-hectare "Gardens by the Bay" (URA 2006). The three waterfront gardens are an integral part of plans to transform the "Garden City" into a "City in the Garden" (URA 2006). Despite costing over S$1 billion (CNA 2011), the government believes that the investment in this green space in the city's new downtown "will enhance the value of the surrounding land, but beyond land value, it will help make the Marina Bay area a distinctive live-work-play environment on the world stage" (URA 2006, p. 13). This conviction in the value of urban green spaces has proven to serve the city state well as it continues to be ranked the most liveable Asian city in the 2010 Mercer Quality of Living Survey.

As the population of the island state continues to grow, the city can only become denser, with little room for expanding city boundaries. As Table 10.1 shows, the per capita green space provision for Singapore seems to be declining as population density increases faster than the city's green space. However, Fuller and Gaston (2009, p. 354) found that the low per capita green space allocation in small-size and high-density cities is due to "more people being packed into the urban matrix, rather than to buildings replacing existing green spaces". In fact, Fuller and Gaston found that in extremely urbanized cities, not unlike Singapore, the relationship between population density and proportion of urban green space is "uncoupled". Instead of showing a decline in liveability, it is possible that in such compact cities, the green space network becomes more robust and people's interactions with nature depend more on street plantings, home gardens, and other landscape outside the formal green space network. Contact with urban biodiversity is still an important indicator of quality of life.

In response to the need to strengthen informal green spaces, Singapore has begun promoting skyrise greenery by relaxing building guidelines and providing incentives for developers to include more sky terraces, balconies, and "gardens in the sky" (URA 2006). The National Parks Board in Singapore has also completed construction of 150 kilometres of park connectors around the island which link residential areas, parks, and nature areas (NParks 2010). This brings people closer to green spaces and provides easy access to recreational spaces for the whole population, as well as natural corridors for wildlife (Lilian, Ho, and Ismail 2002). Public access to green spaces is an important element of liveability and an increasing challenge in many cities (Douglass et al. 2008).

Kuala Lumpur

According to the Kuala Lumpur Structure Plan 2020 published in 2003, total open space and land use for recreational and sport facilities have increased "significantly" by 169.6 per cent from 586 hectares in 1984, to 1,580 hectares in 2000. However, this category of land use, which includes parks and forest reserves, represents only 6.5 per cent of total land use in the capital city. The actual amount of green space available to the public, out of the 6.5 per cent, is even less when golf courses are excluded. Furthermore, the plan noted that despite the increase, there has been a steady decline in public open space in the city centre largely because of conversion to other uses.

Salleh and Ishak (2002) found that widespread urbanization is deteriorating environmental quality in many urban areas in Malaysia. Lilian, Ho, and Ismail (2002) reported that rapid urbanization had spurred local authorities in major cities to adopt the Garden City concept in Malaysia. Satellite towns in the Greater Kuala Lumpur area, such as Petaling Jaya and Putrajaya, were developed, based on principles of Ebenezer Howard's Garden City concept. In fact, 70 per cent of Putrajaya has been reserved as green spaces, including twelve public parks and wetlands. Nonetheless, in a Quality of Life Survey conducted in 1998 by the Kuala Lumpur City Hall, respondents expressed a high level of dissatisfaction with regards to accessibility of recreational facilities and the low level of social interaction and integration in the city (CHKL 2003). Azwar and Ghani (2009) suggest that there are still many areas, especially in the city centre, that are lacking green spaces, while Salleh and Ishak (2002) recommended making urban greening mandatory in development projects to ensure green space provision in the city.

In the Draft Kuala Lumpur City Plan 2020 released in 2008, the city expressed a vision of "a network of high quality, accessible parks and green spaces which promote recreation, health, education and economic regeneration, helping to make Kuala Lumpur a significantly more attractive city in which to live and work" (CHKL 2008). The city plans to increase its parks and open spaces from the current 6.5 per cent of Kuala Lumpur's total area, to 8 per cent in 2020. In fact, the city plans to introduce development control and planning guidelines to ensure private developers provide green spaces for public use in their development projects.

These local plans are further reinforced by the strategies of the nation's Economic Transformation Programme, which plans to transform Malaysia into a high-income nation by 2020 (PEMANDU 2010). One of the strategies is to transform the Greater Kuala Lumpur/Klang Valley area into one of the National Key Economic Areas by enhancing liveability for residents and attracting tourists and investors. To do so, the government plans to revitalize the Klang River banks into a heritage and commercial area, not unlike the transformation of the Singapore River banks over the last thirty years. This is to be implemented by the Kuala Lumpur City Hall and other local authorities. The government also plans to green the area to ensure "every resident enjoys sufficient green space" by planting 100,000 trees and encouraging rooftop greening. This greening is expected to create 3,000 jobs by 2020 and an estimated potential GNI impact of RM1 billion annually (PEMANDU 2010).

Bangkok

A green belt plan was proposed for Bangkok in 1960 which would act as a finger plan, "allocating [a] series of development areas along radial transportation corridors" (Ryan and Wayuparb 2004). This was replaced by a concentric circles plan in 1971 and a 25-kilometre radius green belt in 1982, which is enforced through the Metropolitan Bangkok Regulations. However, this green belt consists primarily of rice fields (Ryan and Wayuparb 2004). To date, 26 per cent of the total land area in Bangkok consists of agricultural land (Thaiutsa et al. 2008).

From the early 1990s, the Bangkok Metropolitan Administration began engaging in active street tree-planting campaigns (Thaiutsa et al. 2008). Thaiutsa et al. (2008) found through a GIS study that excluding agricultural land, only 4.2 per cent of Bangkok's total area of 1,569 km² consists of street trees and naturalized areas, and 1.2 per cent is developed green spaces, such as parks, sports fields, and golf courses. However, half of this small area is private land, such as golf courses, that are "not readily accessible to average citizens of Bangkok". While citywide average green space per capita was 30 per cent higher than central Bangkok's aggregate, 40 per cent of the green space in central Bangkok is actual park space and the rest are street plantings (Thaiutsa et al. 2008, p. 224). Furthermore, Douglass et al. (2008, p. 291) report that there is an increasing trend in the inner zone of Bangkok of parks and playgrounds being outnumbered by entertainment spots, such as pubs, karaoke bars, and massage parlours, by a ratio of one to ten.

Nonetheless public green spaces continue to receive significant attention from the city and national government. In 2002 the eighth Thai National Economic, and Social Development Plan (NESDP) identified resource conservation and provision of public spaces for liveable cities as key issues for the nation (Ryan and Wayuparb 2004). In 2007, in response to the challenges of global climate change, the Bangkok Metropolitan Administration adopted an Action Plan on Global Warming Mitigation 2007–12, which includes the expansion of park areas in the city (BMA 2010). As part of its action plan, the BMA expanded urban greenery by 1,219,200 m² and increased its per capita green space from 3.3 to 3.49 m² per person from 2008 to 2010. To achieve this, the city administration actively converts vacant state land into public parks (BMA 2010). For its plan to make Bangkok into a liveable city, Bangkok received the ASEAN Environmentally Sustainable Cities Award in 2008.

Jakarta

The push for a greener Jakarta dates back to the time of the first president of Indonesia, Sukarno, who was in office from 1945 to 1967. However, there has been little implementation of plans to ensure parks and open spaces in the city (*Jakarta Globe* 2010). In 1965, more than 35 per cent of Jakarta was green space, but with urbanization, population growth, and internal migration, only 9.3 per cent of the city remains as green spaces (*Jakarta Globe* 2010). From 1972 to 2001, 51 per cent of the total land area in Jakarta City was converted from agriculture to urban development (Rustiadi et al. 2001). Furthermore, the proportion of urban green space fell by 23 per cent from 1972 to 1997, with a low percentage of urban green space in the centre of Jakarta and the three surrounding satellite cities, but a high percentage of green spaces remain on the fringes of the metropolitan area (Zain 2001). In the study by Zain (2001), Jakarta was shown to have experienced the most rapid loss of open green space, whereas other Southeast Asian cities such as Bangkok and Manila had shown a more gradual change.

To address the shortage of green spaces, the Jakarta 2010–30 spatial master plan promised a green facelift that would see the development of more green areas. The city administration is working to reclaim natural spaces by tearing down gas stations in the green belt area and setting aside plots of land in 2,500 neighbourhood wards as pocket parks. Despite this effort, the space crunch in the city is proving to be an obstacle for the

government to increase the statistical indicator. In a vicious cycle, the lack
of green spaces and shortage of alternatives drive residents into malls,
which provide sanctuary from the heat and pollution (Douglass et al.
2008). This has led to an increase of "mall culture" in society, resulting in
further encroachment and neglect of parks (*Jakarta Globe* 2010; Kraas 2010).
This phenomenon is not confined to just Jakarta, but widespread across
the developing cities of Southeast Asia (Douglass et al. 2008).

RECOMMENDATIONS

It is increasingly recognized, both in literature and in city plans, that green
spaces play a critical role in ensuring the liveability of cities. As can be
seen from the various case studies, green spaces are not without economic
value and can contribute far greater external returns than perceived.
However, translating theory to praxis proves to be the largest challenge
facing cities due to lack of capabilities, funding, or political will. The
increasing displacement of public green spaces by commercial entities
and shopping malls has not only resulted in limited public access, but
also in the neglect and reduced community use of remaining parks. As
a result, many public parks decline in quality and maintenance, gaining
a negative image, and, in many cities, becoming unsafe for children and
families (Kraas 2010). This vicious cycle needs to be addressed. Below are
some recommendations for cities in Southeast Asia to consider.

Data and Research

One of the key issues that was consistently encountered throughout the
writing of this chapter is the lack of reliable data. There is no standardized
definition of "green space" or "open space" across the cities and nations
of Southeast Asia, much less "urban", which in itself requires further
rigorous defining. Data are either not collected at the city level, or collection
is done independently by the examination of satellite images by various
researchers. Data and research are critical to understanding and improving
the quality and inventory of green spaces in cities. The data also need to
be easily accessible to further research.

   An example of a possible tool for cities to benchmark their biodiversity
conservation efforts is the Singapore Index on Cities' Biodiversity, which
was endorsed by the Tenth Meeting of the Conference of Parties to the
Convention of Biological Diversity in 2010. At the ASEAN Workshop on

the City Biodiversity Index, the tool was introduced to cities in the ASEAN Initiative on Environmentally Sustainable Cities in 2010 (ASEAN Centre for Biodiversity 2010). Through uniform data sets and regular monitoring, the index can be incorporated as one of the potential "green criteria" for the ASEAN Awards for Environmentally Sustainable Cities. Currently the award only evaluates clean land, air, and water, but does not have an official component for evaluating biodiversity conservation and provisions for green spaces in ASEAN cities.

Regional Exchanges

Many cities cite difficulties in finding space and funding when it comes to securing urban green spaces. Regional exchanges amongst cities in the region on creative infrastructure financing and practices to overcome implementation woes may help provide a plethora of solutions for cities to consider. Regional dialogues are often pegged at national levels, while local governments that implement the plans need to be more involved. Beyond best performers, cities that struggle and perform poorly in providing green spaces should also be identified for other cities to offer assistance and consultation. Some international aid agencies have even selected specific cities to be partnered for technical exchanges.

Note

1. Much of the development was originally centred in the downtown area. The surrounding rural areas were plantations and farms. After the 1960s, satellite towns and industrial parks were built around the rest of the island, decentralizing the built-up area from the city.

References

ASEAN Centre for Biodiversity. ASEAN Workshop on City Biodiversity Index. 2010 <http://aseanbiodiversity.org/index.php?option=com_content&view=article&id=578:asean-workshop-on-city-biodiversity-index&catid=62:acb-events)>.

Azwar, D.H. and I. Ghani. "The Importance of Green Space: Towards a Quality Living Environment in Urban Areas". *International Journal of Architectural Research* 3, no. 1 (2009): 245–62.

Bangkok Metropolitan Administration. "Challenges and Opportunities in the Age of Globalisation". Speech made at the World Cities Summit 2010.

Bangkok Post. "4 ASEAN Capitals Join Forces to Turn 'Green'". 4 November 2009.

City Hall Kuala Lumpur. Draft Structure Plan Kuala Lumpur 2020 Book. Malaysia: City Hall Kuala Lumpur (CHKL), 2003.

———. Draft Kuala Lumpur City Plan 2020. Malaysia: City Hall Kuala Lumpur (CHKL), 2008 <http://klcityplan2020.dbkl.gov.my>.

Channel NewsAsia. "Gardens by the Bay Reaches First Milestone". 15 February 2011.

Chiesura, A. "The Role of Urban Parks for the Sustainable City". *Landscape and Urban Planning* 68 (2004): 129–38.

Douglass, M., T.Q. Le, C.K. Lowry, H.T. Nguyen, A.N. Pham, N.D. Thai, et al. "The Livability of Mega-Urban Regions in Southeast Asia — Bangkok, Ho Chi Minh City, Jakarta and Manila Compared". In G.W. Jones and M. Douglass, *Mega-Urban Regions in Pacific Asia.* Singapore: NUS Press, 2008.

Emmanuel, R. "Sustainable Urbanity and Urban Climate Change: Amelioration of UHI's as a Quality-of-Life Agenda for Tropical Mega-Cities". The Seventh International Conference on Urban Climate, 29 June – 3 July 2009, Yokohama, Japan.

Fuller, R.A. and K.J. Gaston. "The Scaling of Green Space Coverage in European Cities". *Biology Letters* 5, no. 3 (2009): 352–55.

Gairola, S. and M.S. Noresah. "Emerging Trend of Urban Green Space Research and the Implications for Safeguarding Biodiversity: A Viewpoint". *Nature and Science* 8, no. 7 (2010): 43–49.

Jakarta Globe. "Green Jakarta: Great Idea. How Do We Get Some?" 23 June 2010.

Koh, K.L. "Singapore: Fashioning Landscape for 'The Garden City'". In IUCN, *Landscape Conservation Law: Present Trends and Perspectives in International and Comparative Law,* 2000.

Kraas, F. "Urban Public Space and Governance — Bridging the Gap between Theory and Praxis". Presentation at the "ForUm — Network for Urban Future in Southeast Asia on Urban Public Spaces and Governance in Southeast Asia", 2010.

Kuchelmeister, G. "Urban Forestry: Present Situation and Prospects in the Asia and Pacific region". In *FAO Asia-Pacific Forestry Sector Outlook Study.* FAO Working Paper No: APFSOS/WP/44. Food and Agriculture Organization of the United Nations, Rome, 1998.

Kwang, H.F., W. Fernandez and S. Tan. *Lee Kuan Yew: The Man & His Ideas.* Singapore: Times Edition, 1998.

Laquian, A.A. "The Planning and Governance of Asia's Mega-Urban Regions". United Nations Expert Group Meeting on Population Distribution, Urbanization, Internal Migration and Development. 21–23 January 2008, New York.

Lerner, S. and W. Poole. *The Economic Benefits of Parks and Open Space: How Land Conservation Helps Communities Grow Smart and Protect the Bottom Line.* The Trust for Public Land, 1999.

Lilian, T.Y.C., C.S. Ho, and S. Ismail. "Some Planning Consideration of Garden City Concept Towards Achieving Sustainable Development". Proceedings of the Regional Symposium on Environment and Natural Resources, 2002. Vol. 1, pp. 261–69.

Lim, W.S. "Livable Urban Spaces in Singapore". In *Cities for People: Reflections of a Southeast Asian Architect*. Singapore: Select Books, 1990.

Mamas, S.G. and R. Komalasari. "Jakarta — Dynamics of Change and Livability". In *Mega-Urban Regions in Pacific Asia: Urban Dynamics in a Global Era*, edited by G.W. Jones, and M. Douglass. Singapore: NUS Press, 2008.

NParks. *National Parks Board Annual Report 2002/2003*. Singapore: NParks, 2003.

———. *National Parks Board Annual Report 2009/2010*. Singapore: NParks, 2010.

———. "Eleven Parks in Northern Singapore Now Connected — Northern Explorer PCN is the Third Loop of Park Connectors to be Completed", 2010 <http://www.nparks.gov.sg/cms/index.php?option=com_news&task=view&id=240&Itemid=50>.

Olembo, R. and P.D. Rham. "In Two Different Worlds". *Unasylva — No. 155 — Urban Forestry: Cities, Trees and People*, 39, 1987.

PEMANDU. "Developing Greater Kuala Lumpur/Klang Valley as an Engine of Economic Growth". In *Economic Transformation Programme: A Roadmap for Malaysia*. Malaysia: Performance Management and Development Unit (PEMANDU), 2010.

PPS. "Enrique Peñalosa". Retrieved from Project for Public Spaces — Placemaking for Communities <http://www.pps.org/articles/epenalosa-2/> (accessed 7 Dec. 2010).

Ryan, P. and N, Wayuparb. "Green Space Sustainability in Thailand". *Sustainable Development* 12 (2004): 223–37.

Rustiadi, E., A.M. Zain, B.H. Trisasongko, and I. Carolita. *Land Cover Change in Jabotabek Region*. Indonesia: Institut Pertanian Bogor, 2001.

Salleh, M.N. and Ishak, M.Y. "Greening Our Cities: Challenges and Opportunities". Paper presented at the 18th EAROPH World Planning Congress, Kuala Lumpur, Malaysia, 7–10 October 2002.

Siemens. Asian Green City Index: Manila, Philippines. Siemens, 2011.

Straits Times. "Making Republic a 'First World Oasis' Helped Woo Investors, Says MM Lee", 7 May 2009.

Tan, Y.S. *Clean, Green and Blue: Singapore's Journey Towards Environmental and Water Sustainability*. Singapore: Institute of Southeast Asian Studies, 2009.

Thaiutsa, B., L. Puangchit, R. Kjelgren, and W. Arunpraparut. "Urban Green Space, Street Tree and Heritage Large Tree Assessment in Bangkok, Thailand". *Urban Forestry & Urban Greening* 7 (2008): 219–29.

Tzoulas, K. and P. James. "Our Natural Heritage: Urban Parks". 2004.

UN-HABITAT. *State of the World's Cities 2008/2009 — Harmonious Cities*. London: Earthscan, 2008.

URA. A City in a Garden. *Skyline*, January–February 2006, pp. 10–15.

Vietnews. "HCMC Loses Half Greenery Area Within a Decade", 31 December 2009 <http://www.vietnewsonline.vn/News/Society/Environment/10561/HCMC-loses-half-greenery-area-within-a-decade.htm>.

Zain, A.M. "Distribution, Structure and Function of Urban Green Space in Southeast Asian Mega-cities with Special Reference to Jakarta Metropolitan Region (Jabotabek)". PhD dissertation, Department of Agricultural and Environmental Biology, Graduate School of Agricultural and Life Sciences, University of Tokyo, 2001.

11

DECENTRALIZED WASTE WATER MANAGEMENT FOR THE WASTE WATER REVOLUTION IN URBAN AREAS TO SUPPORT THE ENGINES OF DEVELOPMENT IN SOUTHEAST ASIA

Felix Seebacher and Ti Le-Huu

Untreated sewage is one of the main causes for deteriorating water bodies in urban areas of Southeast Asia, and is leading to a complete neglect of these once beautiful environments and undermining the engines of development and growth in one of the most dynamic regions of the globe. Due to climate change, increasing demand for water as a result of urbanization, and other demographic and economic trends, the available per capita water in a given watershed area is rapidly dropping in many parts of the world, including Southeast Asia.

At the same time, the production of waste water in total and per capita is significantly increasing. This problem will become even more acute if the supply of safe drinking water to households and its consumption continue to increase at the current pace. An increase in water supply will result in an increase in sewage, which, without proper treatment, will end up untreated in the nearest water body or aquifer. By now the natural self-purification processes in water bodies have been exhausted and the receiving waters have partly become open sewers.

The goal for many cities and towns is to stop the discharge of untreated sewage into water bodies by treating the sewage at the source at the household and neighbourhood level. Returning a water body to its former pristine or more semi-natural state is a challenging undertaking. There is still hope, as water fronts at large and impressive rivers have become major attractions in many cities (for example, Singapore, Phnom Penh) and are now a focus of upscale development. Smaller urban water courses are, however, severely neglected. These water bodies once provided opportunities for cultivation and fishery, recreation, open space, and areas for water storage during flood seasons, but also served as effective drainage system during heavy downpours.

River training works started early and can be dated back to at least two thousand years ago. Many rivers became harnessed on a large scale during the late nineteenth and twentieth centuries. More and more small to medium-sized watercourses were trained as cities expanded. This trend is still ongoing today. Excessive river training and the discharge of liquid and solid wastes into rivers have led to a significant deterioration of many water bodies, and are affecting most urban streams. The deterioration of water bodies is exceptionally high in the Asia-Pacific region, and particularly in its fast growing urban areas. Business as usual will undermine the prospect of prosperity of the region, as well as the sustainability of economic achievements from development efforts in the past several decades.

It is in the best interest of most urban and rural stakeholders to improve water quality and rehabilitate the remaining existing water bodies in urban and non-urban areas, because the quality of water bodies is essential for sustainable development. Efforts must be made to treat and manage wastewater at all levels, especially at the local and community levels before it enters a river or lake. This is one of the major starting points to enhance the ecological efficiency of the urban environment. For this reason, the United Nations Secretary General's Advisory Board (UNSGAB) recently initiated a programme entitled, "Wastewater Revolution in Asia", for major investment in this important issue of wastewater management.

The Second Hashimoto Action Plan (HAP II) of UNSGAB calls for "action on wastewater to protect human health, economic development and ecosystems while also alleviating growing water scarcity in many regions". HAP II pointed out that "since developing countries treat just a fraction of their wastewater, we need to encourage a move beyond toilets to the other side of sanitation — collecting, reusing and disposing of municipal waste as well as storm water". In line with HAP II, UNESCAP is promoting the integration of this concept into socio-economic development processes through its programme, "Development of Eco-efficient Water Infrastructure in Asia and the Pacific". Through pilot projects in several countries, innovative approaches for the treatment of wastewater have been promoted for the rehabilitation of urban water bodies and rivers. In Southeast Asia, the implementation of country projects has started in Indonesia, the Philippines, Malaysia, and Vietnam.

This chapter examines the challenges of the wastewater revolution in the Asia-Pacific, with relevance to the Southeast Asian region; it discusses its strategic dimensions, including investment magnitude and trend of decentralized wastewater management, and the initial efforts to move the wastewater revolution forward.

EXTENTS OF THE PROBLEM

Urban Population Affected by Polluted Urban Water Bodies

The world is undergoing the largest wave of urban growth in history. Its fastest growing cities in the 2000s were found predominantly in Asia and Africa. Between 2000 and 2010, urban populations grew by an annual average of 3.3 per cent in the Middle East and Africa, and by 2.7 per cent in Asia and the Pacific, compared with a global urban growth rate of 2.1 per cent. In most of the world, urban population growth is driven mostly by natural population growth, but the urban growth in Asia and the Pacific is mainly driven by rural migration. Urbanization is not just a shift in the number of people living in urban and rural areas; it has many socio-economic consequences, including changes in consumption patterns. The largely unplanned and informal nature of urban growth in the developing world also amplifies environmental and social hazards, and increases risks to the business environment.

The UNEP/UN-HABITAT 2010 publication, *Sick Water?*, states that globally an estimated total of two billion cubic metres of sewage and industrial and agricultural waste are discharged into the world's waterways. Exact information on the amount of untreated wastewater in urban areas in the Asia-Pacific region or in Southeast Asia is not available, but can be estimated. The average daily consumption of drinking water per person is currently approximately 150 litres (with a wide scatter of values from a few litres up to over 300 litres). It can be assumed that about 80 to 90 per cent (or about 120 to 135 litres) of the actually supplied drinking water is used within a household and converted into grey or black water. The remaining 10 to 20 per cent is used for watering gardens and other activities that do not produce wastewater. Thus, Southeast Asia, with an urban population of almost 250 million, would produce more than 30 million cubic metres of wastewater daily. These estimates do not include wastewater released from small and medium-sized enterprises and industries located within urban areas. If we take these untreated releases into account, the total amount of untreated wastewater in urban areas may double.

Much of the produced urban wastewater is not properly treated and discharged untreated directly into open watercourses or seeps into the ground, but exact data are not available. The available data on existing wastewater treatment facilities show higher treatment ratios, but, if investigated in depth, it becomes apparent that most treatment plants do not operate even approximately at their designed parameters, but on much lower throughputs. This can be explained in various ways: the sewer network may not yet be in place and therefore the sewage does not reach the facility, or the facility is in place, but is not properly maintained and operated. In brief, available data show that the wastewater problem is severe and needs to be addressed to improve the living conditions of the urban population.

How Many Urban Water Bodies Are Possibly Affected?

Very little is known about the actual number, length, and extent of urban water bodies and their gradual disappearance in the urbanization process. Urbanization is leading to a reduction in the length of river courses, and the number of lakes, ponds, and wetlands because of the construction of roads, rail links, housing, parking lots, etc., the filling of minor tributaries, piped drainage, river training, the lowering of the groundwater table due to over-extraction, and many other developments.

The density of water bodies (that is, of watercourses measured in kilometre length per square kilometre) is decreasing. Studies show that the higher the degree of urbanization, the lower the river density. This is due not only to the increase in paved and impervious surfaces and hence higher run-off values and significantly faster flows, but also to the concentration of these increased flow rates on fewer and shorter watercourses. This can lead to a significant and clearly noticeable increase in urban flooding. Climate change, with a tendency to more pronounced and intensified precipitation, worsens the situation. Longer rivers and wetlands, ponds, lakes, and even swilleys in the landscape, can withhold water, but their absence and shorter rivers lead to a reduction of water storage capacity and hence an increase of flood water run-off.

Smaller urban watercourses, which in the "old days" were often the centre of pre-urban life, are particularly neglected. Many small waterways are covered to allow more space for roads or commercial areas, put into concrete beds, used mostly to facilitate storm water run-offs or, in many cases, simply used as open sewers. The main water source of urban water bodies are the outflows of untreated sewage from households and small to medium sized businesses, and small water courses are generally extremely polluted and form a permanent threat for the riparian population. Besides being a hazard to human health, the watercourses are eyesores and hence there is a tendency to throw solid waste into the ditches, which leads to even more contamination.

A solution to these problems is decentralized wastewater treatment. Today, technology for compact, small wastewater treatment plants has improved significantly and the requirement for space has been very much reduced so that even in crowded urban spaces, these units can operate. There are many advantages associated with decentralized, small-scale treatment plants: rapid decision-making and implementation at a local level is feasible; unit costs are within an affordable range; the length and diameter of the pipes of the collection system can be minimized, significantly lowering the overall project cost.

Whatever the number, length, and extent of urban water bodies affected, rivers, creeks, canals, ponds, lakes, and wetlands have deteriorated significantly and they need to be upgraded and rehabilitated. As a first step, the inflowing water quality needs to be improved and the inflow of untreated sewage needs to be eradicated. In the process of rehabilitation, the water bodies need to undergo a general clean-up from rubbish, be dredged, and have morphological improvements made on them. The creation of ecological niches, stabilization of banks, establishment of amenities along the water body, and access to the water, recreational parks, and other public and private facilities could follow.

To address the problem of these very small urban water bodies, UNESCAP developed "Draft Guidelines for Sustainable Rehabilitation of Small Urban Water Bodies". The draft guidelines provide objectives, concepts, and actual sample approaches at city or district levels to enable planners to convert deteriorated water bodies to sustainable and rehabilitated waters from which the entire population can benefit.

SCALE OF INVESTMENT NEEDED AND BENEFITS EXPECTED

Evaluation of Investment Costs per Unit of Treatment Capacity

Collecting and publishing cost or unit cost data for any kind of construction is generally not an easy undertaking since the costs depend on a very wide range of externalities and other parameters. Many different sources of unit costs for decentralized wastewater treatment systems (also known by its acronym DEWATS) were used, covering the wide arch of the Asia-Pacific region, from Indonesia to Japan.

To express a common unit for cost estimates, one cubic metre of wastewater treated per day and investment cost in U.S. dollars were used as a basis [US\$/m^3/day]. Often the actual design criteria for a plant were given in m^3/day. According to the used design values and the literature on this topic, the daily wastewater produced per person is in the range of 100 to 200 litres, but the actual value depends on many factors, such as the existence of reliable water supply, climate, culture, religion, household income, type of sanitation, etc. The target wastewater treatment plant is the compact, efficient, and space-saving type suitable within an urban and peri-urban environment. If land is cheap and readily available, the treatment facilities have generally a lower unit price per one cubic metre of wastewater treated than where land is in short supply. The unit costs generally do not include the cost of laying the collecting pipes from the buildings, nor the pipe from the decentralized treatment plant to the receiving water body. The costs of operation and maintenance are also not included because it is difficult to obtain reliable operation and maintenance costs for different treatment plant designs.

As expected, the unit costs for wastewater treatment vary significantly. There are strong economies of scale: larger units have lower unit costs per cubic metre of treated wastewater than smaller plants, but even the unit investment cost for similar plant sizes can vary two to threefold. Legally or ecologically required effluent standards are an important cost determining factor: there is a price to be paid for achieving a higher standard by adding a second or even third treatment stage. Treatment at source to the highest possible standard is generally the most efficient form of treatment since the flow is well defined and limited, and the concentrations (per unit flow) are still relatively high.

If we look at total cost to society of treating wastewater, it is generally more expensive to clean up polluted water bodies than to treat wastewater at source since polluted water bodies have a higher flow rate of the mixture of polluted and unpolluted water and hence mostly dilute the existing pollution. Treatment plants to treat the water of polluted water bodies specifically usually require a large dimension and are not as efficient as the proposed array of compact decentralized treatment plants for households, condominiums, and small communities.

To facilitate rough investment cost estimates during the planning process, these collected and evaluated cost data from different units, technologies, and installations in different countries are summarized in Figure 11.1. Although they are possibly cheaper, septic tanks with leach field, cesspools, wastewater lagoons or ponds, and constructed wetlands were not considered because of the emanating smells, the water quality parameters, and the high cost of land in urban areas. The costs do not include the purchase of land, the collecting pipe system, or the pipe to the receiving waters. It does include the principal electric installation (blower, motor for rotor, etc.) where required.

In the graph in Figure 11.1, an area of the range of unit cost has been delineated. As can be seen, the installation of single-household treatment units with a throughput of about 1 m^3/day is the most expensive, and ranges from US$3,500 to US$10,000/m^3, whereas treatment plants with a capacity to treat 100 m^3/day, serving approximately 500 to 1,000 people, cost in the range of US$300 to US$900/m^3. The total investment costs for such a 100 m^3/day treatment plant range from US$30,000 to US$90,000. The typical capacity of DEWATS is in the range of 10 m^3/day to 100 m^3/day.

To estimate the costs of rehabilitating urban water bodies is similarly difficult and depends on a long array of boundary conditions, constraints,

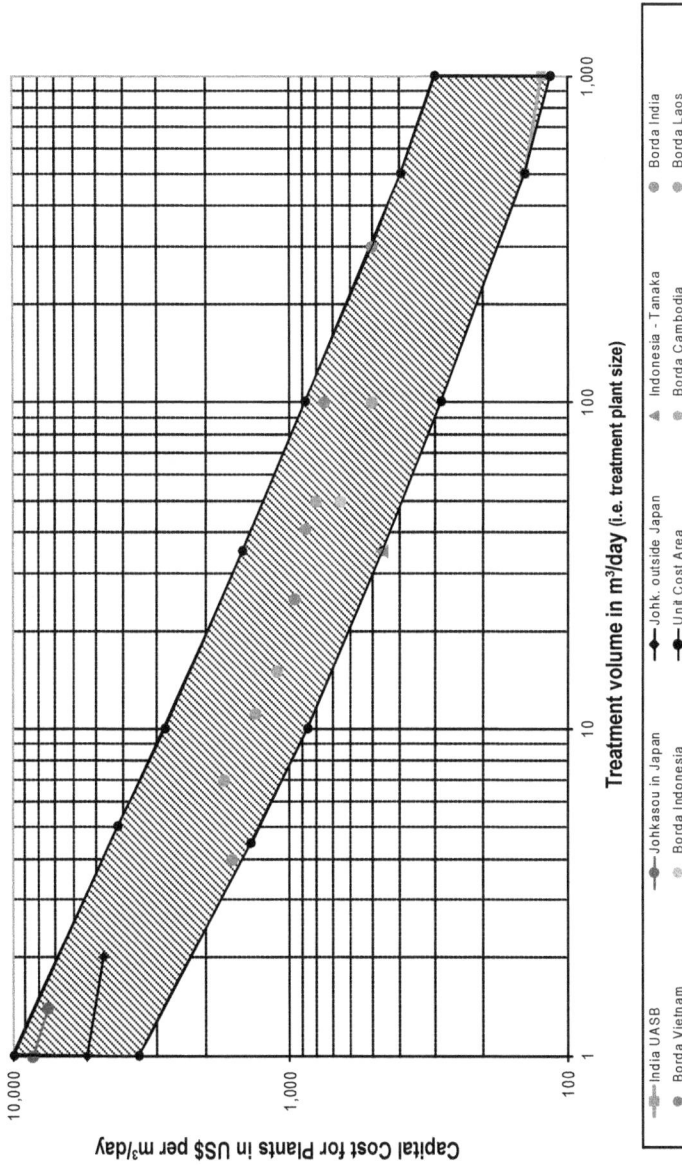

Figure 11.1
Capital Cost for DEWATS per Unit of Treatment (without cost for land)

Note: Unit investment cost for compact wastewater treatment plants surveyed in Asia-Pacific, price base: 2010.

the size of the water body, climate, construction material and labour cost, geomorphological and geotechnical conditions, and demands by the local population, just to name a few. At this stage in time, with a lack of reliable data on costs and a proper inventory of water bodies, it is not appropriate to try to estimate the overall costs to rehabilitate all affected and deteriorated water bodies. However, the order of the magnitude involved will be in a similar range as the investment costs for treating untreated urban wastewater.

Expected Benefits

Without doubt, participating citizens and communities will benefit from clean water at their doorstep. One of the main effects of introducing decentralized wastewater treatment is the reduction of faecal bacteria and nutrients in streams and other water bodies. It is hard to gauge exactly the impact that a reduction in faecal bacteria contamination will have on public health as many cases of waterborne infection are not reported or are sometimes incorrectly attributed to other sources. However, the incidence of infection from pollutant sources, through contact with surface waters, should be reduced considerably, and this should be clearly noticed by the community, doctors, and primary health care centres.

Major savings in health care costs and gains in productive days can be realized by improving access to basic sanitation. According to the World Bank, investing in sanitation brings very large economic returns of up to 2 per cent of a country's gross domestic product, or even more in some specific country contexts. According to the WHO, 88 per cent of the cases of diarrhoea worldwide are attributable to unsafe drinking water, inadequate sanitation, or insufficient hygiene. Childhood malnutrition causes about 35 per cent of all deaths of children under the age of five years worldwide; it is estimated that 50 per cent of childhood malnutrition is associated with repeated diarrhoea or intestinal nematode infections as a result of unsafe water and inadequate sanitation.

Studies by WHO, UN-HABITAT, and UNICEF and other published data show that the benefits of clean urban water bodies include improvement in public health, increased school attendance, significant reduction in child death, reduction of waterborne diseases, and increased worker productivity and economic activity. Investing in clean water will pay multiple dividends, from overcoming poverty to assisting in meeting the Millennium Development Goals. Wastewater treatment also makes economic sense. According to UNEP's *Green Economy Initiative Report*, every dollar invested in safe water and sanitation has a payback of US$3 to US$34, depending on the region and the technology deployed.

Improvement of urban water bodies is generally combined with an integrated water resource management approach, and has added components of flood mitigation and protection. Hence, it helps to reduce the amount of future flood damages. From an ecological point of view, conservation of natural resources helps to improve aquatic, semi-aquatic, and riparian habitats because a healthy riparian buffer benefits the aquatic habitat and aquatic life in the same stream. Vegetated buffers that are established reduce sediment and nutrient transported to the stream from upslope locations.

To make a wastewater treatment and rehabilitation project more attractive to the riparian community, improved recreational facilities should be part of the project. Such rehabilitation projects also create direct economic opportunities for food vendors, restaurants, and tourism, and can even improve small-scale, organic agricultural production. Improvements in water quality and the riparian environment also have a significant effect on real estate values. Just the planting of trees along roads and watercourses will increase these values. Data from the region suggest that if a watercourse is clean, rehabilitated, and attractive, land value can increase up to tenfold.

The success of any urban water rehabilitation project depends on community participation and support, the embracing of the project idea by a local champion or the riparian community as a whole, voluntary actions, such as an annual day for the clean-up of the water body by the affected population and streamside property owners, and involvement of local schools and businesses. The community or individual citizens will be able to find outside project support through NGOs, international organizations, partner communities, or by simply taking advantage of cost-sharing and tax incentive programmes to restore urban water bodies. A general quantification of all these benefits is, however, difficult to make.

THE WASTEWATER REVOLUTION IN ASIA

In February 2010, at the UN Water Meeting in Hamilton, Canada, the Sanitation Working Group co-chairperson, Margaret Catley-Carlson, briefed members on the Omega Alliance, a coalition of the willing working to provoke a revolution in wastewater collection, treatment, and reuse. Currently, the principal organizations of the alliance are the Asian Development Bank (ADB), the International Water Association (IWA), and UNSGAB. These three organizations agreed to initiate a number of activities. ADB agreed to launch a regional technical assistance project; IWA will compile a technology inventory cataloguing examples where innovative wastewater treatment approaches are being used; and UNSGAB will provide a guiding vision statement.

A wastewater revolution is necessary to make cities and their environment more liveable and sustainable because: (1) water pollution is becoming increasingly serious and turning into a limiting factor to economic growth in Asia; (2) recent developments in technology and management offer better and affordable approaches to wastewater management; (3) there is a need to transform society, culture, philosophy, and technology much more than political systems; these transformations are often known as social revolutions. The key to success is a blend of immediate action and long-term thinking and the wastewater issue must be brought into the wider dialogues of urban planning and management.

The wastewater revolution, as proposed by UNSGAB, has become possible because of the availability of a novel, cost-efficient, and modular approach that can lead to significant improvements in the living environment of the population. The immediate effect of wastewater treatment can be seen and experienced by the local population due to the improvement in the quality of the water bodies at their doorsteps. A significant reduction of bad odours, an increase in the transparency of the water, an improvement of ecology affecting fish, birds, and plants, should lead to a rapid acceptance of the technology within the immediate neighbourhood. The wastewater revolution is expected to be driven by a new approach that links decentralized wastewater treatment with the rehabilitation of urban water bodies, based on positive experiences in these two fields.

In view of the immense challenges and scale of investments required, the wastewater revolution in the Asia-Pacific region requires concerted efforts by many parties, and it is necessary to ensure the continuity of these efforts, as well as synergies of initiatives. Under the leadership of UNSGAB, the wastewater revolution relies on a wide range of partners and supporters: the UN family (in particular WHO, UNICEF, UNESCO, UN-HABITAT, UNEP, UNDP); financial institutions (ADB, World Bank, and others); international advocacy groups such as the International

Water Association, the World Toilet Organization, and the Global Water Partnership; the Asia-Pacific Water Forum and its knowledge hubs; international state aid organizations; foundations and funds such as the Aga Khan Foundation and OPEC Fund for International Development; the Japanese Sanitation Consortium, the Korea Water Forum, the Japan Water Forum, and wastewater treatment-dedicated NGOs such as BORDA.

Comprehensive and sustained wastewater management, in combination with sanitation and hygiene, is central to good health, food security, economic development, and employment generation. In terms of public spending on health issues, investing in improved wastewater management and in the supply of safe water provides particularly high returns. However, solutions must be innovative, adaptable, affordable, and bring about partnerships between the private and public sectors. Support for project development, the availability of financial resources, and the development of partnerships, should create favourable conditions for the successful implementation of the new wastewater management concept and generate the necessary support of the local population and the required change in the mindsets of local and community leaders towards wastewater management.

Capacity building at all levels is key for successful wastewater management and rehabilitation projects. To disseminate information on, promote, and raise awareness for the new combined approach of decentralized wastewater treatment and water body rehabilitation, the following three activities are suggested:

1. Creation of a "Community Wastewater Revolution Award";
2. Mobilization of resources to start and maintain the process;
3. Implementation of pilot projects to prove the success of the proposed approaches.

Similar to UN-HABITAT's annual "World Habitat Awards", or ADB's "Water Champion", the "Community Wastewater Revolution Award" should recognize communities for their efforts to clean up and rehabilitate their immediate environment. The possibility of high-level recognition and winning an award, including possible funding, should encourage communities to bring forward their most pressing cause to improve their deteriorated environment by improving sanitation and rehabilitating polluted urban water bodies.

Successful and sustained wastewater management will need entirely new dimensions and approaches of investments. A combination of public and private funding, possible commercial credit lines, tax incentives, and direct subsidies will have to be developed. These financial instruments and incentives will have to be adjusted to local, economical, cultural, and religious circumstances and settings.

Through the implementation of well-chosen and suitable pilot projects, the success story of improved living conditions due to the effective treatment of wastewater and the improvement of the urban environment will have to be demonstrated. The cleaning efforts have to follow the flow of water, from upstream to downstream, to achieve a measurable and visible impact. There already exists an array of different and well-documented pilot sanitation projects that have demonstrated the effectiveness of particular approaches, technologies, or management and operation tools. However, the combination of one of these projects with an improvement in the urban environment at the doorstep of the affected population has up to now not been applied.

CONCLUSION

Decentralized wastewater management as a tool to implement the wastewater revolution in urban areas, and to support the engines of development in the Asia-Pacific, has proven to be a convergence of recent regional trends and efforts. This convergence is especially true in terms of the improvement of the eco-efficiency of wastewater infrastructure development on the one hand, and the need to achieve the Millennium Development Goals on sanitation in a sustainable manner on the other. The implementation of the wastewater revolution in the Asia-Pacific will provide opportunities to strengthen partnerships in the water and sanitation sectors, so as to sustain a high level of economic growth in the region, while building on its collective strength for prosperity.

This trend is fully recognized within the context of the green growth approach promoted by ESCAP. The executive secretary of ESCAP in her inaugural address at the Regional Dialogue on Wastewater Management in Kuala Lumpur in June 2010 pointed out that:

> As a region, we must build upon our collective strengths if we are not only to achieve the MDGs, but also build the foundations for a more

inclusive and sustainable society for all peoples of Asia-Pacific. I would therefore like to call on you all to contribute to the achievement of the objectives of this Regional Dialogue, particularly in terms of exploring possibilities of promoting this initiative of Wastewater Revolution for the Green Growth of Asia and the Pacific.

References

BORDA and Water, Engineering and Development Centre. Decentralized Wastewater Treatment Systems (DEWATS) and Sanitation in Developing Countries — A practical Guide. 2010.

Euromonitor Global Market Research Blog, "World's Fastest Growing Cities are in Asia and Africa", 2 March 2010 <http://blog.euromonitor.com/2010/03/special-report-worlds-fastest-growing-cities-are-in-asia-and-africa.html>.

Iovanna, R. and C. Griffiths. "Clean Water, Ecological Benefits, and Benefits Transfer: A work in progress at the U.S. EPA". *Ecological Economics* 60 (2006): 473–82.

Tanaka, N. et al. "Development of a Model System for Participatory Community Waste Water Treatment Using Low-cost, Space-saving Technology in Densely Populated Area of Yogyakarta Special Province". 2010.

UNEP/UN-HABITAT. *Sick Water? The Central Role of Wastewater Management in Sustainable Development — A Rapid Response Assessment*. 2010.

Hashimoto Action Plan II — Strategy and Objectives through 2012. The United Nations Secretary-General's Advisory Board on Water and Sanitation (UNSGAB), 2010 <http://www.unsgab.org/HAP-II/HAP-II_en.pdf>.

WHO. "Safer Water, Better Health — Costs, Benefits and Sustainability of Interventions to Protect and Promote Health". 2008.

———. "Global Annual Assessment of Sanitation and Drinking-water (GLAAS) Report 2010: Targeting resources for better results". UN-Water initiative, 2010.

WHO/UNICEF. Joint Monitoring Programme (JMP) for Water Supply and Sanitation. Update 2010.

Zhou, H. et al. "Impacts of Rapid Urbanization on River Network and Flood Hazard in Shenzhen Region, China". 2010.

Governance, Decentralization, and Urbanization

12

DECENTRALIZATION AND GOOD URBAN GOVERNANCE IN SOUTHEAST ASIA
Focus on the Philippines, Indonesia, and Thailand

Alex B. Brillantes, Jr. and Herisadel P. Flores

Over the past decades decentralization has been adopted as a strategy among many nations in the region to promote good governance. The fundamental ideology here is democratization and people participation: in accordance with the fundamental principle of subsidiarity, decisions are most responsive to the specific and unique needs of the people if they are made as close to the people as possible. Therefore, governments must be brought closer to the people to make the delivery of public services more responsive.

The problems and challenges are even more critical for rapidly urbanizing areas. The argument here is that basic challenges — ranging from the delivery of basic services to the protection of the environment — and the imperative of regulation to address the problems brought about by congestion and a burgeoning population, are best addressed under a decentralized politico-administrative system.

This chapter discusses the relationship between and among economic growth, urbanization, and the imperative to decentralize. It adheres to the observation that growth and urbanization are mutually reinforcing. In fact it could be argued that these trends can lead to a "virtuous cycle" if managed well, or a "vicious spiral" to diminishing living standards if not harnessed properly. Decentralization is presented as both a logical and necessary response to urbanization in Southeast Asia.

The experience of three countries in the region in decentralizing their respective governments is recounted to provide a picture of how these countries pursued decentralization as a national policy, and includes a discussion of some of the issues and challenges they faced along the way. This is followed by a retelling of success stories from four local governments from the three focus countries, which demonstrate that good urban governance can flourish under a decentralized set-up. Various lessons are derived from these good practices, which can be emulated by other local governments in the region confronted by the challenge of rapid urbanization.

In the concluding section, a call is made to establish a regional body that would seek out, recognize, document, and disseminate good urban practices in the region. A regional alliance of cities is also sought to strengthen cooperation among city governments in the region through *sister city* and other similar arrangements.

ECONOMIC GROWTH, URBANIZATION, AND THE NEED TO DECENTRALIZE

It is not a coincidence that most Southeast Asian countries felt the pressure to decentralize roughly the same time they started to experience accelerating urbanization. Neither is it by chance that growth in the size (in terms of area and/or population) and number of urban areas almost always came at the heels of significant and sustained economic growth. These phenomena broadly suggest a relationship among economic growth, urbanization, and decentralization (White and Smoke 2005, p. 4).

The concentration of population and the intensification of economic activities in urbanized areas increase the demand for public infrastructure, goods and services, and new ways of delivering them. The rise of new economic centres also calls for localized regulation of commercial activities.

This new urban order of things, at the least, requires reforms in the old system of centralized government planning and administration. Most often the challenges to administer service effectively in the face of burgeoning needs in a particular area make it imperative for national governments to empower subnational institutions. Empirical evidence actually shows that for developing and developed countries alike, growth in per capita income is associated with a declining share in public investment by the central government (White and Smoke 2005, p. 4). In short, when faced with the complex challenges brought about by economic growth and urbanization, the central governments' frequent response is to resort to decentralization.

In addition to urbanization, democratization appears to be an important factor that triggers decentralization. After the sudden collapse of the authoritarian regimes of President Marcos in the Philippines (1986) and President Soeharto in Indonesia (1997), decentralization became a national policy as calls for legitimate, local representation grew louder (White and Smoke 2005, p. 4).

The concentration of large numbers of people in urban areas also has negative externalities, such as various kinds of congestion (from traffic to sewers to schools to recreation areas), waste, pollution, and unemployment. In the end, it is the residents of these localities who suffer from poorer health and lower overall standards of living. Of all the sections of the urban population, it is the poor, and especially their children, who are most vulnerable to these negative impacts (Yap 2010, pp. 2–5).

More than ever, Southeast Asian countries today face the challenge of urbanization and the societal and environmental changes that it brings about. The United Nations estimates that around thirty-four million people, or 6 per cent of the total population of Southeast Asia, today live in urban areas of more than five million or more inhabitants, that is, the large cities of Bangkok, Ho Chi Minh City, Jakarta, and Manila. Furthermore, almost half of the population of Southeast Asia (48.2 per cent) live in urban settlements of any size. Many of the urban residents live in urban informal settlements where they face the threat of eviction and a lack of access to basic utilities such as potable water and sanitation. These "slum-dwellers" add up to an estimated 72 million, or a quarter of the region's urban population.

Despite all its potential ill effects, urbanization is not necessarily evil. It is often the result of economic growth and a characteristic of a country on the path of development. More than this, it could be said that urbanization is necessary to sustain economic growth, largely because of the potential of urban areas to attract local and foreign investments. What is needed, therefore, is well-managed urbanization.

Decentralization — with its basic principles of responsiveness, democratic processes, and citizen participation — provides us with a logical approach, and tool, to manage urbanization effectively so that we can minimize its negative impacts, and instead harness its potential for bringing about sustainable development. Thus today, more than ever, Southeast Asian countries must recognize the need to decentralize.

DECENTRALIZATION: DEFINITION AND FORMS

Decentralization, broadly defined, is the government tendency to move away from the centre and refocus its efforts on local-level institutions (Brillantes 2003, p. 2). As pointed out by Friedman (1983, pp. 40–41), the level and extent of decentralization is subject to the interpretation of the uses and functions of local institutions by more powerful governing authorities in society. As such, the perceived *needs* of the central government determine the powers and functions assigned to local governments (Friedman 1983, pp. 40–41). This results in various forms of decentralization within and across countries which fall within a spectrum of four decentralization variants: *deconcentration, delegation, devolution,* and *debureaucratization.*

Let us describe briefly each of these variants. Deconcentration, which is also referred to as administrative decentralization, means the decentralization of functions of central government ministries, departments, and offices to subnational governments, which act as agents (or branches) of the centre (White and Smoke 2005, p. 6). It is a limited form of decentralization since decision-making remains at the centre. The role of lower levels of government — in this case, the field offices of the national government agencies — is largely limited to transmitting orders and implementing decisions of centrally based authorities (Brillantes 2009, p. 23).

Under delegation, the subnational governments do not act as branches of central government agencies. Instead they assume responsibility for delivering certain services. However, it is still the centre that determines what should be spent and sets minimum service standards. Subnational governments, on their part, are left to define the details. It is therefore the design of intergovernmental fiscal transfers and the degree and nature of central monitoring that determine the balance between central and local decision-making under delegation (White and Smoke 2005, p. 6).

Devolution, or political decentralization, involves the transfer of decision-making powers and responsibilities from national government agencies to local governments (Brillantes 2009, p. 23). Considered as the most complete form of decentralization, devolution assigns to subnational governments the responsibility of delivering legally determined public services, as well as of imposing fees and taxes required to finance these services. Generally, subnational governments under a devolved set-up have elected executive and legislative officials who enjoy a high degree of independence from central government supervision (White and Smoke 2005, p. 6).

Under debureaucratization, which is being presented as a fourth decentralization variant (but is not discussed here), the participation of the private sector and non-governmental organizations in the delivery of services is harnessed through various modalities, including contracting out, private-public partnership, and joint ventures (Brillantes 2009, p. 23).

Whatever the form or approach taken, the common aim of decentralization is to make the politico-administrative system more responsive to the needs and aspirations of citizens and thereby bring about better governance (Brillantes 2003, p. 1). Its intention is to move public decision-making processes closer to the people most affected by those decisions (Sarosa 2006, p. 157).

DECENTRALIZATION IN SOUTHEAST ASIA

As Southeast Asia marches into the twenty-first century, decentralization has been adopted by most governments in one form or another to make public services more responsive to the changing needs of citizens. Table 12.1 summarizes the legal bases and thrusts of the various decentralization reforms adopted by ASEAN member-countries, except Singapore and Brunei Darussalam — which are too small to decentralize — and Myanmar, which remains one of the most centralized states in the world (Fritzen and Lim 2006, p. 1).

This chapter focuses on the Philippines, Indonesia, and Thailand as the three countries that pursued decentralization relatively more extensively than their neighbours in Southeast Asia, although in different forms. The Philippines and Indonesia pursued devolution in their respective decentralization policies, while Thailand adopted a careful, if not shaky,

Table 12.1
Legal Bases and Thrusts of Decentralization Reforms of
ASEAN Member Countries

Country	Legal Basis	Thrust of Decentralization Reform
Cambodia	Commune Law of 2001	Significant elements of decentralization at the formal policy and legislative levels were established, but there has been limited progress in implementation. Commune councils were elected for the first time in the country's history in 2002, but were given only limited functions and resources. Nevertheless, decentralization and deconcentration policies in several pilot areas gave local authorities increased responsibility for managing urban growth, particularly in providing urban infrastructure and services, with minimal assistance and intervention from the central government. Development reforms included the Social Fund and SEILA (Khmer word for stone, which implies sustainable) programmes, through which all overseas assistance and aid were coordinated to support the decentralization and deconcentration policies of the government.
Indonesia	Law 32/2004 (on Local Governance) Law 33/2004 (on Fiscal Balance between National and Local Governments)	Law 22/1999 and Law 25/1999 (later amended by Law 32/2004 and Law 33/2004, respectively) brought about what is usually referred to as "Big Bang" decentralization. Local governments were given regulatory authority, as well as wider control over natural resources. The fiscal balance between central and local governments was reformed to give more room for democratic principles, public participation, equality, and justice. Almost all government functions were transferred to local governments, with only a handful being left to the centre. The increased responsibility, however, has not been met with adequate funds; thus there is pressure for local governments to increase revenue to cover the costs of development.
Laos	Prime Minister's Decree No. 01 (2000)	In 2000 the Prime Minister's Decree No. 01/PM identified provincial governments as strategic development units, district governments as budgetary and planning units, and village councils

Country	Legal Basis	Thrust of Decentralization Reform
	Law on Local Administration (2003)	as implementing units. The Local Administration Law, passed in 2003, set out the rights and duties of provincial, district, municipal, and village authorities, establishing the framework for local decision-making, and, to some extent, local budgeting in the process. They will require the issuance of further decrees and instructions to actually empower them.
Malaysia	Items 4 and 5 of the 9th Schedule of the Federal Constitution	Policy reforms to make local governments more responsive to the needs of the population have been more administrative than political. Recent reforms to depoliticize local governments have even reinforced centralization.
Philippines	1987 Constitution Local Government Code of 1991	The Local Government Code of 1991 devolved to local governments certain regulatory powers, as well as the responsibility of delivering a wide range of basic services, including health care, social services, environmental protection, agricultural extension, public works, education, tourism, telecommunication, and housing. The resource base of local governments was greatly expanded by broadening their taxing powers on top of increased shares in national wealth and internal revenues. The Code also provided legal and institutional infrastructure for civil society participation in local governance, and laid the foundation for a more "entrepreneurial-oriented" local government.
Thailand	Decentralization Plan and Process Act of 1999 2007 Constitution	The Constitution established significant elements of decentralization at the formal policy and legislative levels, mainly through the Decentralization Plan and Process Act of 1999. However, limited progress had been made in terms of implementation. Nonetheless, 245 central public services were transferred to local entities along with civil employees. Local revenue increased significantly through the reassignment of revenue sources and a higher share in total government revenue.

continued on next page

Table 12.1 — *cont'd*

Country	Legal Basis	Thrust of Decentralization Reform
Vietnam	1992 Constitution (and its revised clauses of 2001) Law on the Organization of the People's Councils and People's Committees of 1994	Vietnam's decentralization policy has mainly focused on the delegation of administrative functions (with emphasis on administrative and fiscal responsibilities) by the central government to three distinct levels of local government: provinces, districts, and communes. More recently, some government functions have also been delegated to the private and civil society sectors. Local administrative bodies, which are responsible for the delivery of almost all public services, are accountable to both popularly elected bodies and to higher levels of administrative units. Provincial budgets are determined annually through negotiation with the central government. The provinces, in turn, assign tax shares to the districts, which assign shares to the communes. The system of assigning revenues to lower levels of local government varies from province to province.

Note: Table constructed from data in various reports, including Khemro 2006; Suhardjo Undated; Mabbitt 2006; Phang 2008; Mahakanjana 2006; Fumio, Ozaki, Kimata 2007; Adam Fforde and Associates 2003; and Vo-Tong et al. 2001.

mix of deconcentration, delegation, and devolution. While differences in culture and history led to the adoption of distinct brands of decentralization by each country, the Philippines, Indonesia, and Thailand arguably represent the most advanced forms of decentralization in the region, characterized by a conscious effort to democratize government processes at the subnational level.

A closer look at the decentralization experiences of these pioneering member countries can provide the rest of ASEAN with an opportunity to learn from their successes, as well as from the challenges that they faced. More particularly, they can learn how to utilize decentralized structures to confront urbanization. It is important to note, however, that the urbanization trends and challenges are very similar in some respects and very different in others.

The Philippines

In 2005, the Philippine population was estimated at 84.6 million, of which 62.7 per cent lived in urban areas. With the rapid urban population growth rate of 3.04 per cent per year, it was estimated that two thirds of Filipinos will be living in urban areas by 2010. At present, the problems associated with poorly managed urbanization — pollution, inadequate water supply, weak sewage infrastructure and waste disposal, high unemployment and crime rates, concentration of informal settlers in slums, and traffic congestion — have clearly already crept up in the urban areas, particularly in Metro Manila and in other major economic centres in the country (Mangahas 2006, p. 288).

Indonesia

Back in 2005, the Indonesian population of more than 226 million was almost equally distributed between urban and rural areas, with the latter having a slight advantage. An annual urban population growth rate of 3.34 per cent, however, has swung the balance to urban areas. Rapid urbanization is largely brought about by the concentration of industrialization and economic growth in some major urban areas.

At present most city governments are poorly prepared for rapid urbanization that has led to a scarcity of urban employment opportunities; inadequate urban infrastructure and services; unavailability of affordable, decent housing for the urban poor; the need for slum improvement; unaffordable land for urban development; lack of security of tenure; inadequate land-use planning and development control; lack of financing for urban development; the need for urban environment regulation; safety concerns; etc. (Sarosa 2006, pp. 158–61).

Thailand

Thailand's population was estimated at sixty-three million in 2005, with 32.3 per cent living in urban areas; by 2010, this proportion had grown to 34 per cent. The slow growth of urban population is in large part brought about by the overall low rate of natural population increase, which was estimated at 0.66 per cent. Among the challenges brought about by urbanization is substandard housing for poorer households exemplified by those found in the new slums in urban fringe areas and around secondary cities. Declining environmental conditions (including air pollution and solid waste) pose various threats to public health (Vorratnchaiphan and Villenueve 2006, p. 347). Much of the urban growth in Thailand is occurring outside the municipal boundaries and at the expense of adjacent

arable lands, which are being transformed into newly urbanized zones
(pp. 343–44).

Table 12.2 summarizes the demographic indicators of urbanization
of the three countries and compares them with those of Southeast Asia
as a whole.

Observing decentralization in Asia during the early 1980s, Friedman
(1983, p. 41) remarked that local governments were generally seen as
mere bureaucratic instruments of implementation (Friedman 1983,
p. 41). He noted that throughout the continent, local government leaders
were perceived as lower-level bureaucrats who were mere recipients
of communications, implementers of policies devised elsewhere, and
supporters of higher authorities (p. 55). But even then and earlier, several
authors identified emerging forms of decentralization in the Southeast
Asian region.

Friedman (1983, p. 39) reported that before the declaration of martial
law in 1972, the Philippines had constitutionally mandated provincial
governments and a variety of governing bodies and officials elected at
the municipal and barrio levels. Although these local governments had
very limited resources, intergovernmental transfers through a complicated
system of grants made them more autonomous than their counterparts
in other Asian countries. He perceived the Philippine local government
system as having the potential for continued political development not
found anywhere else as it generated its own leadership, addressed its
own needs, and solved its own problems. Under martial law, however, the
local governments were subjected to tightened central controls through
technocratic bureaucratization, despite guarantees in the 1973 Constitution
for local government autonomy and the Marcos regime's rhetoric of
increasing self-government (p. 39).

Indonesia's second five-year national development plan (REPELITA
II) paid significant attention to regional development. Under REPELITA[1]
II, provincial governments prepared their own development plans which,
together with the regional development strategy formulated centrally,
helped determine budgetary allocations for sectoral projects and local
government subsidies (Mathur 1983, p. 65). In Thailand, provincial
development planning was introduced in 1977. This made the province
the key unit in subnational development. The Provincial Development
Planning Committee, chaired by the governor, drew up a five-year social
and economic plan for the province, allocated funds for projects to local

Table 12.2
Demographic Indicators of Urbanization in Southeast Asia, Indonesia, the Philippines, and Thailand

	Total Population ('000)			Urban Population ('000)			Percentage Urban (%)		Urban Annual Growth Rate (%)		Total Annual Growth Rate (%)	
	2005	2010		2005	2010		2005	2010	2005–2010	2010–2015	2005–2010	2010–2015
Southeast Asia	557,669	594,214		245,895	286,579		44.1	48.2	3.06	2.63	1.27	1.11
Indonesia	226,063	239,600		108,828	128,634		48.1	53.7	3.34	2.70	1.16	0.97
Philippines	84,566	93,001		53,032	61,731		62.7	66.4	3.04	2.60	1.90	1.67
Thailand	63,003	65,125		20,352	22,118		32.3	34.0	1.66	1.75	0.66	0.50

Note: Generated from the United Nation's *World Urbanization Prospects: The 2007 Revision Population Database*, 28 May 2010 <http://esa.un.org/unup/p2k0data.asp>.

administration units, and submitted performance reports to the Central Committee on Provincial Development (p. 60).

Beginning in the latter part of the 1980s, however, important developments on the social, economic, and political fronts occurred in these three countries. Regime transitions ushered in changes in various areas of governance. In all three countries, significant strides were taken towards more meaningful decentralization, as summarized in the following:

The Philippines

Five years after the relatively peaceful "1986 People Power Revolution" that brought down President Marcos' authoritarian regime, the Local Government Code of 1991 (LGC) was enacted in the Philippines. This was in accordance with a provision in the 1987 Constitution, which declared that "the State shall ensure the autonomy of local governments". Most sectors of society welcomed this development, especially after decades of putting up with an over-centralized politico-administrative system, which concentrated most significant political and administrative decisions in the national capital. The enactment of the LGC finally transferred the responsibility of delivering basic services, such as agricultural extension, health care, social services, environmental protection, and public works to local government units (LGUs), together with the appropriate personnel, assets, equipment, programmes, and projects (Brillantes 2003, p. 8).

Aside from providing the legal mandate for government decentralization, the LGC contributed much to the policy framework for regional planning and development, which is part of the functions and responsibilities devolved to the LGUs. For instance, the LGC encourages local governments to group themselves, build alliances, and forge partnerships with civil society organizations in managing development. It also recognizes the potential of metropolitan arrangements consisting of clusters of relatively urbanized LGUs (Mangahas 2006, p. 279).

The LGC provides for the transfer of national income to LGUs through the internal revenue allotment (IRA). At present the IRA represents 40 per cent of the internal taxes collected by the national government (computed against the third preceding year's collection). For most LGUs, this is their main source of funds, which they use to finance the delivery of public services. The LGC gives LGUs access to other financial resources, besides the IRA, by broadening their revenue-generating and taxation powers and by providing them with a specific share of the national resources extracted in their area, such as charges for mining, fisheries, and forestry (Mangahas 2006, p. 279).

Indonesia

Almost three years after Soeharto resigned from the presidency, Indonesia adopted what has later been called a "Big Bang" decentralization on 1 January 2001. This came after decades of debate and delay in implementing decentralization and democratization. The term "Big Bang" decentralization came about since the preparation took only one year and the degree of decentralization was extensive. What used to be a very strong central government was decentralized directly to the districts (*kabupaten*) and municipalities (*kota*). All government authority was devolved to local governments, except for monetary and fiscal affairs, religious affairs, the judicial system, foreign affairs, and national security (Brodjonegoro 2009, p. 103).

Decentralization in Indonesia was initiated through the enactment of two important laws: Law 22/1999 on Local Governance and Law 25/1999 on Fiscal Balance between National and Local Governments. The law on local governance, commonly referred to as the decentralization law, transferred a large number of the government's obligatory functions from the national government to local governments. The accompanying fiscal decentralization law (the law on fiscal balance), meanwhile, aimed to provide the necessary financial resources for local governments to carry out their newly expanded responsibilities. Together with the transfer of functions and financial resources, decentralization also led to the transfer of 2.3 million staff from departmental offices to local governments. All this was done in the span of one year (Sarosa 2006, p. 166).

In 2004 Law 22/1999 on Local Governance was amended by Law 32/2004. This modification was deemed necessary to clarify some provisions of the earlier law, especially with regard to the specific responsibilities of the local governments. It also addresses the confusion brought about by the dual roles of the provinces, which perform the deconcentration function as the representatives of the central government in their particular regions and the decentralized function as autonomous entities. Nonetheless the fundamental principle of transferring a wide range of government functions to provincial as well as local governments remained intact. The amendment also set the record straight on the misconception that there is a non-hierarchical relationship between provinces and districts, which was thought to be a hindrance to necessary regional cooperation. In addition, the new law was intended to promote the democratization process further. For instance, while Law 22/1999 provided that district heads should be elected by their respective local councils, Law 32/2004 specified that they should be directly elected by the citizens (Sarosa 2006, p. 166).

With the devolution of almost all government functions, the people of Indonesia can expect that decision-making on the development processes will be much closer to them and that their aspirations will be better heard by the decision-makers. In some districts, decentralization has gone even further than what Law 32/2004 required, with some functions of the district government being transferred to lower levels of governments (*kecamatan*, *kelurahan*, or villages), in combination with lump sum financial grants to ensure that the functions transferred can be implemented effectively (Sarosa 2006, p. 166).

Thailand

The promulgation of the 1997 Constitution was a major turning point for both the extensive reform of the local authority system and the decentralization process. It defined decentralization as a national basic policy, leading to the enactment in 1999 of a Decentralization Plan and Process Act (the Decentralization Act of 1999). The act created a National Decentralization Committee (NDC), which was convened at the start of 2000. The committee led the drafting of the Decentralization Plan made up of a Master Plan and an Action Plan. The Decentralization Act of 1999 called for an increase in the percentage of local authority expenditures to at least 20 per cent of total government expenditure by 2001, and further to at least 35 per cent by 2006. This indicated an intergovernmental transfer of services supported by fiscal decentralization as a legal mandate (Nagai, Ozaki, and Kimata 2007, p. 7).

The Decentralization Act of 1999 mandates the Thai Government to complete the decentralization process in four years. Should it fail to do so, a maximum period of ten years was allowed. The Decentralization Plan identified a total of fifty central government departments and 245 public services for decentralization. As of the beginning of 2007, however, only 180 functions had been transferred, or were in the process of being transferred to local authorities. This means that one in every four functions had remained with the central government. Furthermore, the proportion of local authority revenue to total government revenue stood at 24.1 per cent in 2006. This fell far short of the 35 per cent targeted by the end of that year. Instead, an amendment to the Decentralization Act of 1999 lowered the target to 25 per cent, to be attained by the end of 2007. The previous target of 35 per cent was downgraded to a non-binding target in the same amendment (Nagai, Ozaki, and Kimata 2007, pp. 12–13).

On the human resources front, the transfer of government personnel from the central offices to local authorities has been stalled since 2005. A total of only 4,459 central government officials and employees were transferred to the local authorities from 2003 to 2004. Thus, it could be said that fiscal decentralization was not accompanied by the transfer of functions or human resources, reflecting a significant deviation from the principles of the Decentralization Plan (Nagai, Ozaki, and Kimata 2007, p. 16).

In the latter part of 2006, a military junta overthrew the government of Prime Minister Thaksin Shinawatra. This paved the way for the drafting and later adoption of the 2007 Constitution. The salient provisions of this new constitution concerning decentralization focused on five vital areas: (1) more explicit and comprehensive extension of local government organizations' duties and powers; (2) a better balance between the supervision of local government organizations and their independence; (3) the development of operational and administrative systems for local government organizations; (4) the provision of public space for people, communities, and civil society to participate in local administration, jointly with the local government organizations; and (5) the implantation of transparency in local politics (Tanchai 2009, p. 58).

DECENTRALIZATION ISSUES AND CHALLENGES

Despite its perceived advantages, decentralization has stirred up major debates as governments went along with its implementation. A case can be made that some of the problems attributed to decentralization were not inherent in decentralized governance, but were the results of a hesitant, if not half-hearted, approach in implementing decentralization. Furthermore, a number of concerns may just be temporary but inevitable consequences of the transition to a decentralized government, which can nonetheless be mitigated. Still, it is clear that some decentralization problems were the result of self-serving actions and behaviour by some sectors that tried to take advantage of the new policy. The following are some of the challenges faced by the three countries as they undertook decentralization:

Deteriorating Public Services

Perhaps the most important measure of success is whether decentralization was able to improve the services that the citizens receive. Feedback on the initial implementation of decentralization in the three countries suggests that this has not been the case. Rather, the perceived deterioration in the quality of public services during the first few years of decentralization threatened to roll back the policy, and quite a few calls for recentralization were made. However, a major shift in governance such as this necessarily requires major adjustments. The deterioration in the quality of services under decentralization was undoubtedly partly caused by half-hearted decision-making on the part of the central government. This is demonstrated by the existence of (1) unfunded mandates of local governments brought about by inadequate financial transfers from the centre, and (2) a lack of manpower and technical capacity of local governments because of the centre's failure to transfer expertise and personnel.

In Indonesia, the nationwide shortage of public sector administrative skills affected the performance of local governments, especially in remote urban centres in the eastern part of the country. These localities have weak health, education, and community facilities, making it extremely difficult for them to attract professionals away from larger urban centres (Sarosa 2006, pp. 166–67). Brodjonegoro (2009, p. 111) commented that the central government should have completed its unfinished homework of setting a national minimum standard for basic public service delivery, especially in basic education, health, and infrastructure, before the introduction of decentralization. This was deemed crucial in guaranteeing that local communities everywhere in Indonesia would not receive less than the national standard in their local public service delivery (Brodjonegoro 2009, p. 111).

The Philippines' Department of the Interior and Local Government (DILG) developed a mechanism to monitor local government compliance with certain performance standards. Its Local Government Performance Measurement System (LGPMS) focuses on five major areas: governance, administration, social services, economic development, and environmental services. The outputs of the LGPMS serve as the basis for "the state of local government" reports prepared by the local governments, and also serve as a guide in the design and implementation of development programmes and projects of the local governments, including capacity building interventions and assistance. The system is currently under review (Brillantes 2009, p. 25).

Lack of Coordination among Local Governments

In Indonesia the euphoria among local governments over their new powers made it difficult for them to work in cooperation with adjacent local governments. This has prevented them from developing a coherent urban strategy; an example is the problems faced by the capital city of Jakarta to find a suitable dump site for its solid waste (Sarosa 2006, p. 164). Meanwhile, the fragmentation of urban areas in Thailand led to uncoordinated urban service delivery. Urban areas suffered from the results of disjointed development and local spatial planning, wherein the former is a function of the local authorities, while the latter is performed by a central government agency (Vorratnchaiphan and Villenueve 2006, p. 347).

Several local governments in the Philippines have entered into various modes of inter-local government alliance or cooperation to address common concerns, ranging from traffic to solid waste management to environment management such as watershed and marine resources management, and the management of inter-local health zones and trade-based agro-industrial zones. Alliances involve both horizontal and vertical cooperation among government agencies, that is, among provinces, cities, or municipalities, or between provinces and their component municipalities (Brillantes 2008, p. 25).

Fragmentation of Local Governments

In Indonesia, the local elite reportedly abused an article in Law 22/1999 and its amending law, Law 32/2004, which provides for the creation of new local governments, by proposing many new local governments. The first eight years after decentralization saw the number of local governments increase from about 340 to 470 (Brodjonegoro 2009, p. 105). This rapid growth in the number of district and provincial government units caused problems in financing, monitoring, and evaluation. It led to a reduction in the per capita allocation of national grants and transfers to established local governments; larger urban governments were the most affected (Sarosa 2006, pp. 166–67). Ironically, the emergence of new local governments only made local governments more heavily dependent on the general allocation fund, the country's main intergovernmental transfer instrument. The role of locally sourced revenues became minor since most of the new local governments do not have a sufficient economic base for local taxes and charges (Brodjonegoro 2009, p. 106).

Brodjonegoro (2009, p. 107) identified two possible solutions to these challenges: inter-local government cooperation and amalgamation of local governments. He suggested that the central government could offer an incentive for neighbouring local governments to merge into one, in the form of additional transfers to merged local governments. However, Indonesia, so far, does not have that kind of incentive (p. 107).

In the Philippines, the fragmentation of provinces has also increased, although this was seen as costly considering the tremendous administrative overhead involved. Despite this, there are still several more proposals to divide provinces, which smack of a variation of gerrymandering. On a more positive note, there have been some successful cases of political amalgamation, albeit among lower-tier local governments. For instance, the Island Garden City of Samal was formed through the amalgamation of five municipalities on the island. Another case was the merger of the city of Sorsogon and the municipality of Bakon (Brillantes 2009, p. 25).

Lack of Coordination between Central and Local Governments

In the Philippines, both central and local governments pursue local and regional development, but their efforts are hardly coordinated. This has resulted in duplication and the misallocation of scarce resources. An example is the weak link between the planning and budgeting processes at central and local government levels. The planning and budgeting processes at the national level are characterized by a sectoral bias and very weak spatial and physical orientation (Mangahas 2006, p. 283).

More recently efforts had been made by the national government to address this problem. Four central government agencies — the Department of the Interior and Local Government (DILG), the National Economic and Development Authority (NEDA), the Department of Budget and Management (DBM), and the Department of Finance (DOF) — issued a joint circular (2007):

1. to provide guidelines on the harmonization and synchronization of local planning, investment programming, revenue administration, budgeting, and expenditure management;

2. to strengthen the interface between LGUs and national government agencies and the coordination between and among all LGU levels in planning, investment programming, revenue administration, budgeting, and expenditure management; and
3. to clarify and spell out the responsibilities of DILG, NEDA, DBM, and DOF relative to local planning, investment programming, revenue administration, budgeting and expenditure management.

This only goes to show that realities on the ground can also influence the policies of higher-level government authorities.

GOOD URBAN GOVERNANCE PRACTICES FROM THE THREE FOCUS COUNTRIES

The governance challenges faced by urban localities in the three focus countries can be summarized as follows: (1) economic pressures including rising unemployment; (2) inadequate public infrastructure and services; (3) environmental degradation; (4) inadequate housing and informal settling; and (5) a worsening safety and security situation. While many local governments continue to struggle in addressing these problems, some have made good use of opportunities that a decentralized set-up has made available to find new and effective solutions to these challenges.

Freeing local officials from the chains of too much central government control, decentralization in the three countries in focus has spawned a lot of good practices in the management of urban localities. The most outstanding of these good practices — those that were able to balance local development with other positive social values such as equity, transparency, accountability, participation, and environmental protection, among others — were also deemed as the most sustainable. Labelled good urban governance (GUG) practices, these are recognized and documented locally and internationally by national government agencies, civil society, and development partner organizations to serve as paradigms that can be emulated by other local governments.

Internationally the 2006 ADB study on *Urbanization and Sustainability in Asia* featured GUG cases of three local governments from each of the twelve Asian countries covered. These cases were selected by country specialists based on their contribution to (1) good governance; (2) urban management; (3) infrastructure and service provision; (4) financing and cost recovery; (5) sustainability, innovation, and change; and (6) leveraging official development assistance (Roberts and Kanaley 2006, p. 7).

In the Philippines, the Gawad Galing Pook gives annual awards to outstanding local government programmes selected using the following criteria: (1) positive results; (2) promotion of people's participation and empowerment; (3) innovation, transferability, and sustainability; and (4) efficiency of programme service delivery. The programmes are documented and disseminated so that they can be replicated by other local governments. In Thailand, the annual Sustainable City Award selects local government awardees based on their demonstration of good governance, sustainability, and innovative urban management practices (Vorratnchaiphan and Villenueve 2006, p. 355).

The GUG practices of three of the four Southeast Asian local governments highlighted in this section were recognized by the above institutions and documented in *Urbanization and Sustainability in Asia*. These local governments are the cities of Marikina and Naga in the Philippines, the island city of Tarakan in Indonesia, and the municipality of Phichit in Thailand.

Marikina is one of the smallest cities within the Philippines' National Capital Region (NCR). It has an area of 21.5 km^2 and a population of about half a million people (City Government of Marikina n.d.). Naga City is located 500 km southeast of NCR and is part of the Bicol Region, one of the poorest regions in the Philippines. It has an area of 84.48 km^2 and a population of more than 160,000. As Bicol's centre for commerce, finance, trade, and services, Naga plays a crucial role in regional development (Mangahas 2006, p. 296). Tarakan is a 251 km^2 island city in East Kalimantan, Indonesia, with a population of around 170,000. The city is a trading centre for fishery, forest products, and domestic goods (Sarosa 2006, p. 175). Phichit Municipality is the capital of Phichit Province, 345 km north of Bangkok. The municipal jurisdiction covers 12 km^2, with a population of around 25,000 (Vorratnchaiphan and Villenueve 2006, pp. 358–59). Below is a summary of their accomplishments in addressing challenges brought about by urbanization:

Economic Pressures

Naga City initiated the formation of the Metro Naga Development Council with fourteen neighbouring towns from the adjacent province of Camarines Sur to facilitate urban-rural linkages. The inter-local government alliance practised area-wide planning to bring about sustainable development in all its member localities. By virtue of a local ordinance, the city government granted incentives to investors in preferred investments in order to generate jobs for Metro Naga residents and promote balanced growth. The Investment Promotions and Action Center was established to implement the objectives set by the city's investment board, market Metro Naga as an investment site, facilitate joint venture projects with local and external investors, and provide assistance to investors (Mangahas 2006, p. 298).

In order to change peoples' wasteful consumption of scarce energy resources, Tarakan City issued a policy that increased local electricity basic rates. The additional income gained from this measure was used to improve the energy supply on the island so that its economic development would not be hindered by electricity outages (Sarosa 2006, p. 177).

Inadequate Public Infrastructure and Services

Tarakan City made human development of its citizens its top priority by allocating more than 30 per cent of its annual budget to education. The local government improved the physical facilities of public elementary, middle, and high schools. It also put up a campus for a local university, which includes a seven-storey library and education information centre. To complement these projects, programmes that improve the welfare and calibre of teachers, as well as the quality of the curriculum, were also implemented (Sarosa 2006, p. 176).

Congestion of the old business district drove Naga City to harness the capacity of the private sector by partnering firms to develop four new satellite markets. These provide alternative commercial centres, which made the old business district dynamic again (Mangahas 2006, p. 298).

Environmental Degradation

The local government cleaned up Marikina's primary river and developed its shores to usher the locality's transformation from a murky, low-profile town into one of the most liveable cities in the country. This paved the way for renewed public support for the local government which then spawned numerous other outstanding local governance programmes (Galing Pook 2003, p. 8).

Tarakan City instituted policies to protect its remaining mangrove forest that had been neglected for years as the commercial centre expanded. The city maintained the island's rich biodiversity by identifying, protecting, and cultivating endangered plant species. A local regulation was passed banning the trade of mangrove wood and protected species (Sarosa 2006, p. 175).

Phichit Municipality linked caring for the environment with the generation of income for the people through various waste recycling projects. Municipal staff collect used paper from offices, which they convert into decorative products. Another project, the Waste Bank, is a waste recycling shop managed by a community committee. It serves as a depot for people who buy recyclable materials from households and subsequently sell them to the Waste Bank. From the profit, the Waste Bank allocates funds to organize social and sporting activities for the community.

Encouraged by these successes, the mayor of Phichit initiated a collaboration for the municipality, the Provincial Administrative Organization, and the Regional Environmental Office to minimize organic waste from the fresh food market. On the technical advice of a local university, the project involves the composting of organic waste to produce fertilizer pellets that are distributed back to the communities either for use or resale. People can trade their organic waste for fertilizer pellets (Vorratnchaiphan and Villenueve 2006, pp. 358–61).

Inadequate Housing and Informal Settling

In an effort to address urban poverty, Marikina City created the Settlements Office, whose main task is to provide decent shelter to the underprivileged. One of its services, the community mortgage programme (CMP), implemented in partnership with the National Home Mortgage Finance Corporation, helps residents in depressed areas acquire the lots they occupy (Galing Pook 2003, p. 8).

Tarakan City introduced tough population regulations to control in-migration and mitigate its negative impacts. New settlers of the island city are required to have a permanent job within six months of their arrival. Otherwise they are asked to return home using the cash deposit they made as new entrants requesting residential permits. This population management approach was replicated from a similar approach by the city of Balikpapan (also in Indonesia); it shows that the transfer, exchange, and sharing of experiences, knowledge, and expertise can and does occur among autonomous local governments (Sarosa 2006, p. 177).

Worsening Safety and Security Situation

Marikina City established within the market premises a Clean Food Laboratory that randomly tests all kinds of food sold in the market to ensure that they are safe for consumption. The city also maintains an emergency hotline for medical, fire, and police assistance. Local authorities guarantee a response time of five minutes immediately after a phone call (Galing Pook 2003, p. 8).

LESSONS FROM GOOD URBAN GOVERNANCE PRACTICES

What the above good urban governance cases tell us is that decentralization can lead to more responsive management of urban areas, resulting in more balanced development and better living standards for citizens. Some valuable lessons can also be culled from these cases. For instance, all the cases cited above involve some degree of departure from the traditional or usual ways of delivering public services. Rather than just collecting and disposing of garbage, the mayor of Phichit saw the potential of recycling for minimizing waste and providing livelihood. She created the Waste Bank. The mayor of Marikina saw the need to ensure that food products from the city public market are safe and clean. He established the Clean Food Laboratory. These officials showed the capacity for vision and innovation, two attributes of effective leadership. Another attribute of effective leadership is the exercise of political will. Increasing local electricity basic rates was certainly not a popular decision, but the mayor of Tarakan still went ahead with the implementation of the policy because he was aware of its ultimate benefits to the city and its inhabitants.

Participation by the private sector, civil society, and citizens is another attribute of good urban governance that was demonstrated in the different cases. Tapping these sectors not only expands the human, financial, and knowledge resources that can be utilized for the implementation of local government programmes, but also enhances the communal sense of ownership of the programmes. With everyone having their stake in the success of the programme, it can be expected that everyone will do his or her share to make the endeavour successful. The success of Naga City in attaining a balanced local economic development can be attributed, to some extent, to the participation of civil society in the various legislative councils and local special bodies. The various waste recycling projects of

Phichit Municipality might not have been that successful if not for the cooperation and patronage of the citizens.

Some urban management concerns transcend jurisdictional boundaries, and one argument against decentralization is the fragmentation of urban areas, leading to disjointed policies and programmes of adjacent localities. There are some quarters, however, who perceive that cities have grown too big to respond effectively to the needs and aspirations of communities. While the debate is still on whether integration or fragmentation is more appropriate in effectively managing continuously growing urban areas, there are clusters of local governments that built alliances on their own initiative to address common problems. Sometimes these cooperative arrangements are even used as venues to promote local economic development in an area encompassing two or more localities. One such alliance is the Metro Naga Development Council that was formed by Naga City and fourteen other municipalities in the Province of Camarines Sur in the Philippines.

In addition to the above, local governments are now realizing that they exist in the interest of the citizens. With urbanization, the number of public services delivered by local governments increases. Aside from the delivery of social services, local governments are increasingly responsible for the regulation of economic transactions and processes. Citizen-centred urban governance ensures that the welfare of citizens is the primary interest of the local government. One expression of this principle is the formulation and publication of a Citizen's Charter or Service Pledge like what Naga City did.

CONCLUDING REMARKS: RECOMMENDATIONS TOWARDS BETTER URBAN GOVERNANCE IN SOUTHEAST ASIA

The preceding sections show us that Southeast Asian cities have the capacity for good urban governance. However, their performance is affected by a myriad of factors, such as inadequate resources, lack of technical capacity, restrictive national policies, excessive central government controls and supervision, and uninspired leadership. Most of these concerns are brought about by the fact that decentralization is still a relatively new approach to governance in Southeast Asia. Thus, there is still a huge demand for capacity building that equips local government officials with the appropriate knowledge and skills on effective urban management approaches. One way ASEAN could meet this demand is to establish a regional award-giving body that would recognize, feature, and document good urban practices of innovative Southeast Asian cities. It could also identify indicators of good urban governance that it can use in selecting the awardees. These indicators could be similar to those that had been used by the ADB in the *Urbanization and Sustainability in Asia* study, and the criteria used by the Gawad Galing Pook in the Philippines and the Sustainable Cities Award in Thailand. Winning programmes could then be published and given as much exposure as possible so that they can be replicated by other local governments.

Another way the flame of local governance innovation is being sustained in the Philippines is through *sister city* arrangements between the governments of a relatively highly developed urban area and a newly urbanizing locality. Such arrangements can facilitate the transfer of knowledge through technical assistance, benchmarking, and peer-to-peer coaching. Sometimes this may even involve financial support.

Establishing a *Southeast Asian Cities Alliance* could help expand the network of local governments from their respective countries to the entire region. The alliance would be responsible for maintaining a databank of good urban governance practices in Southeast Asia that could be used as a portal to promote *sister city* arrangements between cities from different countries in the region. With more cooperation among cities in Southeast Asia, we can look forward to better urban governance in the region within the framework of meaningful decentralization.

Note

1.   Acronym for *Rencana Pembangunan Lima Tahun*, which translates in English to Five-Year Development Plan.

References

Adam Fforde and Associates Pty Ltd. "Decentralisation in Vietnam — Working Effectively at Provincial and Local Government Level — A Comparative Analysis of Long An and Quang Ngai Provinces". Report prepared for the Australian Agency for International Development, November 2003 <http://www.ausaid.gov.au/publications/pdf/decentralisation_vietnam.pdf> (accessed 28 May 2010).

Brillantes, Alex Jr. B. *Innovations and Excellence: Understanding Local Governments in the Philippines*. Quezon City: Center for Local and Regional Governance, National College of Public Administration and Governance, University of the Philippines, 2003.

———. "Decentralization and Local Autonomy in the Philippines: Reflections after 17 Years of Implementation". In *Decentralization and Local Communities: Symposium Report for the 2nd Symposium of the Institute for Comparative Studies in Local Governance (COSLOG)*. Tokyo: COSLOG, National Graduate Institute for Policy Studies (GRIPS), 2009.

Brodjonegoro, Bambang P.S. "Decentralization in Indonesia and its Impacts to Local Community". In *Decentralization and Local Communities: Symposium Report for the 2nd Symposium of the Institute for Comparative Studies in Local Governance (COSLOG)*. Tokyo: COSLOG, National Graduate Institute for Policy Studies (GRIPS), 2009.

City Government of Marikina. Official Website <http://www.marikina.gov.ph/PAGES/Demography.htm> (accessed 28 May 2010).

DILG, NEDA, DBM, and DOF, Republic of the Philippines. Joint Memorandum Circular No. 1 Series of 2007.

Friedman, Harry J. "Decentralized Development in Asia: Local Political Alternatives". In *Decentralization and Development: Policy Implementation in Developing Countries*, edited by G. Shabir Cheema and Dennis A. Rondinelli. Beverly Hills: Sage, 1983.

Fritzen, Scott A. and Patrick W. O. Lim. "Problems and Prospects of Decentralization in Developing Countries". Paper submitted to *Encyclopedia of Public Administration and Public Policy*, May 2006 <http://www.spp.nus.edu.sg> (accessed 28 May 2010).

Galing Pook. *Gawad Galing Pook 2003*. Pasig City: Galing Pook Foundation, 2003.

Khemro, Beng Hong Socheat. "Cambodia". In *Urbanization and Sustainability in Asia: Case Studies of Good Practice*, edited by Brian Roberts and Trevor Kanaley. Manila: Asian Development Bank, 2006.

Mabbitt, Richard. "Lao People's Democratic Republic". In *Urbanization and Sustainability in Asia: Case Studies of Good Practice*, edited by Brian Roberts and Trevor Kanaley. Manila: Asian Development Bank, 2006.

Mahakanjana, Chandra-nuj. "Decentralization, Local Government and Socio-political Conflict in Southern Thailand". East-West Center Washington Working Papers No. 5. Washington, DC: East-West Center, 2006.

Mangahas, Joel V. "The Philippines". In *Urbanization and Sustainability in Asia: Case Studies of Good Practice*, edited by Brian Roberts and Trevor Kanaley. Manila: Asian Development Bank, 2006.

Mathur, Kuldeep. "Administrative Decentralization in Asia". In *Decentralization and Development: Policy Implementation in Developing Countries*, edited by G. Shabir Cheema and Dennis A. Rondinelli. Beverly Hills: Sage, 1983.

Nagai, Fumio, Kazuyo Ozaki, and Yoichiro Kimata. *JICA Program on Capacity Building of Thai Local Authorities: Analysis from a Capacity Development Perspective*. Tokyo: Research Group, Institute for International Cooperation, Japan International Cooperation Agency, 2007.

Phang Siew Nooi. "Transforming Local Government — The Challenge to Centralization". Paper presented at Seminar in Local Government in Malaysia — The Search for New Directions, organized by the Centre for Malaysian Chinese Studies in collaboration with the Institution of China Studies, University of Malaya, 22 May 2008 <http://english.cpiasia.net/index.php?option=com_docman&task=doc_download&gid=218&Itemid=101> (accessed 28 May 2010).

Roberts, Brian and Trevor Kanaley, eds. *Urbanization and Sustainability in Asia: Case Studies of Good Practice*. Manila: Asian Development Bank, 2006.

Sarosa, Wicaksono. "Indonesia". In *Urbanization and Sustainability in Asia: Case Studies of Good Practice*, edited by Brian Roberts and Trevor Kanaley. Manila: Asian Development Bank, 2006.

Suhardjo, Sussongko. "Country Reports on Local Government Systems: Indonesia" <http://www.unescap.org/huset/lgstudy/new-countrypaper/Indonesia/Indonesia.pdf> (accessed 28 May 2010).

Tanchai, Woothisarn. "Decentralization in Thailand: The Case Study of People Participation in Local Government". In *Decentralization and Local Communities: Symposium Report for the 2nd Symposium of the Institute for Comparative Studies in Local Governance (COSLOG)*. Tokyo: COSLOG, National Graduate Institute for Policy Studies (GRIPS), 2009.

United Nations. World Urbanization Prospects: The 2007 Revision Population Database <http://esa.un.org/unup/p2k0data.asp> (accessed 28 May 2010).

Vorratnchaiphan, Chamniern and David Villenueve. "Thailand". In *Urbanization and Sustainability in Asia: Case Studies of Good Practice*, edited by Brian Roberts and Trevor Kanaley. Manila: Asian Development Bank, 2006.

Vo-Tong Xuan et al. "Viet Nam: Country Portfolio Review and Evaluation". Report prepared for the International Fund for Agricultural Development, 2001 <http://www.ifad.org> (accessed 28 May 2010).

White, Roland and Paul Smoke. "East Asia Decentralizes". In World Bank, *East Asia Decentralizes: Making Local Government Work*. Washington, DC: World Bank, 2005.

Yap Kioe Sheng. "Promoting Productive, Inclusive and Sustainable Cities and Towns in Southeast Asia". Singapore: Monograph (draft), 2010.

13

CONTEXTS AND CHALLENGES IN ENGAGING LOCAL GOVERNMENTS FOR SUSTAINABLE URBAN DEVELOPMENT IN SOUTHEAST ASIA

Wicaksono Sarosa and F.P. Anggriani Arifin

This chapter aims to identify key challenges in engaging local governments in the Southeast Asian region in the promotion of sustainable urban development. The engagement with local governments is considered imperative in the context of various macro-level transformations that are currently going on in the region, namely rapid economic growth, urbanization, democratization, and decentralization. These transformations have generally thrust local governments and local communities into prominence in ensuring that rapid urban development in the region is more sustainable, or otherwise allowing the formation of harmful towns, cities, and urban settlements through neglect or lack of capacity.

Therefore, it is crucial that local governments and communities have the necessary awareness and knowledge of the various aspects of sustainable urban development, as well as the needed skills and capacities to make it happen. There are at least two different ways that local governments can take to come to that point or, at least, to start embarking on a path that will lead to sustainable urban development.

One is when local governments or communities become serious in making their cities sustainable without being deliberately and significantly engaged by external parties. There are documented good practices where local leaders and communities became the major driving force for the needed local innovations.[1] However, in many other cases, external parties are needed to instigate and support the initiatives. These can be in the forms of urban-related national policies, international conventions, or donor-supported projects and programmes.

In most cases though, a combination of both internal and external factors exist in the efforts to make urban development in Southeast Asia more sustainble. In addition to the two different ways, distinct political institutional settings from one country to another also engender different methods and approaches in such endeavours. This chapter elaborates on the various ways of engaging local governments in promoting sustainable urban development.

THE CONTEXT FOR INCREASING ROLES OF LOCAL GOVERNMENTS

In the past couple of decades, the Southeast Asian region has been undergoing various transformations, such as rapid economic growth that is naturally followed by urbanization, and democratization that is generally followed by decentralization of authorities to the local governments. There are certainly great variations among countries — and more starkly among cities — in the region with regard to the extent of these transformations.

The first major transformation currently being experienced in the region is the relatively rapid economic growth that goes hand in hand with the opening up of the region's economies. While the economic growth in Southeast Asia may generally be lower than that of China's (estimated at 10.3 per cent in 2010) or India's (8.6 per cent, in 2010; IMF 2010, p. 160), it has been significantly higher than that of many countries in the world, especially during the recent financial crisis in the west. OECD expects that Southeast Asia's economy as a whole will continue to grow at an average of 5–6 per cent, although there are countries in the region that perform much better than their neighbours. In 2010 well-performing countries such as Indonesia, the Lao People's Democratic Republic, Malaysia, the

Philippines, Thailand, and Vietnam grew 6–7.3 per cent (OECD 2010, p. 551), while countries such as Cambodia and Myanmar were calculated to grow at 6.9 per cent and 5.1 per cent respectively (IMF 2010, p. 160). Singapore's 14.5 per cent growth in 2010 is certainly an outlier. The fully urbanized city state has been able to reinvent itself from time to time in order to maintain its economic attractiveness.

While rapid economic growth in itself does not directly propel local governments to play more roles, it does create serious challenges for them, such as meeting the expanding need for infrastructure and services, as well as urban housing. It also instigates urbanization, as more rural people are drawn (rather than pushed) to migrate to industrialized areas, and more rural lands are being transformed into urban uses. New industrial towns — based on both high-tech and low-tech industries — are also developed in various places in the region to boost economic growth.

While not too long ago, Southeast Asia was generally seen as predominantly rural — with an urbanization rate only 14.5 per cent in 1950, and 37.2 per cent in 2000 — the region is projected to be predominantly urban in 2025 by having 53.2 per cent of its population living in cities and towns (Jones 2002). Yet this urbanization is not evenly distributed. The city state of Singapore is 100 per cent urban, Malaysia is 70 per cent, and Indonesia 52 per cent. Thailand is statistically still 33 per cent (very interestingly, considering it has Bangkok as one of the largest metropolises in the world) while Cambodia is still about 22 per cent (all figures are for the year 2008).

The region's estimated average rate of urban population growth of 2.63 per cent for 2010–15 may not seem to be so rapid, yet considering that many parts of the region are still basically rural — such as most parts of the Lao People's Democratic Republic, Myanmar, and Cambodia, as well as some parts of Vietnam and Indonesia — this figure indicates that urban concentrations in the region are increasing. Some urban parts of the region are even expected to grow at a rate of around 4 per cent in 2010–15. Currently about 48.2 per cent of the total population in the region lives in urban areas (see Table 1.1 on p. 11 in the overview chapter by Yap Kioe-Sheng).

Urbanization does not only mean higher population numbers to be serviced by local governments, but it also means that local governments have to deal with various issues related to living in higher density areas, multiple land-use, conflicts over urban space, limited infrastructure and services, influx of unskilled rural migrants, and many other challenges that would not have been seriously found in rural districts. Because urbanization itself is rarely by design,[2] many local governments are actually not ready to manage urban areas, and, at the same time, many urban communities are also not ready to live urban lives with all its implications. Without strong support from their respective national governments, many local governments will not have adequate technical, institutional, or financial capacities to deal with the various and increasing challenges that come with urbanization.

At the national level, rapid urbanization also means more cities and more urban local governments to be engaged. In countries such as Indonesia, the Philippines, Thailand, and Vietnam, urbanization means the emergence of new mega-urban regions around Ho Chi Minh City, Surabaya, and Bandung, in addition to the more-established mega-urban regions such as Jakarta, Manila, and Bangkok (Jones 2002, p. 121). Countries such as Indonesia and Thailand face spatial imbalance: urbanization tends to concentrate on Java island for Indonesia, and around the Bangkok Metropolitan Region for Thailand. The huge diversity certainly poses complex challenges to the national governments in trying to engage their respective local governments in promoting sustainable urban development.

Another parallel transformation that is going on in the region is the democratization of the way the countries, cities, and towns are governed. In essence, it implies civil society participation in practically all public matters. Civil society in the Philippines, Indonesia, and Thailand in particular has been increasingly involved in influencing public decision-making processes, by sending their representatives to legislative councils, through elections, participating directly in the planning and budgeting process (such as the bottom-up "Musrenbang" planning process in Indonesia), conducting independent monitoring of publicly funded activities, or occasionally through public rallies or demonstrations.

While more democratic processes are meant to provide better opportunities for people's aspirations to be voiced and accommodated — and therefore people's actual social, economic, and political needs to be met — the emphasis on democracy's procedures rather than on its delivery has allowed these processes to be captured or dominated by local elites who are publicly vocal, locally popular, or have more means (that is, money) to gain more votes. In the Philippines, and increasingly also in Indonesia, there are popular people, such as actors, actresses, or singers, who won local elections and then hold local leadership or local representative positions. They are, however, not necessarily the most competent people to govern.

One fundamental component that is often missing in such a process is that the people should be able to decide freely on the basis of relatively complete information about the implications of their choices. The paternalistic nature of society (which allows local leaders to dictate to their people), an inadequate level of education (which allows people to be misled), and poverty (which tempts people to sell their votes) have made elections less democratic. While becoming more expensive, elections do not always result in the improvement of public services and collective goods.[3] This characterizes the democratic practices in the Philippines, Indonesia, and Thailand, resulting in the election of some local leaders whose main concern is, ironically, not the maximal improvement of their people's welfare, but rather "the return on their investment" in getting elected.[4]

Paradoxically, local leaders in other parts of the region are not directly elected by the local population, but are instead selected from among the bureaucracy, or by the leaders of the governing party in the upper-level government, and yet the local governments have been able to deliver good services and create improvement in the people's welfare. Malaysia and Singapore provide good examples of governments that deliver services and improve welfare despite limited public participation in the political processes. The outcomes of democratization processes in Vietnam, Cambodia, Myanmar, and the Lao People's Democratic Republic (Lao PDR) are yet to be seen.

The combination of the two situations above has prompted some people to question the implementation of democracy in the region. Yet, the authors of this chapter are of the opinion that it will be a mistake to conclude that democratic local governance does not work in this region and that top-down, yet welfare-oriented, national governments should step up their roles. There are good examples, such as the cities of Tarakan and Solo in Indonesia, Naga City in the Philippines, and Bangkok City in Thailand, where elected local leaders delivered real improvement and benefits to their respective people.[5]

In the long run, as people are getting more educated and better informed, they will demand more say in (s)electing their local leaders, as well as in public decision-making that affects their lives — and this is what democracy is all about. Economic welfare may possibly be served through top-down approaches, but a true sense of justice will more likely be served through the practice of democracy. However, it cannot be denied that effective regulations are needed to curb the increasing costs of getting elected. It also cannot be denied that voters need to be better educated and fully informed about their choices and their implications.

The increasing acknowledgement of the importance of democratization, especially in larger countries, tends to trigger decentralization, similar to the way economic growth triggers urbanization. Democratization and decentralization share the principle of bringing public decision-making processes closer to the people who are most affected by the decisions. However, in the case of decentralization it was commonly preceded by a collective demand by local authorities and communities to be more autonomous, especially when local resources are exploited without significantly benefiting local populations, or when local values, cultures, and characteristics are in danger of being trampled by the uniformity of national policies or global trends.

In Southeast Asia, decentralization was pioneered by the Philippines (in the 1990s), followed by Indonesia and Thailand (in the early 2000s) and later — and to a lesser degree — by Vietnam. Other countries in the region have also been mulling over the concept, if not implementing parts of it. Welfare provision controlled at the central level is considered to be unable to capture the social and economic circumstances of each area, making decentralization the tool that aims at improving local service delivery by local governments. This system of governance gives local governments greater authority in managing their respective administrative domains. In a few cases, decentralization has resulted in good local innovations that would not have happened in a more centralized governing environment.[6]

These transformations have placed local governments and communities at the forefront of efforts to attain sustainable urban environments. Local knowledge and wisdom are amongst assets that are most likely better possessed by local governments and communities than by any national entity. This can be viewed as a modality that local governments possess and will be further discussed in the next section.

APPROACHES AND MODALITIES IN ENGAGING LOCAL GOVERNMENTS

From the number of urban development initiatives throughout Southeast Asia that can be considered as contributing to urban sustainability, this chapter identifies the different ways in which local governments become aware of the urgent need to implement such sustainable practices, and meet the challenges in making such endeavours successful. There are at least five approaches or modalities in engaging local governments to commit to sustainable practices. They are (1) national government policies, programmes, and support, (2) donor-funded or donor-initiated programmes and projects, (3) civil-society-led initiatives, (4) peer-to-peer learning, that is often generated by networks of city governments and communities, (5) visionary and innovative local leaders supported by capable local bureaucracy (see Figure 13.1).

While the first two approaches (national government policies and programmes and donor-funded projects) are driven by external actors or factors, the next two (civil-society-led initiatives and peer-to-peer learning) can be externally and/or internally driven, while the last one (local leaders) is certainly internally driven. The way these modalities work differs from one case to another, depending on which modality is more dominant at play. They are not necessarily exclusive of each other. In fact, in many cases, there are combinations of modalities, approaches, and actors, external and internal.

The first modality to get local governments to engage in sustainable development practices is through national government policies or programmes. In countries where national governments still play strong roles in local development, initiatives as well as technical and financial support for sustainable urban development practices often come from the national governments. This nationally driven approach applies both in countries such as Vietnam and Cambodia that are just developing, as well as in relatively more-developed countries such as Malaysia and Singapore (which actually does not need to be mentioned as it is a city state and the city is therefore directly managed by the national government).

Even in countries that have implemented a decentralization policy such as Indonesia and the Philippines, national governments still play important roles through relevant national policies, as well as nationwide urban infrastructure or housing programmes. The push towards low-cost, high-rise housing — some of them subsidized — that has been gradually changing the urban landscape in some Indonesian major cities since 2007 was basically initiated by then-Vice-President Jusuf Kalla.

A number of Southeast Asian countries such as Indonesia, Thailand, and the Philippines have developed national urban policies with different levels of national intervention and varying degrees of effectiveness in terms of actually effectuating better urban landscape and management.[7]

Figure 13.1
Factors, Contexts, and Modalities in Engaging Local Governments

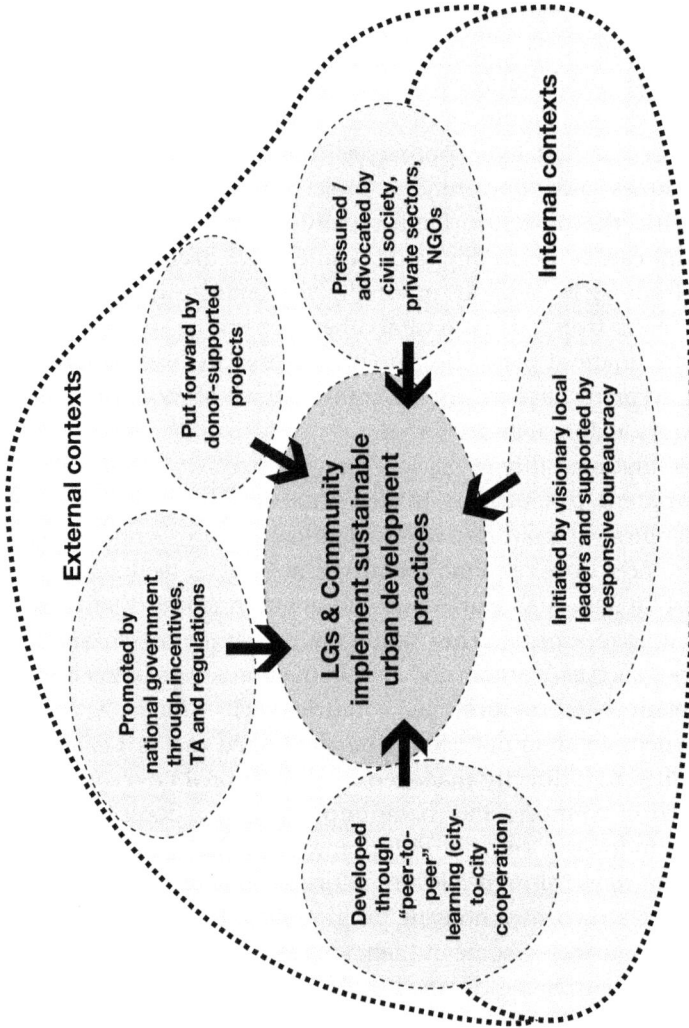

Besides trying to influence urban development at the local level, those national urban policies also commonly try to influence the national urban system. However, national urban policies in Indonesia, Thailand, and the Philippines have been much less effective in reducing the urban domination of their respective capital cities (Jakarta, Bangkok, and Manila).

Another example of heavy national government involvement in city development is Putrajaya City in Malaysia. Considered to be one of the country's largest urban development projects and built as the nation's administrative capital, Putrajaya is intended to be a model city of sustainable development. The Putrajaya wetlands, which are constructed as part of a human-made water management system, demonstrate a successful attempt at urban greening and have attracted interest from other cities, from within the Malaysian boundaries as well as beyond, to learn from this model (see Yuen, Ahmad, and Ho 2006, p. 237).

The second modality or approach in engaging local governments to commit to sustainable urban development is through donor-supported projects or programmes. One classic example has been the World Bank–supported slum upgrading programmes (that were inspired by an earlier version of the locally initiated Jakarta Kampong Improvement Programme in the 1970s). Globally promoted policies that have been adopted by national and/or local governments can also play the role of instigators of such sustainable practices. An example of this is Local Agenda 21, a global action plan for sustainable development, adopted in June 1992 at the United Nations Conference on Environment and Development.

Numerous countries — including those in Southeast Asia — have adopted the agenda and required their local governments to create their own action plans and devise their service strategy. The strategy encompasses ways to develop the local economy, implement national policy, manage environmental, social, and economic infrastructure, and provide services within the area. There are already several countries in the region that have adopted the agenda, such as Thailand and the Philippines, and the agenda serves as guidance for local governments in developing their local urban policies. Some cities such as Tarakan in Indonesia took the initiative — without being officially required by the national government — to develop and adopt their own version of Local Agenda 21.

There are many other donor-supported urban programmes and projects that cannot be even summarized here. They range from policy interventions to support for improvement in urban services, infrastructure, and housing provision. In the past ten years or so, there has also been donor support for a wider range of local governance issues. These include the recently concluded Local Governance Support Programme by USAID in Indonesia, or the Strengthening Local Government Capacities for Planning, Budgeting, and Managing Public Resources by UNDP in Vietnam, as well as many other similar programmes.

The third modality operates through pressure by civil society, which encompasses community organizations, advocacy groups, professional associations, and private-sector corporations through their corporate social responsibility (CSR) programmes. The democratization of public decision-making processes opens up not only civil society participation, but occasionally also civil society's ownership of the initiatives. As pointed out by Mercer in her essay, civil society plays a major role in mobilizing pressure for a political change, especially in the transformative era of democratization (see Mercer 2007, p. 7), as shown by People Power in the Philippines in the 1980s and early 2000s, and in Indonesia in the late 1990s.

There is a plethora of institutes, community-based organizations, and civil society organizations that introduce sustainability practices to society, as well as to local governments. BaliFokus is among the many NGOs that do such promotions. The Bali-based organization has grown from assisting communities in handling solid waste management to developing sanitation programmes for the city of Denpasar as well as other cities on the island and beyond. In doing so, the specialized NGO works in cooperation with local governments and small-scale entrepreneurs or farmers.

Corporate social responsibility is another vehicle through which local governments become engaged in sustainable development practices. Indonesia's state-owned BNI-Bank, for example, is currently financially supporting the revitalization or development of urban forests in a number of Indonesian cities. CSR in Singapore is also significant in promoting sustainable development. Increased consumer awareness of the environmental agenda and award incentives from the government have led to an increase in sustainability reporting within the Global Reporting Initiative (GRI) framework, from zero companies in 2007, to more than twenty in 2010 (*Green Times* 2002).

The fourth modality covers practices that are initiated by local leaders (formal and non-formal political elite and cultural and social leaders) and that are supported by a responsive bureaucracy. Other than the previously discussed cases of Tarakan, Naga, and Bangkok City, the city of Solo in Indonesia also has a story of how the mayor and his local government staff demonstrated that a humanistic approach for relocation is possible, when more than one thousand street vendors were willingly moved to a designated shopping area.

The fifth modality is peer-to-peer learning. Cooperation among local governments — whether they be adjacent to each other, within one country, across countries within Southeast Asia, or even beyond the region — has been mushrooming in order to improve the capacity of the local governments, through the sharing of experiences and the establishment of direct cooperation in particular sectors. Citynet Asia-Pacific is an example of a medium for peer-to-peer learning, committed to helping local governments improve sustainability. It currently has more than 100 members, most of them located in the Asia-Pacific region. Local governments in the Philippines have long been known as very active in networking among themselves. Associations of municipalities have sprung up in most countries in the region. There has been evidence that such forms of cooperation make positive impacts in improving the capacity of the participating local governments.

While the modalities of engaging local governments and communities to commit to more sustainable urban development practices as outlined above have been known, implementation is not as easy as it looks. There are quite a number of challenges to overcome, as summarized below.

CHALLENGES IN ENGAGING LOCAL GOVERNMENTS

The first key challenge is at the technical level. It refers to the lack of resources needed in urban development, such as lack of capacity, finances, skills, technology, and so forth. The transformations which are driven by economic growth often cause growing disassociation between economic and social standards (Mishra 1998, p. 484), and a declining concern for environmental degradation. The lack of capacity of skills and technology to manage urban finance efficiently has also led to deterioration in environmental qualities, a low quality of urban infrastructure and public services, a housing backlog, and diminishing social capital within communities.

The second key challenges lies at the systemic level. It refers to the existing regulatory framework that has not served as a supportive environment for good urban practices. For example, functional decentralization has not generally been adequately followed by fiscal and technical decentralization. When local governments still rely heavily on their national government to generate revenue, the ability to effectuate urban sustainability is certainly very limited. This is especially so in Southeast Asian countries where governments still struggle with unbalanced budgets and an insufficient provision of vital expenditures for services (see Gonzales and Mendoza 2002, p. 211).

National-level policymakers are often also unaware of the close correlation between decentralization/localization and economic growth. Drawing from Asia's experience, we see that localization and growth seem to go together. China had the highest GDP growth per capita in the period of 1990 to 1999, followed by Malaysia. Both countries were committed to providing privileges and facilities required by their cities as a consequence of their designation as engines of growth. In Indonesia, Thailand, and the Philippines, the inability to introduce a thoroughly decentralized infrastructure resulted in slower economic growth rates. In raising revenue, tax reforms are often viewed as the answer, but Indonesia and the Philippines are amongst the countries that have difficulties in raising revenue through better tax administration and fiscal management. Only the Lao PDR, according to World Bank data, managed to implement specific policy measures to improve transparency and efficiency in public budgeting and execution, and revenue collection and control (Gonzales and Mendoza 2002, p. 211).

The third is challenges at the paradigmatic level. It refers to a limited understanding of the chief purposes of decentralization by local governments. The spirit of decentralization is to give larger authority to local governments and communities so that they can ensure optimum public service delivery to their citizens. However, such a notion is sometimes not entirely comprehended by most staff and leadership at the local government level. In most cities of Southeast Asia, regulations are unclear and uncoordinated. This deters investors and opens the door for "elite captures" — a phenomenon where only a small group of local people has access to power and capital, and thus is able to reap the most benefit from decentralization. In a recent survey on decentralization and poverty alleviation in Asia, Das Gaiha claimed that although the growth of the local economy and the expanded resource base of local governments are likely to lead to some efficiency gains and benefits to the poor, it is doubtful whether these are widely shared (Gonzales and Mendoza 2002, p. 208).

Other problems in this category include a lack of willingness on the part of local leaders and/or local bureaucracy to work with the increasingly more dynamic civil society, reluctance to prioritize the quality of public services, a local "ego" and a lack of understanding of the importance of working together with other municipalities, an "inward-looking" attitude, a limited willingness on the part of national government to support local governments, and a "too-paternalistic" approach by the national government. The response to this condition was often the inducing of good urban governance's underlying principles of participation, effectiveness, efficiency, accountability, and transparency to the local governments, through a central government, NGO- or donor-supported programme.

This chapter is fully aware that there are major differences in local governing situations in the region. The town councils in the economically advanced city state of Singapore and the centrally controlled districts in resource-rich Brunei certainly cannot be compared with local governments in Indonesia, Thailand, and the Philippines. The latter group not only deals with larger populations, but also possesses more authority because their leaders are popularly elected. They are generally also cash-strapped relative to their need for services and infrastructure. Again, the governance situation at the local level in Malaysia, Vietnam, Cambodia, and the Lao PDR is different because their local leaders are not directly elected by the people. In Malaysia, many local governments have a mechanism for citizen complaints in place.[8] Therefore it is realized that many of the key challenges depend on the institutional set-ups within the countries concerned.

However, some generalities can be identified about the local governance situation in Southeast Asia. There are basically two different sets of contexts and factors: those that are external to the local institutions and those that are internal (as indicated in Figure 13.1).

The external contexts and influencing factors include the various macro-level transformations, as well as the policies and actions of the national government and support from international donors. Internal contexts and influencing factors include cooperation among local governments and the particular characteristics of local governments (such as visionary leaderships and/or responsive and capable bureaucracy). The capability of the local bureaucracy includes financial and technical capacities, as well as the political-administrative independence of the local government. Meanwhile pressures from intercity cooperation, and civil society in general, are located in-between. The challenge for actors in this context is to establish a sustained capacity in local government to continue externally funded programmes and institutionalize this capacity as part of its independent programmes. In doing so, internal actors face the challenge of limited resources and uncertainty about the strategy to be used that best suits the local context.

Meanwhile there are also a number of challenges related to who initiated the practice and how it was initiated. In the case of external factors and actors, such as a national or donor programme or project, the main pitfall has been the sustainability of the good initiatives. There are numerous cases where externally supported local projects were performing well as long as there was external support. Once the external inputs stopped, the good practices gradually disappeared. It is therefore pertinent that an exit strategy is prepared and implemented long before the actual end of the project or programme.

In the case of internally initiated good practices, their dependency on local leaders has been the main challenge. There are many cases where the acclaimed urban development practice gradually disappeared once the local leader who initiated it retired. It is therefore important that internally initiated good urban practices are institutionalized when the local leader is still in power, for instance, through an enactment into local law or the establishment of a special local institution.

WAYS TO UTILIZE MODALITY IN ADDRESSING THE CHALLENGES

This chapter argues that modalities can be used not only to promote sustainable urban development, but also to overcome the above challenges. Most studies and policy recommendations see an increase in local government capacity as the entry point in addressing technical challenges in sustainable urban development in Southeast Asia. The criteria developed by Manasan, Gonzales, and Gaffud (1999) to monitor good governance at the local level highlights three aspects: capacity of local governments to mobilize and utilize resources, efficient and effective delivery of social services, and the presence of mechanisms to ensure accountability (Gonzales and Mendoza 2002, p. 208). National governments need to provide guidance, opportunity, and facility for local governments to enhance professional technical skills and change the mindset and enhance its ability to engineer a supportive system for good governance practices.

Civil society should respond to the paradigmatic challenges by pressuring local government and advocating the implementation of sustainable urban development principles. Aside from the decentralization of authority, accountability for public service provision needs to prioritized and good governance needs to be seen as a crucial requirement for effectiveness in sustainable urban development. A survey among provinces in Indonesia confirmed that good governance correlates with human development.[9] This means that creating an enabling local environment, promoting transparency and accountability in local administration, and encouraging citizen participation in urban development, ensure better urban service delivery and an increase in quality of life for citizens.

One of the instruments that can be used to do this is the Citizen Report Card, which is a monitoring and evaluation tool that engages citizens. The tool can be used for any kind of purpose, depending on the criteria established in "grading" the local government's performance in urban management. It can combine good governance and sustainable urban development (such as "to what extent citizens have been involved in the decision-making process" in order to grade participation; and "to what extent budgets allocated have been used effectively to rehabilitate the environment" in order to grade effectiveness). The benefit of this tool is that it increases local government accountability, creates a stronger sense of ownership of urban development processes amongst citizens and local government officials, and provides venues for socialization and education in sustainable urban development. Citizen Report Cards can only be effective if conducted not only once, but on a regular basis (annually or biannually).

In employing modalities in facing these key challenges, it is important to note that the ways to respond to these challenges not only differ in accordance to the most prominent challenge, but also to the specific context of the particular country. The nature and extent of utilizing such modalities differ across Southeast Asia. In countries such as Singapore and Malaysia, well-functioning national as well as local governments have been able to play dominant roles in the matter, whereas in countries such as Indonesia, Thailand, and the Philippines, multistakeholder approaches — which involve the government, civil society, and the private sector — have increasingly been becoming the most effective of making things happen in more sustainable ways. In these countries, democratic systems and decentralized structures are more developed and the struggles lie mostly in how to make sure the democratic processes deliver what has been promised.

Younger democracies and transitional states such as Vietnam, the Lao PDR, Cambodia, and Myanmar often focus more on assistance in developing new institutions and adjusting to the transfer of public management. For these newly democratized yet still relatively centralized countries, sustainable development principles were best passed top-down from the central government. As they are more centrally managed, promoting sustainable development could be more easily done by using the existing pipes and lanes, whilst in the already decentralized countries such as the Philippines, Indonesia, and Thailand, these principles would be better sustained if they were developed from the bottom up, and chanelled through local communities. For example, Local Agenda 21, which is practically a combination of national government and donor-driven projects, was generally viewed as too top-down, and thus is less sustainable in Thailand.

Even in the countries where most government functions have been transferred to local governments, such as in Indonesia, the Philippines, and, to a lesser degree, Thailand, there is still the need for a more assertive and effective national urban policy and strategy that is synchronized with the policies and strategies of the local governments. The Southeast Asia region is rapidly urbanizing — and will have more people living in urban areas by 2012 — while the financial, technical, and managerial ability of the national and local governments to meet the demand for public services, infrastructure, and facilities created by the growth is still limited.

A national urban policy is needed because of what is known as "decentralized concentration". Concentrated growth is inevitable, but it should be utilized in a way that works in the country's favour. Instead of distributing resources evenly, they should be strategically allocated to the most capable centres where the return is the highest, that is, to the "graduated" local government (see Figure 13.2). This does not mean that cities and towns where the local governments have limited capacities will not be supported to grow. In this approach, the national government still provides technical assistance in an effort to "level the playing field" and support local governments to compete with the other cities to receive the incentives given by the central government. In such an approach, there will be more and more cities or local governments that "graduate" and become more capable of performing the decentralized tasks, hence securing sustainable local development.

In formulating the national urban policy, Southeast Asian national governments need to define the boundaries of functions to determine accountabilities. Support for the local government should be limited to

Figure 13.2
Sustainable Approach to Promoting SUD by the National Government

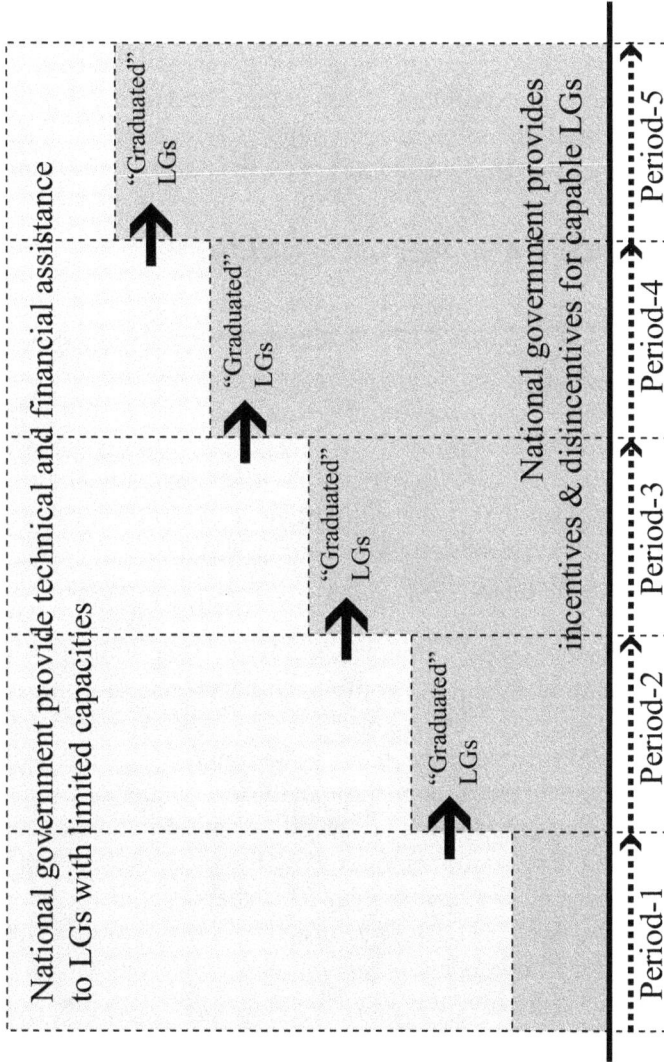

National government provide technical and financial assistance to LGs with limited capacities

National government provides incentives & disincentives for capable LGs

"Graduated" LGs

"Graduated" LGs

"Graduated" LGs

"Graduated" LGs

"Graduated" LGs

Period-1   Period-2   Period-3   Period-4   Period-5

guidance, and not include micromanagement. The roles of the private sector and civic society in sustainable urban development should be enhanced and they should serve as assets for local governments in development. Privatization must be done cautiously as a national government must first establish its degree of intervention, taking into account where the market has failed to serve. As an example, electricity provision in Southeast Asian countries seems best provided through joint efforts of the private sector and the national government, especially in remote areas where private sector entrance needs to be supported by the national government.

CONCLUSIONS AND RECOMMENDATIONS

The ongoing transformations have placed local governments in a role which is crucial in making sustainable urban development possible. Yet most countries in the region are facing several challenges at various levels to have the local government adopt and implement the principles of sustainable urban development. These challenges encompass the limitations of local government itself to perform its functions, as well as the current regulatory climate that is not supportive of sustainable urban practices mushrooming in cities throughout Southeast Asia.

It can be concluded that:

- The challenges are at various levels and they should be addressed by the involvement of a combination of stakeholders, in accordance with the type of challenge.
- The efforts to engage local governments in sustainable urban development can be done through the formulation of a national urban policy that can provide an overall vision of national development (especially in countries that follow the urban-led approach) and to develop a clear urban system. This chapter is of the view that the National Urban Policy should ideally leave room for authority of local governments in mobilizing its resources, while the role of the national government is to facilitate and not micromanage.
- Good governance is the key supporting factor in ensuring sustainable urban development, with internal modalities — urban leaders, civil society, and associations for peer-to-peer learning — being the focus of engagement, while external factors should only add value to the internal factors.

Notes

1.   Among others, see Roberts and Kanaley 2006.
2.   Except in China and a few other countries, urbanization is rarely by design. The People's Republic of China employed the so-called urban-based development approach since 1970 with its open economic policy and the establishment of compact mega-urban regions, encompassing Special Economic Zones (SEZ), coastal cities, and open economic regions. See Choe 2008.
3.   There is a speculation, especially in Indonesia, but it may also happen in the Philippines and Thailand, that fewer genuinely people-oriented and capable local leaders have been elected than those who only use the democratic processes for their own or their group's interests (plus the ones who are actually genuinely people-oriented, but are not capable of bringing about the betterment of public goods and people's welfare). Further study is needed to confirm or reject this statement.
4.   Widespread corruption cases committed by elected local officials in Indonesia have been linked to the high cost of getting elected. See Soehartono 2011.
5.   The elected Tarakan mayor, Dr Jusuf Serang Kasim (period 1999–2007) made the city a local champion for its urban forest and inclusive education service; a similarly admirable accomplishments by Jesse M. Robredo of Naga City in the Philippines (period 1988–98) of strengthening the city's economy led to his receiving numerous awards. Mom Rajawongse Sukhumbhand Paribatra, elected mayor of Bangkok City (period 2009–current), brought the city to a level of resilience that was acknowledged by the UNISDR World Disaster campaign 2010–11 as the champion.
6.   See Robert and Kanaley 2006 for various good local practices across Asia and beyond.
7.   Indonesia has had successive national urban policies in the name of the National Urban Development Strategy (NUDS), first formulated in the mid-1980s and renewed in the 2000s (which was eventually enacted only as a ministerial decree of the Ministry of Public Works that has little power over various urban related programmes from other departments and government agencies). At the time of the writing of this chapter, a new national urban policy and strategy is being formulated. The authors of this chapter had been part of this process. The Philippines has the 1992 Urban Development and Housing Act, National Urban Development and Housing Framework 1999–2004, as well as the National Urban Policy Agenda (NUPA), while Thailand has the National Urban Development Policy Framework, as well as various relevant economic, social, and spatial development plans.
8.   While most of the knowledge about local government situations in various Southeast Asian countries outlined here is collected from secondary sources,

the same understanding cannot be confidently drawn by the authors about the local government situation in Myanmar due to the lack of direct interactions with relevant actors and researchers from this particular country.

9. Partnership Governance Index, a survey in all thirty-three provinces in Indonesia about the implementation of good governance principles in the provinces. See <http://www.kemitraan.or.id>.

References

Roberts, Brian, and Trevor Kanaley, eds. *Urbanization and Sustainability in Asia: Case Studies of Good Practice*. Manila: Asian Development Bank, 2006.

Choe, Kyeong-Ae K. and Aprodicia A. Laquian. *City Cluster Development: Toward an Urban-Led Development Strategy for Asia*. Manila: Asian Development Bank, 2008.

Gonzales E., and Magdalena L. Mendoza. *Governance in Southeast Asia: Issues and Options*. Philippine Institute for Development Studies, 2002.

Green Times (Singapore). "More Companies Embrace SCR in Singapore". 30 September 2010 <http://www.greenbusinesstimes.com/2010/09/30/more-companies-embrace-csr-in-singapore>accessed (accessed 14 February 2011).

International Monetary Fund (IMF). *World Economic Outlook: Rebalancing Growth*. April 2010.

Jones, Gavin W. "Southeast Asian Urbanization and the Growth of Mega-Urban Regions". In *Journal of Population Research* 19, no. 2 (2002).

Mercer, C. "NGO, Civil Society and Democratization: A Critical Review of Literature". *Progress in Development Studies* 2 (2002): 7.

Mishra, R. "Beyond the Nation State: Social Policy in an Age of Globalization". *Social Policy and Administration* 32, no. 5 (1998): 484.

Marsh, I., "Democratization and State Capacity in East and Southeast Asia". *Taiwan Journal of Democracy* 2, no. 2 (2006): 215.

OECD. *Southeast Asian Economic Outlook 2010*. OECD, 2010.

Partnership Governance Index. Available at <http://www.kemitraan.or.id> (accessed 12 November 2010).

Soehartono. "Korupsi di Daerah adalah Kesalahan Kita Bersama" (We All Should Take Responsibility of Corruption at the Local Level). *Kompas* (Jakarta) 2011 (accessed February 2011).

Tonami, A. and Akihisa Mori. "Sustainable Development in Thailand: Lessons from Implementing Local Agenda 21 in Three Cities". *Journal of Environment and Development* (2007): 268–89.

Urban and Regional Development Institute. *Kartu Penilaian Bersama — Tujuan*

Pembangunan Milenium (Citizen report card — millenium development goals). Jakarta: URDI, 2007.

Wikipedia. "Urbanization by Country". <http://en.wikipedia.org/wiki/urbanization by country> (accessed 10 November 2010).

Yuen, B., Supian Ahmad, and Chin Siong Ho. "Malaysia". *Urbanization and Sustainability In Asia: Good Practices Approaches in Urban Region Development*. Manila: ADB, 2006, p. 237.

14

GOVERNANCE AND ACCOUNTABILITY IN SOUTHEAST ASIAN CITIES

Goh Ban Lee

Cities are now touted as engines of development. Although this has been the role of cities since the glory days of Mesopotamia, the Indus Valley, and Huang Ho Plains about 4,000 to 6,000 years ago (Reader 2004), the idea of promoting cities as engines of development is a recent phenomenon.

But the gulf between wanting to promote cities as engines of development and actually achieving success is rather wide. Governance has been identified as an important factor in determining success or failure. The objective of this chapter is to discuss the realities of governance in Southeast Asian cities. The focus is on accountability as it would not be possible to cover all the characteristics of good governance in a short chapter. Besides, accountability, a basic pillar of good governance, is closely linked to transparency and rule of law, two other important pillars.

THE POWER OF CITIES

It was not long ago that cities were seen as centres of crime and moral decay. Suburban development and new towns were popular during the post-war boom days. Political economists even termed cities as "theatres of accumulation" and therefore not friendly to the working class. An example of an extreme anti-urban measure was the clearing of Phnom Penh by the Pol Pot regime in 1975, which caused great miseries and countless deaths. Lately, however, leading urban scholars have been singing the praises of cities.

But the rural poor have always known about the "prosperity" properties of towns and cities. During the Industrial Revolution, the poor of Europe flocked to the towns to be part of the engines of growth. Since then, their cousins in the developing countries in Asia, South America, and Africa have been coming to the cities to try to share in the prosperity and better quality of life. Many have made it. The sizeable and growing middle class is clear testimony to this.

However, many are left behind. Some have suffered even poorer quality of life, largely as a result of discrimination, or the couldn't-care-less attitude of administrators. But for them, there is no turning back. There is hope, if not for themselves, then at least for their children. As Lewis Mumford once said, "the City is a place for multiplying happy chances and making the most of unplanned opportunities" (Mumford and Miller 1986, p. 43).

As such, cities have been growing rapidly. According to the United Nations' *World Population Prospects, the 2010 Revision*, by 2010, more than half the world's population will be living in towns and cities. The term "megacities" was coined to describe cities with ten million people or more. Therefore, it is not surprising that the phrase, "cities as the engines of development", is beginning to be heard in meetings and conferences.

But development is not a natural process. Resources need to be harnessed and directed towards desired ends. Having good development plans is essential. But good governance is equally essential. However, those involved in making development plans and entrusted to manage the cities in most developing countries are still at the learning curve despite the degrees and membership to "professional" institutes. It is hoped publications such as this will hasten the learning process.

LIVEABLE CITIES

Before we go on to discuss governance, it is useful to touch briefly on the state of the cities in Southeast Asia. Despite the millions of dollars in making plans, most ASEAN cities do not rank very high in liveable city indexes conducted by consultant agencies. For instance, according to Mercer Human Resource Consultancy, a Swiss-based consulting firm that conducts an annual ranking of liveable cities, no Asian city is in the top ten. The 2010 top ten liveable cities are: Vienna (1st), Zurich (2nd), Geneva (3rd), Vancouver (4th), Auckland (4th), Dusseldorf (6th), Munich (7th), Frankfurt (7th), Bern (9th), and Sydney (10th). The highest ranked city in Asia is Singapore at 28th position (Mercer 2010). Other Asian cities within the first fifty liveable cities are Tokyo (40th), Yokohama (41st), Kobe (41st), and Osaka (44th). Apart from Singapore, no other ASEAN city is in the top fifty.

Another reputable institution is the Economist Intelligence Unit (EIU) based in Britain. According to its latest report, the top ten liveable cities in 2010 in descending order are: Vancouver, Vienna, Melbourne, Toronto, Calgary, Helsinki, Sydney, Perth, Adelaide, and Auckland.

According to a Location Ranking by ECA International, a private human resources company, based on the views of Asian expatriates, ASEAN cities also do not rank very high except for Singapore, which has topped the quality of life ranking for the last eleven years. Table 14.1 shows liveable city rankings for Southeast Asian cities in 2010 according to ECA International.

Table 14.1
Livable Cities According to ECA International

City	Global Rank	Asia Rank
Singapore	1	1
Kuala Lumpur	62	8
Bangkok	62	8
George Town	62	8
Hanoi	123	20
Ho Chi Minh City	126	22
Metro Manila	142	25
Vientiane	147	28
Phnom Penh	171	36
Jakarta	191	38
Yangon	198	39
Surabaya	210	41

Source: ECA, 2010.

GOOD URBAN GOVERNANCE

The poor showing by Southeast Asian cities in liveable city rankings is not for the lack of plans. Although making city development plans is a costly exercise, most, if not all, cities have plans. Poorer cities usually could get assistance from multilateral organizations to help them prepare development plans. What is seriously lacking is effective urban management. Although every town or city has a government, usually in the form of a local council, it does not necessarily mean that its management is effective, as many local councils in the developing countries are no more than tax collecting agencies to run rudimentary sanitary services and maintain basic infrastructure. The idea of turning basically administrative machines into management bodies using the tools of business corporations to make cities engines of development is of recent coinage. But effective urban management depends on good governance.

Governance generally refers to the processes by which public decisions are made and implemented. For example, John Friedmann (1999), a leading urban planning and city scholar, defines governance as "the social processes by which binding decisions for cities and city-regions are made and carried out". According to UN-ESCAP, it is "the process of decision-making and the process by which decisions are implemented (or not implemented)".

The characteristics of good governance are also well established, although there may be minor differences among scholars and organizations. According to UN-ESCAP, they are accountability, transparency, rule of law, consensus building and participation, effectiveness and efficiency, equitability and inclusiveness, and responsiveness. On the other hand, according to the World Urban Forum (WUF), a vehicle of the United Nations Human Settlements Programme (UN-HABITAT) to spread the importance of urban good governance, the five core principles of good governance are equity, effectiveness, accountability, participation, and security (WUF n.d.).

There is also a general agreement among scholars that the major players in urban governance can be grouped into three major categories: politicians and bureaucrats, civil society, and corporate capital, with the first category standing at the apex of a pyramid, and the other two at the two corners at the base (Friedmann 1999). In the power structure of the triangle, the politicians and bureaucrats who represent the state yield the most power because they are backed by laws. Their decisions are binding, at least theoretically.

Categorizing society into three groups, while useful for analytical purposes, may be an oversimplification. As such, one has to be cautious when making conclusions and generalizations. For instance, in many large cities in the developing countries, corporate capital is increasingly being dominated by international capital. Still, its role in shaping city landscapes could be tremendous because of the close relationship between its owners and the politicians and bureaucrats. The role of property developers is particularly important. The development projects in sensitive terrains will lead fair observers to conclude that the developers must have special relationships with local politicians and bureaucrats.

Furthermore, the role of civil society in urban governance is a contested issue more in Southeast Asian cities than in other countries because citizenship in East and Southeast Asian countries "is less indicative of the rights than of the obligations of citizen-subjects" (Friedmann 1999). He questions whether it even makes sense to speak of civil society acting with "a degree of autonomy in the public sphere" (Friedmann 1999, p. 1). Although this view was expressed more than a decade ago, it is still valid in some countries.

As such, an understanding of governance in each city requires an insight into the agenda of the major players: how they relate to one another and how the players in each category relate among themselves. The challenge is to institute measures that ensure the interests of the society are provided for while each entity pursues its own interests.

The first step is to identify the measures that promote the development of liveable cities. There is no one-size-fit-all strategy as the decision-making process in one city is different from another, even though both may have similar laws. While there are numerous studies of local politics, much is still not known about the workings of the local authorities and it is not possible to make improvements if one does not know how the present process works. As a result, even if there are development control plans prepared by the most reputable consultants, these are usually not implemented because they do not take into consideration governance in the towns or cities.

DIVERSITY IN THE THIRD-TIER GOVERNMENT

Most countries have a three-tier government: national, state or province, and local government. There are exceptions. Some very large cities have metropolitan governments, and, to provide for wider citizen participation in municipal affairs, there are smaller district local governments to take care of specific functions. For example, the capital of Thailand has the Bangkok Metropolitan Administration (BMA) with a governor and sixty council members directly elected by the people. However, to promote wider representation, the BMA has fifty "districts", with each having a "District Council" with elected members, although the heads are appointed by the Bangkok governor (UNDP 2007).

The size of municipalities and roles of the local government also vary from country to country. Local councils in Malaysia tend to cover very large areas, and some city councils have jurisdiction over large "rural" areas. For example, the Seberang Perai Municipal Council in Penang covers an area of more about 740 km^2.

In some countries, national capitals and special cities are under the direct jurisdiction of the national government. Although the local governments in Malaysia are generally under the jurisdiction of the state governments, Kuala Lumpur City Hall comes directly under the federal government. So do Putrajaya the new administrative capital and Labuan, an island off the coast of Sabah that is an offshore financial centre. They come under the charge of the Ministry of Federal Territories and Urban Well-being. Similarly, Hanoi, the capital of Vietnam, comes under the jurisdiction of the central government. This means that even though the residents get to elect the ninety-five deputies in the People's Council, the leaders at the national government have a very large say in the development of the city.

As a general rule, local governments are not sovereign bodies. They are creations of either provincial or state governments, or even the federal government, and their power and roles are decided by their creators.

Generally, local governments are given the responsibility of managing public cleansing and solid waste disposal, food safety, public health, development control, and activities likely to cause nuisance. Some are also responsible for fire brigades, traffic management, education, municipal police, water, electricity, and municipal public transportation.

In the last two decades or so, there has been a trend to decentralize power to local authorities in Southeast Asia. Since the overthrow of the Soeharto government in 1998, the Indonesian Government has enacted Law No. 32/2004 that not only provides a clear system of local government and the elections of local officials, but also allocates specific powers for local leaders to administer their area (UNDP 2007, pp. 101–3). Thailand, the Philippines, Vietnam, and even Cambodia have taken steps to decentralize decision-making to subnational administrative areas (Fritzen 2007).

But Malaysia appears to go in the opposite direction. Here the federal government not only abolished local government elections in 1976, but has also taken over several functions that have been traditionally performed by the local authorities. For example, it took over the management of sewage in the 1980s. In 2007, the parliament enacted two acts to enable the federal government to take over the management of solid waste and public cleansing.

Lately, there appears to be a slight change of heart from Malaysia's national leadership. For example, under the recently unveiled New Economic Model, local authorities are encouraged to develop and support growth initiatives and to compete among themselves (NEAC 2010). However, it is still too early to say for certain that this is the beginning of a devolution of power to the local authorities.

ACCOUNTABILITY

One of the most important characteristics of good governance is accountability. It means that those who hold power and have influence in the decision-making processes that affect the lives of others are held responsible for their actions. This is expected not only of politicians and bureaucrats, but also of those who represent corporate capital and civil society. It also means that there must be a mechanism to remove anyone who fails to fulfil his or her allocated tasks. In serious cases, anyone who breaks the law should be charged in the courts of law and, if found guilty, should be punished.

However, accountability is not something Southeast Asian cities can be proud of. The level of accountability varies greatly, not only among cities, but also among the three categories of actors in a city. Below is a brief account of accountability according to the three categories of decision-makers in cities.

Politicians and Bureaucrats

As a general rule, the people who yield the most power in the towns or cities are the mayors or presidents or governors and councillors. In democratic countries the accepted mechanism of accountability is through periodic elections so that the mayors or presidents or governors and councillors have to have their mandate renewed to make decisions on behalf of the people.

Most local authority leaders in Southeast Asian cities are elected. In theory they are accountable to the people who elect them. But even in this very basic accountability process, there are cities that have no elected representatives. The mayor and members of the Yangon City Development Committee (YCDC) are all appointed by the the the State Law and Order Restoration Council (later renamed the State Peace and Development Council). As such, they are not accountable to the residents of the city.

In Malaysia, which can be described as a democratic country, none of the mayors or presidents or councillors are elected. With the exception of the leaders of the Federal Territories, they are appointed by the respective state governments. In the case of the Federal Territories, namely Kuala Lumpur, Labuan, and Putrajaya, the municipal leaders are appointed by the king on the recommendations of the federal government, more specifically, the minister of federal territories and urban well-being.

There is also no local government election in Brunei Darussalam. As such, the capital of Brunei, Bandar Seri Bagawan, has no elected representatives.

In the case of Yangon, the absence of accountability at the local councils is "understandable" since the national government itself is not an elected one. In the case of Malaysia, while both the federal government and state governments are elected, all local governments are appointed. Local government elections were suspended in 1965 and were abolished in 1976. Although there have been calls for local elections by non-governmental organizations and two political parties, the federal government has turned a deaf ear to these calls.

The leaders of the federal government claim that there is accountability through the state and federal government elections. Although the elections for these two levels of government are basically fair, the absence of local government elections is a black mark in the accountability process at the local government level (Goh Ban Lee 2005; 2010).

However, it is important to note that having elections alone does not necessarily mean accountability to the people. The whole electoral process, including eligibility to be candidates, election campaigns, and the voting and counting processes should be taken into consideration. It is clear that the integrity of the whole election process in Southeast Asia is not uniform.

Although the deputies in the local authorities in Vietnam, officially named People's Councils, are elected by "universal suffrage, equality, directness and secret ballot", the candidates standing for local elections, whether they are party or non-party members, are vetted and approved by a range of institutions, such as the Fatherland Front that is closely linked to the Communist Party of Vietnam (UNDP 2007, p. 34). It is fair to conclude that only those deemed suitable to the higher political echelons are allowed to become candidates to be elected to the People's Councils. In such circumstance, the deputies are only partially accountable to the voters as they have to keep an eye on the wants and needs of those who approve their candidatures.

There is also no guarantee that elected mayors and councillors are fully accountable to the people and have only their interests at heart. Elections are seldom thoroughly fair, especially in developing countries. Even in countries that have independent election commissions, the ruling parties — especially those in power for decades — are usually given more leeway to push the envelope during election campaigns. For instance, although Cambodia has come a long way since the local government elections in 1993 organized by the United Nations, the fairness of elections has been questioned (Fritzen 2007).

It usually takes a large amount of funds to run effective campaigns. Again, in many ASEAN countries where there are clearly dominant political parties, the contributions by businessmen are usually very disproportionate among the political parties. Successful local politicians are not "indebted" only to the voters, but also to their financial supporters. Besides, since voters are individuals with only one vote to each man, the elected mayors and councillors or deputies tend to be more accountable to a few prominent individuals, such as party leaders, financial supporters, and local community leaders, than to the people at large.

The accountability of bureaucrats is supposed to be clear-cut — implement the law and policies set by the politicians without fear or favour or be punished for negligence of duty. Although the actions of government officers are regulated by thick administrative orders, acts of non-compliance are common with the possible exception of those in Singapore. In a study of bureaucratic efficiency in selected Asian countries by the Hong Kong based Political and Economic Risk Consultancy (PERC), the rankings of some Southeast Asian countries are nothing to be proud of. Of the twelve countries ranked, Singapore was ranked first, with Thailand placed third, after Hong Kong. The rest of the ranking in descending order are South Korea, Japan, Malaysia, Taiwan, Vietnam, China, the Philippines, and Indonesia, with India at the bottom of the heap (*The Sun*, 3 June 2009).

ASEAN countries also do not fare well in the Corruption Perceptions Index published by Transparency International. In 2008, Indonesia was given a 2.6 score, making it ranked 126th out of the 180 countries surveyed. Malaysia fared better with a score of 5.1 and ranked 47th, while the Philippines did badly with a score of 2.3 and ranked 141st. Singapore, with a score of 9.2, was ranked fourth, while Myanmar, with a score of 1.3, was at the bottom (Transparency International 2009). The rankings of Southeast Asian countries are in Table 14.2.

Much has been written about corruption as a cause for poor urban management in developing countries. While there is no doubt that acts of bribery are serious among the bureaucrats in ASEAN town and cities, it is not fair to blame them alone for the lack of enforcement actions against people who break municipal rules. Interference by politicians, including appointed councillors, state assemblymen, and Members of Parliament, also play a big role (Goh Ban Lee 2002).

There are of course rules that define the roles of politicians and administrators. But in countries where politicians and political parties

Table 14.2
Corruption Perceptions Index 2008

Rank	Country	Score
4	Singapore	9.2
47	Malaysia	5.1
82	Thailand	3.5
121	Vietnam	2.7
126	Indonesia	2.6
141	Philippines	2.3
145	Timur-Leste	2.2
151	Laos	2.0
166	Cambodia	1.8
178	Myanmar	1.3

Source: Transparency International (2009, pp 397–400).

have been in the government for a very long time, it is very difficult for bureaucrats to resist interference by politicians. Even if the politicians cannot sack officers they do not like, there are ways to make their lives very difficult, such as transferring them to obscure places. Fritzen (2007) states that Cambodia's bureaucracy is determined to be largely politicized because it is dominated by political appointees, even for low-level officials.

As a whole, there is not much accountability by politicians and government officers simply because the administrative procedures are vague. One is not sure if an incompatible development project is the result of a wrong decision by planners, or the corruption of those who sit in committees that approve applications to undertake the development.

Corporate Capital

In capitalist societies, including those that have the word "Socialist" embedded in their names, those who own capital do have an important role in urban decision-making processes. Property developers quickly come to mind as it is very hard to understand how development projects can be approved in ecologically sensitive areas, or areas that block access to scenic areas. But financiers, chief executive officers of multinational corporations, and leaders of chambers of commerce all have a role. Too little is known about the role of the corporate capital in the decision-making process of the local authorities.

While there is no doubt that corruption and bribery do take place in the relationship between the holders of capital and the politicians or bureaucrats, it is also important to stress that the powerful role of corporate capital does not just lie in the use of money alone. Many agendas of property developers or managers of multinational corporations get conveyed to the power holders simply because they have more opportunities to be in contact with one another through social or official functions, or even chance meetings at airport business class or first class lounges. The power of corporate capital is not just the meeting opportunities. The owners of capital also have the means to employ professional consultants to argue their cases. Indeed, their professional consultants are not limited only to those with technical expertise, such as architects and engineers, but also include advertising and media consultants.

The importance of the role of corporate capital in local government decision-making is not well known because their participation is often conducted in closed-door meetings, or in restaurants or exclusive clubs or even on golf courses. Unlike the NGOs, they do not go public to trumpet their success stories.

There is nothing inherently wrong in owners of corporate capital pushing their agenda. What is not good for the society is that they are accountable for their actions to only a handful of people, the shareholders of their companies — meaning only the upper echelons of the society. Even in public-listed companies, it only takes a control of 30 per cent of the shares to dominate the decisions of the board of directors. The 30 per cent is owned by a family or a few persons.

The recent emergence of corporate social responsibility is promising. Some leaders of multinational corporations are beginning to be interested in showing that the activities of their companies are not causing environmental pollution or problems to their neighbours.

Civil Society

Those who are grouped in this category in the decision-making process include households and NGOs, the latter including clan associations, religious organizations, and race-based pressure groups. The voices of civil society, especially the NGOs, are getting louder with the spread of the Internet. This is especially the case in countries that have oppressive laws regulating the production of newspapers and magazines.

In Malaysia the NGOs are the most vocal in calling for local government elections. Two political parties, namely the Democratic Action Party (DAP) and Peoples' Justice Party (PKR), were also very vocal in calling for local government elections. Since 2008 they have been part of the coalition governments in two out of the thirteen states in Malaysia, namely Penang and Selangor.

The growing roles of civil society have been facilitated by resolutions in international conferences, such as the United Nations Conference on Environment and Development, popularly known as the Rio Conference, in 1992, and the adoption of Agenda 21 that calls for local authorities to consult their communities when formulating development plans. Indeed, with assistance from UNDP, many towns and cities have adopted Local Agenda 21 or LA21 as one of their planning tools. Many projects have been successfully implemented by municipal councils and NGOs.

In practice, however, people participation is often a briefing of government projects to local residents rather than real consultations in formulating development plans or projects. Much more effort is needed to educate government officers on the process and mechanics of consultation and to empower households and NGOs on the whole process of people participation. As noted by Friedmann (1999), "For the most part, civil society is too preoccupied with daily survival issues to mobilize in politically effective ways."

That said, it is also important to take note that the accountability of NGO leaders and other pressure groups has not been well studied. Many NGOs are single-issue bodies and even if the leaders are true to the causes of their members, the voices of these people do not necessarily reflect the wishes of the majority of the people. In Kuala Lumpur and surrounding areas, as a reaction to growing criminality, many neighbourhoods have decided to place boom gates and security guards on public roads. But these are causing problems of access to residents of adjacent areas.

More worrisome are NGOs that are registered as private companies. The number of members is limited and selective. Some leaders have remained in their positions for years and even decades! There is little accountability. As such, it is not easy to know whether the opinions of NGO leaders are the voices of the people or their members, or just their own. Furthermore the causes of NGOs are not necessarily noble or good. There are NGOs advocating racial superiority or religious extremism. Effective participation of NGOs is not necessarily good for the society as a whole.

NON-COMPLIANCE — FAILURE OF ACCOUNTABILITY

Although accountability has been a much used word in conferences, seminars, and meetings related to urban governance, it is not easy to put the concept into practice. The clearest signs of the lack of accountability are the ubiquitous acts of non-compliance in almost all Southeast Asian cities. These include indiscriminate discarding of litter, bags of household waste, and even loads of construction waste, indiscriminate parking, incompatible building use, illegal building extensions, and illegal hawking and operation of businesses or even factories. Strictly speaking, the acts themselves are not indicators of lack of accountability. It is the absence or lack of action against the culprits.

The fact that the acts of non-compliance with municipal rules and development plans are not nipped in the bud means that the bureaucrats who are tasked to enforce the law are sleeping on the job. The chain of non-compliance often goes up even higher to the politicians: the councillors, mayors, or governors or presidents of local authorities, the apex of the compliance ladder. They neglect their duty of ensuring that bureaucrats perform their duties and acts of non-compliance on the streets are punished.

Often the failure of the politicians is even more serious than just not taking actions against bureaucrats. They are often the reasons why actions are not taken against those who break the law. They interfere in the enforcement actions (Goh Ban Lee 2002). Although it is suspected that the reasons of acts of non-compliance in many Southeast Asian cities are similar, there is a serious need to conduct a series of studies on this very important issue in different towns and cities.

However, non-compliance is a neglected agenda in urban governance. A major weakness in the study of governance in developing countries is the tendency to focus on formal structures and systems of governance, including the laws, by-laws, and development plans. This is especially so in works done by professional consultant firms because this is much easier than trying to understand governance on the streets. The structure and system of governance and the laws and plans are neatly stored on shelves in government offices and can be understood in a relatively short time and often in a comfortable environment. While this approach to study urban governance may be acceptable in developed countries, such as Germany, Switzerland, and Norway, it is not so in developing countries, including those of Southeast Asia, with the exception of Singapore, because the rules and plans are not followed.

There is no doubt that acts of non-compliance are the main reasons Southeast Asian cities are not among the top internationally recognized liveable cities. But as shown by Singapore, this "disease" can be cured. It needs committed and unwavering leaders. The case of Michael Fay is a good case study of such commitment.

Fay, an American youth, was found guilty of vandalism and was fined and ordered to be caned. Despite protests and criticisms by writers and even the White House and President Bill Clinton, Singapore went ahead to cane him, but the number of strokes was reduced from six to four. When a *Time* correspondent asked Lee Kuan Yew, then a senior minister, whether it was necessary to cane Fay, the reply was:

> Can we govern if we let him off and not cane him? Can we then cane any other foreigner or our own people? We'll have to close shop. That's my view. I am an old-style Singaporean who believes that to govern you

must have a certain moral authority. If we do not cane him because he is an American, I believe we'll lose our moral authority and our right to govern (*Time*, 9 May 1994).

That was perhaps the "Ah-ha" moment that made Singapore what it is today — the ability not only to make good plans and laws, but also have the commitment to implement them.

Despite its success in urban management, Singapore has not become an example for the others. There is a notion that in a country where the prime minister knows practically every road and lane, its success is unique. But what is interesting is that China is beginning to enforce compliance with municipal and sanitary rules and regulations. The campaign to make the citizens of Beijing obey the law just before the 2008 Olympic Games did show results. Even the BBC, a liberal news network not accustomed to praising communist leaders, published complimentary stories about the successful efforts (BBC News, 20 February 2007).

But not all Southeast Asian countries are like China, a one-party state. Can the citizens of democratic countries be educated to comply with municipal rules and standards in democratic countries in a relatively short time?

Phisanulok, a medium-size city north of Bangkok, provides some hope. The city is clean. The townspeople appear to comply with their cleanliness regulations, including accepting the fact that there are no municipal waste bins in the towns. They have also participated enthusiastically in recycling. The town has a recycling rate of about 80 per cent (Goh Ban Lee 2009). It has been officially proclaimed "The City of Recycling" by the provincial governor.

URGENT ISSUES

There is a serious and urgent need to understand the issue of the lack of accountability in governance in ASEAN cities. But an effective solution to the issue of non-compliance needs a thorough understanding of not only the laws of each city, but the social-economic and cultural values of the residents.

At the wider level, there is the mistaken belief that municipal leaders in Southeast Asia can simply implement the various characteristics of good governance after attending some conferences, seminars, or even workshops. Leaving existing laws and by-laws aside, we are expecting too much to believe that seasoned politicians who are elected mayors and governors can suddenly be converted into practising democrats, and implement measures for effective public participation in municipal activities.

In the case of Malaysia, where all the mayors or presidents of local authorities are senior government officers, it will take more than seminars or conferences to make them corporate managers who adopt all the concepts of corporate management after years of strict adherence to administrative procedures that are basically a top-down system to get things done.

There is also much to be done in efforts to introduce good urban governance in the cities and towns of Southeast Asia. Generally those who are well versed in the workings of local government know little about good urban governance. Those who are "experts" in the concept of good governance usually do not know the intricacies of the workings of local authorities.

WHAT CAN ASEAN DO?

For cities in ASEAN countries to become engines of development, they will have to be notable liveable cities. Accountability in urban management is crucial. A collaborative project under the sponsorship of the ASEAN Secretariat should be carried out to study accountability in cases of non-compliance, and to propose steps that can be implemented to foster good governance. As each country, indeed each city, is unique, the recommendations for improving compliance should not be one-size-fits-all. More specifically, there is a need for in-depth study on non-compliance in ASEAN cities, otherwise all the calls for liveable cities will be wasted.

Furthermore there is a serious need to ensure that decisions made at seminars and conferences are implementable and realistic. ASEAN can facilitate collaborative studies. As a beginning, ASEAN must set up a resource centre as a depository for all studies conducted in member countries. It should also house copies of conference or seminar papers held in member countries. Ideally these materials should be in digital version so as to facilitate access. This is to solve the difficulties of access to unpublished studies and conference papers.

CONCLUSION

By now, many mayors or governors or presidents in Southeast Asia want their cities to become engines of development. Many want them to be education hubs or centres of creativity or be known as cities of tourism and sports, or some other ideas they have heard from study tours or learned from conferences and seminars.

There is no way they can accomplish their dreams by just pulling their own bootstraps. They need concrete ideas on good governance that are suitable to their local situations. They need collaborative efforts from people who know the "hardware" (roads, buildings, factories, telecommunications, etc.) and the "software' (governance) to make the dreams of their cities as engines of development come true.

References

Brookfield, Harold and Yvonne Byron, eds. *South-East Asia's Environmental Future — the Search for Sustainability.* Tokyo: UNU Press, 1993.

Cherry, Gordon. *The Evolution of British Town Planning.* London: Leonard Hill Books, 1974.

Douglass, M. and Ooi Ling. *Industrializing Cities and the Environment in Pacific Asia: Towards a Policy Framework and Agenda for Action.* USAID Development Expression Clearinghouse, 1999.

ECA. "Singapore Retains Pole Position as No. 1 Place for Asians to Live for 11th Consecutive Year". March 2010 <http//www.eca-international.com/showpressrelease.aspx?ArtilcesID=7140> (accessed 24 May 2010).

EIU. *Global Liveability Report,* January 2010 <www.eiu.com/site_info.asp?info_name=The_Global_Liveability_Report&rf=0> (accessed 24 May 2010).

Friedmann, John. "The Governance of City-Regions in East and Southeast Asia". Paper presented at an international conference on cities in Asia, Hiroshima, Japan, December 1999.

———. "Cities Unbound: The Intercity Network in the Asia-Pacific Region". Discussion Paper Series no. 23, Management of Social Transformation (MOST), 1997 <www.unesco.org/most/friedmann/htm>.

Fritzen, Scott. "Discipline and Democratize: Patterns of Bureaucratic Accountability". In *International Journal of Public Administration,* no. 30 (2007): 1435–57.

Goh Ban Lee. *Non-compliance — A Neglected Agenda in Urban Governance.* Skudai: Institut Sultan Iskandar, 2002.

———. "The Demise of Local Government Elections and Urban Politics". In *Elections and Democracy in Malaysia,* edited by Mavis Puthucheary and Norani Othman. Bangi: Penerbit Universiti Kebangsaan Malaysia, 2005.

———. "Planning Livable Cities in an Environment of Non-compliance". Paper presented at the International Conference on Liveable Cities, organized by the Federal Department of Town and Country Planning Department, Ministry of Housing and Local Government, Kuala Lumpur, 8–9 November 2006.

————. *Counselling Local Councils*. Petaling Jaya: Federation of Malaysian Consumers' Association (FORMCA), 2007.

————. "Phisanulok — the City of Recycling". *The Sun*, 24 July 2009.

————. "Local Govt Elections Can Wait". *The Sun*, 9 February 2010.

Hall, Peter. "The City of Theories". In *The City Reader*, 4th ed., edited by Richard LeGates and Frederic Stout. London: Routledge, 2007.

Hamer, Andrew. "Economic impacts of Third World Mega-cities: Is Size the Issue?". In *Mega-City Growth and the Future*, edited by Roland Fuchs et al. Tokyo: United Nations University, 1994, pp. 172–91.

Howard, Ebenezer. *Garden Cities of Tomorrow*. MIT Press, 1965.

Laquian, Aprodicio. "The Planning and Governance of Asia's Mega-Urban Regions". Paper presented at the United Nations expert group meeting on population distribution, urbanization, internal migration and development, UN/POP?EGM-URB/2008/04, 2008.

Levi, Margeret. *Consent, Dissent and Patriotism*. Cambridge: Cambridge University Press, 1997.

Mercer. "Quality of Living Worldwide City Ranking 2010". Mercer Survey <http://www,mercer.com/qualityoflivingpr#City_Ranking_Table> (accessed 1 June 2010).

Mumford, Lewis and Donald Miller. *The Lewis Mumford Reader*. Pantheon, 1986.

NEAC. "New Economic Model for Malaysia". Putrajaya: National Economic Advisory Council, 2010.

Peerenboon, Randall, ed. *Asian Discources of Rule of Law: Theories and Implementation of Rule of Law in Twelve Asian Countries, France and the United States*. London: Routledge, 2004.

Reader, John. *Cities*. Vintage Books, 2004.

Roula Majdalani. "Municipal Governance and Expanded NGOs Role in Selected Countries in the Middle East", 1999 <http://www.lcps-lebanon.org/coaf/00/mdf3/papers/majdalani/pdf>.

Transparency International. *Global Corruption Report 2009 — Corruption and the Private Sector*. Cambridge: Cambridge University Press, 2009.

UNDP. *Designing Inclusive and Accountable Local Democratic Institutions — A Practitioners' Guide*. Bangkok: UNDP Regional Centre, 2007.

WUF. "Global Campaign on Urban Governance". Progress Report of the executive director, HS/UF/1/13 — Dialogue/1/Paper 7 <http://2085_72479_wuf_progress_report.doc>.

Urbanization from an
ASEAN Perspective

15

PROMOTING AN INTEGRATED APPROACH TO URBANIZATION IN ASEAN COUNTRIES

Rony Soerakoesoemah and Moe Thuzar

When an integrated regional approach on addressing urbanization in ASEAN countries is being considered, the question that most readily comes to mind is why a regional approach is necessary for this issue. Past practice in ASEAN has not shown that the association's members feel an urgent need to tackle the issue regionally. Urbanization is still largely seen as a national responsibility rather than an issue with regional implications. When the topic does come up for discussion, there is a tendency to dismiss its cross-sectoral relevance.

It would be relevant to bear in mind, however, the role of regional institutions in pushing action at national levels. Dua and Esty (1997) highlight that the regional level represents a critical middle ground between global and national scales. Regional cooperation mechanisms — by their very nature, a peer process — can thus facilitate the formulation and implementation of necessary policies and measures at several levels, including the national and subregional. Although referring to environmental governance, Kimball (1999) has made the same emphasis on regional systems (of environmental management) being "essential" to securing agreements for, and implementation of, specific action programmes.

The challenge here is whether urbanization presents the same imperative for action and "management". Koh and Robinson (2002) argue that ASEAN does not have a core bureaucracy, with its permanent secretariat in Jakarta playing a largely limited role in facilitating the implementation of regional agreements. However, with the entry into force of the ASEAN Charter in December 2008, there is a wider scope for the ASEAN Secretary-General and officers of the ASEAN Secretariat "to facilitate and monitor the progress in implementation of ASEAN agreements and decisions" (Article 11, paragraph 2). The Protocol (1992) amending the 1976 Agreement on the Establishment of the ASEAN Secretariat details the functions and powers of the Secretary-General, including to "initiate, advise, coordinate and implement ASEAN activities" and "develop and provide the regional perspective on subjects and issues before ASEAN".

This indicates the existence of a window for ASEAN to consider urbanization issues as part of the regional cooperation agenda. The question then arises as to which among the plethora of ASEAN meetings and mechanisms would take up the challenge, or whether setting up a new regional mechanism is feasible.

The Senior Officials on Development Planning (SOMDP) would seem to be the ideal forum for urbanization and its multifaceted implications as it brings together representatives of planning agencies responsible for national development plans. The SOMDP's discussion agenda, however, focuses on the integration of regional plans and priorities into national development agendas and does not specifically look at urbanization.

The only ASEAN body that has taken up the topic at the regional level is the ASEAN Working Group on Environmentally Sustainable Cities, which takes the environment protection perspective on urbanization and cities. Yet the implications of urban policies are multidimensional: ASEAN's economic, sociocultural, and political spheres are all affected by the increasing rate of urbanization in ASEAN member states.

This chapter proposes that an integrated regional approach to urbanization is possible for ASEAN, and that the vehicle for coordinating national efforts can be found in the Initiative for ASEAN Integration (IAI).

ASEAN INTEGRATION AIMS

The Initiative for ASEAN Integration (IAI) was inaugurated in 2000 at the Fourth Informal ASEAN Summit in Singapore. Built on the premise that integration cannot fully take place when a development gap exists between the member states of ASEAN, the IAI aims to expedite greater economic integration, promote equitable economic development and help alleviate poverty in ASEAN member states, and help newer members (Cambodia, the Lao PDR, Myanmar, and Vietnam, collectively referred to as "CLMV") develop more rapidly in order to participate in and benefit from regional integration.

Achieving a common regional market or an ASEAN Economic Community (AEC) is the major goal for economic integration. The AEC vision is to create by 2015 a stable, prosperous, and highly competitive ASEAN economic region in which there is a free flow of goods, services, investment, and a freer flow of capital, equitable economic development, and reduced poverty and socio-economic disparities. ASEAN adopted a blueprint to achieve the AEC goals in November 2007 at the 13th ASEAN Summit in Singapore. This was followed by the adoption of blueprints for the two other community pillars of ASEAN — the ASEAN Political Security Community and the ASEAN Sociocultural Community — at the 14th ASEAN Summit in Thailand the following year. The three blueprints and the second IAI Work Plan (IAI Work Plan II) are now referred to as the "Roadmap for an ASEAN Community" and have an implementation time frame of 2009 to 2015.

ASEAN has subsequently adopted a master plan on regional connectivity to "promote economic growth, narrow development gaps, ASEAN integration and Community-building process [sic], enhance competitiveness of ASEAN, promote deeper social and cultural understanding as well as greater people mobility and connect its Member States within the region and with the rest of the world".

The main thrust of regional integration in ASEAN still lies in economic integration. The greatest challenge to this is the development divide among the members. ASEAN members are at very different stages of economic development. This gap is manifested not only in terms of GDP per capita, but also in human development indicators such as incidence of poverty, life expectancy, literacy, and public expenditure in health and education. A 2007 UN-ESCAP study on challenges and opportunities for ASEAN Integration finds that there are still large disparities in development outcomes among the countries in economic, poverty, education, gender, health, environment, energy, and IT and physical infrastructure indicators (Figure 15.1).

In addition, cities in the region are now faced with the strategic choice of whether economic dynamism comes at the cost of liveability. The United Nations Population Division estimates that 65 per cent of the population in Southeast Asia will live in urban areas by 2050. Today, the region's urban population accounts for over 40 per cent, although not all are concentrated in the mega-urban areas. Challenges commonly faced in large urban agglomerations include shelter, security, infrastructure, employment, and services, highlighting that the quality of urban development affects development prospects (Thuzar 2011).

URBAN ISSUES IN ASEAN COUNTRIES

The overview paper of the seminars on which this book is based states that "almost half of the population of Southeast Asia (48.2 per cent) lives in urban settlements [and this figure] is projected to increase to 70% in 30 years' time". The fact that CLMV countries are largely rural and agriculture-based, with limited availability/access to financial resources only reinforces that claim. As ASEAN progresses with its integration efforts, urbanization and urban development will be a growing concern for these countries as their populations move into settlements that promise more economic opportunities and a better life.

The governments' response is to ensure that growth does not come at the cost of environmental stress, overcrowding, and widening income gaps. Effective urban planning will require efforts that foster physical infrastructure development and realize effective connectivity in key areas such as transport, information, and communication technology, and energy sectors.

With regard to promoting quality living standards in urban areas, the ASEAN Initiative on Environmentally Sustainable Cities (AIESC), endorsed by the ASEAN Environment Ministers in 2005, assists participating ASEAN cities to pursue environmental sustainability. The programme includes regional activities to build capacity in clean water projects and twinning partnerships such as Ilo-Ilo–Phnom Penh (on hygiene promotion), Putrajaya–Ha Long (on waste water treatment operation and management), and Manila–Danang (on water quality).

Figure 15.1

Inequality between ASEAN Countries by Indicator (Gini Index 1990–2006)

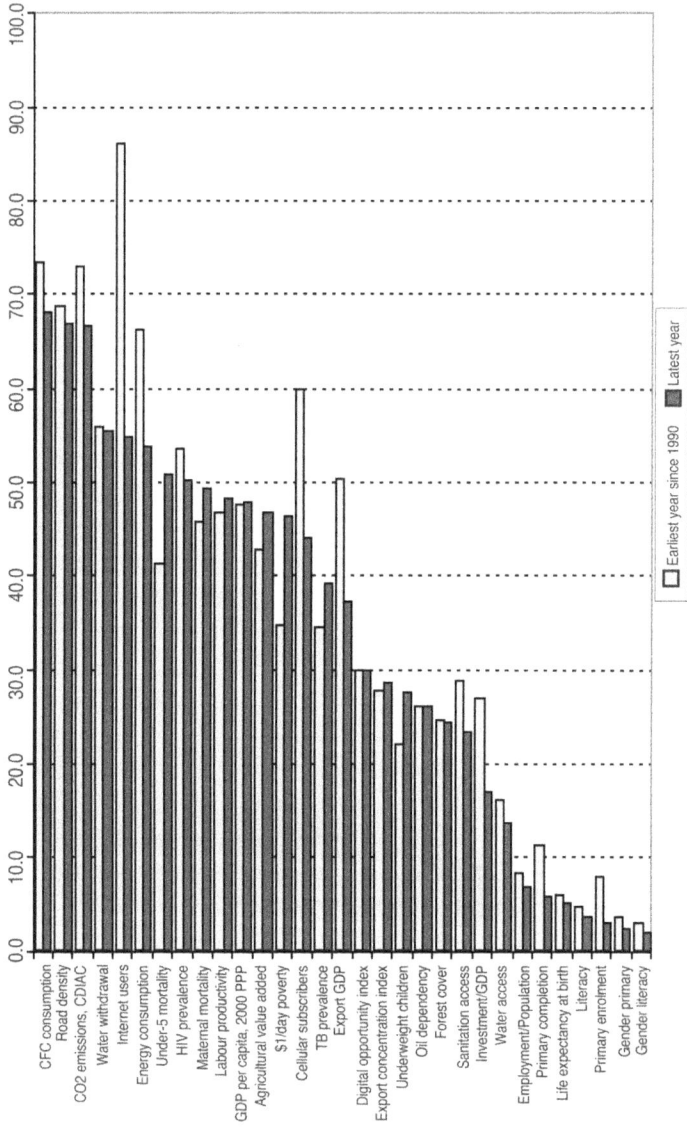

Source: UN-ESCAP (2007).

The ASEAN Environmentally Sustainable City (ESC) Award programme was initiated in 2008 to promote ASEAN cities that had undertaken exemplary measures to keep their cities clean, green, and liveable, even as they continue to grow as centres of economic and industrial activity. Recipients of the ASEAN ESC Award 2008 are mostly secondary cities and towns: Brunei Darussalam: Temburong District; Cambodia: Municipality of Phnom Penh; Indonesia: Palembang City; Lao PDR: Luang Prabang District; Malaysia: North Kuching City Hall; Myanmar: Taunggyi City; the Philippines: Puerto Princesa City; Singapore: South West Community Development Council; Thailand: Bangkok City; and Vietnam: Ha Long City.

THE IAI AND URBANIZATION

A mid-term review of the first IAI work plan was carried out in 2005. It recommended that the scope of the IAI be broadened to address energy, tourism, investment climate, poverty reduction, and improving the quality of life. The first work plan had initially four priority thrusts: infrastructure development, information and communications technology, human resource development, and regional economic integration. These topics — both the original four priorities and the recommended additional areas — are relevant to the region's urbanization processes.

A number of initiatives in the IAI Work Plan II (2009–15) can be identified with attempting to address the concerns of urbanization. The work plan lists specific actions for infrastructure development to improve living standards in ASEAN cities and urban areas. It should be pointed out, however, that the initiatives listed in the work plan are separate activities implemented by different ASEAN committees and working groups, independent of one another. The activities, therefore, do not follow a coherent theme of addressing urbanization in ASEAN cities. Progress is also reported individually, through each of the overarching "Community Councils" and the ASEAN Coordinating Council,[1] to the ASEAN leaders at their annual summit meetings.

The IAI remains the main instrument to narrow the development gap in ASEAN and is primarily directed towards accelerating economic integration of the newer members of ASEAN (Cambodia, Lao PDR, Myanmar, and Vietnam). ASEAN leaders have emphasized that narrowing the development gap will remain an important task to ensure the benefits of ASEAN integration. Activities under the IAI have been devoted largely to "soft" infrastructure. However, development of physical transport and communication infrastructure networks, completion of the physical road, rail, and air and sea linkages within ASEAN, such as the Singapore-Kunming Rail Link, and efforts in building the hard infrastructure are becoming key activities, particularly with the consolidation of these priorities into the Master Plan on ASEAN Connectivity.

This master plan is the latest initiative by ASEAN towards regional integration by 2015. The plan's executive summary cites the vision for an ASEAN Community 2015 as being premised on "a well-connected region" that is essential in bringing "peoples, goods, services and capital together". Implicit in the master plan is the importance of encouraging the competitiveness and resilience of cities and subregions (or city-regions) in this process of enhanced connectivity. Through implementation of the plan, cities and towns in the ASEAN region can be brought together under a coherent strategy that will stimulate economic growth and bridge regional disparities, ultimately establishing closer links with countries in the rest of Asia (Thuzar 2011).

In this drive for enhanced regional connectivity, the IAI and especially its second Work Plan (IAI Work Plan II) are an opportunity to improve the way ASEAN goes about regional integration. The IAI Work Plan II takes into account the need for better designed projects that serve specific country requirements in the CLMV; creative approaches for the delivery of the activities; and a change in mindset of the people involved to overcome the constraints faced in implementation. IAI projects have had positive outcomes, but admittedly the work plan's narrow focus, insufficient inter-agency coordination, and weak ownership in the CLMV countries, have held back significant progress.

There are some fundamental issues that need to be addressed if the work plan is to be used as a vehicle to coordinate regional responses to urbanization (and other development cooperation) issues in ASEAN:

1. **Technical assistance implemented under IAI may need to be country-specific.** This is necessary to ensure effectiveness in building capacities in the respective countries. By being precise, projects will have long-term continuity and sustainability, and build a sense of ownership of the activities, so countries do not have to rely too much on external assistance that may be donor-driven.

2. **Cross-cutting issues.** Adopting a thematic cluster approach can provide space for specific detailed discussions based on thematic areas and present a new paradigm for local economic development. The approach can establish linkages among existing sectoral activities to help improve coordination of related measures.

3. **Infrastructure development**. Improvement of physical transport and communication infrastructure networks and the completion of the physical road, rail, air and sea linkages within ASEAN need to be key activities in the IAI Work Plan.

4. **Monitoring and evaluation of activities/projects**. ASEAN has so far been weak in the area of monitoring and evaluating the impact of regional projects and activities. Admittedly, institutions such as the ASEAN Secretariat do not have the capacity to track the progress of "soft" projects — which are mainly focused on capacity building of government officials — beyond their immediate implementation time frame. However, measuring impact and evaluating benefits of the activities will yield useful information for ASEAN and can help develop a set of key parameters representative of how the development gap is bridged. Overall an enhanced assessment of IAI activities will improve implementation of the IAI (and other regional programmes).

5. **Coordination.** Encouraging information exchange among stakeholders will improve coordination among donors (from within ASEAN as well as dialogue and development partners) with the IAI. Donor coordination is important in-country, that is, among and within the CLMV countries; between those countries and the donors; and among divisions in the ASEAN Secretariat which deal with the respective sectors of cooperation.

AN INTEGRATED APPROACH FOR ASEAN ON URBANIZATION: RECOMMENDATIONS

There are a number of cross-cutting and thematic issues and emerging priorities that require (horizontal) coordination of efforts of sectoral bodies across the three community pillars, which cannot be adequately addressed individually by any of the community councils that coordinate the work of each community pillar. In addition to climate change, disaster management, energy and food security, emerging infectious diseases, poverty alleviation, the Millennium Development Goals (MDG), and financial crises, urbanization and urban development is one cross-cutting issue that has not yet been recognized. Special attention is needed to help make ASEAN's sprawling urban areas more sustainable, competitive, inclusive, and environmentally friendly.

The issues facing the CLMV countries — as well as the other six ASEAN members — regarding urbanization and urban development, require a well-coordinated and integrated implementation plan among the relevant ASEAN sectoral bodies.

One way is to take up cross-cutting or thematic issues to promote dialogue and discussions among various sectors. Thematic clustering is not intended to create new institutional bodies as they will build on existing ASEAN mechanisms and provide further support and impetus to related initiatives.

By adopting a cluster approach, ASEAN can synergize current sectoral initiatives, give the individual activities more purpose, and steer towards a common objective. Gradually, coordination among related ASEAN committees will improve and eventually help formulate infrastructure and policy investments that will have the greatest development impact on urbanization.

The Cluster Approach

Addressing specific cross-cutting issues will require the involvement of relevant sectoral bodies in ASEAN within and across the three communities. There needs to be more consultation among these sectoral bodies in planning their actions. This is to ensure complementarity of effort, harmonize objectives as much as possible, and mobilize resources efficiently. The proposed cluster approach will help coordinate efforts and ensure an integrated response to a specific theme. At the risk of creating yet another ASEAN mechanism, the cluster approach could be in the form of an ASEAN Cluster on Urbanization that brings together senior officials from, among others, the environment, transportation, energy, health, and science and technology sectors.

The cluster should aim at facilitating coordination and promoting synergy among the key sectoral bodies on common and related issues of urbanization. The cluster would thus undertake the following:

1. Plan and develop an integrated and cohesive implementation work programme and its strategic schedule based on the blueprint actions relevant to specific issues;

2. Map the initiatives of the various sectors represented in the cluster that could lead to adjustments to the work programmes of the concerned sectoral bodies;
3. Conduct strategic resource planning and mobilization, including donor coordination, to mobilize resources for the timely implementation of activities;
4. Prioritize, coordinate, and assess the progress of implementation of agreed programmes and related activities; and
5. Conduct consultations among member states and other stakeholders to develop a regional strategy on urbanization.

IAI on Urbanization: Possible Next Steps

Before undertaking any form of cluster approach, a comprehensive study would be necessary to take stock of ASEAN's activities in the various related sectors that address urbanization challenges. The study would provide an overview of what ASEAN has done with respect to the issue of urbanization, and will help establish whether ASEAN has done enough to tackle the problems and challenges brought about by the process of urbanization. The study would also list further needs, including priorities for implementation.

Results of the study would need to be shared among the relevant ASEAN officials to obtain policy support for related activities in the various sectors. Doing so will also add urgency to activities deemed important.

To do this, an ASEAN Regional Forum on Urbanization could be established as a regional platform for discussion and exchange on urbanization issues. It would serve as the regional platform for the ASEAN Cluster on Urbanization to present its recommendations. It would also institutionalize a network of urban experts, policymakers, and practitioners to raise urbanization issues to a higher level of priority on the regional agenda. The forum can build on the informal network created by the joint initiative of the ASEAN Studies Centre at the Institute of Southeast Asian Studies and the Centre for Liveable Cities, which brought together academics, experts, and practitioners from the region to start discussions on urbanization in Southeast Asia.

Putting all this together will require resources beyond the capacity of member states and ASEAN. The regional forum would help obtain additional sources of funding to implement the various strategies and recommendations, but resources are also necessary to get the forum going.

Alternatively, the existing platform of the IAI Development Cooperation Forum (IDCF) could be used to promote ASEAN's needs to tackle urbanization challenges collectively. Through the IDCF, ASEAN's dialogue and development partners can extend their support to the IAI in mobilizing resources for the implementation of plans related to urbanization. The IDCF was established in 2002 to serve as the main venue for engaging ASEAN's dialogue partners and other donors (from a range of regional and international organizations, corporations, and foundations) in a collective dialogue on the IAI Work Plan. Three forums have since been organized. The scope of partnerships now include other subregional frameworks such as the ADB's Greater Mekong Subregion Economic Cooperation Programme (GMS Programme), the ASEAN Mekong Basin Development Cooperation (AMBDC), the Ayeyawaddy-Chaopraya-Mekong Economic Cooperation Strategy (ACMECS), BIMP-EAGA, and IMT-GT.

Note

1. The ASEAN Charter, which came into force in December 2008, established four new ministerial bodies to coordinate regional cooperation activities better within and across sectors. The ASEAN Coordinating Council (ACC) comprises the ASEAN Foreign Ministers and has the responsibility to provide support for ASEAN Summit meetings and oversee overall implementation and coordination of projects and activities towards the ASEAN Community. The three community pillars each have a council that coordinates sectoral work in each sphere of cooperation: ASEAN Political-Security Community Council, ASEAN Economic Community Council, and ASEAN Sociocultural Community Council.

References

ASEAN Secretariat. "1992 Protocol Amending the Agreement on the Establishment of the ASEAN Secretariat", 22 July 1992 <http://cil.nus.edu.sg/1992/1992-protocol-amending-the-agreement-on-the-establishment-of-the-asean-secretariat-signed-on-22-july-1992-in-manila-the-philippines-by-the-foreign-ministers/> (accessed January 2011).
———. "Press Statement by the Chairman of the 4th ASEAN Informal Summit, Singapore", 25 November 2000 <http://www.asean.org/5310.htm> (accessed February 2011).
———. "Hanoi Declaration for Narrowing Development Gap for Closer ASEAN Integration". Issued at the 34th ASEAN Ministerial Meeting in Hanoi, 23 July 2001.

————. Discussion Paper presented at the 2nd IAI Development Cooperation Forum, Hanoi, 12 June 2007.

————. "Initiative for ASEAN Integration (IAI) Strategic Framework and IAI Work Plan 2, 2009–2015", 2009.

————. "Status Update of the IAI Work Plan I, 2002–2008". Presented at the 35th Meeting of the IAI Task Force, Jakarta, 17 October 2009 <http://www.aseansec.org/documents/Status-Update-IAI-WP-2002-2008.pdf> (accessed March 2010).

————. "Master Plan on ASEAN Connectivity", 2010 <www.asean.org/documents/MPAC.pdf> (accessed December 2010).

————. "Bridging the Development Gap Among Members of ASEAN". Initiative for ASEAN Integration Unit <http://www.aseansec.org/14683.htm> (accessed March 2010).

————. "Report on the Mid-Term Review of the IAI Work Plan I" <http://www.aseansec.org/18201.htm> (accessed December 2010).

Koh, Kheng Lian and Nicholas A. Robinson. "Regional Environmental Governance: Examining the Association of Southeast Asian Nations (ASEAN) Model". In *Global Environmental Governance: Options and Opportunities*, edited by Daniel C. Esty and Maria H. Ivanova. Yale School of Forestry and Environmental Studies, 2002.

Ooi, Giok Ling and Belinda Yuen, eds. *World Cities: Achieving Liveability and Vibrancy*. Singapore: World Scientific, 2010.

Thuzar, Moe. "Urbanisation in Southeast Asia: Developing Smart Cities for the Future?" In *Regional Outlook: Southeast Asia 2011–2012*, edited by Michael J. Montesano and Lee Poh Onn. Singapore: Institute of Southeast Asian Studies, 2011.

UN-HABITAT. "Ten as One: Challenges and Opportunities for ASEAN Integration". United Nations Economic and Social Commission for Asia and the Pacific (UN-ESCAP), 2007.

————. *Global Report on Human Settlements 2009: Planning Sustainable Cities*. United Nations Human Settlements Programme (UN-HABITAT), 2009.

————. "State of the World's Cities 2010/2011: Bridging the Urban Divide". United Nations Human Settlements Programme (UN-HABITAT), 2010.

Yap Kioe Sheng. "Promoting Productive, Inclusive and Sustainable Cities and Towns in Southeast Asia", Overview Paper presented at the 2nd Regional Workshop on Urbanisation in Southeast Asian Countries, Singapore, March 2010.

Index

www.ingramcontent.com/pod-product-compliance
Lightning Source LLC
Chambersburg PA
CBHW072043020426
42334CB00017B/1376